Praise for *Delta Lake: The Definitive Guide*

Delta Lake has revolutionized data architectures by combining the best of data lakes and warehouses into the lakehouse architecture. This definitive guide by O'Reilly is an essential resource for anyone looking to harness the full potential of Delta Lake. It offers deep insights into building scalable, reliable, high-performance data architectures. Whether you're a data engineer, scientist, or practitioner, this book will empower you to tackle your toughest data challenges with confidence and precision.

—Matei Zaharia, associate professor of computer science at UC Berkeley and cofounder and chief technologist at Databricks

This book not only provides excellent code examples for Delta Lake but also explains what happens behind the scenes. It's a resource I'll continue to rely on as a practical reference for Delta Lake APIs. Furthermore, it covers the latest exciting innovations within the Delta Lake ecosystem.

—Ryan Zhu, founding developer of Delta Lake, cocreator of Delta Sharing, Apache Spark PMC member, Delta Lake maintainer

The authors of this book fuse deep technical knowledge with pragmatism and clear exposition to allow readers to bring their Spark data lakehouse aspirations to life with the Delta Lake framework.

—Matt Housley, CTO and coauthor of Fundamentals of Data Engineering

Open table formats are the future. If you are invested in Delta Lake, this book will take you from zero to 100, including use cases, integrations, and how to overcome hiccups.

—Adi Polak, author of Scaling Machine Learning with Spark

There are two types of people in data: those who believe they understand what Delta Lake is and those who read this book.

—*Andy Petrella, part of the second group, author of* Fundamentals of Data Observability, *and founder of Kensu*

Look no further if you want to master all things Delta Lake. Denny, Tristen, Scott, and Prashanth have gone above and beyond to give you more experience than you could ever imagine.

—*Jacek Laskowski, freelance Data(bricks) engineer*

Delta Lake is much more than Apache Parquet with a commit log. *Delta Lake: The Definitive Guide* takes the mystery out of streaming, data governance, and design patterns.

—*Bartosz Konieczny,* waitingforcode.com

Delta Lake: The Definitive Guide

Modern Data Lakehouse Architectures
with Data Lakes

Denny Lee, Tristen Wentling,
Scott Haines, and Prashanth Babu
Forewords by Michael Armbrust and Dominique Brezinski

Delta Lake: The Definitive Guide

by Denny Lee, Tristen Wentling, Scott Haines, and Prashanth Babu

Published by O'Reilly Media, Inc., 1005 Gravenstein Highway North, Sebastopol, CA 95472.

O'Reilly books may be purchased for educational, business, or sales promotional use. Online editions are also available for most titles (*https://oreilly.com*). For more information, contact our corporate/institutional sales department: 800-998-9938 or *corporate@oreilly.com*.

Acquisitions Editor: Aaron Black	**Indexer:** BIM Creatives, LLC
Development Editor: Gary O'Brien	**Interior Designer:** David Futato
Production Editor: Gregory Hyman	**Cover Designer:** Karen Montgomery
Copyeditor: Arthur Johnson	**Illustrator:** Kate Dullea
Proofreader: Emily Wydeven	

November 2024:   First Edition

Revision History for the First Edition
2024-10-29:   First Release

See *http://oreilly.com/catalog/errata.csp?isbn=9781098151942* for release details.

978-1-098-15194-2

[LSI]

Table of Contents

Foreword by Michael Armbrust

The Delta protocol was first conceived when I met Dominique Brezinski at Spark Summit 2017. As he described to me the scale of data processing that he was envisioning, I knew that, through our collaborative approach to running Apache Spark, Databricks had already laid down the building blocks of the cloud-scale computing environment necessary to make him successful. Yet I also knew that these fundamentals would inevitably prove to be insufficient without us introducing a novel system to manage the complexities of transactional access to the ever-growing lake of data that Dom had been collecting in his private cloud. Recognizing that Apache Spark itself could serve as the engine of scalable transaction consistency enforcement was the key insight that underpins the ongoing success of Delta Lake. That is, to simplify and scale, we treated the metadata like how we processed and queried the data.

Translating this single insight and the resulting protocol into Delta Lake, a comprehensive toolset for developers to use in any streaming data management solution, has been a long road, with many collaborations along the way. Becoming an open source project allowed Delta Lake to evolve through community input and contributions. The robust ecosystem that has resulted now includes multiple implementations of the Delta protocol, in multiple frameworks, such as Flink, Trino, Presto, and Pulsar, and in multiple languages, including Rust, Go, Java, Scala, Hive, and Python.

To celebrate and further build on this vibrant open source community, I'm now excited to present *Delta Lake: The Definitive Guide*. This guide details Delta Lake's architecture, use cases, and best practices, catering to data engineers, scientists, and analysts alike. It encapsulates years of innovation in data management, offering a comprehensive resource for unlocking Delta Lake's full potential. As you explore this book, you'll gain the knowledge to leverage Delta Lake's capabilities in your projects. I'm eager to see how you'll use it to drive innovation and achieve your data goals.

Welcome to the shore of the Delta Lake. The water is great—let's take a swim!

— Michael Armbrust
Creator of Delta Lake, Spark PMC Member,
Delta Lake TSC and Maintainer

Foreword by Dominique Brezinski

Delta Lake emerged from Michael and my discussions about the challenges I encountered when building a high-scale streaming ETL system using Apache Spark, EC2, and S3. We faced the same challenges at Apple in processing vast amounts of data for intrusion monitoring and threat response. We needed to build a system that could do not only streaming ingestion but also streaming detection and support performant queries over a long retention window of large datasets. From these requirements Delta Lake was created to support ACID transactions and seamless integration of batch and streaming processes, allowing us to handle petabytes of daily data efficiently.

This guide reveals Delta Lake's architectural fundamentals, practical applications, and best practices. Whether you're a data engineer, scientist, or business leader, you'll find valuable insights to leverage Delta Lake effectively.

I'm excited for you to explore this guide and witness how Delta Lake can propel your own innovations. Together, we're shaping the future of data management, enabling the construction of reliable and performant data lakehouses.

— Dominique Brezinski
Distinguished Engineer, Apple
Delta Lake Technical Steering Committee Member

Preface

Welcome to *Delta Lake: The Definitive Guide*! Since it became an open source project in 2019, Delta Lake has revolutionized how organizations manage and process their data. Designed to bring reliability, performance, and scalability to data lakes, Delta Lake addresses many of the inherent challenges traditional data lake architectures face.

Over the past five years, Delta Lake has undergone significant transformation. Originally focused on enhancing Apache Spark, Delta Lake now boasts a rich ecosystem with integrations across various platforms, including Apache Flink, Trino, and many more. This evolution has enabled Delta Lake to become a versatile and integral component of modern data engineering and data science workflows.

Who This Book Is For

As a team of production users and maintainers of the Delta Lake project, we're thrilled to share our collective knowledge and experience with you. Our journey with Delta Lake spans from small-scale implementations to internet-scale production lakehouses, giving us a unique perspective on its capabilities and how to work around any complexities.

The primary goal of this book is to provide a comprehensive resource for both newcomers and experts in data lakehouse architectures. For those just starting with Delta Lake, we aim to elucidate its core principles and help you avoid the common mistakes we encountered in our early days. If you're already well versed in Delta Lake, you'll find valuable insights into the underlying codebase, advanced features, and optimization techniques to enhance your lakehouse environment.

Throughout these pages, we celebrate the vibrant Delta Lake community and its collaborative spirit! We're particularly proud to highlight the development of the Delta Rust API and its widely adopted Python bindings, which exemplify the community's innovative approach to expanding Delta Lake's capabilities. Delta Lake has evolved significantly since its inception, growing beyond its initial focus on Apache Spark to embrace a wide array of integrations with multiple languages and frameworks. To reflect this diversity, we've included code examples featuring Flink, Kafka, Python, Rust, Spark, Trino, and more. This broad coverage ensures that you'll find relevant examples regardless of your preferred tools and languages.

While we cover the fundamental concepts, we've also included our personal experiences and lessons learned. More importantly, we go beyond theory to offer practical guidance on running a production lakehouse successfully. We've included best practices, optimization techniques, and real-world scenarios to help you navigate the challenges of implementing and maintaining a Delta Lake–based system at scale.

Whether you're a data engineer, architect, or scientist, our goal is to equip you with the knowledge and tools to leverage Delta Lake effectively in your data projects. We hope this guide serves as your companion in building robust, efficient, and scalable lakehouse architectures.

How This Book Is Organized

We organized the book so that you can move from chapter to chapter—introducing concepts, demonstrating key concepts via example code snippets, and providing full code examples or notebooks in the book's GitHub repository (*https://oreil.ly/ dldg_code*). The earlier chapters provide the fundamentals on how to install Delta Lake, its essential operations, understanding its ecosystem, building native Delta Lake applications, and maintaining your Delta Lake; the later chapters expand on these fundamentals and dive deeper into the features before coming back up to review how you can architect this all together for your production workloads:

Chapter 1, "Introduction to the Delta Lake Lakehouse Format"
    We explain Delta Lake's origins, what it is and what it does, its anatomy, and the transaction protocol. We impress upon you that the Delta transaction log is the single source of truth and is subsequently the single source of the relationship between its metadata and data.

Chapter 2, "Installing Delta Lake"
    We discuss the various ways to install Delta Lake, whether through pip or through Docker implementations for Rust, Python, and Apache Spark.

Chapter 3, "Essential Delta Lake Operations"
    In this chapter we look at CRUD operations, merge operations, conversion from Parquet to Delta, and management of Delta Lake metadata.

Chapter 4, "Diving into the Delta Lake Ecosystem"

We delve into the Delta Lake ecosystem, discussing the many frameworks, services, and community projects that support Delta Lake. This chapter includes code samples for the Flink DataStream Connector, Kafka Delta Ingest, and Trino.

Chapter 5, "Maintaining Your Delta Lake"

While Delta Lake provides optimal reading and writing out of the box, developers reading this book will want to further tweak Delta Lake configuration and settings to get even more performance. This chapter looks at using table properties, optimizing your table with Z-Ordering, table tuning and management, and repairing/restoring your table.

Chapter 6, "Building Native Applications with Delta Lake"

The delta-rs project was built from scratch by the community starting in 2020. Together, we built a Delta Rust API using native code, thus allowing developers to take advantage of Delta Lake's reliability without needing to install or maintain the JVM (Java virtual machine). In this chapter, we will dive into this project and its popular Python bindings.

 We'd like to give a shout-out to R. Tyler Croy, who not only contributed to and helped with this entire book but also is the author of Chapter 6.

Chapter 7, "Streaming In and Out of Your Delta Lake"

We discuss the importance of streaming and Delta Lake and dive deeper into streaming with Apache Flink, Apache Spark, and delta-rs. We also discuss streaming options, advanced usage with Apache Spark, and Change Data Feed.

Chapter 8, "Advanced Features"

Delta Lake contains advanced features such as generated columns and deletion vectors, which support a novel approach for Merge-on-Read (MoR).

Chapter 9, "Architecting Your Lakehouse"

Taking a 10,000-meter view, how should you architect your lakehouse with Delta Lake? Answering that question involves understanding the lakehouse architecture, transaction support, the medallion architecture, and the streaming medallion architecture.

Chapter 10, "Performance Tuning: Optimizing Your Data Pipelines with Delta Lake"

This is probably our most fun chapter! In it, we further discuss Z-Ordering, liquid clustering, table statistics, and performance considerations.

Chapter 11, "Successful Design Patterns"
To help you build a successful production environment, we look at slashing compute costs, efficient streaming ingestion, and coordinating complex systems.

Chapter 12, "Foundations of Lakehouse Governance and Security", and Chapter 13, "Metadata Management, Data Flow, and Lineage"
Next, we have detailed chapters on lakehouse governance! From access control and the data asset model to unifying data warehousing and lake governance, data security, metadata management, and data flow and lineage, these two chapters set the foundation for your governance story.

Chapter 14, "Data Sharing with the Delta Sharing Protocol"
Delta Sharing is an open protocol for secure, real-time data sharing across organizations and computing platforms. It allows data providers to share live data directly from their Delta Lake tables without the need for data replication or copying to another system. In this chapter, we explore these topics further.

Conventions Used in This Book

The following typographical conventions are used in this book:

Italic
Indicates new terms, URLs, email addresses, filenames, and file extensions.

`Constant width`
Used for program listings, as well as within paragraphs to refer to program elements such as variable or function names, databases, data types, environment variables, statements, and keywords.

`Constant width bold`
Used to call attention to code snippets of particular interest, within the context of the discussion.

`Constant width italic`
Shows text that should be replaced with user-supplied values or by values determined by context.

 This element signifies a tip or suggestion.

This element signifies a general note.

 This element indicates a warning or caution.

Using Code Examples

Supplemental material (code examples, exercises, etc.) is available for download at *https://oreil.ly/dldg_code*.

If you have a technical question or a problem using the code examples, please send email to *support@oreilly.com*.

This book is here to help you get your job done. In general, if example code is offered with this book, you may use it in your programs and documentation. You do not need to contact us for permission unless you're reproducing a significant portion of the code. For example, writing a program that uses several chunks of code from this book does not require permission. Selling or distributing examples from O'Reilly books does require permission. Answering a question by citing this book and quoting example code does not require permission. Incorporating a significant amount of example code from this book into your product's documentation does require permission.

We appreciate, but generally do not require, attribution. An attribution usually includes the title, author, publisher, and ISBN. For example: "*Delta Lake: The Definitive Guide* by Denny Lee, Tristen Wentling, Scott Haines, and Prashanth Babu (O'Reilly). Copyright 2025 O'Reilly Media, Inc., 978-1-098-15194-2."

If you feel your use of code examples falls outside fair use or the permission given above, feel free to contact us at *permissions@oreilly.com*.

O'Reilly Online Learning

 For more than 40 years, *O'Reilly Media* has provided technology and business training, knowledge, and insight to help companies succeed.

Our unique network of experts and innovators share their knowledge and expertise through books, articles, and our online learning platform. O'Reilly's online learning platform gives you on-demand access to live training courses, in-depth learning paths, interactive coding environments, and a vast collection of text and video from O'Reilly and 200+ other publishers. For more information, visit *https://oreilly.com*.

How to Contact Us

Please address comments and questions concerning this book to the publisher:

O'Reilly Media, Inc.
1005 Gravenstein Highway North
Sebastopol, CA 95472
800-889-8969 (in the United States or Canada)
707-829-7019 (international or local)
707-829-0104 (fax)
support@oreilly.com
https://www.oreilly.com/about/contact.html

We have a web page for this book, where we list errata, examples, and any additional information. You can access this page at *https://oreil.ly/DeltaLakeDefGuide*.

For news and information about our books and courses, visit *https://oreilly.com*.

Find us on LinkedIn: *https://linkedin.com/company/oreilly-media*.

Watch us on YouTube: *https://youtube.com/oreillymedia*.

Acknowledgments

This book has truly been a team effort and a labor of love. As authors, we were driven by a strong desire to share our lessons learned and best practices with the community. The journey of bringing this book to life has been immensely rewarding, and we are deeply grateful to everyone who contributed along the way.

First and foremost, we would like to extend our heartfelt thanks to some of the early contributors who played a pivotal role in making Delta Lake a reality. Our sincere gratitude goes out to Ali Ghodsi, Allison Portis, Burak Yavuz, Christian Williams, Dominique Brezinski, Florian Valeye, Gerhard Brueckl, Matei Zaharia, Michael Armbrust, Mykhailo Osypov, QP Hou, Reynold Xin, Robert Pack, Ryan Zhu, Scott Sandre, Tathagata Das, Thomas Vollmer, Venki Korukanti, and Will Jones; your vision and dedication laid the foundation for this project, and without your efforts, this book would not have been possible.

We are also incredibly thankful to the numerous reviewers who provided us with invaluable guidance. Their diligent and constructive feedback, informed by their technical expertise and perspectives, has shaped this book into a valuable resource for learning about Delta Lake. Special thanks to Adi Polak, Aditya Chaturvedi, Andrew Bauman, Andy Petrella, Bartosz Konieczny, Holden Karau, Jacek Laskowski, Jobinesh Purushothaman, Matt Housley, and Matt Powers; your insights have been instrumental in refining our work.

A massive shout-out goes to R. Tyler Croy, who started as a reviewer of this book and eventually joined the author team. His contributions have been invaluable, and his work on Chapter 6, "Building Native Applications with Delta Lake", is a testament to his dedication and expertise. Thank you, Tyler, for your unwavering support and for being an integral part of this journey.

Last but certainly not least, we want to thank the Delta Lake community. As of this book's release, it has been a little more than five years since Delta Lake became open source. Throughout this time, we have experienced many ups and downs, but we have grown together to create an amazing project and community. Your enthusiasm, collaboration, and support have been the driving force behind our success.

Thank you all for being a part of this incredible journey!

Denny

On a personal note, I would like to express my deepest gratitude to my wonderful family and friends. Your unwavering support and encouragement have been my anchor throughout this journey. A special thank-you to my amazing children, Katherine, Samantha, and Isabella, for your patience and love. And to my partner and wonderful wife, Hua-Ping, I could not have done this without you or your constant support and patience.

Tristen

I could not have made it through the immense effort (and many hours) required to pour myself into this book without the many people who helped me become who I am today. I want to thank my wife, Jessyca, for her loving and patient endurance, and my children, Jake, Zek, and Ada, for always being a motivation and a source of inspiration to keep going the distance. I would also like to thank my good friend Steven Yu for helping to guide and encourage me over the years we've known each other; my parents, Kirk and Patricia, for always being encouraging; and the numerous colleagues with whom I have shared many experiences and conversations.

Scott

Getting to the end of a book as an author is a fascinating journey. It requires patience and dedication, but even more, you leave part of yourself behind in the pages you write, and in a very real sense you leave the world behind as you write. Finding the time to write is a balancing act that tries the patience of your friends and family. To my wife, Lacey: thanks for putting up with another book. To my dogs, Willow and Clover: I'm sorry I missed walks and couch time. To my family: thanks for always being there, and for pretending to get excited as I talk about distributed data (your glassy eyes give you away every time). To my friends: I owe all of you more personal time now and promise to drive up to the Bay Area more often. Last, I lost my little sister Meredith while writing this book, and as a means of memorializing her, I've hidden inside jokes and things that would have made her laugh throughout the book and in the examples and data. I love you, Meredith.

Prashanth

I extend my deepest gratitude to my wife, Kavyasudha, for her unwavering support, patience, and love throughout the journey. Your belief in me, even during the most challenging times, has been my anchor. To our curious and joyful child, Advaith, thank you for your infectious laughter and understanding, which have provided endless motivation and joy. Your curiosity and energy remind me daily of the importance of perseverance and passion. To both of you, I extend all my love and appreciation.

## CHAPTER 1

Introduction to the Delta Lake Lakehouse Format

This chapter explains Delta Lake's origins and how it was initially designed to address data integrity issues around petabyte-scale systems. If you are familiar with Delta Lake's history and instead want to dive into what Delta Lake is, its anatomy, and the Delta transaction protocol, feel free to jump ahead to the section "What Is Delta Lake?" on page 6 later in this chapter.

The Genesis of Delta Lake

In this section, we'll chart the course of Delta Lake's short evolutionary history: its genesis and inspiration, and its adoption in the community as a lakehouse format, ensuring the integrity of every enterprise's most important asset: its data. The Delta Lake lakehouse format was developed to address the limitations of traditional data lakes and data warehouses. It provides ACID (atomicity, consistency, isolation, and durability) transactions (*https://oreil.ly/gjn55*) and scalable metadata handling and unifies various data analytics tasks, such as batch and streaming workloads, machine learning, and SQL, on a single platform.

Data Warehousing, Data Lakes, and Data Lakehouses

There have been many technological advancements in data systems (high-performance computing [HPC] and object databases, for example); a simplified overview of the advancements in querying and aggregating large amounts of business data systems over the last few decades would cover data warehousing, data lakes, and lakehouses. Overall, these systems address online analytics processing (OLAP) workloads.

Data warehousing

Data warehouses are purpose-built to aggregate and process large amounts of structured data quickly (Figure 1-1). To protect this data, they typically use relational
databases to provide ACID transactions, a step that is crucial for ensuring data
integrity for business applications.

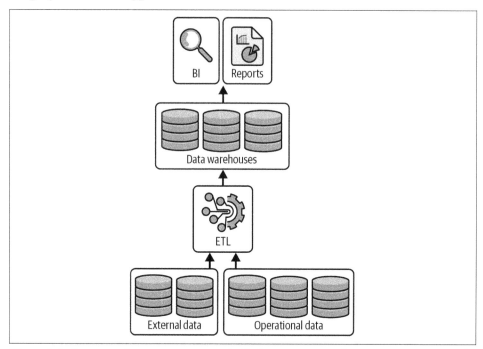

*Figure 1-1. Data warehouses are purpose-built for querying and aggregating structured
data*

Building on the foundation of ACID transactions, data warehouses include management features (backup and recovery controls, gated controls, etc.) to simplify the
database operations as well as performance optimizations (indexes, partitioning,
etc.) to provide reliable results to the end user more quickly. While robust, data
warehouses are often hard to scale to handle the large volumes, variety of analytics
(including event processing and data sciences), and data velocity typical in big data
scenarios. This limitation is a critical factor that often necessitates using more scalable
solutions such as data lakes or distributed processing frameworks like Apache Spark.

Data lakes

Data lakes are scalable storage repositories (HDFS, cloud object stores such as Amazon S3, ADLS Gen2, and GCS, and so on) that hold vast amounts of raw data
in their native format until needed (see Figure 1-2). Unlike traditional databases,

data lakes are designed to handle an internet-scale volume, velocity, and variety of data (e.g., structured, semistructured, and unstructured data). These attributes are commonly associated with big data. Data lakes changed how we store and query large amounts of data because they are designed to scale out the workload across multiple machines or nodes. They are file-based systems that work on clusters of commodity hardware. Traditionally, data warehouses were scaled up on a single machine; note that massively parallel processing data warehouses have existed for quite some time but were more expensive and complex to maintain. Also, while data warehouses were designed for structured (or tabular) data, data lakes can hold data in the format of one's choosing, providing developers with flexibility for their data storage.

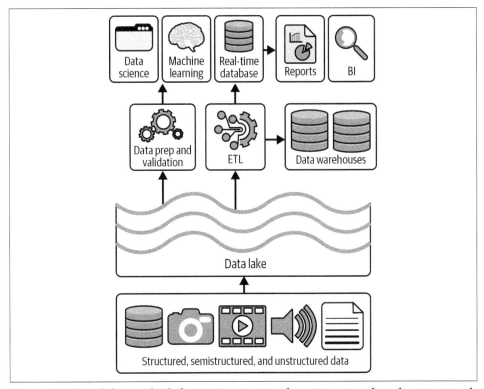

Figure 1-2. Data lakes are built for storing structured, semistructured, and unstructured data on scalable storage infrastructure (e.g., HDFS or cloud object stores)

While data lakes could handle all your data for data science and machine learning, they are an inherently unreliable form of data storage. Instead of providing ACID protections, these systems follow the BASE model—basically available, soft-state, and eventually consistent (*https://oreil.ly/eAqrW*). The lack of ACID guarantees means the storage system processing failures leave your storage in an inconsistent state with orphaned files. Subsequent queries to the storage system include files that should not result in duplicate counts (i.e., wrong answers).

Together, these shortcomings can lead to an infrastructure poorly suited for BI queries, inconsistent and slow performance, and quite complex setups. Often, the creation of data lakes leads to unreliable data swamps instead of clean data repositories due to the lack of transaction protections, schema management, and so on.

Lakehouses (or data lakehouses)

The lakehouse combines the best elements of data lakes and data warehouses for OLAP workloads. It merges the scalability and flexibility of data lakes with the management features and performance optimization of data warehouses (see Figure 1-3). There were previous attempts to allow data warehouses and data lakes to coexist side by side. But such an approach was expensive, introducing management complexities, duplication of data, and the reconciliation of reporting/analytics/data science between separate systems. As the practice of data engineering evolved, the concept of the *lakehouse* was born. A lakehouse eliminates the need for disjointed systems and provides a single, coherent platform for all forms of data analysis. Lakehouses enhance the performance of data queries and simplify data management, making it easier for organizations to derive insights from their data.

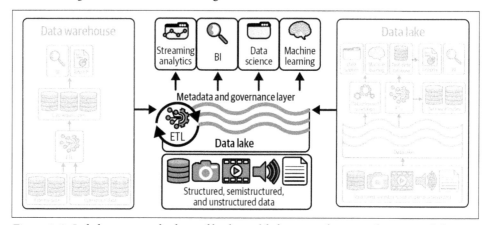

Figure 1-3. Lakehouses are the best of both worlds between data warehouses and data lakes

Delta Lake, Apache Iceberg, and Apache Hudi are the most popular open source lakehouse formats. As you can guess, this book will focus on Delta Lake.[1]

---

1 To learn more about lakehouses, see the 2021 CIDR whitepaper "Lakehouse: A New Generation of Open Platforms That Unify Data Warehousing and Advanced Analytics" (*https://oreil.ly/ObS0C*).

Project Tahoe to Delta Lake: The Early ~~Years~~ Months

The 2021 online meetup From Tahoe to Delta Lake (*https://oreil.ly/52sIg*) provided a nostalgic look back at how Delta Lake was created. The panel featured "old school" developers and Delta Lake maintainers Burak Yavuz, Denny Lee, Ryan Zhu, and Tathagata Das, as well as the creator of Delta Lake, Michael Armbrust. It also included the "new school" Delta Lake maintainers who created the delta-rs project, QP Hou and R. Tyler Croy.

The original project name for Delta Lake was "Project Tahoe," as Michael Armbrust had the initial idea of providing transactional reliability for data lakes while skiing at Tahoe in 2017. Lake Tahoe is an iconic and massive lake in California, symbolizing the large-scale data lake the project aimed to create. Michael is a committer/PMC member of Apache Spark™; a Delta Lake maintainer; one of the original creators of Spark SQL, Structured Streaming, and Delta Lake; and a distinguished software engineer at Databricks. The transition from "Tahoe" to "Delta Lake" occurred around New Year's 2018 and came from Jules Damji. The rationale behind changing the name was to invoke the natural process in which rivers flow into deltas, depositing sediments that eventually build up and create fertile ground for crops. This metaphor was fitting for the project, as it represented the convergence of data streams into a managed data lake, where data practitioners could cultivate valuable insights. The Delta name also resonated with the project's architecture, which was designed to handle massive and high-velocity data streams, allowing the data to be processed and split into different streams or views.

But why did Armbrust create Delta Lake? He created it to address the limitations of Apache Spark's file synchronization. Specifically, he wanted to handle large-scale data operations and needed robust transactional support. Thus, his motivation for developing Delta Lake stemmed from the need for a scalable transaction log that could handle massive data volumes and complex operations.

Early in the creation of Delta Lake are two notable use cases that emphasize its efficiency and scalability. Comcast utilized Delta Lake to enhance its data analytics and machine learning platforms and manage its petabytes of data. This transition reduced its compute utilization from 640VMs to 64VMs and simplified job maintenance from 84 to 3 jobs. By streamlining its processing with Delta Lake, Comcast reduced its compute utilization by 10x, with 28x fewer jobs. Apple's information security team employed Delta Lake for real-time threat detection and response, handling over 300 billion events per day and writing hundreds of terabytes of data daily. Both cases illustrate Delta Lake's superior performance and cost-effectiveness compared to traditional data management methods. We will look at additional use cases in Chapter 11.

What Is Delta Lake?

Delta Lake is an open source storage layer that supports ACID transactions, scalable metadata handling, and unification of streaming and batch data processing. It was initially designed to work with Apache Spark and large-scale data lake workloads.

With Delta Lake, you can build a single data platform with your choice of high-performance query engine to address a diverse range of workloads, including (but not limited to) business intelligence (BI), streaming analytics/complex event processing, data science, and machine learning, as noted in Figure 1-4.

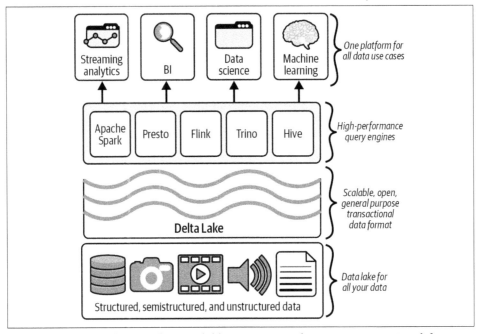

Figure 1-4. Delta Lake provides a scalable, open, general-purpose transactional data format for your lakehouse

However, as it has evolved, Delta Lake has been optimally designed to work with numerous workloads (small data, medium data, big data, etc.). It has also been designed to work with multiple frameworks (e.g., Apache Spark, Apache Flink, Trino, Presto, Apache Hive, and Apache Druid), services (e.g., Athena, Big Query, Databricks, EMR, Fabric, Glue, Starburst, and Snowflake), and languages (.NET, Java, Python, Rust, Scala, SQL, etc.).

Common Use Cases

Developers in all types of organizations, from startups to large enterprises, use Delta Lake to manage their big data and AI workloads. Common use cases include:

Modernizing data lakes
> Delta Lake helps organizations modernize their data lakes by providing ACID transactions, scalable metadata handling, and schema enforcement, thereby ensuring data reliability and performance improvements.

Data warehousing
> There are both data warehousing technologies and *techniques*. The Delta Lake lakehouse format allows you to apply data warehousing techniques to provide fast query performance for various analytics workloads while also providing data reliability.

Machine learning/data science
> Delta Lake provides a reliable data foundation for machine learning and data science teams to access and process data, enabling them to build and deploy models faster.

Streaming data processing
> Delta Lake unifies streaming and batch data processing. This allows developers to process real-time data and perform complex transformations on the fly.

Data engineering
> Delta Lake provides a reliable and performant platform for data engineering teams to build and manage data pipelines, ensuring data quality and accuracy.

Business intelligence
> Delta Lake supports SQL queries, making it easy for business users to access and analyze data and thus enabling them to make data-driven decisions.

Overall, Delta Lake is used by various teams, including data engineers, data scientists, and business users, to manage and analyze big data and AI workloads, ensuring data reliability, performance, and scalability.

Key Features

Delta Lake comprises the following key features that are fundamental to an open lakehouse format (please see the VLDB research article "Delta Lake: High-Performance ACID Table Storage over Cloud Object Stores" (*https://oreil.ly/PaRNO*) for a deeper dive into these features):

ACID transactions
> Delta Lake ensures that data modifications are performed atomically, consistently, in isolation, and durably, i.e., with ACID transaction protections. This means that when multiple concurrent clients or tasks access the data, the system maintains data integrity. For instance, if a process fails during a data modification, Delta Lake will roll back the changes, ensuring that the data remains consistent.

Scalable metadata
> The metadata of a Delta Lake table is the transaction log, which provides transactional consistency per the aforementioned ACID transactions. With a petabyte-scale table, the table's metadata can itself be exceedingly complicated to maintain. Delta Lake's scalable metadata handling feature is designed to manage metadata efficiently for large-scale datasets without its operations impacting query or processing performance.

Time travel
> The Delta Lake time travel feature allows you to query previous versions of a table to access historical data. Made possible by the Delta transaction log, it enables you to specify a version or timestamp to query a specific version of the data. This is very useful for a variety of use cases, such as data audits, regulatory compliance, and data recovery.

Unified batch/streaming
> Delta Lake was designed hand in hand with Apache Spark Structured Streaming to simplify the logic around streaming. Instead of having different APIs for batch and streaming, Structured Streaming uses the same in-memory Datasets/DataFrame API for both scenarios. This allows developers to use the same business logic and APIs, the only difference being latency. Delta Lake provides the ACID guarantees of the storage system to support this unification.

Schema evolution/enforcement
> Delta Lake's schema evolution and schema enforcement ensure data consistency and quality by enforcing a schema on write operations and allowing users to modify the schema without breaking existing queries. They also prevent developers from inadvertently inserting data with incorrect columns or types, which is crucial for maintaining data quality and consistency.

Audit history

This feature provides detailed logs of all changes made to the data, including information about who made each change, what the change was, and when it was made. This is crucial for compliance and regulatory requirements, as it allows users to track changes to the data over time and ensure that data modifications are performed correctly. The Delta transaction log makes all of this possible.

DML operations

Delta Lake was one of the first lakehouse formats to provide data manipulation language (DML) operations. This initially extended Apache Spark to support various operations such as insert, update, delete, and merge (or CRUD operations). Today, users can effectively modify the data using multiple frameworks, services, and languages.

Open source

The roots of Delta Lake were built within the foundation of Databricks, which has extensive experience in open source (the founders of Databricks were the original creators of Apache Spark). Shortly after its inception, Delta Lake was donated to the Linux Foundation to ensure developers have the ability to use, modify, and distribute the software freely while also promoting collaboration and innovation within the data engineering community.

Performance

While Delta Lake is a lakehouse storage format, it is optimally designed to improve the speed of your queries and processing for both ingestion and querying using the default configuration. While you can continually tweak the performance of Delta Lake, most of the time the defaults will work for your scenarios.

Ease of use

Delta Lake was built with simplicity in mind right from the beginning. For example, to write a table using Apache Spark in Parquet file format, you would execute:

```
data.write.format("parquet").save("/tmp/parquet-table")
```

To do the same thing for Delta, you would execute:

```
data.write.format("delta").save("/tmp/delta-table")
```

Anatomy of a Delta Lake Table

A Delta Lake table or Delta table comprises several key components that work together to provide a robust, scalable, and efficient data storage solution. The main elements are as follows:

Data files

> Delta Lake tables store data in Parquet file format. These files contain the actual data and are stored in a distributed cloud or on-premises file storage system such as HDFS (Hadoop Distributed File System), Amazon S3, Azure Blob Storage (or Azure Data Lake Storage [ADLS] Gen2), GCS (Google Cloud Storage), or MinIO. Parquet was chosen for its efficiency in storing and querying large datasets.

Transaction log

> The transaction log, also known as the Delta log, is a critical component of Delta Lake. It is an ordered record of every transaction performed on a Delta Lake table. The transaction log ensures ACID properties by recording all changes to the table in a series of JSON files. Each transaction is recorded as a new JSON file in the *_delta_log* directory, which includes metadata about the transaction, such as the operation performed, the files added or removed, and the schema of the table at the time of the transaction.

Metadata

> Metadata in Delta Lake includes information about the table's schema, partitioning, and configuration settings. This metadata is stored in the transaction log and can be retrieved using SQL, Spark, Rust, and Python APIs. The metadata helps manage and optimize the table by providing information for schema enforcement and evolution, partitioning strategies, and data skipping.

Schema

> A Delta Lake table's schema defines the data's structure, including its columns, data types, and so on. The schema is enforced on write, ensuring that all data written to the table adheres to the defined structure. Delta Lake supports schema evolution (add new columns, rename columns, etc.), allowing the schema to be updated as the data changes over time.

Checkpoints

> Checkpoints are periodic snapshots of the transaction log that help speed up the recovery process. Delta Lake consolidates the state of the transaction log by default every 10 transactions. This allows client readers to quickly catch up from the most recent checkpoint rather than replaying the entire transaction log from the beginning. Checkpoints are stored as Parquet files and are created automatically by Delta Lake.

Figure 1-5 is a graphical representation of the structure of a Delta Lake table.

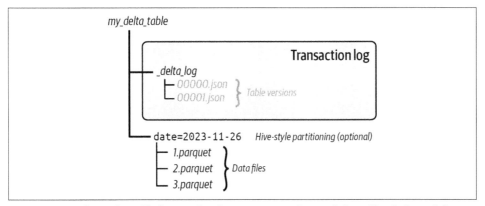

Figure 1-5. Delta Lake table layout for the transaction log and data files (adapted from an image by Denny Lee)[2]

Delta Transaction Protocol

In the previous section, we described the anatomy of a Delta Lake table. The Delta transaction log protocol (*https://oreil.ly/CPxmm*) is the specification defining how clients interact with the table in a consistent manner. At its core, all interactions with the Delta table must begin by reading the Delta transaction log to know what files to read. When a client modifies the data, the client initiates the creation of new data files (i.e., Parquet files) and then inserts new metadata into the transaction log to commit modifications to the table. In fact, many of the original Delta Lake integrations (*https://oreil.ly/vfuS2*) (delta-spark, Trino connector, delta-rust API, etc.) had codebases maintained by different communities. A Rust client could write, a Spark client could modify, and a Trino client could read from the same Delta table without conflict because they all independently followed the same protocol.

Implementing this specification brings ACID properties to large data collections stored as files in a distributed filesystem or object store. As defined in the specification, the protocol was designed with the following goals in mind:

Serializable ACID writes
Multiple writers can modify a Delta table concurrently while maintaining ACID semantics.

---

2 Denny Lee, "Understanding the Delta Lake Transaction Log at the File Level" (*https://oreil.ly/X5p5R*), *Denny Lee* (blog), November 26, 2023.

Snapshot isolation for reads
> Readers can read a consistent snapshot of a Delta table, even in the face of concurrent writes.

Scalability to billions of partitions or files
> Queries against a Delta table can be planned on a single machine or in parallel.

Self-describing
> All metadata for a Delta table is stored alongside the data. This design eliminates the need to maintain a separate metastore to read the data and allows static tables to be copied or moved using standard filesystem tools.

Support for incremental processing
> Readers can tail the Delta log to determine what data has been added in a given period of time, allowing for efficient streaming.

Understanding the Delta Lake Transaction Log at the File Level

To better understand this in action, let's look at what happens at the file level when a Delta table is created. Initially, the table's transaction log is automatically created in the *_delta_log* subdirectory. As changes are made to the table, the operations are recorded as ordered *atomic commits* in the transaction log. Each commit is written out as a JSON file, starting with *000...00000.json*. Additional changes to the table generate subsequent JSON files in ascending numerical order, so that the next commits are written out as *000...00001.json*, *000...00002.json*, and so on. Each numeric JSON file increment represents a new version of the table, as described in Figure 1-5.

Note how the structure of the data files has not changed; they exist as separate Parquet files generated by the query engine or language writing to the Delta table. If your table utilizes Hive-style partitioning, you will retain the same structure.

The Single Source of Truth

Delta Lake allows multiple readers and writers of a given table to all work on the table at the same time. It is the central repository that tracks all user changes to the table. This concept is important because, over time, processing jobs will invariably fail in your data lake. The result is partial files that are not removed. Subsequent processing or queries will not be able to ascertain which files should or should not be included in their queries. To show users correct views of the data at all times, the Delta log is the *single source of truth*.

The Relationship Between Metadata and Data

As the Delta transaction log is the single source of truth, any client who wants to read or write to your Delta table *must* first query the transaction log. For example, when inserting data while creating our Delta table, we initially generate two Parquet files: *1.parquet* and *2.parquet*. This event would automatically be added to the transaction log and saved to disk as commit *000...00000.json* (see A in Figure 1-6).

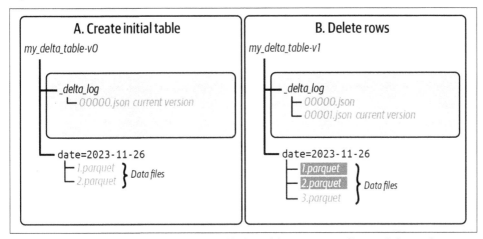

Figure 1-6. (left) Creating a new Delta table by adding Parquet files and their relationship with the Delta transaction log; (right) deleting rows from this Delta table by removing and adding files and their relationship with the Delta transaction log

In a subsequent command (B in Figure 1-6), we run a DELETE operation that results in the removal of rows from the table. Instead of modifying the existing Parquet files (*1.parquet, 2.parquet*), Delta creates a third file (*3.parquet*).

Multiversion Concurrency Control (MVCC) File and Data Observations

For deletes on object stores, it is faster to create a new file or files comprising the unaffected rows rather than modifying the existing Parquet file(s). This approach also provides the advantage of multiversion concurrency control (MVCC). MVCC is a database optimization technique that creates copies of the data, thus allowing data to be safely read and updated concurrently. This technique also allows Delta Lake to provide time travel. Therefore, Delta Lake creates multiple files for these actions, providing atomicity, MVCC, and speed.

> We can speed up this process by using deletion vectors, an approach we will describe in Chapter 8.

The removal/creation of the Parquet files shown in B in Figure 1-6 is wrapped in a single transaction recorded in the Delta transaction log in the file *000...00001.json*. Some important observations concerning atomicity are:

- If a user were to read the Parquet files without reading the Delta transaction log, they would read duplicates because of the replicated rows in all the files (*1.parquet, 2.parquet, 3.parquet*).

- The remove and add actions are wrapped in the single transaction log *000...00001.json*. When a client queries the Delta table at this time, it records both of these actions and the filepaths for that snapshot. For this transaction, the filepath would point only to *3.parquet*.

- Note that the remove operation is a soft delete or tombstone where the physical removal of the files (*1.parquet, 2.parquet*) has yet to happen. The physical removal of files will happen when executing the VACUUM command.

- The previous transaction *000...00000.json* has the filepath pointing to the original files (*1.parquet, 2.parquet*). Thus, when querying for an older version of the Delta table via time travel, the transaction log points to the files that make up that older snapshot.

Observing the Interaction Between the Metadata and Data

While we now have a better understanding of what happens at the *individual* data file and metadata file level, how does this all work together? Let's look at this problem by following the flow of Figure 1-7, which represents a common data processing failure scenario. The table is initially represented by two Parquet files (*1.parquet* and *2.parquet*) at t_0.

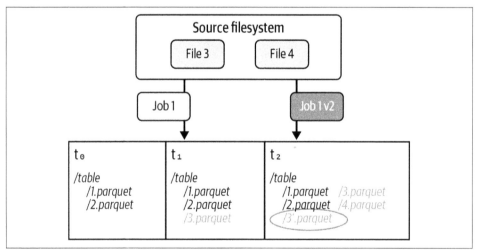

Figure 1-7. A common data processing failure scenario: partial files

At t_1, job 1 extracts file 3 and file 4 and writes them to storage. However, due to some error (network hiccup, storage temporarily offline, etc.), an incomplete portion of file 3 and none of file 4 are written into *3.parquet*. Thus, *3.parquet* is a partial file, and this incomplete data will be returned to any clients that subsequently query the files that make up this table.

To complicate matters, at t_2, a new version of the same processing job (job 1 v2) successfully completes its task. It generates a new version of *3.parquet* and *4.parquet*. But because the partial *3'.parquet* (circled) exists alongside *3.parquet*, any system querying these files will result in double counting.

However, because the Delta transaction log tracks which files are valid, we can avoid the preceding scenario. Thus, when a client reads a Delta Lake table, the engine (or API) initially verifies the transaction log to see what new transactions have been posted to the table. It then updates the client table with any new changes. This ensures that any client's version of a table is always synchronized. Clients cannot make divergent, conflicting changes to a table.

Let's repeat the same partial file example on a Delta Lake table. Figure 1-8 shows the same scenario in which the table is represented by two Parquet files (i.e., *1.parquet* and *2.parquet*) at t_0. The transaction log records that these two files make up the Delta table at t_0 (Version 0).

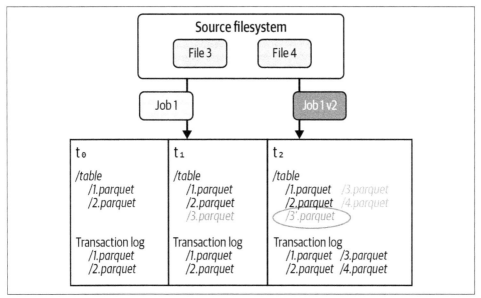

Figure 1-8. Delta Lake avoids the partial files scenario because of its transaction log

At t_1, job 1 fails with the creation of *3.parquet*. However, because the job failed, the transaction was *not* committed to the transaction log. No new files are recorded;

notice how the transaction log has only *1.parquet* and *2.parquet* listed. Any queries against the Delta table at t_1 will read only these two files, even if other files are in storage.

At t_2, job 1 v2 is completed, and its output is the files *3.parquet* and *4.parquet*. Because the job was successful, the Delta log includes entries only for the two successful files. That is, *3'.parquet* is *not* included in the log. Therefore, any clients querying the Delta table at t_2 will see only the correct files.

Table Features

Originally, Delta tables used protocol versions (*https://oreil.ly/xkjRV*) to map to a set of features to ensure user workloads did not break when new features in Delta were released. For example, if a client wanted to use Delta's Change Data Feed (CDF) option (*https://oreil.ly/dJeON*), users were required to upgrade their protocol versions and validate their workloads to access new features (Figure 1-9). This ensured that any readers or writers incompatible with a specific protocol version were blocked from reading or writing to that table to prevent data corruption.

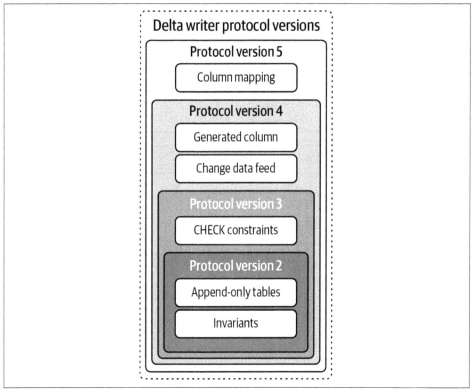

Figure 1-9. Delta writer protocol versions

But this process slows feature adoption because it requires the client and table to support *all* features in that protocol version. For example, with protocol version 4, your Delta table supports both generated columns (*https://oreil.ly/E7sBs*) and CDF. For your client to read this table, it must support both generated columns and Change Data Feed even if you only want to use CDF. In other words, Delta connectors have no choice but to implement all features just to support a single feature in the new version.

Introduced in Delta Lake 2.3.0 (*https://oreil.ly/Apr1l*), *Table Features* replaces table protocol versions to represent features a table uses so connectors can know which features are required to read or write a table (Figure 1-10).

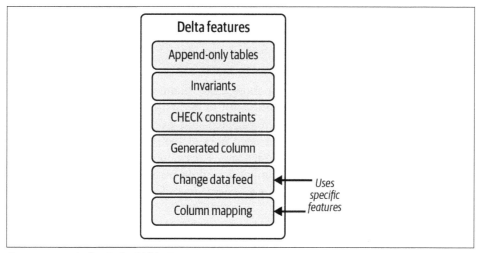

Figure 1-10. Delta Lake Table Features

The advantage of this approach is that any connectors (or integrations) can selectively implement certain features of their interest, instead of having to work on all of them. A quick way to view what table features are enabled is to run the query SHOW TBLPROPERTIES:

```
SHOW TBLPROPERTIES default.my_table;
```

The output would look similar to the following:

```
Key (String)                            Value (String)
delta.minReaderVersion                  3
delta.minWriterVersion                  7
delta.feature.deletionVectors           supported
delta.enableDeletionVectors             true
delta.checkpoint.writeStatsAsStruct     true
delta.checkpoint.writeStatsAsJson       false
```

To dive deeper, please refer to "Table Features" in the GitHub page for the Delta transaction protocol (*https://oreil.ly/wjBBu*).

Delta Kernel

As previously noted, Delta Lake provides ACID guarantees and performance across many frameworks, services, and languages. As of this writing, every time new features are added to Delta Lake, the connector must be rewritten entirely, because there is a tight coupling between the metadata and data processing. Delta Kernel (*https://oreil.ly/0P0zv*) simplifies the development of connectors by abstracting out all the protocol details so the connectors do not need to understand them. Kernel itself implements the Delta transaction log specification (per the previous section). This allows the connectors to build only against the Kernel library, which provides the following advantages:

Modularity
  Creating Delta Kernel allows for more easily maintained parity between Delta Lake Rust and Scala/JVM, enabling both to be first-class citizens. All metadata (i.e., transaction log) logic is coordinated and executed through the Kernel library. This way, the connectors need only to focus on how to perform their respective frameworks/services/languages. For example, the Apache Flink/Delta Lake connector needs to focus only on reading or modifying the specific files provided by Delta Kernel. The end client does not need to understand the semantics of the transaction log.

Extensibility
  Delta Kernel decouples the *logic* for the metadata (i.e., transaction log) from the data. This allows Delta Lake to be modular, extensible, and highly portable (for example, you can copy the entire table with its transaction log to a new location for your AI workloads). This also extends (pun intended) to Delta Lake's extensibility, as a connector is now, for example, provided the list of files to read instead of needing to query the transaction log directly. Delta Lake already has many integrations (*https://oreil.ly/nlO4w*), and by decoupling the logic around the metadata from the data, it will be easier for all of us to maintain our various connectors.

Delta Kernel achieves this level of abstraction through the following requirements:

It provides narrow, stable APIs for connectors.
  For a table scan query, a connector needs to specify only the query schema, so that the Kernel can read only the required columns, and the query filters for Kernel to skip data (files, rowgroups, etc.). APIs will be stable and backward compatible. Connectors should be able just to upgrade the Delta Kernel version

without rewriting their client code—that is, they automatically get support for an updated Delta protocol via Table Features.

It internally implements the protocol-specific logic.
Delta Kernel will implement all of the following operations:

- Read JSON files
- Read Parquet log files
- Replay log with data skipping
- Read Parquet data and DV files
- Transform data (e.g., filter by DVs)

While Kernel internally implements the protocol-specific logic, better engine-specific implementations can be added (e.g., Apache Spark or Trino may have better JSON and Parquet reading capabilities).

It provides APIs for plugging in better performance.
These include *Table APIs* for connectors to perform table operations such as data scans and *Engine APIs* for plugging in connector-optimized implementations for performance-sensitive components.

As of this writing, Delta Kernel is still in the early stages, and building your own Kernel connector is outside the scope of this book. If you would like to dive deeper into how to build your own Kernel connector, please refer to the following resources:

- "[Umbrella Feature Request] Delta Kernel APIs to simplify building connectors for reading Delta tables" (*https://oreil.ly/a6Qn9*)
- Delta Kernel—Java (*https://oreil.ly/_KRTc*)
- Delta Kernel—Rust (*https://oreil.ly/Yx4-a*)
- "Delta Kernel: Simplifying Building Connectors for Delta" (*https://oreil.ly/u3FpF*)

Delta UniForm

As noted in the section "Lakehouses (or data lakehouses)" on page 4, there are multiple lakehouse formats. Delta Universal Format, or UniForm, is designed to simplify the interoperability among Delta Lake, Apache Iceberg, and Apache Hudi. Fundamentally, lakehouse formats are composed of metadata and data (typically in Parquet file format).

What makes these lakehouse formats different is how they create, manage, and maintain the *metadata* associated with this data. With Delta UniForm, the metadata of other lakehouse formats is generated concurrently with the Delta format. This way, whether you have a Delta, Iceberg, or Hudi client, it can read the data, because all of their APIs can understand the metadata. Delta UniForm includes the following support:

- Apache Iceberg support as part of Delta Lake 3.0.0 (*https://oreil.ly/BheSC*) (October 2023)
- Apache Hudi support as part of Delta Lake 3.2.0 (*https://oreil.ly/MgmwB*) (May 2024)

For the latest information on how to enable these features, please refer to the Delta UniForm documentation (*https://oreil.ly/1hQoF*).

Conclusion

In this chapter, we explained the origins of Delta Lake, what it is and what it does, its anatomy, and the transaction protocol. We emphasized that the Delta transaction log is the single source of truth and thus is the single source of the relationship between its metadata and data. While still early, this has led to the development of Delta Kernel as the foundation for simplifying the building of Delta connectors for Delta Lake's many frameworks, services, and community projects. The core difference between the different lakehouse formats is their metadata, so Delta UniForm unifies them by generating all formats' metadata.

## CHAPTER 2

Installing Delta Lake

In this chapter, we will show you how to set up Delta Lake and walk you through the simple steps to start writing your first standalone application.

There are multiple ways you can install Delta Lake. If you are just starting, using a single machine with the Delta Lake Docker image is the best option. If you want to skip the hassle of a local installation, the Databricks Community Edition, which includes the latest version of Delta Lake, is free. Various free trials of Databricks, which natively provides Delta Lake, are also available; check your cloud provider's documentation for additional details. Other options discussed in this chapter include the Delta Rust Python bindings, the Delta Rust API, and Apache Spark. In this chapter, we also create and verify the Delta Lake tables for illustrative purposes. Delta Lake table creation and other CRUD operations are covered in depth in Chapter 3.

Delta Lake Docker Image

The Delta Lake Docker image contains all the necessary components to read and write with Delta Lake, including Python, Rust, PySpark, Apache Spark, and Jupyter Notebooks. The basic prerequisite is having Docker installed on your local machine (you can find installation instructions at Get Docker (*https://oreil.ly/nZTFH*)). Once you have Docker installed, you can either download the latest prebuilt version of the Delta Lake Docker image from DockerHub (*https://oreil.ly/cG0K_*) or build the Docker image yourself by following the instructions from the Delta Lake Docker GitHub repository (*https://oreil.ly/-BNl0*). Once the image has been built or you have downloaded the correct image, you can then move on to running the quickstart in a notebook or shell. The Docker image is the preferred option to run all the code snippets in this book.

Please note this Docker image comes preinstalled with the following:

Apache Arrow

Apache Arrow (*https://oreil.ly/qbJoo*) is a development platform for in-memory analytics and aims to provide a standardized, language-independent columnar memory format for flat and hierarchical data, as well as libraries and tools for working with this format. It enables fast data processing and movement across different systems and languages, such as C, C++, C#, Go, Java, JavaScript, Julia, MATLAB, Python, R, Ruby, and Rust.

DataFusion

Created in 2017 and donated to the Apache Arrow project in 2019, DataFusion (*https://oreil.ly/K6Rv0*) is a fast, extensible query engine for building high-quality data-centric systems written in Rust that uses the Apache Arrow in-memory format.

ROAPI

ROAPI (*https://oreil.ly/qrCcK*) is a no-code solution to automatically spin up read-only APIs for Delta Lake and other sources; it builds on top of Apache Arrow and DataFusion.

Rust

Rust (*https://oreil.ly/J7mSl*) is a statically typed, compiled language that offers performance akin to C and C++, but with a focus on safety and memory management. It's known for its unique ownership model that ensures memory safety without a garbage collector, making it ideal for systems programming in which control over system resources is crucial.

 We're using Linux/macOS in this book. If you're running Windows, you can use Git Bash, WSL, or any shell configured for bash commands. Please refer to the implementation-specific instructions for using other software, such as Docker.

We will discuss each of the following interfaces in detail, including how to create and read Delta Lake tables with each one:

- Python
- PySpark Shell
- JupyterLab Notebook

- Scala Shell
- Delta Rust API
- ROAPI

Run Docker Container

To start a Docker container with a bash shell:

1. Open a bash shell.

2. Run the container from the build image with a bash entrypoint using the following command in bash:

```
docker run --name delta_quickstart --rm -it \
--entrypoint bash delta_quickstart
```

Delta Lake for Python

First, open a bash shell and run a container from the built image with a bash entrypoint.

Next, use the `python3` command to launch a Python interactive shell session. The following code snippet will create a Pandas DataFrame (*https://oreil.ly/SxmKt*), create a Delta Lake table, generate new data, write by appending new data to this table, and finally read and then show the data from this Delta Lake table:

```
# Python
import pandas as pd
from deltalake.writer import write_deltalake
from deltalake import DeltaTable

df = pd.DataFrame(range(5), columns=["id"])      # Create Pandas DataFrame
write_deltalake("/tmp/deltars_table", df)        # Write Delta Lake table
df = pd.DataFrame(range(6, 11), columns=["id"])  # Generate new data
write_deltalake("/tmp/deltars_table", \
        df, mode="append")                       # Append new data
dt = DeltaTable("/tmp/deltars_table")            # Read Delta Lake table
dt.to_pandas()                                   # Show Delta Lake table
```

The output should look similar to the following:

```
# Output
    0
0   0
1   1
... ...
8   9
9   10
```

With these Python commands, you have created your first Delta Lake table. You can validate this by reviewing the underlying filesystem that makes up the table. To do that, you can list the contents within the folder of your Delta Lake table that you saved in */tmp/deltars-table* by running the following ls command after you close your Python process:

```bash
# Bash
$ ls -lsgA /tmp/deltars_table
total 12
4 -rw-r--r-- 1 NBuser 1610 Apr 13 05:48 0-...-f3c05c4277a2-0.parquet
4 -rw-r--r-- 1 NBuser 1612 Apr 13 05:48 1-...-674ccf40faae-0.parquet
4 drwxr-xr-x 2 NBuser 4096 Apr 13 05:48 _delta_log
```

The *.parquet* files contain the data you see in your Delta Lake table, while the *_delta_log* contains the Delta table's transaction log. We will discuss the transaction log in more detail in Chapter 3.

PySpark Shell

First, open a bash shell and run a container from the built image with a bash entrypoint.

Next, launch a PySpark interactive shell session:

```bash
# Bash
$SPARK_HOME/bin/pyspark --packages io.delta:${DELTA_PACKAGE_VERSION} \
--conf "spark.sql.extensions=io.delta.sql.DeltaSparkSessionExtension" \
--conf \
"spark.sql.catalog.spark_catalog=org.apache.spark.sql.delta.catalog.DeltaCatalog"
```

Let's run some basic commands in the shell:

```python
# Python
# Create a Spark DataFrame
data = spark.range(0, 5)

# Write to a Delta Lake table
(data
    .write
    .format("delta")
    .save("/tmp/delta-table")
)

# Read from the Delta Lake table
df = (spark
        .read
        .format("delta")
        .load("/tmp/delta-table")
        .orderBy("id")
    )
```

```
# Show the Delta Lake table
df.show()
```

To verify that you have created a Delta Lake table, you can list the contents within your Delta Lake table folder. For example, in the preceding code, you saved the table in */tmp/delta-table*. Once you close your pyspark process, run a list command in your Docker shell, and you should see something similar to the following:

```
# Bash
$ ls -lsgA /tmp/delta-table
total 36
4 drwxr-xr-x 2 NBuser 4096 Apr 13 06:01 _delta_log
4 -rw-r--r-- 1 NBuser  478 Apr 13 06:01 part-00000-56a2c68a-f90e-4764-8bf7-
a29a21a04230-c000.snappy.parquet
4 -rw-r--r-- 1 NBuser   12 Apr 13 06:01 .part-00000-56a2c68a-f90e-4764-8bf7-
a29a21a04230-c000.snappy.parquet.crc
4 -rw-r--r-- 1 NBuser  478 Apr 13 06:01 part-00001-bcbb45ab-6317-4229-
a6e6-80889ee6b957-c000.snappy.parquet
4 -rw-r--r-- 1 NBuser   12 Apr 13 06:01 .part-00001-bcbb45ab-6317-4229-
a6e6-80889ee6b957-c000.snappy.parquet.crc
4 -rw-r--r-- 1 NBuser  478 Apr 13 06:01 part-00002-9e0efb76-
a0c9-45cf-90d6-0dba912b3c2f-c000.snappy.parquet
4 -rw-r--r-- 1 NBuser   12 Apr 13 06:01 .part-00002-9e0efb76-
a0c9-45cf-90d6-0dba912b3c2f-c000.snappy.parquet.crc
4 -rw-r--r-- 1 NBuser  486 Apr 13 06:01 part-00003-909fee02-574a-47ba-9a3b-
d531eec7f0d7-c000.snappy.parquet
4 -rw-r--r-- 1 NBuser   12 Apr 13 06:01 .part-00003-909fee02-574a-47ba-9a3b-
d531eec7f0d7-c000.snappy.parquet.crc
```

JupyterLab Notebook

Open a bash shell and run a container from the built image with a JupyterLab entrypoint:

```
# Bash
docker run --name delta_quickstart --rm -it \
-p 8888-8889:8888-8889 delta_quickstart
```

The command will output a JupyterLab notebook URL. Copy the URL and launch a browser to follow along in the notebook and run each cell.

Scala Shell

First, open a bash shell and run a container from the built image with a bash entrypoint. Next, launch a Scala interactive shell session:

```
# Bash
$SPARK_HOME/bin/spark-shell --packages io.delta:${DELTA_PACKAGE_VERSION} \
--conf "spark.sql.extensions=io.delta.sql.DeltaSparkSessionExtension" \
--conf \
"spark.sql.catalog.spark_catalog=org.apache.spark.sql.delta.catalog.DeltaCatalog"
```

Let's run some basic commands in the shell:

```scala
// Scala
// Create a Spark DataFrame
val data = spark.range(0, 5)

// Write to a Delta Lake table
(data
    .write
    .format("delta")
    .save("/tmp/delta-table")
)

// Read from the Delta Lake table
val df = (spark
            .read
            .format("delta")
            .load("/tmp/delta-table")
            .orderBy("id")
        )

// Show the Delta Lake table
df.show()
```

For instructions on verifying the Delta Lake table, please refer to "PySpark Shell" on page 24.

Delta Rust API

First, open a bash shell and run a container from the built image with a bash entrypoint.

Next, execute *examples/read_delta_table.rs* to review the metadata and files of the covid19_nyt Delta Lake table; this command will list useful output, including the number of files written and their absolute paths, among other information:

```bash
# Bash
cd rs
cargo run --example read_delta_table
```

Finally, execute *examples/read_delta_datafusion.rs* to query the covid19_nyt Delta Lake table using DataFusion:

```bash
# Bash
cargo run --example read_delta_datafusion
```

Running the above command should list the schema and five rows of the data from the covid19_nyt Delta Lake table.

ROAPI

The rich open ecosystem around Delta Lake enables many novel utilities, such as ROAPI, which is included in the quickstart container. With ROAPI, you can spin up read-only APIs for static Delta Lake datasets without a single line of code. You can query your Delta Lake table with Apache Arrow and DataFusion using ROAPI, which is also preinstalled in the Docker image.

Open a bash shell and run a container from the built image with a bash entrypoint:

```
# Bash
docker run --name delta_quickstart --rm -it \
 -p 8080:8080 --entrypoint bash delta_quickstart
```

The API calls are pushed to the *nohup.out* file. If you haven't created the `deltars_table` in your container, create it via the option described in the section "Delta Lake for Python" on page 23. Alternatively, you may omit `--table 'deltars_table=/tmp/deltars_table/,format=delta'` from the command, as well as any steps that call the `deltars_table`.

Start the ROAPI utility using the following `nohup` command:

```
# Bash
nohup roapi --addr-http 0.0.0.0:8080 \
--table 'deltars_table=/tmp/deltars_table/,format=delta' \
--table 'covid19_nyt=/opt/spark/work-dir/rs/data/COVID-19_NYT,format=delta' &
```

Next, open another shell and connect to the same Docker image:

```
# Bash
docker exec -it delta_quickstart /bin/bash
```

Run the next three steps in the bash shell you launched in the previous step.

Check the schema of the two Delta Lake tables:

```
# Bash
curl localhost:8080/api/schema
```

The output of the preceding command should be along the following lines:

```
# Output
{
    "covid19_nyt":{"fields":[{"name":"date","data_type":"Utf8","nulla-
ble":true,"dict_id":0,"dict_is_ordered":false},
{"name":"county","data_type":"Utf8","nulla-
ble":true,"dict_id":0,"dict_is_ordered":false},
{"name":"state","data_type":"Utf8","nulla-
ble":true,"dict_id":0,"dict_is_ordered":false},
{"name":"fips","data_type":"Int32","nulla-
ble":true,"dict_id":0,"dict_is_ordered":false},
{"name":"cases","data_type":"Int32","nulla-
ble":true,"dict_id":0,"dict_is_ordered":false},
```

```
{"name":"deaths","data_type":"Int32","nulla-
ble":true,"dict_id":0,"dict_is_ordered":false}]},
    "deltars_table":{"fields":[{"name":"0","data_type":"Int64","nulla-
ble":true,"dict_id":0,"dict_is_ordered":false}]}
}
```

Query the `deltars_table`:

```
# Bash
curl -X POST -d "SELECT * FROM deltars_table"  localhost:8080/api/sql
```

The output of the preceding command should be along the following lines:

```
# Output
[{"0":0},{"0":1},{"0":2},{"0":3},{"0":4},{"0":6},{"0":7},{"0":8},{"0":9},
{"0":10}]
```

Query the `covid19_nyt` Delta Lake table:

```
# Bash
curl -X POST \
-d "SELECT cases, county, date FROM covid19_nyt ORDER BY cases DESC LIMIT 5" \
localhost:8080/api/sql
```

The output of the preceding command should be along the following lines:

```
# Output
[
{"cases":1208672,"county":"Los Angeles","date":"2021-03-11"},
{"cases":1207361,"county":"Los Angeles","date":"2021-03-10"},
{"cases":1205924,"county":"Los Angeles","date":"2021-03-09"},
{"cases":1204665,"county":"Los Angeles","date":"2021-03-08"},
{"cases":1203799,"county":"Los Angeles","date":"2021-03-07"}
]
```

Native Delta Lake Libraries

While Delta Lake's core functionality is deeply integrated with Apache Spark, the underlying data format and transaction log are designed to be language agnostic. This flexibility has spurred the development of native Delta Lake libraries in various programming languages, offering direct interaction with Delta Lake tables without the overhead of Spark.

These libraries provide lower-level access to Delta Lake's features, enabling developers to build highly optimized and specialized applications in a language-agnostic way. Developers can choose the language that best suits their needs and expertise. We discuss this in more detail in Chapter 6.

Multiple Bindings Available

The Rust library provides a strong foundation for other non-JVM-based libraries to build pipelines with Delta Lake. The most popular and prominent of those bindings are the Python bindings, which expose a `DeltaTable` class and optionally integrate seamlessly with Pandas or PyArrow. At the time of this writing, the Delta Lake Python package is compatible with Python versions 3.7 and later and offers many prebuilt wheels (*https://oreil.ly/JVvZO*) for easy installation on most major operating systems and architectures.

Multiple communities have developed bindings on top of the Rust library, exposing Delta Lake to Ruby, Node, or other C-based connectors. None have yet reached the maturity presently seen in the Python package, partly because none of the other language ecosystems have seen a level of investment in data tooling like that in the Python community. Pandas, Polars, PyArrow, Dask, and more provide a very rich set of tools for developers to read from and write to Delta tables.

More recently, there has been experimental work on a so-called Delta Kernel initiative (*https://oreil.ly/0P0zv*), which aims to provide a native Delta Lake library interface for connectors that abstracts away the Delta protocol into one place. This work is still in an early phase but is expected to help consolidate support for native (C/C++, for example) and higher-level engines (e.g., Python or Node) so that everybody can benefit from the more advanced features, such as deletion vectors, by simply upgrading their underlying Delta Kernel versions.

Installing the Delta Lake Python Package

Delta Lake provides native Python bindings based on the delta-rs project (*https://oreil.ly/ZtPkY*) with Pandas integration (*https://oreil.ly/SxmKt*). This Python package can be easily installed with the following command:

```Bash
# Bash
pip install deltalake
```

After installation, you can follow the same steps as outlined in "Delta Lake for Python" on page 23.

Apache Spark with Delta Lake

Apache Spark is an open source engine designed for the processing and analysis of large-scale datasets. It's architected to be both rapid and versatile and is capable of managing a variety of analytics, both batch and real-time. Spark provides an interface for programming comprehensive clusters, offering implicit data parallelism and fault tolerance. It leverages in-memory computations to enhance speed and data processing over MapReduce operations.

Spark offers multilingual support, which allows developers to construct applications in several languages, including Java, Scala, Python, R, and SQL. Spark also incorporates numerous libraries that enable a wide array of data analysis tasks encompassing machine learning, stream processing, and graph analytics.

Spark is written predominantly in Scala, but its APIs are available in Scala, Python, Java, and R. Spark SQL also allows users to write and execute SQL or HiveQL queries. For new users, we recommend exploring the Python API or SQL queries to get started with Apache Spark.

Check out *Learning Spark* (O'Reilly) or *Spark: The Definitive Guide* (O'Reilly) for a more detailed introduction to Spark.

Setting Up Delta Lake with Apache Spark

The steps in this section can be executed on your local machine in either of the following ways:

Interactive execution
    Start the Spark shell (with `spark-shell` for Scala language, or with `pyspark` for Python) with Delta Lake and run the code snippets interactively in the shell. In this chapter, we will focus on interactive execution.

Run them as a project
    If, instead of code snippets, you have code in multiple files, you can set up a Maven or sbt project (*https://oreil.ly/gqTDS*) (Scala or Java) with Delta Lake, with all the source files, and run the project. You could also use the examples provided in the GitHub repository (*https://oreil.ly/Qo0mz*).

For all the following instructions, make sure to install the version of Spark or PySpark that is compatible with Delta Lake 2.3.0. See the release compatibility matrix (*https://oreil.ly/4VkQ1*) for details.

Prerequisite: Set Up Java

As noted in the official Apache Spark installation instructions (*https://oreil.ly/NFI_5*), you must ensure that a valid Java version (8, 11, or 17) has been installed and configured correctly on your system using either the system `PATH` or the `JAVA_HOME` environmental variable.

Readers should make sure to use the Apache Spark version that is compatible with Delta Lake 2.3.0 and above.

Setting Up an Interactive Shell

To use Delta Lake interactively within the Spark SQL, Scala, or Python shells, you need a local installation of Apache Spark. Depending on whether you want to use SQL, Python, or Scala, you can set up either the SQL, PySpark, or Spark shell, respectively.

Spark SQL shell

The Spark SQL shell, also referred to as the Spark SQL CLI, is an interactive command-line tool designed to facilitate the execution of SQL queries directly from the command line.

Download the compatible version of Apache Spark (*https://oreil.ly/4VkQ1*) by following instructions in the Spark documentation (*https://oreil.ly/NFI_5*), either by using pip or by downloading and extracting the archive and running `spark-sql` in the extracted directory:

```
# Bash
bin/spark-sql --packages io.delta:delta-core_2.12:2.3.0 --conf \
"spark.sql.extensions=io.delta.sql.DeltaSparkSessionExtension" --conf \
"spark.sql.catalog.spark_catalog=org.apache.spark.sql.delta.catalog.DeltaCatalog"
```

To create your first Delta Lake table, run the following in the Spark SQL shell prompt:

```
-- SQL
CREATE TABLE delta.`/tmp/delta-table` USING DELTA AS
SELECT col1 AS id FROM VALUES 0, 1, 2, 3, 4;
```

You can read back the data written to the table with another simple SQL query:

```
-- SQL
SELECT * FROM delta.`/tmp/delta-table`;
```

PySpark shell

The PySpark shell, also known as the PySpark CLI, is an interactive environment that facilitates engagement with Spark's API using the Python programming language. It serves as a platform for learning, testing PySpark examples, and conducting data analysis directly from the command line. The PySpark shell operates as a Read-Eval-Print Loop (REPL), providing a convenient environment for swiftly testing PySpark statements.

Install the PySpark version that is compatible with the Delta Lake version by running the following in the command prompt:

```
# Bash
pip install pyspark==<compatible-spark-version>
```

Next, run PySpark with the Delta Lake package and additional configurations:

```bash
# Bash
pyspark --packages io.delta:delta-core_2.12:2.3.0 --conf \
"spark.sql.extensions=io.delta.sql.DeltaSparkSessionExtension" --conf \
"spark.sql.catalog.spark_catalog=org.apache.spark.sql.delta.catalog.DeltaCatalog"
```

Finally, to create your first Delta Lake table, run the following in the PySpark shell prompt:

```python
# Python
data = spark.range(0, 5)
data.write.format("delta").save("/tmp/delta-table")
```

You can read back the data written to the table with a simple PySpark code snippet:

```python
# Python
df = spark.read.format("delta").load("/tmp/delta-table")
df.show()
```

Spark Scala shell

The Spark Scala shell, also referred to as the Spark Scala CLI, is an interactive platform that allows users to interact with Spark's API using the Scala programming language. It is a potent tool for data analysis and serves as an accessible medium for learning the API.

Download the compatible version of Apache Spark (*https://oreil.ly/4VkQ1*) by following instructions in the Spark documentation (*https://oreil.ly/HYwom*), either by using pip or by downloading and extracting the archive and running spark-shell in the extracted directory:

```bash
# Bash
bin/spark-shell --packages io.delta:delta-core_2.12:2.3.0 --conf \
"spark.sql.extensions=io.delta.sql.DeltaSparkSessionExtension" --conf \
"spark.sql.catalog.spark_catalog=org.apache.spark.sql.delta.catalog.DeltaCatalog"
```

To create your first Delta Lake table, run the following in the Scala shell prompt:

```scala
// Scala
val data = spark.range(0, 5)
data.write.format("delta").save("/tmp/delta-table")
```

You can read back the data written to the table with a simple PySpark code snippet:

```scala
// Scala
val df = spark.read.format("delta").load("/tmp/delta-table")
df.show()
```

PySpark Declarative API

A PyPi package (*https://oreil.ly/ZPzSi*) containing the Python APIs for using Delta Lake with Apache Spark is also available. This could be very useful for setting up a Python project and, more importantly, for unit testing. Delta Lake can be installed using the following command:

```Bash
# Bash
pip install delta-spark
```

And `SparkSession` can be configured with the `configure_spark_with_delta_pip` utility function in Delta Lake:

```Python
# Python
from delta import *
builder = (
  pyspark.sql.SparkSession.builder.appName("MyApp").config(
    "spark.sql.extensions",
    "io.delta.sql.DeltaSparkSessionExtension"
  ).config(
    "spark.sql.catalog.spark_catalog",
    "org.apache.spark.sql.delta.catalog.DeltaCatalog"
  )
)
```

Databricks Community Edition

With the Databricks Community Edition (*https://oreil.ly/WnJeY*), Databricks has provided a platform for personal use that gives you a cluster of 15 GB memory, which might be just enough to learn Delta Lake with the help of notebooks and the bundled Spark version.

To sign up for Databricks Community Edition, go to the Databricks sign-up page (*https://oreil.ly/FccCw*), fill in your details on the form, and click Continue. Choose Community Edition by clicking on the "Get started with Community Edition" link on the second page of the registration form.

After you have successfully created your account, you will be sent an email to verify your email address. After completing the verification, you can log in to Databricks Community Edition to view the Databricks workspace.

Create a Cluster with Databricks Runtime

Start by clicking on the Compute menu item in the left pane. All the clusters you create will be listed on this page. If this is the first time you are logging in to this account, the page won't list any clusters since you haven't yet created any.

Clicking on Create Compute will bring you to a new cluster page. Databricks Runtime 13.3 LTS is, at the time of this writing, selected by default. You can choose any of the latest (preferably LTS) Databricks Runtimes for running the code. For this example, we chose Databricks Runtime 13.3 LTS. For more information on Databricks Runtime releases and the compatibility matrix, please check the Databricks website (*https://oreil.ly/IqhD1*).

Next, choose any name you'd like for your cluster; we chose "Delta_Lake_DLDG" (see Figure 2-1). Then hit the Create Cluster button at top to launch the cluster.

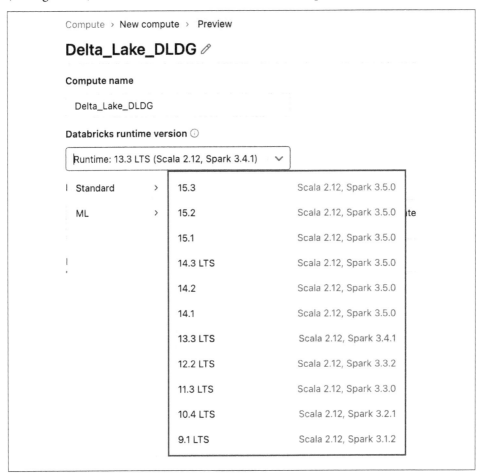

Figure 2-1. Selecting a Databricks Runtime for a new cluster in Databricks Community Edition

You can create only one cluster at a time with Databricks Community Edition. If a cluster already exists, you will need to either use it or delete it before you can create a new cluster.

Your cluster should be up and running within a few minutes, as shown in Figure 2-2.

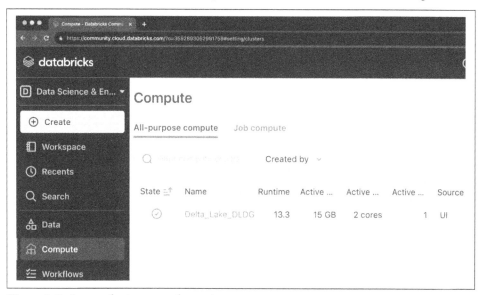

Figure 2-2. A new cluster up and running

 Delta Lake is bundled in the Databricks Runtime, so you don't need to install Delta Lake explicitly either through pip or by using the Maven coordinates of the package to the cluster.

Importing Notebooks

For brevity and ease of understanding, we will use the Jupyter Notebook we saw in the section "JupyterLab Notebook" on page 25. This notebook is available in the delta-docs GitHub repository (*https://oreil.ly/woPgT*). Please copy the notebook link and keep it handy, as you will import the notebook in this step.

Go to Databricks Community Edition and click on Workspace, and then click on the three stacked dots at top right, as shown in Figure 2-3.

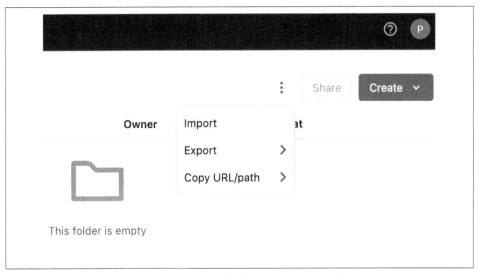

Figure 2-3. Importing a notebook in Databricks Community Edition

In the dialog box, click on the URL radio button, paste in the notebook URL, and click Import. This will render the Jupyter Notebook in Databricks Community Edition.

Attaching Notebooks

Now select the Delta_Lake_DLDG cluster you created earlier to run this notebook, as shown in Figure 2-4.

Figure 2-4. Choosing the cluster you want to attach to the notebook

You can now run each cell in the notebook and press Control + Enter on your keyboard to execute the cell. When a Spark Job is running, Databricks Community Edition shows finer details directly in the notebook. You can also navigate to the Spark UI from here.

You will be able to write to and read from the Delta Lake table within this notebook.

Conclusion

In this chapter, we explored the various approaches you can take to get started with Delta Lake, including Delta Docker, Delta Lake for Python, Apache Spark with Delta Lake, PySpark Declarative API, and finally Databricks Community Edition. We showed how easily you can run a simple notebook or a command shell to write to and read from Delta Lake tables. The next chapter will cover writing and reading operations in more detail.

Finally, we showed you how to use any of these approaches to install Delta Lake and the many different ways in which Delta Lake is available. You also learned how to use SQL, Python, Scala, Java, and Rust programming languages through the API to access Delta Lake tables. In the next chapter, we'll cover the essential operations you need to know to use Delta Lake.

Essential Delta Lake Operations

This chapter explores the essential operations of using Delta Lake for your data management needs. Since Delta Lake functions as the storage layer and participates in the interaction layer of data applications, it makes perfect sense to begin with the foundational operations of persistent storage systems. You know that Delta Lake provides ACID guarantees already,[1] but focusing on CRUD operations (see Figure 3-1) will point us more toward the question "How do I use Delta Lake?"[2] This would be a woefully short story (and consequently this would be a short book) if that was all that you needed to know, however, so we will look at several additional things that are vital to interacting with Delta Lake tables: merge operations, conversion from so-called *vanilla* Parquet files, and table metadata.

 Except where specified, *SQL* will refer to the Spark SQL syntax (*https://oreil.ly/NXS90*) for simplicity's sake. If you are using Trino or some other SQL engine with Delta Lake, you can find additional details either in Chapter 4, which explores more of the Delta Lake ecosystem, or in the relevant documentation.[3] The Python examples will all use the Spark-based Delta Lake API (*https://oreil.ly/CTla3*) for the same reason. Equivalent examples are presented for both throughout. It is also possible to leverage the equivalent operations using PySpark (*https://oreil.ly/1gt26*), and examples of that are shown where it makes sense to do so.

---

1 ACID transactions are discussed in Chapter 1.

2 For a comparison of variant approaches or different types of applications, start with the Wikipedia article on CRUD operations (*https://oreil.ly/-mOVx*).

3 See the Trino SQL documentation (*https://oreil.ly/U5w84*), for example.

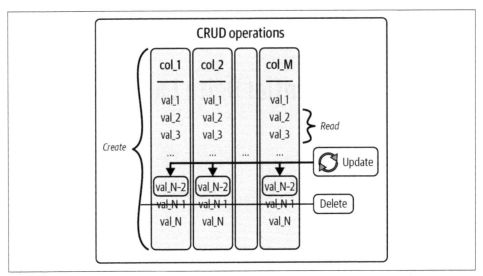

Figure 3-1. Create, read, update, and delete (CRUD) operations are among the most fundamental operations required for any persistent storage data system

We can perform operations with Delta Lake tables using the top-level directory path of a Delta Lake table or by accessing it via a catalog, like the Hive Metastore commonly used with Apache Spark, or the more advanced Unity Catalog (*https://oreil.ly/21G-5*).[4] You will see both methods used throughout this chapter; your choice of which method to use will depend primarily on personal preference and the features of the systems you are working with. Generally speaking, if you have a catalog available in the environment you use, it simplifies both the readability of your code and potential future transactions (imagine if you change a table's location). Note that if you use a catalog, you can set a location for the database object or individually for each table.

Create

Before much else can be done, you need to create a table so there's something to interact with. The actual creation operation can occur in different forms, as many engines will handle something like a nonexistent table simply by creating it as part of the processing during certain actions (such as an append operation in Spark SQL). "What gets created during this process?" you might ask. At its core, Delta Lake could not exist without Parquet, so one of the things you will see created is the Parquet file

---

4 For a technical review of the Hive Metastore, including its design and the interaction operations that are fundamental to its operation, see the Apache Hive documentation (*https://oreil.ly/dEOVj*).

directory and data files, as if you had used Parquet to create the table. However, one of the new things you should notice is another file called _delta_log_.

Creating a Delta Lake Table

To create an empty Delta Lake table, you need to define the table's schema.[5] Using SQL, this will look just like any database table definition, except you will also specify that your table is based on Delta Lake by including the USING DELTA parameter:

```
-- SQL
CREATE TABLE exampleDB.countries (
    id LONG,
    country STRING,
    capital STRING
) USING DELTA;
```

 All the examples and other supporting code for this chapter can be found in the book's GitHub repository (*https://oreil.ly/2m8Kv*).

In Python, you will start with the TableBuilder object yielded by the method Delta Table.create and then add attributes like the table name and the definitions of the columns to be included. The execute command combines the definition into a query plan and puts it into action:

```
# Python
from pyspark.sql.types import *
from delta.tables import *

delta_table = (
    DeltaTable.create(spark)
    .tableName("exampleDB.countries")
    .addColumn("id", dataType=LongType(), nullable=False)
    .addColumn("country", dataType=StringType(), nullable=False)
    .addColumn("capital", dataType=StringType(), nullable=False)
    .execute()
    )
```

In either the Python or the SQL method of defining the table, the process itself is essentially just a matter of creating a named table object with a specification of the column names and types. One other element you might have noticed in the Python dialect is that we also have the option to specify nullability in Apache Spark. This setting will be ignored for Delta Lake tables, as it applies only to JDBC sources. An

---

5 Type support does vary by engine to some degree, though most engines support most data types. For an example of the types supported by Azure Databricks, see the documentation page (*https://oreil.ly/P38y9*).

additional item you might commonly include during a create statement is the IF NOT EXISTS qualifier in SQL or the alternative method createIfNotExists in Python. Their use is purely at your discretion.

 Many of the examples throughout this chapter take the use of table objects accessed through a catalog for granted, but most of the essential operations here are well supported with direct file access methods. One of the key differences for Spark SQL is that it uses the path accessor delta.`<TABLE>` (note the backticks) in place of a table name. With the DeltaTable API, you will typically just swap out the forPath method in place of forName. In PySpark you'll have to turn to alternative methods at times as well, such as using save with a path argument in place of saveAsTable with a table name. Refer to Delta Lake's Python documentation (*https://oreil.ly/ CTla3*) for additional details that might need to be configured for path-based access in some cases (e.g., cloud provider–specific security configuration arguments).

Loading Data into a Delta Lake Table

Assuming you have a Delta table, the most common operations will consist of reading or writing, and naturally, before you read from a table you will probably want to write to it first so that there is something to read. This brings us to one of the most prominent differences between using SQL and using Python APIs with Delta Lake. With either method, you will first define a table and then put rows into that table, but between the two the syntax for doing this is a little different. With SQL you need to use an INSERT statement, whereas with Python you can use the similar insertInto method or use Spark append operations instead.

INSERT INTO

When you have an empty Delta Lake table, you can load data into it using the INSERT INTO command. The idea is to define where you are inserting data and then what you are inserting by providing the VALUES for each row with all the specific info of the columns:

```
-- SQL
INSERT INTO exampleDB.countries VALUES
(1, 'United Kingdom', 'London'),
(2, 'Canada', 'Toronto')
```

With PySpark DataFrame syntax, you just need to specify that inserting records into a specific table is the destination of a write operation with insertInto (note that columns are aligned positionally, so column names will be ignored with this method):

```
# Python
data = [
    (1, "United Kingdom", "London"),
    (2, "Canada", "Toronto")
    ]

schema = ["id", "country", "capital"]

df = spark.createDataFrame(data, schema=schema)

(
df
.write
.format("delta")
.insertInto("exampleDB.countries")
)
```

There might be cases in which you already have the required data (with the same schema and headers) in other formats such as CSV or Parquet. You can specify that the source is a file and select from it or even directly specify another table. This data, via a SELECT statement, can be swapped out with the VALUES argument in the INSERT INTO operation. You need to specify which columns you are selecting from the new data source or specify that you are selecting an entire table with SELECT TABLE <table name> instead:

```
-- SQL
INSERT INTO exampleDB.countries
SELECT * FROM parquet.`countries.parquet`;
```

This provides one way of appending preexisting data into a Delta Lake table. Another way will be through the append mode option for Spark DataFrame write operations.

Append

In addition to the insertInto method for a DataFrame, we can add new data to a Delta Lake table using append mode. In SQL, this just happens as part of the INSERT INTO operation, but for the DataFrameWriter you will explicitly set writing mode with the syntax .mode(append), or with its longer specification .option("mode", "append"). This informs the DataFrameWriter that you are only adding additional records to the table. When a DataFrame is written with the mode set to append and the table already exists, data gets appended to it; however, if the table didn't exist before, it will be created:

```
# Python
# Sample data
data = [(3, 'United States', 'Washington, D.C.') ]

# Define the schema for the Delta table
schema = ["id", "country", "capital"]
```

```
# Create a DataFrame from the sample data and schema
df = spark.createDataFrame(data, schema=schema)

# Write the DataFrame to a Delta table in append mode
# (if the table doesn't exist, it will be created)
(df
.write
.format("delta")
.mode("append")
.saveAsTable("exampleDB.countries")
)
```

> If the mode is not set, Delta Lake assumes you are creating a table
> by default, but if a table with that name already exists, you will
> receive the following error message (*https://oreil.ly/AHqPt*):
>
> ```
> AnalysisException: [TABLE_OR_VIEW_ALREADY_EXISTS] Can-
> not create table or view `exampleDB`.`countries`
> because it already exists.
> ```
>
> ```
> Choose a different name, drop or replace the existing
> object, add the IF NOT EXISTS clause to tolerate pre-
> existing objects, or add the OR REFRESH clause to
> refresh the existing streaming table.
> ```

For PySpark users, this is the most common method of appending data to a table
because it provides a little more flexibility in the event you might like to specify
different write modes at different points in development. It also uses the table specification to align column names from the incoming DataFrame, unlike the `insertInto`
method.

CREATE TABLE AS SELECT

With append operations in PySpark, we noted that if you appended to a table that did
not yet exist, then one would be created. In SQL with `INSERT INTO`, this is not the
case. You must define the destination table to which you want to append the records
before trying to insert records into it. One way to get behavior more like the append
operation is to use a CTAS (Create Table As Select) statement to combine the creation
of the table and the insertion of data into a single operation:

```
-- SQL
CREATE TABLE exampleDB.countries2 AS
SELECT * FROM exampleDB.countries
```

Using CTAS statements to create your tables gives you some additional simplicity for
your table definitions. One of the biggest benefits is that you get to skip the step of
defining the schema in cases where you don't need granular control over the type
or over other column-level information. Whether you want to use this method or

standard CREATE and INSERT operations is up to you; for the most part, they will yield pretty much the same result. The main area in which the two methods differ is that they require a different number of transactions and will be represented separately in the transaction log you will see next.

The Transaction Log

When your table is created, you get a subdirectory within the Parquet structure called *_delta_log*. This is the transaction log that tracks all of the change history for a table.[6] If you inspect the file structure of the *_delta_log* directory, you will find that it contains JSON files:

```
# Bash
!tree countries.delta/_delta_log

countries.delta/_delta_log
└── 00000000000000000000.json
```

These files provide a record of all the operations that happen to the table and make some kind of change (i.e., not read operations). Each creation, insertion, or append action will add another JSON file to the transaction log and increment the version number of the table. The exact structure of the transaction log varies by implementation, but some of what you will commonly find within the transaction records is information about the creation of the table (such as what processing engine was used to create it, the number of records, or other metrics from write operations to the table), records of maintenance operations, and deletion information.[7]

While it may seem like a small thing, you should understand that the transaction log is the core component that makes Delta Lake work. Some might even go so far as to say that the transaction log *is* Delta Lake. The record of transactions and the way processing engines interact with it are what set Delta Lake apart from Parquet and provide ACID guarantees, the possibilities of exactly-once stream processing, and all the other magic Delta Lake provides to you. One example of the magic that comes from the transaction log is *time travel*, which is described in the next section.

The details may differ depending on where and how you are using Delta Lake, but the key takeaway is that you need to know that the transaction log exists and where to find it. Owing to the richness of the information often included in the transaction log, you may find it an invaluable tool for investigating processes, diagnosing errors, and monitoring the health of your data pipelines. Don't neglect the information available at your fingertips!

---

6 Chapter 1 includes a detailed review of the transaction log, but this is a critical concept.

7 Matthew Powers provides a handy reference (*https://oreil.ly/mnxcO*) to many implementations of the Delta Lake transaction log, if you want to compare what information might be available to each.

Read

Reading is such a fundamental operation in data processing that one could almost assume there is no need to look into it. However, there are several things concerning reading from Delta Lake tables that are worth focusing on, including a high-level understanding of how partition filtering works (which is explored much more deeply in Chapters 5 and 10) and how the transaction log allows querying views of the data from previous versions with time travel.

Querying Data from a Delta Lake Table

Just as with the rich database systems you might have encountered in the past, there are many kinds of SQL tricks you can use to manipulate data read from a Delta Lake table. What is central to getting to more advanced practices, however, is understanding that everything builds on top of basic read operations. In SQL this usually takes the form of a SELECT statement, whereas with the DeltaTable API, you will load an object and convert it to a Spark DataFrame:

```
-- SQL
SELECT * FROM exampleDB.countries

# Python
from delta.tables import DeltaTable

delta_table = DeltaTable.forName(spark, "exampleDB.countries")
delta_table.toDF()
```

Both methods will yield all table records, with the output limited only by the processing engine you're using (e.g., the default value of show in Spark gives 20 records). Often you will want to select just a subset of the data; this could be a single record, an entire file partition, or an arbitrary collection of records from disparate locations throughout the table.[8] To facilitate this, you just need to add a filtering action to the query or DataFrame definition:

```
-- SQL
SELECT * FROM exampleDB.countries
WHERE capital = "London"

# Python
delta_table_df.filter(delta_table_df.capital == 'London')
```

---

8 The concept of partitioning is a supported part of the Parquet file structure. For an in-depth exploration of partitioning, we suggest checking out the Spark documentation covering Parquet files (*https://oreil.ly/w_xj_*).

This will give you all the results from your table that match the filtering condition. This is true even when the values don't exist. If a value is specified as a filtering condition but does not exist in the table, the result will be no records returned. In Spark, this will be an empty `DataFrame` object that still shares the originating table schema. You might also wish to select a subset of columns in conjunction with filters or just to perform other operations. To do so, just specify the columns required:

```
-- SQL
SELECT
    id,
    capital
FROM
    exampleDB.countries

# Python
delta_table_df.select("id", "capital")
```

While the operations themselves are simple, more is going on under the covers. Just like Parquet files, Delta Lake includes statistics on the underlying files to make these queries more efficient where possible. The amount of statistics can be controlled and varies by implementation (Chapter 12 focuses on these statistics and on how you can optimize performance). Parquet itself is a columnar file structure, so reading subsets of columns will often be more efficient overall. One area in which the transaction log comes into play and offers a distinct advantage over traditional Parquet files is the ability to read data from the past.

Reading with Time Travel

Courtesy of the transaction log in Delta Lake, you have additional table parameters that you can use to accomplish some otherwise difficult tasks. One thing made possible through the log is the ability to view or restore older versions of a table. This means you can check on previous versions or on what the data in a table looked like at a certain time, with less effort required to create backups of files, and without relying on native cloud service backup utilities.

 The DeltaTable API used throughout this chapter does not directly support time travel. However, that feature is still available to Python users via PySpark. The API supports restoration actions, which are covered in "Repairing, Restoring, and Replacing Table Data" on page 108. You will also find some more advanced operations regarding deletion of data. In light of this limitation, equivalent expressions with PySpark are presented alongside the SQL expressions for time travel.

To view a previous version of a table in SQL, just add a qualifier to the query. There are two different options for specifying this. One is to specify the VERSION AS OF with a particular version number. For example, if you want to see which values of id existed as part of a specific version of the table, you might combine a DISTINCT query with time travel to version 1 of the table:

```
-- SQL
SELECT DISTINCT id FROM exampleDB.countries VERSION AS OF 1
```

```
# Python
(
spark
.read
.option("versionAsOf", "1")
.load("countries.delta")
.select("id")
.distinct()
)
```

Or if you want to see how many records existed before the current date without having to check the version number, you can use TIMESTAMP AS OF instead and specify the current date:[9]

```
-- SQL
SELECT count(1) FROM exampleDB.countries TIMESTAMP AS OF "2024-04-20"
```

```
# Python
(
spark
.read
.option("timestampAsOf", "2024-04-20")
.load("countries.delta")
.count()
)
```

While extremely useful as a feature, time travel is just a by-product of proper versioning on your table. It does exemplify the protections that you get for your data in terms of transaction guarantees and atomicity, though. So really, time travel is not the full benefit but a window into the protections provided by ACID transactions available in Delta Lake.[10]

---

9 This "same day" behavior does depend on the way Spark converts a date to a timestamp—i.e., in the examples, 2024-04-20 = 2024-04-20 00:00:00.

10 To read more about retention timelines and versioning, see Chapter 5.

Update

Being able to create a table, add data to it, and read the data from it are all great capabilities. Sometimes, though, maybe while reading the data, an error in a name could be discovered. Or perhaps integration with a business system requires the abbreviation of a country name.

Suppose your sales team decides that it wants to use country abbreviations in place of the full names because they are shorter and display better in the graphs in sales reports. In this case, you would need to update the column value of "United Kingdom" to "U.K." in the table from the examples. To make these kinds of changes, all you need is an UPDATE statement that specifies what you want to change with SET and where you want to change it with a WHERE clause:

```
-- SQL
UPDATE exampleDB.countries
SET { country = 'U.K.' }
WHERE id = 1;

# Python
delta_table_df.update(
    condition = "id = 1",
    set = { "country": "'U.K.'" } )
```

Using UPDATE makes it easy to fix a specific value in a table. You can also use this to update many values in your table by using a less specific filtering clause. Omitting the WHERE clause completely would allow you to update values across the entire Delta Lake table. Each update action will increment the version of the table in the transaction log.

Delete

Deleting data from a table is the last of the CRUD operations to be explored here. Deletions can happen for many reasons, but a few of the most common ones are to remove specific records (e.g., right to be forgotten[11]), to replace erroneous or stale data (e.g., daily table refresh), or to trim a table time window (most often when the same data might be available elsewhere but you wish to keep a reporting table or similar to a trimmed length for performance or as part of the basis for calculations). For some of these, you would want to give explicit commands to remove values; in other cases, you might be able to let the system handle the deletion on your behalf.

---

11 The right to be forgotten (*https://oreil.ly/IBEs2*) or right to erasure is part of the EU's General Data Protection Regulation (GDPR). If this law applies to your data practices, we suggest you thoroughly review the EU's "Complete Guide to GDPR Compliance" (*https://oreil.ly/zMIkN*).

The two usual ways to achieve this are to use the DELETE command or to specify overwriting behavior.

Deleting Data from a Delta Lake Table

All that is required to delete records from a Delta Lake table is the DELETE statement. Functionally, it works very similarly to a SELECT statement in that you apply filtering with a WHERE clause to get the appropriate level of selectivity for determining the records to be deleted. This has the handy application of being able to first select and review the records that would be deleted from the table by simply switching between SELECT and DELETE in a SQL query. With the Python API, you do not have this same swappable parity (swapping SELECT for DELETE) to make reviewing records easier, but what *is* similar is supplying the condition on which to delete. It is still just an expression specifying matching criteria for the operation. One enhancement you gain with the Python API is that the expression itself can be a string containing an expression in SQL or can use functions out of the PySpark libraries. This can give you additional flexibility in the way you write your code:

```
-- SQL
DELETE FROM exampleDB.countries
WHERE id = 1;

# Python
from pyspark.sql.functions import col

delta_table.delete("id = 1")        # uses SQL expression
delta_table.delete(col("id") == 2) # uses PySpark expression
```

 Adequate care should be taken to specify the WHERE clause so as to prevent unintentional deletion of additional data. Failure to include a WHERE clause will result in the deletion of all table records. Similar care should also be used when using overwrite mode with writes to a table. If this happens to you accidentally, you will need to restore a prior version of the table (see Chapter 5 for more details on how to do this).

Deleting many records from a table works similarly to deleting a single record. In cases in which the value in the expression matches multiple records, all those records will get deleted. You could also use inequality-based expressions to delete based on thresholds. An example of this kind of expression might look something like "transaction_date <= date_sub(current_date(), 7)", which would trim the table values to have only values within the last week. Deleting large amounts of data from a table can often be associated with replacing the data in that table with a whole new set of records. Rather than doing this as a two-step operation, there may be cases in which you would like to *overwrite* the data instead.

Overwriting Data in a Delta Lake Table

Delta Lake makes it very easy to overwrite data in a table. This is both a feature and a warning for you. Overwrite mode allows you to replace the data in a table, no matter the size or number of files, with a new result set.[12] The exception is when you specify that you want to overwrite only a specific partition of the data, but even in this case, you should be deliberate about what you are doing, as partitions can also contain many files that might be overwritten during the process. With that in mind, overwriting tables is a fairly common process and can be used for updating records in a table when they are recomputed regularly, when an error occurs and you wish to replace some or all of a table as a result, or when you wish to change the structure of a table. Overwriting is included within this section's discussion since a core component of any of the outlined methods is implicitly deleting any preexisting data. Each approach to interacting with Delta Lake via Spark uses a different method to overwrite data. The DeltaTable API has a unique `replace` method, while PySpark and Spark SQL both have a way to specify overwriting as an operation mode.

The replace method

When using the DeltaTable Python API, there are distinct methods that allow for replacing the entire contents of a table. You can use either `replace` or `createOr Replace` to replace the contents of a table. Both methods are direct handlers that let you use the same `TableBuilder` object to define a new table structure over the top of the existing one:

```python
# Python
delta_table2 = (
    DeltaTable.replace(spark)
    .tableName("countries.delta")
    .addColumns(data_df.schema)
    .execute()
    )
```

Working with the DeltaTable API allows you to overwrite the table schema with the column definitions coming from a DataFrame called `data_df`. Overall, if you are already working with Spark, you might find it easier to use the overwrite mode specification from the Spark `DataFrameWriter` instead.

Overwrite mode

Overwriting data by changing the output mode on a Spark `DataFrameWriter` can be a quick and efficient method for wholly replacing part or all of a dataset in Delta Lake. The overwrite mode parameter is a mirror of the append mode parameter used

---

12 More detailed discussion of overwrite semantics can be found in Chapter 5.

to add data to a Delta Lake table. In this case, instead of data being added to the table's preexisting data, the contents of the current DataFrame will just replace what is already in the table. All of the prior data will be removed and only the current data will be available going forward, unless you restore the table to the prior version:

```python
# Python
(
spark
.createDataFrame(
    [
    (1, 'India', 'New Delhi'),
    (4, 'Australia', 'Canberra')
    ],
    schema=["id", "country", "capital"]
    )
.write
.format("delta")
.mode("overwrite") # specify the output mode
.saveAsTable("exampleDB.countries")
)
```

Using this method gives you the ability to switch between the two different output modes by changing just one word, which can be particularly useful during development and testing. You can do something similar in Spark SQL with INSERT OVERWRITE.

INSERT OVERWRITE

As a companion to INSERT INTO, INSERT OVERWRITE can be used in the same way as the overwrite mode with PySpark DataFrame syntax.[13] These two query-based commands function in the same way as append and overwrite modes in PySpark; that is, they allow you to switch between the INTO and OVERWRITE parameters without making other changes to your queries:

```sql
-- SQL
INSERT OVERWRITE exampleDB.countries
VALUES (3, 'U.S.', 'Washington, D.C.');
```

As with the overwrite mode or the replace method, using INSERT OVERWRITE will remove all previous data from the target table. This means you should exercise caution when using it and make sure you know what you are overwriting. As with the INSERT INTO command, you have a large amount of freedom with regard to the contents you want to insert into the target table. You can use specific values, other tables, or files as a source for writing over a target table.

---

13 Due to the way Trino interacts with files, it does not directly support INSERT OVERWRITE.

Merge

Combining inserts, updates, and/or deletes in processing data is common enough to warrant creating "shortcuts" for those actions. MERGE is a great example of such a shortcut, as it allows you to chain together multiple operations on a set of data with a unified set of matching conditions across the chain. It allows you to conditionally control actions based on the degree of matching or not matching as you specify. When the operations are limited only to combining inserts and updates, merging is also commonly called *upserting*.[14] This can be used to great advantage with practice, as many day-to-day data engineering patterns align with merge behavior.[15]

If you have many records to insert into a table but also need to update previously existing records, you may need to combine and perform several different queries. To accomplish this, you would need to identify which records are already in the table, update those records, and then take the additional records and insert those into the same target. MERGE lets you combine these actions into a single operation by conditionally qualifying the logic in your query based on how it matches against specified values in the table. In essence, you get to specify different actions based on whether or not particular values already exist in the key columns of the table.

The number of ways in which you can create combinations within a MERGE query is enormous, but generally speaking, you will define a set of matching criteria between a target table (the one you want to make changes to) and some source data (from a file or another table, for example). With matching criteria defined, you can take different actions depending on the matching status of each record coming from the source data:

WHEN MATCHED
> When the conditions are matched, you can either DELETE matching records or UPDATE with the entire new record or from specified columns.

WHEN NOT MATCHED
> When conditions are not matched, you can INSERT unmatched records either in their entirety or from specified columns.

WHEN NOT MATCHED BY SOURCE
> When no new records from the source match records in the target, you can DELETE those records or UPDATE with either the entire new record or from specified columns.

---

14 For a more in-depth exploration of its history and implementation comparisons across multiple SQL dialects, we recommend the "Merge (SQL)" Wikipedia article (*https://oreil.ly/5QSGj*) as a jumping-off point.

15 For a dedicated exploration of Delta Lake merge semantics, we suggest Nick Karpov's blog post (*https://oreil.ly/Qlkwx*).

With SQL, you simply combine the actions to build your entire `MERGE` query and execute it as a single statement. You start by specifying the target to merge into, the source to merge from, and the conditions on which you want to base your matching logic. Then, for an upsert, you will just define the update operation and insert operation details:

```
-- SQL
MERGE INTO exampleDB.countries A
USING (select * from parquet.`countries.parquet`) B
ON A.id = B.id
WHEN MATCHED THEN
  UPDATE SET
    id = A.id,
    country = B.country,
    capital = B.capital
WHEN NOT MATCHED
  THEN INSERT (
    id,
    country,
    capital
  )
  VALUES (
    B.id,
    B.country,
    B.capital
  )
```

With the DeltaTable API, you will use a new class called the `DeltaMergeBuilder` to specify these conditions and actions. Unlike in the SQL syntax, each combination of matching status and subsequent action to take has its own method to use. You can find the full list of supported combinations in the documentation (*https://oreil.ly/-KtwU*). We recommend you combine multiple actions and just chain them together into a single transaction to help you break down the logical path of any particular record. Here is what it might look like if you wanted to do an upsert operation with a DataFrame containing new records; notice that, starting with the DeltaTable object, you first apply `MERGE` to specify the new record source and the matching conditions and then apply `whenMatchedUpdate` and `whenNotMatchedInsert` to cover both cases:

```
# Python
idf = (
    spark
    .createDataFrame([
        (1, 'India', 'New Delhi'),
        (4, 'Australia', 'Canberra')],
        schema=["id", "country", "capital"]
        )
    )

delta_table.alias("target").merge(
    source = idf.alias("source"),
```

```
    condition = "source.id = target.id"
).whenMatchedUpdate(set =
{
"country": "source.country",
"capital": "source.capital"
}
).whenNotMatchedInsert(values =
{
"id": "source.id",
"country": "source.country",
"capital": "source.capital"
}
).execute()
```

Overall, using MERGE can help you simplify what otherwise would require several
distinct queries with different kinds of join logic and associated actions.

Other Useful Actions

There are a couple more essential operations to be aware of with Delta Lake. One
is a conversion that can simplify moving to Delta Lake from other file formats, and
the other is a review of the functions you need to inspect several different kinds of
metadata about your tables. Both can be highly valuable to you for many applications.

Parquet Conversions

Even in cases where you establish Delta Lake as the file format underlying all your
data activities, you are still likely to encounter datasets coming from legacy systems,
third-party providers, or other sources that use different formats. For a couple of file
types, namely the Parquet and the Parquet-based Iceberg formats, there is a simple
conversion method you can use to simplify some of your operations. The CONVERT
TO DELTA command is the recommended approach for transforming an Iceberg or
Parquet directory into a Delta table.

Regular Parquet conversion

Since a Delta Lake table is composed of Parquet files internally, the transaction log is
the biggest difference when converting a Parquet table to a Delta Lake table. To create
a log for an existing Parquet file, you just need to run CONVERT TO DELTA in SQL, or
convertToDelta with the DeltaTable API, with the directory:

```
-- SQL
CONVERT TO DELTA parquet.`countries.parquet`

# Python
from delta.tables import DeltaTable
```

```
delta_table = (
    DeltaTable
    .convertToDelta(
        spark,
        "parquet.`countries.parquet`"
        )
    )
```

This command scans all Parquet files within the specified directory, infers the schema from the types stored in the Parquet files, and builds the Delta Lake transaction log _delta_log. If the Parquet directory is partitioned, you will also need to specify the partitioning columns using a PARTITIONED BY parameter in the SQL query or a SQL string as an additional argument for convertToDelta.

Iceberg conversion

Like Delta Lake, Apache Iceberg (*https://oreil.ly/ubgsB*) is composed of Parquet files internally. Is it possible to again use CONVERT TO DELTA in SQL, or convertToDelta, to convert Iceberg files? Partly yes and partly no. The DeltaTable API does not support the Iceberg conversion. Spark SQL, however, can support the conversion with CONVERT TO DELTA, but you will also need to install support for the Iceberg format in your Spark environment:

```
-- SQL
CONVERT TO DELTA iceberg.`countries.iceberg`
```

You should be able to accomplish this by installing an additional JAR file (*delta-iceberg*) to the cluster you are using.[16] Unlike with Parquet files, when converting Iceberg you will not need to specify the partitioning structure of the table, as it will infer this information from the source.[17]

There's one more thing you should know about this conversion process. An interesting side effect exists in converted Iceberg tables. Since both Iceberg and Delta Lake maintain distinctly separate transaction logs, none of the new files added through interactions via Delta Lake will be registered on the Iceberg side. However, since the Iceberg log is not removed, the new Delta Lake table will still be readable and accessible as an Iceberg table.[18]

---

16 For further exploration of using Apache Iceberg with Apache Spark, we suggest starting with the official quickstart guide (*https://oreil.ly/JAlrU*).

17 There are some caveats to being able to convert Iceberg based on different feature usage. You should look at the documentation (*https://oreil.ly/WIT5B*) to check whether this might affect your specific situation.

18 This is different from Delta UniForm (Universal Format), which we discussed in Chapter 1.

Delta Lake Metadata and History

Often you will want to quickly check some information about the metadata related to one of your Delta Lake tables. It can be useful to review information such as the schema of a table, which reader or writer version is implemented for a table, or any other properties that might be set. To review this information, you only need to use `DESCRIBE DETAIL` in Spark SQL or `detail` with the DeltaTable API:

```
-- SQL
DESCRIBE DETAIL exampleDB.countries

# Python
delta_table.detail()
```

This will give you all the metadata details listed, as well as additional things such as the last time the table was modified or the number of files in the table. You can find a reference for the entire schema returned in the documentation (*https://oreil.ly/z-lqu*).

Similarly, you might wish to check not just the most recent values of this metadata but also the metadata for each transaction. There are a couple of ways to easily access the information stored in the transaction log, which can provide a rich history of the changes that have taken place in the table over time. This has many potential applications, such as monitoring the frequency and size of `append` operations to a table or checking the source of a particular deletion.

In this case, instead of the detail, you will want the history of the table:

```
-- SQL
DESCRIBE HISTORY exampleDB.countries

# Python
delta_table.history()
```

Similar to the metadata, the table history contains a great deal of different transaction-level metadata and, depending on the type of transaction, many associated metrics. You can find an overview of the available information in the documentation (*https://oreil.ly/D7Tme*) as well.

Conclusion

The essential operations of Delta Lake provide a robust interaction layer for creating, reading, updating, and deleting data in tables, going well beyond traditional data lake capabilities. With ACID transactions, time travel, merge operations, and easy conversion from Parquet and Iceberg formats, Delta Lake offers a powerful storage and data management layer. By understanding the essential operations covered in this chapter—from basic CRUD actions to more advanced merge logic and transaction log introspection—you can effectively use Delta Lake to build reliable, high-performance data pipelines and applications.

Diving into the Delta Lake Ecosystem

Over the last few chapters, we've explored Delta Lake from the comfort of the Spark ecosystem. The Delta protocol, however, offers rich interoperability not only across the underlying table format but within the computing environment as well. This opens the doors to an expansive universe of possibilities for powering our lakehouse applications, using a single source of table truth. It's time to break outside the box and look at the connector ecosystem.

The connector ecosystem is a set of ever-expanding frameworks, services, and community-driven integrations enabling Delta to be utilized from just about anywhere. The commitment to interoperability enables us to take full advantage of the hard work and effort the growing open source community provides without sacrificing the years we've collectively poured into technologies outside the Spark ecosystem.

In this chapter, we'll discover some of the more popular Delta connectors while learning to pilot our Delta-based data applications from outside the traditional Spark ecosystem. For those of you who haven't done much work with Apache Spark, you're in luck, since this chapter is a love song to Delta Lake without Apache Spark and a closer look at how the connector ecosystem works.

We will be covering the following integrations:[1]

- Flink DataStream Connector
- Kafka Delta Ingest
- Trino Connector

---

[1] For the full list of evolving integrations, see "Delta Lake Integrations" (*https://oreil.ly/nlO4w*) on the Delta Lake website.

In addition to the four core connectors in this chapter, support for Apache Pulsar, ClickHouse, FINOS Legend, Hopsworks, Delta Rust, Presto, StarRocks, and general SQL import to Delta is also available at the time of writing.

What are connectors, you ask? We will learn all about them next.

Connectors

As people, we don't like to set limits for ourselves. Some of us are more adventurous and love to think about the unlimited possibilities of the future. Others take a more narrow, straight-ahead approach to life. Regardless of our respective attitudes, we are bound together by our pursuit of adventure, search for novelty, and desire to make decisions for ourselves. Nothing is worse than being locked in, trapped, with no way out. From the perspective of the data practitioner, it is also nice to know that what we rely on today can be used tomorrow without the dread of contract renegotiations! While Delta Lake is not a person, the open source community has responded to the various wants and needs of the community at large, and a healthy ecosystem has risen up to ensure that no one will have to be tied directly to the Apache Spark ecosystem, the JVM, or even the traditional set of data-focused programming languages like Python, Scala, and Java.

The *mission of the connector ecosystem* is to ensure frictionless interoperability with the Delta protocol. Over time, however, fragmentation across the current (`delta < 3.0`) connector ecosystem has led to multiple independent implementations of the Delta protocol and divergence across the current connectors. To streamline support for the future of the Delta ecosystem, Delta Kernel (*https://oreil.ly/a6Qn9*) was introduced to provide a common interface and expectations that simplify true interoperability within the Delta ecosystem.

Kernel provides a seamless set of read- and write-level APIs that ensures correctness of operation and freedom of expression for the connector API implementation. This means that the behavior across all connectors will leverage the same set of operations, with the same inputs and outputs, while ensuring each connector can quickly implement new features without lengthy lead times or divergent handling of the underlying Delta protocol. Delta Kernel is introduced in Chapter 1.

There are a healthy number of connectors and integrations that enable interoperability with the Delta table format and protocols, no matter where we trigger operations from. Interoperability and unification are part of the core tenets of the Delta project and helped drive the push toward UniForm (introduced along with Delta 3.0), which provides cross-table support for Delta, Iceberg, and Hudi.

In the sections that follow, we'll take a look at the most popular connectors, including Apache Flink, Trino, and Kafka Delta Ingest. Learning to utilize Delta from your favorite framework is just a few steps away.

Apache Flink

Apache Flink (*https://oreil.ly/h5DWQ*) is "a framework and distributed processing engine for stateful computations over unbounded and bounded data streams...[that] is designed to run in all common cluster environments [and] perform computations at in-memory speed and at any scale." In other words, Flink can scale massively and continue to perform efficiently while handling every increasing load in a distributed way, and while also adhering to exactly-once semantics (if specified in the Checkpoin tingMode) for stream processing, even in the case of failures or disruptions at runtime to a data application.

 If you haven't worked with Flink before and would like to, there is an excellent book by Fabian Hueske and Vasiliki Kalavri called *Stream Processing with Apache Flink* (O'Reilly) that will get you up to speed in no time.

The assumption from here going forward is that we either (a) understand enough about Flink to compile an application or (b) are willing to follow along and learn as we go. With that said, let's look at how to add the delta-flink connector to our Flink applications.

Flink DataStream Connector

The Flink/Delta Connector (*https://oreil.ly/A1cV7*) is built on top of the Delta Standalone library (*https://oreil.ly/ZvcMu*) and provides a seamless abstraction for reading and writing Delta tables using Flink primitives such as the DataStream and Table APIs. In fact, because Delta Lake uses Parquet as its common data format, there really are no special considerations for working with Delta tables aside from the capabilities introduced by the Delta Standalone library.

The standalone library provides the essential Java APIs for reading the Delta table metadata using the DeltaLog object. This allows us to read the full current version of a given table, or to begin reading from a specific version, or to find the approximate version of the table based on a provided ISO-8601 timestamp. We will cover the basic capabilities of the standalone library as we learn to use DeltaSource and DeltaSink in the following sections.

The full Java application referenced in the following sections is located in the book's Git repository under */ch04/flink/dldg-flink-delta-app/* (*https://oreil.ly/2m8Kv*).

As a follow-up for the curious reader, unit tests for the application provide a glimpse at how to use the Delta standalone APIs. You can walk through these under */src/test/* within the Java application.

Installing the Connector

Everything starts with the connector. Simply add the `delta-flink` connector to your data application using Maven (*https://oreil.ly/9Nby-*), Gradle (*https://oreil.ly/Q_h3T*), or sbt (*https://oreil.ly/gqTDS*). The following example shows how to include the `delta-flink` connector (*https://oreil.ly/FdHci*) dependency in a Maven project:

```
<dependency>
  <groupId>io.delta</groupId>
  <artifactId>delta-flink</artifactId>
  <version>${delta-connectors-version}</version>
</dependency>
```

It is worth noting that Apache Flink is officially dropping support for the Scala programming language. The content for this chapter is written using Flink 1.17.1, which officially no longer has published Scala APIs. While you can still use Scala with Flink, Java and Python will be the only supported variants as we move toward the Flink 2.0 release. All of the examples, as well as the application code in the book's GitHub repository (*https://oreil.ly/2m8Kv*), are therefore written in Java.

The connector ships with classes for reading and writing to Delta Lake. Reading is handled by the `DeltaSource` API, and writing is handled by the `DeltaSink` API. We'll start with the `DeltaSource` API, move on to the `DeltaSink` API, and then look at an end-to-end application.

The value of the `delta-connectors-version` property will change as new versions are released. For simplicity, all supported connectors are officially included in the main Delta repository (*https://oreil.ly/Kc5Y8*). This change was made at the time of the Delta 3.0 release.

DeltaSource API

The `DeltaSource` API provides static builders to easily construct sources for bounded or unbounded (continuous) data flows. The big difference between the two variants is specific to the bounded (batch) or unbounded (streaming) operations on the source Delta table. This is analogous to the batch or microbatch (unbounded) processing with Apache Spark. While the behavior of these two processing modes differs, the configuration parameters differ only slightly. We'll begin by looking at the bounded source and conclude with the continuous source, as there are more configuration options to cover in the latter.

Bounded mode

To create the `DeltaSource` object, we'll be using the static `forBoundedRowData` method from the `DeltaSource` class. This builder takes the path to the Delta table and an instance of the application's Hadoop configuration, as shown in Example 4-1.

Example 4-1. Creating the `DeltaSource` bounded builder

```
% Path sourceTable = new Path("s3://bucket/delta/table_name")
  Configuration hadoopConf = new Configuration()
  var builder: RowDataBoundedDeltaSourceBuilder = DeltaSource.forBoundedRowData(
    sourceTable
    hadoopConf);
```

The object returned in Example 4-1 is a builder. Using the various options on the builder, we specify how we'd like to read from the Delta table, including options to slow down the read rates, filter the set of columns read, and more.

Builder options.   The following options can be applied directly to the builder:

`columnNames` *(string ...)*
> This option provides us with the ability to specify the column names on a table we'd like to read while ignoring the rest. This functionality is especially useful on wide tables with many columns and can help alleviate unnecessary memory pressure for columns that will go unused anyway:
>
> ```
> % builder.columnNames("event_time", "event_type", "brand", "price");
>   builder.columnNames(
>       Arrays.asList("event_time", "event_type", "brand", "price"));
> ```

`startingVersion` *(long)*
> This option provides us with the ability to specify the exact version of the Delta table's transaction to start reading from (in the form of a numeric `Long`). This option and the `startingTimestamp` option are mutually exclusive, as both provide a means of supplying a cursor (or transactional starting point) on the Delta table:
>
> ```
> % builder.startingVersion(100L);
> ```

`startingTimestamp` *(string)*

> This option provides the ability to specify an approximate timestamp to begin reading from in the form of an ISO-8601 `string`. This option will trigger a scan of the Delta transaction history looking for a matching version of the table that was generated at or after the given timestamp. In the case where the entire table is newer than the timestamp provided, the table will be fully read:

```
% builder.startingTimestamp("2023-09-10T09:55:00.001Z");
```

> The timestamp string can represent time with low precision—for example, as a simple date like `"2023-09-10"`—or with millisecond precision, as in the previous example. In either case, the operation will result in the Delta table being read from a specific point in table time.

`parquetBatchSize` *(int)*

> This option takes an integer controlling how many rows to return per internal batch, or generated split within the Flink engine:

```
% builder.option("parquetBatchSize", 5000);
```

Generating the bounded source. Once we finish supplying the options to the builder, we generate the `DeltaSource` instance by calling `build`:

```
% final DeltaSource<RowData> source = builder.build();
```

With the bounded source built, we can now read batches of our Delta Lake records off our tables—but what if we wanted to continuously process new records as they arrived? In that case, we can just use the continuous mode builder!

Continuous mode

To create this variation of the DeltaSource object, we'll use the static `forContinuous RowData` method on the `DeltaSource` class. The builder is shown in Example 4-2, and we provide the same base parameters as were provided to the `forBoundedRowData` builder, which makes switching from batch to streaming super simple.

Example 4-2. Creating the `DeltaSource` continuous builder

```
% var builder = DeltaSource.forContinuousRowData(
    sourceTable,
    hadoopConf);
```

The object returned in Example 4-2 is an instance of the `RowDataContinuousDelta SourceBuilder`, and just like the bounded variant, it enables us to provide options for controlling the initial read position within the Delta table based on the `starting Version` or `startingTimestamp`, as well as some additional options that control the frequency with which Flink will check the table for new entries.

Builder options. The following options can be applied directly to the continuous builder; additionally, all the options of the bounded builder (columnNames, starting Version, parquetBatchSize, and startingTimestamp) apply to the continuous builder as well:

updateCheckIntervalMillis *(long)*

This option takes a numeric Long value representing the frequency to check for updates to the Delta table, with a default value of 5,000 milliseconds:

```
% builder.updateCheckIntervalMillis(60000L);
```

If we know the table we are reading from is updated only periodically, then we can essentially reduce unnecessary I/O by using this setting. For example, if we know that new data will only ever be written on a one-minute cadence, then we can take a breather and set the frequency to check every minute. We can always modify this setting if there is a need to process faster, or slower, based on the behavior of the upstream Delta table.

ignoreDeletes *(boolean)*

Setting this option allows us to ignore deleted rows. It is possible that your streaming application will never need to know that data from the past has been removed. If we are processing data in real time and considering the feed of data from our tables as append-only, then we are focused on the head of the table and can safely ignore the tail changes as data ages out.

ignoreChanges *(boolean)*

Setting this option allows us to ignore changes to the table that occur upstream, including deleted rows, and other modifications to physical table data or logical table metadata. Unless the table is overwritten with a new schema, then we can continue to process while ignoring modifications to the table structure.

Generating the continuous source. Once we finish configuring the builder, we generate the DeltaSource instance by calling build:

```
% final DeltaSource<RowData> source = builder.build();
```

We have looked at how to build the DeltaSource object and have seen the connector configuration options, but what about table schema or partition column discovery? Luckily, there is no need to go into too much detail about those, since both are automatically discovered using the table metadata.

Table schema discovery

The Flink connector uses the Delta table metadata to resolve all columns and their types. For example, if we don't specify any columns in our source definition, all columns from the underlying Delta table will be read. However, If we specify a collection of column names using the `DeltaSource` builder method (`columnNames`), then only that subset of columns will be read from the underlying Delta table. In both cases, the `DeltaSource` connector will discover the Delta table column types and convert them to the corresponding Flink types. This process of conversion from the internal Delta table data (Parquet rows) to the external data representation (Java types) provides us with a seamless way to work with our datasets.

Using the DeltaSource

After building the `DeltaSource` object (bounded or unbounded), we can now add the source into the streaming graph of our `DataStream` using an instance of the `StreamingExecutionEnvironment`.

Example 4-3 creates a simple execution environment instance and adds the source of our stream (`DeltaSource`) using `fromSource`. When we build the `StreamExecution Environment` instance, we provide a `WatermarkStrategy`. Watermarks in Flink are similar in concept to watermarks for Spark Structured Streaming: they enable late-arriving data to be honored for a specific amount of time before they are considered too late to process and therefore dropped (ignored) for a given application.

Example 4-3. Creating the `StreamExecutionEnvironment` for our DeltaSource

```
% final StreamExecutionEnvironment env =
      StreamExecutionEnvironment.getExecutionEnvironment();
  env.setRuntimeMode(RuntimeExecutionMode.AUTOMATIC);
  env.enableCheckpointing(2000, CheckpointingMode.EXACTLY_ONCE);

  DeltaSource<RowData> source = ...
  env.fromSource(source, WatermarkStrategy.noWatermarks(), "delta table source")
```

We now have a live data source for our Flink job supporting Delta. We can choose to add additional sources, join and transform our data, and even write the results of our transforms back to Delta using the `DeltaSink`, or anywhere else our application requires us to go.

Next, we'll look at using the `DeltaSink` and then connect the dots with a full end-to-end example.

DeltaSink API

The `DeltaSink` API provides a static builder to egress to Delta Lake easily. Following the same pattern as the `DeltaSource` API, the `DeltaSink` API provides a builder class. Construction of the builder is shown in Example 4-4.

Example 4-4. Creating the DeltaSink builder

```
% Path deltaTable = new Path("s3://bucket/delta/table_name")
  Configuration hadoopConf = new Configuration()
  RowType rowType = …

  RowDataDeltaSinkBuilder sinkBuilder = DeltaSink.forRowData(
    sourceTable,
    hadoopConf,
    rowType);
```

The builder pattern for the delta-flink connector should already feel familiar at this point. The only difference with crafting this builder is the addition of the RowType reference.

RowType

Similar to the StructType from Spark, the RowType stores the logical type information for the fields within a given logical row. At a higher level, we can think about this in terms of a simple DataFrame. It is an abstraction that makes working with dynamic data simpler.

More practically, if we have a reference to the source, or transformation, that occurred prior to the DeltaSink in our DataStream, then we can dynamically provide the RowType using a simple trick. Through some casting tricks, we can apply a conversion between TypeInformation<T> and RowData<T>, as seen in Example 4-5.

Example 4-5. Extracting the RowType via TypeInformation

```
% public RowType getRowType(TypeInformation<RowData> typeInfo) {
  InternalTypeInfo<RowData> sourceType = (InternalTypeInfo<RowData>) typeInfo;
  return (RowType) sourceType.toLogicalType();
}
```

The getRowType method converts the provided typeInfo object into Internal TypeInfo and uses toLogicalType, which can be cast back to a RowType. In Example 4-6 we see how to use this method to gain an understanding of the power of Flink's RowData.

Example 4-6. Extracting the RowType from our DeltaSource

```
% DeltaSource<RowData> source = …
              TypeInformation<RowData> typeInfo = source.getProducedType();
              RowType rowTypeForSink = getRowType(typeInfo);
```

If we have a simple streaming application, chances are we've managed to get along nicely for a while without spending a lot of time manually crafting plain old Java objects (POJOs) and working with serializers and deserializers; or maybe we've

---

decided to use alternative mechanisms for creating our data objects, such as Avro or Protocol Buffers. It's also possible that we've never had to work with data outside of traditional database tables. No matter what the use case, working with columnar data means we have the luxury of simply reading the columns we want in the same way that we would with a SQL query.

Take the following SQL statement:

```
% select name, age, country from users;
```

While we could read all columns on a table using select *, it is always better to take only what we need from a table. This is the beauty of columnar-oriented data. Given the high likelihood that our data application won't need everything, we save compute cycles and memory overhead and provide a clean interface between the data sources we read from.

The ability to dynamically read and select specific columns—known as *SQL projection*—via our Delta Lake table means we can trust in the table's schema, which is not something we could always say of just any data living in the data lake. While a table schema can and will change over time, we won't need to maintain a separate POJO to represent our source table. This might not seem like a large lift, but the lower the number of moving parts, the simpler it is to write, release, and maintain our data applications. We only need to express the columns we expect to have, which speeds up our ability to create flexible data processing applications, as long as we can trust that the Delta tables we read from use backward compatible schema evolution. See Chapter 5 for more information on schema evolution.

Builder options

The following options can be applied directly to the builder:

withPartitionColumns *(string ...)*
> This builder option takes an array of strings that represent the subset of columns. The columns must exist physically in the stream.

withMergeSchema *(boolean)*
> This builder option must be set to *true* in order to opt into automatic schema evolution. The default value is false.

In addition to discussing the builder options, it is worth covering the semantics of exactly-once writes using the delta-flink connector.

Exactly-once guarantees

The DeltaSink does not immediately write to the Delta table. Rather, rows are appended to flink.streaming.sink.filesystem.DeltaPendingFile—not to be confused with Delta Lake—as these files provide a mechanism to buffer writes (deltas) to the filesystem as a series of accumulated changes that can be committed together. The pending files remain open for writing until the checkpoint interval is met (Example 4-7 shows how we set the checkpoint interval for our Flink applications), and the pending files are rolled over, which is the point at which the buffered records will be committed to the Delta log. We specify the write frequency to Delta Lake using the interval supplied when we enable checkpointing on our `DataStream` object.

Example 4-7. Setting the checkpoint interval and mode

```
% StreamExecutionEnvironment
  .getExecutionEnvironment()
  .enableCheckpointing(2000, CheckpointingMode.EXACTLY_ONCE);
```

Using the checkpoint config above, we'd create a new transaction every two seconds at most, at which point the `DeltaSink` would use our Flink application `appId` and the `checkpointId` associated with the pending files. This is similar to the use of `txnAppId` and `txnVersion` for idempotent writes and will likely be unified in the future.

End-to-End Example

Now we'll look at an end-to-end example that uses the Flink DataStream API to read from Kafka and write to Delta. The application source code and Docker-compatible environment are provided in the book's GitHub repository under */ch04/flink/* (*https:// oreil.ly/2m8Kv*), including steps to initialize the `ecomm.v1.clickstream` Kafka topic, write (produce) records to be consumed by the Flink application, and ultimately write those records into Delta. The results of running the application can be seen in Figure 4-1, which shows the Flink UI and represents the end state of the application.

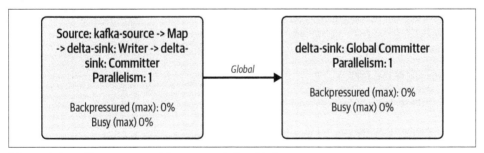

Figure 4-1. `KafkaSource` writing to our `DeltaSink`

Let's define our `DataStream` using the `KafkaSource` connector and the `DeltaSink` from earlier in this section within the scope of Example 4-8.

Example 4-8. KafkaSource to DeltaSink DataStream

```
% public DataStreamSink<RowData> createDataStream(
    StreamExecutionEnvironment env) throws IOException {

    final KafkaSource<Ecommerce> source = this.getKafkaSource();
    final DeltaSink<RowData> sink =
        this.getDeltaSink(Ecommerce.ECOMMERCE_ROW_TYPE);

    final DataStreamSource<Ecommerce> stream = env
        .fromSource(source, WatermarkStrategy.noWatermarks(), "kafka-source");

    return stream
        .map((MapFunction<Ecommerce, RowData>) Ecommerce::convertToRowData)
        .setParallelism(1)
        .sinkTo(sink)
        .name("delta-sink")
        .setDescription("writes to Delta Lake")
        .setParallelism(1);
}
```

The example takes binary data from Kafka representing ecommerce transactions in JSON format. Behind the scenes, we deserialize the JSON data into ecommerce rows and then transform from the JVM object into the internal RowData representation required for writing to our Delta table. Then we simply use an instance of the DeltaSink to provide a terminal point for our DataStream.

Next, we call execute after adding some additional descriptive metadata to the resulting DataStreamSink, as we'll see in Example 4-9.

Example 4-9. Running the end-to-end example

```
% public void run() throws Exception {
    StreamExecutionEnvironment env = this.getExecutionEnvironment();
    DataStreamSink<RowData> sink = createDataStream(env);
    sink
      .name("delta-sink")
      .setParallelism(NUM_SINKS)
      .setDescription("writes to Delta Lake");

    env.execute("kafka-to-delta-sink-job");
}
```

We've just scratched the surface on how to use the Flink connector for Delta Lake, and it is already time to take a look at another connector.

To run the full end-to-end application, just follow the step-by-step overview in the book's GitHub repository under *ch04/flink/README.md* (*https://oreil.ly/LBU42*).

In a similar vein as our end-to-end example with Flink, we'll next be exploring how to ingest the same ecommerce data from Kafka; however, this time we'll be using the Rust-based *kafka-delta-ingest* library.

Kafka Delta Ingest

The connector name sums up exactly what this little powerful library does. It reads a stream of records from a Kafka topic, optionally transforms each record (the data stream)—for example, from raw bytes to the deserialized JSON or Avro payload—and then writes the data into a Delta table. Behind the scenes, a minimal amount of user-provided configuration helps mold the connector to fulfill each specific use case. Due to the simplicity of the `kafka-delta-ingest` client, we reduce the level of effort required for one of the most critical phases of the data engineering life cycle—initial data ingestion into the *lakehouse* via Delta Lake.

Apache Kafka in a Nutshell

While Kafka has been around in the open source community since 2011, it is worth mentioning the basics before diving into the ingestion library. Feel free to skip this sidebar if you already are familiar with the basic Kafka components and architecture and just want to understand how to get the connector to work for you.

Kafka is a distributed event store and stream processing framework that provides a unified, high-throughput, low-latency platform for handling real-time data feeds.

Rather than being composed of *tables*, the Kafka architecture is built upon the notion of *topics*. In a similar fashion to our Delta tables, each topic has the ability to scale in an unbounded way (at the cost of storage space and cluster utilization). Each Kafka topic is partitioned between multiple *brokers* within a *cluster*, and each cluster can scale to meet the needs of the constituent topics contained within.

The real icing on the distributed cake is that Kafka is ultra reliable through simple configurations enabling high-availability and fault-tolerant topics through the use of what are called *in-sync replicas* (ISRs). Each replica stores a complete copy of one or more partitions within each unique Kafka topic, so if the broker is wiped out (e.g., it goes offline or becomes unavailable via network partitioning), the Kafka topic can delegate another broker to take over as the lead in the cluster, and a new broker can step up to receive an additional copy of the entire topic or a select number of partitions (ISRs). In this way, we can guarantee that the data flowing through a given

---

topic will not be lost unless a critical failure occurs across the entire cluster—and if that happens, then we can only hope that a good disaster recovery (DR) plan has been set up to mitigate the risk of data loss.

Last, there are some invariants that make Kafka invaluable, especially for time-series data. Each Kafka topic has the ability to guarantee synchronous insertion within each topic partition without requiring the entire topic to coordinate insertion order across all partitions. This means that when the cluster is running in a normal state, you can trust the event order, which reduces stream processing complexity. This probably goes without saying, but not requiring expensive rereads and sorting when working with time-series data paves the path to analysis peace of mind when it comes to working with data supplied via a Kafka source into our Delta tables. Now, back to the `kafka-delta-ingest` connector.

The `kafka-delta-ingest` connector (*https://oreil.ly/ivqMr*) provides a daemon that simplifies the common step of streaming Kafka data into our Delta Lake tables. Getting started can also be done in four easy steps:

1. Install Rust.
2. Build the project.
3. Create your Delta table.
4. Run the ingestion flow.

Install Rust

This can be done using the `rustup` toolchain:

```
% curl --proto '=https' --tlsv1.2 -sSf https://sh.rustup.rs | sh
```

Once `rustup` is installed, running `rustup update` will ensure we are on the latest stable version of Rust available.

Build the Project

This step ensures we have access to the source code.

Using `git` on the command line, simply clone the connector:

```
% git clone git@github.com:delta-io/kafka-delta-ingest.git \
    && cd kafka-delta-ingest
```

Set up your local environment

From the root of the project directory, run the Docker setup utility:

```
% docker compose up setup
```

After the setup flow completes, we have `localstack` (which runs a local Amazon Web Services [AWS] instance), `kafka` (redpandas), and the `confluent schema registry`, as well as `azurite` for local Azure Storage. Having access to run our cloud-based workflows locally greatly reduces the pain of moving from the design phase of our applications into production.

Build the connector

Rust uses `cargo` for dependency management and to build your project. The `cargo` utility is installed for us by the `rustup` toolchain. From the project root, execute the following command:

```
% cargo build
```

At this point we'll have the connector built and the Rust dependencies installed, and we can choose to either run the examples or connect to our own Kafka brokers and get started. The last section on using `kafka-delta-ingest` will cover running the end-to-end ingestion.[2]

Run the Ingestion Flow

For the ingestion application to function, we need to have two things—a source Kafka topic and a destination Delta table. There is a caveat with the generation of the Delta table, especially if you are familiar with Apache Spark–based Delta workflows: we must first create our destination Delta table in order to successfully run the ingestion flow.

There are a handful of variables that can modify the `kafka-delta-ingest` application. We will begin with a tour of the basic environment variables in Table 4-1, and then Table 4-2 will provide us with some of the runtime variables (args) that are available to us when using this connector.

Table 4-1. Using environment variables

Environment variable	Description	Default
KAFKA_BROKERS	The Kafka broker string; can be used to overwrite the location of the brokers for local testing, or for triage and recovery applications	local host:9092
AWS_ENDPOINT_URL	Used to run local tests via LocalStack	none
AWS_ACCESS_KEY_ID	Used to provide the application identity	test
AWS_SECRET_ACCESS_KEY	Used to authenticate the application identity	test
AWS_DEFAULT_REGION	Can be useful for running LocalStack or for bootstrapping separate S3 bucket locations	none

---

2 The full ingestion flow application is available in the book's GitHub repository under *ch04/rust/kafka-delta-ingest* (*https://oreil.ly/ML145*).

Table 4-2. Using command-line arguments

Argument	Description	Example
`allowed_latency`	Used to specify how long to fill the buffer and await new data before processing	`--allowed_latency 60`
`app_id`	Used to run local tests via LocalStack	`--app_id ingest-app`
`auto_offset_reset`	Can be `earliest` or `latest`; this affects whether you read from the tail or the head of the Kafka topic	`--auto_offset_reset earliest`
`checkpoints`	Will record the Kafka metadata for each processed ingestion batch; this allows for you to easily stop the application and start it back up again without data loss (unless Kafka deletes the data between runs, which can be checked in the delete policy for the topic)	`--checkpoints`
`consumer_group_id`	Provides a unique consumer name for the Kafka brokers; using the group ID, the brokers can distribute the processing of a large topic among multiple consumer applications without duplication	`--consumer_group_id ecomm-ingest-app`
`max_mes sages_per_batch`	Use this option to throttle the number of messages per application tick (loop); this can help keep your applications from running out of memory if there is an unexpected increase in the volume of the records being written to the topic	`--max_messages_per _batch 1600`
`min_bytes_per_file`	Use this option to ensure that the underlying Delta table doesn't become riddled with small files	`--min_bytes_per_file 64000000`
`kafka`	Used to pass the Kafka broker string to the ingest application	`--kafka 127.0.0.1:29092`

Now all that is left to do is to run the ingestion application. If we are running the application using our environment variables, then the simplest command would provide the Kafka topic and the Delta table location. The command signature is as follows:

```
% cargo run ingest <topic> <delta_table_location>
```

Next, we'll see a complete example:

```
% cargo run \
  ingest ecomm.v1.clickstream file:///dldg/ecomm-ingest/ \
  --allowed_latency 120 \
  --app_id clickstream_ecomm \
  --auto_offset_reset earliest \
  --checkpoints \
  --kafka 'localhost:9092' \
  --max_messages_per_batch 2000 \
  --transform 'date: substr(meta.producer.timestamp, `0`, `10`)' \
  --transform 'meta.kafka.offset: kafka.offset' \
  --transform 'meta.kafka.partition: kafka.partition' \
  --transform 'meta.kafka.topic: kafka.topic'
```

With the simple steps we've explored together, we can now easily ingest data from our Kafka topics. We have set ourselves up for success by ensuring that the folks consuming our data do so with a high level of reliability. The more we can automate, the lower the chance of human error getting in the way and resulting in incidents or in the dreaded data loss.

In the next section, we are going to explore Trino. Both prior examples play nice alongside the Trino ecosystem, as they reduce the level of effort to ingest and transform data prior to writing solid tables that can be analyzed through more traditional SQL tooling.

Trino

Trino is a distributed SQL query engine designed to seamlessly connect to and interoperate with a myriad of data sources. It provides a connector ecosystem that supports Delta Lake natively.

 Trino is the community-supported fork of the Presto project and was initially designed and developed in-house at Facebook. Trino was known as PrestoSQL before it was given its present name in 2020.

To learn more about Trino, check out *Trino: The Definitive Guide* (O'Reilly).

Getting Started

All we need to get started with Trino and Delta Lake is any version of Trino newer than version 373. At the time of writing, Trino is currently at version 459.

Connector requirements

While the Delta connector is natively included in the Trino distribution, there are still additional things we need to consider to ensure a frictionless experience.

Connecting to OSS or Databricks Delta Lake:

- Delta Tables written by Databricks Runtime 7.3 LTS, 9.1 LTS, 10.4 LTS, 11.3 LTS, and >= 12.2 LTS.
- Deployments using AWS, HDFS, Azure Storage, and Google Cloud Storage (GCS) are fully supported.
- Network access from the coordinator and workers to the Delta Lake storage.
- Access to the Hive Metastore (HMS).

- Network access to HMS from the coordinator and workers. Port 9083 is the default port for the Thrift protocol used by HMS.

Working locally with Docker:

- Trino Image
- Hive Metastore (HMS) service (standalone)
- Postgres or supported relational database management system (RDBMS) to store the HMS table properties, columns, databases, and other configurations (can point to managed RDBMS like RDS for simplicity)
- Amazon S3 or MinIO (for object storage for our managed data warehouse)

The Docker Compose configuration in Example 4-10 shows how to configure a simple Trino container for local testing.

Example 4-10. Basic Trino Docker Compose

```
services:
  trinodb:
    image: trinodb/trino:426-arm64
    platform: linux/arm64
    hostname: trinodb
    container_name: trinodb
    volumes:
      - $PWD/etc/catalog/delta.properties:/etc/trino/catalog/delta.properties
      - $PWD/conf:/etc/hadoop/conf/
    ports:
      - target: 8080
        published: 9090
        protocol: tcp
        mode: host
    environment:
      - AWS_ACCESS_KEY_ID=$AWS_ACCESS_KEY_ID
      - AWS_SECRET_ACCESS_KEY=$AWS_SECRET_ACCESS_KEY
      - AWS_DEFAULT_REGION=${AWS_DEFAULT_REGION:-us-west-1}
    networks:
      - dldg
```

The example in the next section assumes we have the following resources available to us:

- *Amazon S3 or MinIO (bucket provisioned, with a user, and roles set to allow read, write, and delete access).* Using local MinIO to mock S3 is a simple way to try things out without any upfront costs. See the docker compose examples in the book's GitHub repository under *ch04/trinodb/* (*https://oreil.ly/990GC*).

- *MySQL or PostgreSQL.* This can run locally, or we can set it up on our favorite cloud provider; for example, AWS RDS is a simple way to get started.

- *Hive Metastore (HMS) or Amazon Glue Data Catalog.*

Next, we'll learn how to configure the Delta Lake connector so that we can create a Delta catalog in Trino. If you want to learn more about using the Hive Metastore (HMS), including how to configure the *hive-site.xml*, how to include the required JARs for S3, and how to run HMS, you can read through "Running the Hive Metastore". Otherwise, skip ahead to "Configuring and Using the Trino Connector" on page 79.

Running the Hive Metastore

If you already have a reliable metastore instance setup, you can modify the connection properties to use that instead. If you are looking to have a local setup, then we can begin with the creation of the *hive-site.xml*, which is shown in Example 4-11 and which is required to connect to both MySQL and Amazon S3.

Example 4-11. hive-site.xml for HMS

```
<configuration>
  <property>
    <name>hive.metastore.version</name>
    <value>3.1.0</value>
  </property>
  <property>
    <name>javax.jdo.option.ConnectionURL</name>
    <value>jdbc:mysql://RDBMS_REMOTE_HOSTNAME:3306/metastore</value>
  </property>
  <property>
    <name>javax.jdo.option.ConnectionDriverName</name>
    <value>com.mysql.cj.jdbc.Driver</value>
  </property>
  <property>
    <name>javax.jdo.option.ConnectionUserName</name>
    <value>RDBMS_USERNAME</value>
  </property>
  <property>
    <name>javax.jdo.option.ConnectionPassword</name>
    <value>RDBMS_PASSWORD</value>
  </property>
  <property>
    <name>hive.metastore.warehouse.dir</name>
    <value>s3a://dldgv2/delta/</value>
  </property>
   <property>
      <name>fs.s3a.access.key</name>
      <value>S3_ACCESS_KEY</value>
```

```
        </property>
        <property>
           <name>fs.s3a.secret.key</name>
           <value>S3_SECRET_KEY</value>
        </property>
      <property>
        <name>fs.s3.path-style-access</name>
        <value>true</value>
      </property>
      <property>
        <name>fs.s3a.impl</name>
        <value>org.apache.hadoop.fs.s3a.S3AFileSystem</value>
      </property>
</configuration>
```

The configuration provides the nuts and bolts we need to access the metadata database, using the JDBC connection URL, username, and password properties, as well as the data warehouse, using the `hive.metastore.warehouse.dir` and the properties prefixed with `fs.s3a`.

Next, we need to create a Docker Compose file to run the metastore, which we do in Example 4-12.

Example 4-12. Docker Compose for the Hive Metastore

```
version: "3.7"

services:
  metastore:
    image: apache/hive:3.1.3
    platform: linux/amd64
    hostname: metastore
    container_name: metastore
    volumes:
      - ${PWD}/jars/hadoop-aws-3.2.0.jar:/opt/hive/lib/
      - ${PWD}/jars/mysql-connector-java-8.0.23.jar:/opt/hive/lib/
      - ${PWD}/jars/aws-java-sdk-bundle-1.11.375.jar:/opt/hive/lib/
      - ${PWD}/conf:/opt/hive/conf
    environment:
      - SERVICE_NAME=metastore
      - DB_DRIVER=mysql
      - IS_RESUME="true"
    expose:
      - 9083
    ports:
      - target: 9083
        published: 9083
        protocol: tcp
        mode: host
    networks:
      - dldg
```

With the metastore running, we are now in the driver's seat to understand how to take advantage of the Trino connector for Delta Lake.

Configuring and Using the Trino Connector

Trino uses configuration files called *catalogs*. They are used to describe the catalog type (`delta_lake`, `hive`, and many more), and they enable us to tune a given catalog to optimize for reads and writes and to manage additional connector configurations. The minimum configuration for the Delta connector requires an addressable Hive Metastore location `thrift:hostname:port` (if using HMS). The other supported catalog at the time of writing is AWS Glue (*https://oreil.ly/iBcfi*).

The code in Example 4-13 configures the connector pointing to the Hive Metastore.

Example 4-13. The Delta Lake connector properties

```
connector.name=delta_lake
hive.metastore=thrift
hive.metastore.uri=thrift://metastore:9083
delta.hive-catalog-name=metastore
delta.compression-codec=SNAPPY
delta.enable-non-concurrent-writes=true
delta.target-max-file-size=512MB
delta.unique-table-location=true
delta.vacuum.min-retention=7d
```

> The property `delta.enable-non-concurrent-writes` must be set to `true` if there is a chance of multiple writers making nonatomic changes to a table. This is most often the case with Amazon S3; setting the property to `true` ensures that the table remains consistent.

The property file from Example 4-13 can be saved as *delta.properties*. As long as the file is copied into the Trino catalog directory (*/etc/trino/catalog/*), then we'll be able to read, write, and delete from the underlying `hive.metastore.warehouse.dir`, and do a whole lot more.

Let's look at what's possible.

Using Show Catalogs

Using `show catalogs` is a simple first step to ensure that the Delta connector has been configured correctly and shows up as a resource:

```
trino> show catalogs;

Catalog
---------
```

```
delta
...
(6 rows)
```

As long as we see `delta` in the list, we can move on to creating a schema. This confirms that our catalog is correctly configured.

Creating a Schema

The notion of a schema is a bit overloaded. We have schemas that represent the structured data describing the columns of our tables, but we also have schemas representing traditional databases. Using `create schema` enables us to generate a managed location within our data warehouse that can act as a boundary for access and governance, as well as to separate the physical table data among bronze, silver, and golden tables. We'll learn more about the medallion architecture in Chapter 9, but for now let's create a `bronze_schema` to store some raw tables:

```
trino> create schema delta.bronze_schema;

CREATE SCHEMA
```

> If we are greeted by an exception rather than seeing CREATE SCHEMA returned, then it's likely due to permissions issues writing to the physical warehouse. The following is an example of such an exception:
>
> ```
> Query 20231001_182856_00004_zjwqg failed: Got excep-
> tion: java.nio.file.AccessDeniedException s3a://com.new-
> front.dldgv2/delta/bronze_schema.db: getFileStatus
> on s3a://com.newfront.dldgv2/delta/bronze_schema.db:
> com.amazonaws.services.s3.model.AmazonS3Exception: For-
> bidden (Service: Amazon S3; Status Code: 403;
> ```
>
> We can fix the problem by modifying our identity and access management (IAM) permissions or by ensuring we are using the correct IAM roles.

Show Schemas

This command allows us to query a catalog to view available schemas:

```
trino> show schemas from delta;

Schema
--------------------
 default
 information_schema
 bronze_schema
(3 rows)
```

If the schema we are looking for exists, then we are ready to move on to creating some tables.

Working with Tables

Table compatibility between the Trino and Delta ecosystems requires that we follow some guidelines. We'll look at data type interoperability and then create a table, add some rows, and view the Delta metadata, including the transaction history and tracking changes for Change Data Feed (CDF)–enabled tables. We'll conclude by looking at table optimization and vacuuming.

Data types

There are a few caveats to creating tables using Trino, especially when it comes to type mapping (*https://oreil.ly/iIbzt*) differences between Trino and Delta Lake. The table shown in Table 4-3 can be used to ensure that the appropriate types are used and to steer clear of incompatibility if our aim is interoperability.

Table 4-3. Delta to Trino type mapping

Delta data type	Trino data type
BOOLEAN	BOOLEAN
INTEGER	INTEGER
BYTE	TINYINT
SHORT	SMALLINT
LONG	BIGINT
FLOAT	REAL
DOUBLE	DOUBLE
DECIMAL(p,s)	DECIMAL(p,s)
STRING	VARCHAR
BINARY	VARBINARY
DATE	DATE
TIMESTAMPNTZ (TIMESTAMP_NTZ)	TIMESTAMP(6)
TIMESTAMP	TIMESTAMP(3) WITH TIME ZONE
ARRAY	ARRAY
MAP	MAP
STRUCT(...)	ROW(...)

CREATE TABLE options

The supported table options (shown in Table 4-4) can be applied to our table using the WITH clause of the CREATE TABLE operation. This enables us to specify options on our tables that Trino wouldn't otherwise understand. In the case of partitioning,

Trino won't automatically discover partitions, which could be a problem when it comes to the performance of SQL queries.

Table 4-4. CREATE TABLE options

Property name	Description	Default
location	Filesystem location uniform resource identifier (URI) for table. *This option is deprecated.*	Will use a managed table mapped to the location of the hive.metastore.warehouse.dir or Glue Catalog equivalent
partitioned_by	Columns to partition the table by	No partitions
checkpoint_interval	How often to commit changes to Delta Lake	Every 10 for open source software (OSS), and every 100 for Databricks (DBR)
change_data_feed_enabled	Track changes made to the table for use in change data capture (CDC)/Change Data Feed (CDF) applications	false
column_mapping_mode	How to map the underlying Parquet columns: options (ID, name, none)	none

Creating tables

We can create tables using the longform <catalog>.<schema>.<table> syntax, or the shortform syntax <table> after calling use delta.<schema>. Example 4-14 provides an example using the shortform create.

Example 4-14. Creating a Delta table with Trino

```
trino> use delta.bronze_schema;
CREATE TABLE ecomm_v1_clickstream (
  event_date DATE,
  event_time VARCHAR(255),
  event_type VARCHAR(255),
  product_id INTEGER,
  category_id BIGINT,
  category_code VARCHAR(255),
  brand VARCHAR(255),
  price DECIMAL(5,2),
  user_id INTEGER,
  user_session VARCHAR(255)
)
WITH (
    partitioned_by = ARRAY['event_date'],
    checkpoint_interval = 30,
    change_data_feed_enabled = false,
    column_mapping_mode = 'name'
);
```

The table generated using the DDL statement in Example 4-14 creates a managed table in our data warehouse that will be partitioned daily. The table structure represents the ecommerce data from the "Apache Flink" on page 61 section earlier in this chapter.

Listing tables

Using `show tables` will allow us to view the collection of tables within a given schema in the Delta catalog:

```
trino:bronze_schema> show tables;

Table
---------------------
 ecomm_v1_clickstream
(1 row)
```

Inspecting tables

If we are not the owners of a given table, we can use `describe` to learn about the table through its metadata:

```
trino> describe delta.bronze_schema."ecomm_v1_clickstream";

    Column      |     Type      | Extra | Comment
----------------+---------------+-------+---------
 event_date     | date          |       |
 event_time     | varchar       |       |
 event_type     | varchar       |       |
 product_id     | integer       |       |
 category_id    | bigint        |       |
 category_code  | varchar       |       |
 brand          | varchar       |       |
 price          | decimal(5,2)  |       |
 user_id        | integer       |       |
 user_session   | varchar       |       |
(10 rows)
```

Using INSERT

Rows can be inserted directly using the command line, or through the use of the Trino client:

```
trino> INSERT INTO delta.bronze_schema."ecomm_v1_clickstream"
    VALUES
        (DATE '2023-10-01', '2023-10-01T19:10:05.704396Z', 'view', ...),
        (DATE('2023-10-01'), '2023-10-01T19:20:05.704396Z', 'view', ...);
INSERT: 2 rows
```

Querying Delta tables

Using the `select` operator allows you to query your Delta tables:

```
trino> select event_date, product_id, brand, price
  -> from delta.bronze_schema."ecomm_v1_clickstream";

 event_date | product_id |  brand  | price
------------+------------+---------+--------
 2023-10-01 |   44600062 | nars    |  35.79
 2023-10-01 |   54600062 | lancome | 122.79
(2 rows)
```

Updating rows

The standard `update` operator is available:

```
trino> UPDATE delta.bronze_schema."ecomm_v1_clickstream"
   -> SET category_code = 'health.beauty.products'
   -> where category_id = 2103807459595387724;
```

Creating tables with selection

We can create a table using another table. This is referred to as CREATE TABLE AS, and it allows us to create a new physical Delta table by referencing another table:

```
trino> CREATE TABLE delta.bronze_schema."ecomm_lite"
    AS select event_date, product_id, brand, price
    FROM delta.bronze_schema."ecomm_v1_clickstream";
```

Table Operations

There are many table operations to consider for optimal performance, and for decluttering the physical filesystem in which our Delta tables live. Chapter 5 covers the common maintenance and table utility functions, and the following section covers what functions are available within the Trino connector.

Vacuum

The vacuum operation will clean up files that are no longer required in the current version of a given Delta table. In Chapter 5 we go into more detail about why vacuuming is required, as well as the caveats to keep in mind to support table recovery and rolling back to prior versions with time travel.

With respect to Trino, the Delta catalog property `delta.vacuum.min-retention` provides a gating mechanism to protect a table in case of an arbitrary call to vacuum with a low number of days or hours:

```
trino> CALL delta.system.vacuum('bronze_schema', 'ecomm_v1_clickstream', '1d');
```

```
Retention specified (1.00d) is shorter than the minimum retention configured
in the system (7.00d). Minimum retention can be changed with delta.vacuum.min-
retention configuration property or delta.vacuum_min_retention session property
```

Otherwise, the vacuum operation will delete the physical files that are no longer
needed by the table.

Table optimization

Depending on the size of the table parts created as we make modifications to our
tables with Trino, we run the risk of creating too many small files representing our
tables. A simple technique to combine the small files into larger files is bin-packing
optimize (which we cover in Chapter 5 and in the performance-tuning deep dive in
Chapter 10). To trigger compaction, we can call ALTER TABLE with EXECUTE:

```
trino> ALTER TABLE delta.bronze_schema."ecomm_v1_clickstream" EXECUTE optimize;
```

We can also provide more hints to change the behavior of the optimize operation.
The following will ignore files greater than 10 MB:

```
trino> ALTER TABLE delta.bronze_schema."ecomm_v1_clickstream"
    -> EXECUTE optimize(file_size_threshold => '10MB')
```

The following will only attempt to compact table files within the partition
(event_date = "2023-10-01"):

```
trino> ALTER TABLE delta.bronze_schema."ecomm_v1_clickstream" EXECUTE optimize
WHERE event_date = "2023-10-01"
```

Metadata tables

The connector exposes several metadata tables for each Delta Lake table that contain
information about their internal structure. We can query these tables to learn more
about our tables and to inspect changes and recent history.

Table history

Each transaction is recorded in the <table>$history metadata table:

```
trino> describe delta.bronze_schema."ecomm_v1_clickstream$history";

       Column        |              Type             | Extra | Comment
---------------------+-------------------------------+-------+---------
 version             | bigint                        |       |
 timestamp           | timestamp(3) with time zone   |       |
 user_id             | varchar                       |       |
 user_name           | varchar                       |       |
 operation           | varchar                       |       |
 operation_parameters | map(varchar, varchar)        |       |
 cluster_id          | varchar                       |       |
 read_version        | bigint                        |       |
```

```
isolation_level    | varchar                      |     |
is_blind_append    | boolean                      |     |
```

We can query the metadata table. Let's look at the last three transactions for our
`ecomm_v1_clickstream` table:

```
trino> select version, timestamp, operation
    -> from delta.bronze_schema."ecomm_v1_clickstream$history";

 version |          timestamp          |  operation
---------+-----------------------------+--------------
       0 | 2023-10-01 19:47:35.618 UTC | CREATE TABLE
       1 | 2023-10-01 19:48:41.212 UTC | WRITE
       2 | 2023-10-01 23:01:13.141 UTC | OPTIMIZE
(3 rows)
```

Change Data Feed

The Trino connector provides functionality for reading Change Data Feed (CDF)
entries to expose row-level changes between two versions of a Delta Lake table. When
the `change_data_feed_enabled` table property is set to `true` on a specific Delta Lake
table, the connector records change events for all data changes on the table:

```
trino> use delta.bronze_schema;
CREATE TABLE ecomm_v1_clickstream (
  ...
)
WITH (
    change_data_feed_enabled = true
);
```

Now each row of each transaction is recorded (with the operation type), enabling us
to rebuild the state of a table or to walk through the changes to a table after a specific
point in time.

For example, if we'd like to view all changes since version 0 of a table, we could
execute the following:

```
trino> select event_date, _change_type, _commit_version, _commit_timestamp
from TABLE(
  delta.system.table_changes(
    schema_name => 'bronze_schema',
    table_name => 'ecomm_v1_clickstream',
    since_version => 0
  )
);
```

and view the changes made. In the example use case, we've simply inserted two rows:

```
event_date | _change_type | _commit_version |       _commit_timestamp
-----------+--------------+-----------------+-----------------------------
2023-10-01 | insert       |               1 | 2023-10-01 19:48:41.212 UTC
2023-10-01 | insert       |               1 | 2023-10-01 19:48:41.212 UTC
(2 rows)
```

Viewing table properties

It is useful to be able to view the table properties associated with our tables. We can use the metadata table `<table>$properties` to view the associated Delta TBLPROPERTIES:

```
trino> select * from  delta.bronze_schema."ecomm_v1_clickstream$properties";

              key                | value
---------------------------------+-------
 delta.enableChangeDataFeed      | true
 delta.columnMapping.maxColumnId | 10
 delta.columnMapping.mode        | name
 delta.checkpointInterval        | 30
 delta.minReaderVersion          | 2
 delta.minWriterVersion          | 5
```

Modifying table properties

If we want to modify the underlying table properties of our Delta table, we'll need to use the Delta connectors alias for the supported table properties. For example, `change_data_feed_enabled` will map to the `delta.enableChangeDataFeed` property:

```
trino> ALTER TABLE delta.bronze_schema."ecomm_v1_clickstream"
SET PROPERTIES "change_data_feed_enabled" = false;
```

Deleting tables

Using the `DROP TABLE` operation, we can permanently remove a table that is no longer needed:

```
trino> DROP TABLE delta.bronze_schema."ecomm_lite";
```

There is a lot more that we can do with the Trino connector that is out of scope for this book; for now we will say goodbye to Trino and conclude this chapter.

Conclusion

During the time we spent together in this chapter, we learned how simple it can be to connect our Delta tables as either the source or the sink for our Flink applications. We then learned to use the Rust-based *kafka-delta-ingest* application to simplify the data ingestion process that is the bread and butter of most data engineers working with high-throughput streaming data. By reducing the level of effort required to simply read a stream of data and write it into our Delta tables, we end up in a much better place in terms of cognitive burden. When we start to think about all data in terms of tables—*bounded* or *unbounded*—the mental model can be applied to tame even the most wildly data-intensive problems. On that note, we concluded the chapter by exploring the native Trino connector for Delta. We discovered how simple configuration opens up the doors to analytics and insights, all while ensuring we continue to have a single source of data truth residing in our Delta tables.

Maintaining Your Delta Lake

The process of keeping our Delta Lake tables running efficiently over time is akin to any kind of preventative maintenance for a car or motorcycle or any alternative mode of transportation (a bike, a scooter, rollerblades). We wouldn't wait for our tires to go flat before assessing the situation and finding a solution—we'd take action. We would start with simple observations, look for leaks, and ask ourselves, "Does the tire need to be patched? Could the problem be as simple as adding more air, or is this situation more dire, and the whole tire will need to be replaced?" The process of monitoring the situation, finding a remedy when we detect a problem, and applying the solution can be applied to our Delta Lake tables as well and is all part of the general process of maintaining the tables. In essence, we just need to think in terms of *cleaning*, *monitoring*, *tuning*, *repairing*, and *replacing*.

In the sections that follow, we'll learn to take advantage of the Delta Lake utility methods and learn about their associated configurations (aka table properties). We'll walk through some common methods for cleaning, tuning, repairing, and replacing our tables, in order to lend a helping hand while optimizing the performance and health of our tables, and ultimately build a firm understanding of the cause-and-effect relationships among the actions we take.

Using Delta Lake Table Properties

Delta Lake provides many utility functions to assist with the general maintenance (cleaning and tuning), repair, restoration, and even replacement of our critical tables, all of which are valuable capabilities for any data engineer. We'll begin this chapter with an introduction to some of the common maintenance-related Delta Lake table properties, and a simple exercise showcasing how to apply, modify, and remove table properties.

Delta Lake Table Properties Reference

The metadata stored alongside our table definitions includes `TBLPROPERTIES`. The common properties are presented in Table 5-1 and are used to control the behavior of our Delta tables. These properties enable automated preventative maintenance. When combined with the Delta Lake table utility functions, they also provide incredibly simple control over otherwise complex tasks. We simply add or remove properties to control the behavior of our tables.

Bookmark Table 5-1 for whenever you need a handy reference to these properties. Each row provides the property name, the internal data type, and the associated use case pertaining to cleaning, tuning, repairing, or replacing your Delta Lake tables.

Table 5-1. Delta Lake table properties reference

Property	Data type	Use with	Default
delta.logRetentionDuration	CalendarInterval	Cleaning	interval 30 days
delta.deletedFileRetentionDuration	CalendarInterval	Cleaning	interval 1 week
delta.setTransactionRetentionDuration	CalendarInterval	Cleaning, Repairing	(none)
delta.targetFileSize[a]	String	Tuning	(none)
delta.tuneFileSizesForRewrites[a]	Boolean	Tuning	(none)
delta.autoOptimize.optimizeWrite[a]	Boolean	Tuning	(none)
delta.autoOptimize.autoCompact	Boolean	Tuning	(none)
delta.dataSkippingNumIndexedCols	Int	Tuning	32
delta.checkpoint.writeStatsAsStruct	Boolean	Tuning	(none)
delta.checkpoint.writeStatsAsJson	Boolean	Tuning	true
delta.randomizeFilePrefixes	Boolean	Tuning	false

[a] Properties (*https://oreil.ly/sksjG*) exclusive to Databricks.

The beauty behind using *table properties* is that they affect only the metadata of our tables and in most cases don't require any changes to the physical table structure. Additionally, being able to opt in, or opt out, allows us to modify Delta Lake's behavior without the need to go back and change any existing pipeline code, and in most cases without needing to restart, or redeploy, our streaming applications (the batch applications will simply read the revised properties on their next run).

The general behavior when adding or removing table properties is no different than using common data manipulation language (DML) operators, which consist of insert, delete, update, and, in more advanced cases, upsert, which will insert or update a row based on a match. Chapter 10 will cover more advanced DML patterns with Delta.

Any table changes will take effect or become visible during the next transaction—automatically in the case of batch, and immediately with our streaming applications.

With streaming Delta Lake applications, changes to the table, including changes to the table metadata, are treated like any ALTER TABLE command. Other changes to the table that don't modify the physical table data, such as with the utility functions vacuum and optimize, can be externally updated without breaking the flow of a given streaming application.

Changes to the physical table or table metadata are treated equally and generate a versioned record in the Delta log. The addition of a new transaction results in the local synchronization of the deltaSnapshot for any out-of-sync (stale) processes. This is all due to the fact that Delta Lake supports multiple concurrent writers, allowing changes to occur in a decentralized (distributed) way, with central synchronization at the table's Delta log.

There are other use cases that fall under the maintenance umbrella and require intentional action by humans and the courtesy of a heads-up to downstream consumers. As we close out this chapter, we'll look at using REPLACE TABLE to add partitions. This process can break active readers of our tables, as the operation rewrites the physical layout of the Delta Lake table.

To follow along, the rest of the chapter will be using the covid_nyt dataset included in the book's GitHub repo (*https://oreil.ly/2m8Kv*), along with the companion Docker environment. To get started, execute the following:

```
$ export DLDG_DATA_DIR=~/path/to/delta-lake-definitive-guide/datasets/
$ export DLDG_CHAPTER_DIR=~/path/to/delta-lake-definitive-guide/ch05
$ docker run --rm -it \
  --name delta_quickstart \
  -v $DLDG_DATA_DIR/:/opt/spark/data/datasets \
  -v $DLDG_CHAPTER_DIR/:/opt/spark/work-dir/ch05 \
  -p 8888-8889:8888-8889 \
  delta_quickstart
```

This command will spin up the JupyterLab environment locally. Using the URL provided to you in the output, open up the JupyterLab environment and click into */ch05/ch05_notebook.ipynb* to follow along.

Create an Empty Table with Properties

We've created tables many ways throughout this book, so let's simply generate an empty table with the SQL CREATE TABLE syntax. In Example 5-1, we create a new table with a single date column and one default table property, delta.logRetention Duration. We will cover how this property is used later in the chapter.

Example 5-1. Creating a Delta Lake table with default table properties

```
$ spark.sql("""
    CREATE TABLE IF NOT EXISTS default.covid_nyt (
      date DATE
    ) USING DELTA
     TBLPROPERTIES('delta.logRetentionDuration'='interval 7 days');
""")
```

 It is worth pointing out that the covid_nyt dataset has six columns. In Example 5-1, we are purposefully being lazy, since we can steal the schema of the full covid_nyt table while we import it in the next step. This will teach us how to evolve the schema of the current table by filling in missing columns in the table definition.

Populate the Table

At this point, we have an empty Delta Lake table. This is essentially a promise of a table; it contains only the */{tablename}/_delta_log* directory and an initial log entry with the schema and metadata of our empty table. If you want to run a simple test to confirm, you can run the following command to show the backing files of the table:

```
$ spark.table("default.covid_nyt").inputFiles()
```

The inputFiles command will return an empty list. That is expected but also feels a little lonely. Let's go ahead and bring some joy to this table by adding some data. We'll execute a simple read-through operation of the covid_nyt Parquet data directly into our managed Delta Lake table (the empty table from before).

From your active session, execute the following block of code to merge the covid_nyt dataset into the empty default.covid_nyt table:

```
$ from pyspark.sql.functions import to_date
    (spark.read
      .format("parquet")
      .load("/opt/spark/work-dir/rs/data/COVID-19_NYT/*.parquet")
      .withColumn("date", to_date("date", "yyyy-MM-dd"))
      .write
      .format("delta")
      .saveAsTable("default.covid_nyt")
    )
```

The COVID-19 dataset has the `date` column represented as a `STRING`. For this exercise, we have set the `date` column to a `DATE` type, and we use `withColumn("date", to_date("date", "yyyy-MM-dd"))` to respect the existing data type of the table.

You'll notice the operation fails to execute:

```
$ pyspark.sql.utils.AnalysisException: Table default.covid_nyt already exists
```

We just encountered an *AnalysisException*. Luckily for us, this exception is blocking us for the right reasons. In the prior code block, the exception is thrown due to the default behavior of the `DataFrameWriter` (*https://oreil.ly/kE1vl*) in Spark, which defaults to `errorIfExists` (*https://oreil.ly/IwmG1*). This is done for our benefit, to protect our precious data. So if the table exists, we raise an exception rather than trying to do anything that could damage the existing table.

To get past this speed bump, we'll need to change the write mode of the operation to append. This changes the behavior of our operation by stating that we are intentionally adding records to an existing table.

Let's go ahead and configure the write mode as `append`:

```
(spark.read
    ...
    .write
    .format("delta")
    .mode("append")
    ...
)
```

OK, we made it past one hurdle and are no longer being blocked by the "table already exists" exception. However, we were met with yet another `AnalysisException`:

```
$ pyspark.sql.utils.AnalysisException: A schema mismatch detected when writing
to the Delta table (Table ID: xxxxxxxx-xxxx-xxxx-xxxx-xxxxxxxxxxxx)
```

This time the `AnalysisException` is thrown due to a schema mismatch. This is how the Delta protocol protects us (the operator) from blindly making changes when there is a mismatch between the expected (committed) table schema that currently has one column and our local schema (from reading the `covid_nyt` Parquet data) that is currently uncommitted and has six columns. This exception is another guardrail in place to block the accidental pollution of our table schema, a process known as *schema enforcement*.

Schema Enforcement and Evolution

Delta Lake utilizes a technique from traditional data warehouses called *schema-on-write*. This simply means that there is a process in place to check the schema of the writer against the existing table prior to a write operation being executed. This two-step process provides a single source of truth for a table schema based on prior transactions:

Schema enforcement

This is the controlling process that checks an existing schema before allowing a write transaction to occur and results in throwing an exception in the case of a mismatch.

Schema evolution

This is the process of intentionally modifying an existing schema in a way that enables backward compatibility. This is traditionally accomplished using ALTER TABLE {t} ADD COLUMN(S), which is also supported in Delta Lake, along with the ability to enable the mergeSchema option on write.

Evolve the Table Schema

The last step required to add the covid_nyt data to our existing table is to explicitly state that we approve of the schema changes we are bringing to the table, and that we intend to commit both the actual table data and the modifications to the table schema:

```
$ (spark.read
    .format("parquet")
    .load("/opt/spark/work-dir/rs/data/COVID-19_NYT/*.parquet")
    .withColumn("date", to_date("date", "yyyy-MM-dd"))
    .write
    .format("delta")
    .mode("append") ❶
    .option("mergeSchema", "true") ❷
    .saveAsTable("default.covid_nyt")
)
```

Success! We now have a table to work with, the result of executing the preceding code. As a short summary, we needed to add two modifiers to our write operation, for the following reasons:

❶ We updated the write mode to an append operation. This was necessary given that we created the table in a separate transaction, and the default write mode (errorIfExists) short-circuits the operation when the Delta Lake table already exists.

❷ We updated the write operation to include the `mergeSchema` option, enabling us to modify the `covid_nyt` table schema by adding the five additional columns required by the dataset within the same transaction in which we also physically added the `covid_nyt` data.

With everything said and done, we now have actual data in our table, and we evolved the schema from the Parquet-based `covid_nyt` dataset in the process.

You can take a look at the complete table metadata by executing the following `DESCRIBE` command:

```
$ spark.sql("describe extended default.covid_nyt").show(truncate=False)
```

You'll see the complete table metadata after executing the `DESCRIBE` command, including the columns (and comments) and partitioning (in our case, none), as well as all available `tblproperties`. Using `DESCRIBE` is a simple way of getting to know our table, or frankly any table you'll need to work with in the future.

Alternatives to Automatic Schema Evolution

In the preceding example, we used `.option("mergeSchema", "true")` to modify the behavior of the Delta Lake writer. While this option simplifies how we evolve our Delta Lake table schema, it comes at the price of our not being fully aware of the changes to our table schema. In cases in which there are unknown columns being introduced from an upstream source, you'll want to know which columns are intended to be brought forward and which columns can be safely ignored.

If we knew that we had five missing columns on our `default.covid_nyt` table, we could run an `ALTER TABLE` to add the missing columns:

```
$ spark.sql("""
  ALTER TABLE default.covid_nyt
  ADD COLUMNS (
    county STRING,
    state STRING,
    fips INT,
    cases INT,
    deaths INT
  );
  """)
```

This process may seem cumbersome given that we learned how to automatically merge modifications to our table schema, but it is ultimately more expensive to rewind and undo surprise changes. With a little up-front work, it isn't difficult to explicitly opt out of automatic schema changes:

```
(spark.read
    .format("parquet")
    .load("/opt/spark/work-dir/rs/data/COVID-19_NYT/*.parquet")
```

```
            .withColumn("date", to_date("date", "yyyy-MM-dd"))
            .write
            .format("delta")
            .option("mergeSchema", "false")
            .mode("append")
            .saveAsTable("default.covid_nyt"))
        )
```

And voila! We get all the expected changes to our table intentionally, with zero surprises, which helps keep our table clean and tidy.

Add or Modify Table Properties

The process of adding or modifying existing table properties is simple. If a property already exists, then any changes will blindly overwrite the existing property. Newly added properties will be appended to the set of table properties.

To showcase this behavior, execute the following ALTER TABLE statement in your active session:

```
$ spark.sql("""
  ALTER TABLE default.covid_nyc
  SET TBLPROPERTIES (
     'engineering.team_name'='dldg_authors',
     'engineering.slack'='delta-users.slack.com'
  )
  """)
```

This operation adds two properties to our table metadata: a pointer to the team name (dldg_authors), and the Slack organization (delta-users.slack.com) for the authors of this book. Anytime we modify a table's metadata, the changes are recorded in the table history. To view the changes made to the table, including the change we just made to the table properties, we can call the history method on the DeltaTable Python interface:

```
$ from delta.tables import DeltaTable
  dt = DeltaTable.forName(spark, 'default.covid_nyt')
  dt.history(10).select("version", "timestamp", "operation").show()
```

The preceding will output the changes made to the table:

```
+-------+--------------------+-----------------+
|version|           timestamp|        operation|
+-------+--------------------+-----------------+
|      2|2023-06-07 04:38:...|SET TBLPROPERTIES|
|      1|2023-06-07 04:14:...|            WRITE|
|      0|2023-06-07 04:13:...|     CREATE TABLE|
+-------+--------------------+-----------------+
```

To view (or confirm) the changes from the prior transaction, you can call SHOW TBLPROPERTIES on the covid_nyt table:

```
$ spark.sql("show tblproperties default.covid_nyt").show(truncate=False)
```

Or you can execute the detail() function on the DeltaTable instance from earlier:

```
$ dt.detail().select("properties").show(truncate=False)
```

To round out this section, we'll learn how to remove unwanted table properties; then we can continue our journey by learning to clean and optimize our Delta Lake tables.

Remove Table Properties

There would be no point in only being able to add table properties, so let's look at how to use ALTER TABLE table_name UNSET TBLPROPERTIES.

Let's say we accidentally misspelled a property name—for example, delta.loRgeten tionDuratio rather than the actual property delta.logRetentionDuration; while this mistake isn't the end of the world, there would be no reason to keep it around.

To remove the unwanted (or misspelled) property, we can execute UNSET TBLPROPER TIES on our ALTER TABLE command:

```
$ spark.sql("""
    ALTER TABLE default.covid_nyt
    UNSET TBLPROPERTIES('delta.logRetentionDuration')
    """)
```

And just like that, the unwanted property is no longer taking up space in the table properties.

We just learned to create Delta Lake tables using default table properties at the point of initial creation (see Example 5-1) and relearned the rules of schema enforcement and how to intentionally evolve our table schemas, as well as how to add, modify, and remove properties. Next we'll explore keeping our Delta Lake tables clean and tidy.

(Spark Only) Default Table Properties

Once you become more familiar with the nuances of the various Delta Lake table properties, you can provide your own default set of properties to the SparkSession using the following Spark config prefix:

```
spark.databricks.delta.properties.defaults.<conf>
```

While this works only for Spark workloads, you can probably imagine many scenarios in which the ability to automatically inject properties into your pipelines could be useful:

```
spark...delta.defaults.logRetentionDuration=interval 2 weeks
spark...delta.defaults.deletedFileRetentionDuration=interval 28 days
```

Speaking of useful, table properties can be used for storing metadata about a table owner, an engineering team, communication channels (Slack and email), and essentially anything else that helps to extend the utility of the descriptive table metadata. Utilizing table metadata can lead to simplified data discovery and capture information about the owners and humans accountable for dataset ownership. As we saw earlier, the table metadata can store a wealth of information extending well beyond simple configurations.

Table 5-2 lists some example table properties that can be used to augment any Delta Lake table. The properties are broken down into prefixes and provide additional data catalog–style information alongside your existing table properties.

Table 5-2. Using table properties for data cataloging

Property	Description
catalog.team_name	Provides the team name and answers the question, "Who is accountable for the table?"
catalog.engineering .comms.slack	Provides the Slack channel for the engineering team—use a permalink like *https:// delta-users.slack.com/archives/CG9LR6LN4*, since channel names can change over time
catalog.engineering .comms.email	Provides the email address for the engineering team—for example, *dldg_authors@gmail.com* (note that this isn't a real email address, but you get the point)
catalog.table .classification	Can be used to declare the type of table—examples: pii, sensitive-pii, general, all-access, etc.; these values can be used for role-based access as well (integrations are outside the scope of this book)

Delta Lake Table Optimization

Are you familiar with the idea that, for every action, there is an equal and opposite reaction?[1] Echoing the laws of physics, changes can be felt as new data is inserted (appended), modified (updated), merged (upserted), or removed (deleted) from our Delta Lake tables (the action). The reaction in the system is to record each operation as an atomic transaction (version, timestamp, operations, and more), ensuring not only that the table continues to serve its current use cases but also that it retains enough history to allow us to rewind (time travel) back to an earlier state (point in the table's time) and fix (overwrite) or recover (replace) the table in case larger problems are introduced to the table.

However, before we get into the more complicated maintenance operations, let's first look at common problems that can sneak into a table over time. Among the best known of these is the small file problem. Let's walk through the problem and its solution now.

The Problem with Big Tables and Small Files

When we talk about the small file problem, we are talking about a problem that isn't actually unique to Delta Lake but rather is an issue with network IO and the associated high open cost for unoptimized tables consisting of way too many small files. Small files can be classified as any files under 64 kb.

How can too many small files hurt us? The answer is "in many different ways," but the common thread among all problems is that they sneak up over time and require modifications to the layout of the physical files encapsulating our tables. Not recognizing when our tables begin to slow down and suffer under the weight of themselves can lead to potentially costly increases to distributed compute in order to efficiently open and execute a query.

One strategy for ensuring our tables remain in tip-top shape is to employ table-level monitoring. We cover some strategies for metadata-only monitoring in Chapter 13. These strategies can be extended to handle monitoring of the number of files for the current table snapshot, or to track how many versions of the table remain on disk. In the end, monitoring is a tool to help raise awareness of issues that pop up regularly and can be a lifeline with respect to your maintenance strategy.

---

1 This is Newton's third law of motion.

There is a true cost in terms of the number of operational steps required before the table is physically loaded into memory, which tends to increase over time until the point where a table can no longer be efficiently loaded. This tends to be a result of cloud object storage, where each operation comes with its own variable latency, operational concurrency limits, and ultimately higher cost of doing business.

 This is felt much more in traditional Hadoop-style ecosystems, such as MapReduce and Spark, where the unit of distribution is bound to a task, a file consists of "blocks," and each block takes one task. If we have one million files in a table and the files are 1 GB each, and we have a block size of 64 MB, then we will need to distribute a whopping 15.65 million tasks to read the entire table. It is ideal to optimize the target file size of the physical files in our tables to reduce filesystem IO and network IO. When we encounter unoptimized files (the small files problem), then the performance of our tables suffers greatly because of it. For a solid example, say we had the same large table (~1 TB), but the files making up the table were evenly split at around 5 kb each. This means we'd have 200k files per 1 GB, and around 200 million files to open before loading our table. In most cases the table would never open.

For fun, we are going to re-create a very real small files problem and then figure out how to optimize the table. To follow along, head back to the session from earlier in the chapter, as we'll continue to use the covid_nyt dataset in the following examples.

Creating the small file problem

The covid_nyt dataset has over a million records. The total size of the table is less than 7mb split across eight partitions, which is a small dataset:

```
$ ls -lh \
  /opt/spark/work-dir/ch05/spark-warehouse/covid_nyt/*.parquet | wc -l
8
```

What if we flipped the problem around and had nine thousand or even one million files representing the covid_nyt dataset? While this use case is extreme, we'll learn later in the book (Chapter 7) that streaming applications are a typical culprit with respect to creating tons of tiny files!

Let's create another empty table named default.nonoptimal_covid_nyt and run some simple commands to unoptimize the table. For starters, execute the following command:

```
$ from delta.tables import DeltaTable
  (DeltaTable.createIfNotExists(spark)
    .tableName("default.nonoptimal_covid_nyt")
    .property("description", "table to be optimized")
```

```
  .property("catalog.team_name", "dldg_authors")
  .property("catalog.engineering.comms.slack",
        "https://delta-users.slack.com/archives/CG9LR6LN4")
  .property("catalog.engineering.comms.email","dldg_authors@gmail.com")
  .property("catalog.table.classification","all-access")
  .addColumn("date", "DATE")
  .addColumn("county", "STRING")
  .addColumn("state", "STRING")
  .addColumn("fips", "INT")
  .addColumn("cases", "INT")
  .addColumn("deaths", "INT")
  .execute())
```

Now that we have our table, we can easily create way too many small files using the normal default.covid_nyt table as our source. The total number of rows in the table is 1,111,930. If we repartition the table from the existing eight partitions to, say, nine thousand partitions, this will split the table into an even nine thousand files at around 5 kb per file:

```
$ (spark
  .table("default.covid_nyt")
  .repartition(9000)
  .write
  .format("delta")
  .mode("overwrite")
  .saveAsTable("default.nonoptimal_covid_nyt")
  )
```

 If you want to view the physical table files, you can run the following command:

```
WAREHOUSE_DIR=/opt/spark/work-dir/ch05/spark-warehouse
FILE_PATH=$WAREHOUSE_DIR/nonoptimal_covid_nyt/*parquet

docker exec -it delta_quickstart bash \
-c "ls -l ${FILE_PATH} | wc -l"
```

You'll see that there are exactly nine thousand files.

We now have a table we can optimize. Next we'll introduce OPTIMIZE. As a utility, consider it to be your friend. It will help you painlessly consolidate the many small files representing our table into a few larger files, and all in the blink of an eye.

Using OPTIMIZE to Fix the Small File Problem

OPTIMIZE is a Delta utility function that comes in two variants: Z-Order and bin-packing. The default is bin-packing. As we look into fixing the small file problem, it is worth pointing out that the reverse can also be true—you may find yourself with many large files that need to be broken down in order to provide efficient processing.

OPTIMIZE

What exactly is *bin-packing*? At a high level, this is a technique that is used to coalesce many small files into fewer large files across an arbitrary number of bins. A bin is defined as a file of a maximum file size (the default for Spark Delta Lake is 1 GB; for Delta Rust, it's 250mb).

The OPTIMIZE command can be tuned using a mixture of configurations.[2]

For tuning the OPTIMIZE thresholds, there are a few considerations to keep in mind:

- *(Spark only)* `spark.databricks.delta.optimize.minFileSize` (long) is used to group together files smaller than the threshold (in bytes) before being rewritten into a larger file by the OPTIMIZE command.

- *(Spark only)* `spark.databricks.delta.optimize.maxFileSize` (long) is used to specify the target file size produced by the OPTIMIZE command.

- *(Spark only)* `spark.databricks.delta.optimize.repartition.enabled` (bool) is used to change the behavior of OPTIMIZE and will use repartition(1) instead of coalesce(1) when reducing.

- *(delta-rs)* The table property `delta.targetFileSize` (string)—an example being 250mb—can be used with the `delta-rs` client but is currently not supported in the OSS delta release.

The OPTIMIZE command is deterministic and aims to achieve an evenly distributed Delta Lake table (or specific subset of a given table).

To see OPTIMIZE in action, we can execute the optimize function on the non optimal_covid_nyt table. Feel free to run the command as many times as you want; OPTIMIZE will take effect a second time only if new records are added to the table:

```
$ results_df = (DeltaTable
    .forName(spark, "default.nonoptimal_covid_nyt")
    .optimize()
    .executeCompaction())
```

The results of running the optimize operation are returned locally in a DataFrame (results_df) and are available via the table history as well. To view the OPTIMIZE stats, we can use the history method on our DeltaTable instance:

```
$ from pyspark.sql.functions import col
(
    DeltaTable.forName(spark, "default.nonoptimal_covid_nyt")
    .history(10)
```

---

2 For the Spark ecosystem, Delta Lake >= 3.1.0 includes the option for auto compaction, using `delta.auto Optimize.autoCompact`.

```
    .where(col("operation") == "OPTIMIZE")
    .select(
            "version", "timestamp", "operation",
            "operationMetrics.numRemovedFiles",
            "operationMetrics.numAddedFiles"
    )
    .show(truncate=False))
```

The resulting output will produce the following table:

```
+-------+-----------------------+---------+---------------+-------------+
|version|timestamp              |operation|numRemovedFiles|numAddedFiles|
+-------+-----------------------+---------+---------------+-------------+
|2      |2023-06-07 06:47:28.488|OPTIMIZE |9000           |1            |
+-------+-----------------------+---------+---------------+-------------+
```

The important column for our operation shows that we removed nine thousand files
(numRemovedFiles) and generated one compacted file (numAddedFiles).

Z-Order Optimize

Z-Ordering (*https://oreil.ly/hbj9g*) is a technique for colocating related information
in the same set of files. The related information is the data residing in your table's
columns. Consider the covid_nyt dataset. If we knew we wanted to quickly calculate
the death rate by state over time, then utilizing ZORDER BY would allow us to *skip*
opening files in our tables that don't contain relevant information for our query.
This colocality is automatically used by the Delta Lake data-skipping algorithms. This
behavior dramatically reduces the amount of data that needs to be read.

For tuning ZORDER BY:

- delta.dataSkippingNumIndexedCols (int) is the table property responsible for
  reducing the number of stats columns stored in the table metadata. This defaults
  to 32 columns.

- delta.checkpoint.writeStatsAsStruct (bool) is the table property responsible
  for enabling writing of columnar stats (per transaction) as Parquet data. The
  default value is false, as not all vendor-based Delta Lake solutions support reading the struct-based stats.

> Chapter 10 will cover performance tuning in more detail, so for
> now we will just dip our toes in and cover general maintenance
> considerations.

Table Tuning and Management

We just covered how to optimize our tables using the OPTIMIZE command. In many cases, where you have a table smaller than 1 GB, it is perfectly fine to use OPTIMIZE; however, it is common for tables to grow over time, and eventually we'll have to consider partitioning our tables as a next step for maintenance.

Partitioning Your Tables

Table partitions can work for you or, oddly enough, against you, not unlike the behavior we observed with the small files problem; too many partitions can create a similar problem, but through directory-level isolation instead. Luckily, there are some general guidelines and rules to live by that will help you manage your partitions effectively, or at least provide you with a pattern to follow when the time comes.

Table partitioning rules

The following rules will help you understand when to introduce partitions:[3]

If your table is smaller than 1 TB, don't add partitions; just use OPTIMIZE *to reduce the number of files.*
> If bin-packing optimize isn't providing the performance boost you need, talk with your downstream data customers and learn how they commonly query your table; you may be able to use Z-Order Optimize and speed up their queries with data colocation.

If you need to optimize, how do you delete?
> GDPR and other data governance rules mean that table data is subject to change. More often than not, abiding by data governance rules mean that you'll need to optimize how you delete records from your tables, or even retain tables, as in the case of legal hold. One simple use case is N-day delete—for example, 30-day retention. The use of daily partitions, while not optimal depending on the size of your Delta Lake table, can simplify common delete patterns, such as for data older than a given point in time. In the case of 30-day delete, given a table partitioned by the column datetime, you could run a simple job calling delete from {table} where datetime < current_timestamp() - interval 30 days.

---

[3] For the complete list of rules, you can always reference the Databricks documentation (*https://oreil.ly/fek2A*).

Choose the right partition column

The following advice will help you select the correct column (or columns) to use when partitioning. The most commonly used partition column is `date`. Follow these two rules of thumb for deciding what column to partition by:

Is the cardinality of a column very high?
> If so, do not use that column for partitioning. For example, if you partition by a column `userId` and there can be more than a million distinct user IDs, then that is a bad partitioning strategy.

How much data will exist in each partition?
> You can partition by a column if you expect data in that partition to be at least 1 GB.

The correct partitioning strategy may not immediately present itself, and that is OK; there is no need to optimize until you have the correct use cases (and data) in front of you.

Given the rules we just set forth, let's go through the following use cases: defining partitions on table creation, adding partitions to an existing table, and removing (deleting) partitions. This process will provide a firm understanding of using partitioning—and after all, this is required for the long-term preventative maintenance of our Delta Lake tables.

Defining Partitions on Table Creation

Let's create a new table called `default.covid_nyt_by_day` that will use the `date` column to automatically add new partitions to the table with zero intervention:

```
$ from pyspark.sql.types import DateType
  from delta.tables import DeltaTable
  (DeltaTable.createIfNotExists(spark)
    .tableName("default.covid_nyt_by_date")
    ...
    .addColumn("date", DateType(), nullable=False)
    .partitionedBy("date")
    .addColumn("county", "STRING")
    .addColumn("state", "STRING")
    .addColumn("fips", "INT")
    .addColumn("cases", "INT")
    .addColumn("deaths", "INT")
    .execute())
```

What's going on in the creation logic is almost exactly the same as in the last few examples; the difference is the introduction of the `partitionBy("date")` on the DeltaTable builder. To ensure the `date` column is always present, the data definition language (DDL) includes a non-nullable flag, since the column is required for partitioning.

Partitioning requires the physical files representing our table to be laid out using a unique directory per partition. This means all of the physical table data must be moved in order to honor the partition rules. Doing a migration from a nonpartitioned table to a partitioned table doesn't have to be difficult, but supporting live downstream customers can be a little tricky.

As a general rule of thumb, it is always better to come up with a plan to migrate your existing data customers to the new table—in this example, that would be the new partitioned table—rather than introducing a potential breaking change into the current table for any active readers.

Given the best practice at hand, we'll learn how to accomplish this next.

Migrating from a Nonpartitioned to a Partitioned Table

With the table definition for our partitioned table in hand, it becomes trivial to simply read all the data from our nonpartitioned table and write the rows into our newly created table. What makes it even easier is that we don't need to specify how we intend to partition since the partition strategy already exists in the table metadata:

```
$ (
    spark
    .table("default.covid_nyt")
    .write
    .format("delta")
    .mode("append")
    .option("mergeSchema", "false")
    .saveAsTable("default.covid_nyt_by_date"))
```

This process creates a fork in the road. We currently have the prior version of the table (nonpartitioned) as well as the new (partitioned) table, and this means we have a copy. During a normal cut-over, you typically need to continue to dual-write until your customers inform you they are ready to be fully migrated. Chapter 7 will provide you with some useful tricks for doing more intelligent incremental merges, and in order to keep both versions of the prior table in sync, using merge and incremental processing is the way to go.

Partition metadata management

Because Delta Lake automatically creates and manages table partitions as new data is being inserted and older data is being deleted, there is no need to manually call `ALTER TABLE table_name [ADD | DROP PARTITION] (column=value)`. This means you can focus your time elsewhere rather than manually working to keep the table metadata in sync with the state of the table itself.

Viewing partition metadata

To view the partition information, as well as other table metadata, we can create a new DeltaTable instance for our table and call the `detail` method; this will return a DataFrame that can be viewed in its entirety or filtered down to the columns you need to view:

```
$ (DeltaTable.forName(spark,"default.covid_nyt_by_date")
    .detail()
    .toJSON()
    .collect()[0]
)
```

The above command converts the resulting DataFrame into a JSON object and then converts that into a List (using `collect()`) so we can access the JSON data directly:

```
{
  "format": "delta",
  "id": "8c57bc67-369f-4c84-a63e-38b8ac19bdf2",
  "name": "default.covid_nyt_by_date",
  "location": "file:/opt/spark/work-dir/ch05/spark-warehouse/covid_nyt_by_date",
  "createdAt": "2023-06-08T05:35:00.072Z",
  "lastModified": "2023-06-08T05:50:45.241Z",
  "partitionColumns": ["date"],
  "numFiles": 423,
  "sizeInBytes": 17660304,
  "properties": {
    "description": "table with default partitions",
    "catalog.table.classification": "all-access",
    "catalog.engineering.comms.email": "dldg_authors@gmail.com",
    "catalog.team_name": "dldg_authors",
    "catalog.engineering.comms.slack": "https://delta-users.slack.com/..."
  },
  "minReaderVersion": 1,
  "minWriterVersion": 2,
  "tableFeatures": ["appendOnly", "invariants"]
}
```

With the introduction to partitioning complete, it is time to focus on two critical techniques under the umbrella of Delta Lake table life cycle and maintenance: repairing and replacing tables.

Repairing, Restoring, and Replacing Table Data

Let's face it: even with the best intentions in place, we are all human and make mistakes. In your career as a data engineer, one thing you'll be required to learn is the art of data recovery. The process of recovering data is commonly called *replaying*, since the action we are taking is to roll back the clock, or rewind to an earlier point in time. This enables us to remove problematic changes to a table and replace the erroneous data with the "fixed" data.

Recovering and Replacing Tables

While it is possible to recover a table, the catch is that there needs to be a data source available that is in a better state than your current table. In Chapter 9, we'll be learning about the medallion architecture, which is used to define clear, quality boundaries between your raw (bronze), cleansed (silver), and curated (gold) datasets. For the purpose of this chapter, we will assume we have raw data available in our bronze database table that can be used to replace data that became corrupted in our silver database table.

One technique for replacing corrupt or otherwise poor table partitions is to use the `replaceWhere` option alongside `overwrite` mode. Say, for example, that data was accidentally deleted from our table for 2021-02-17. There are other ways to restore accidentally deleted data (which we will learn next), but in the case where data is permanently deleted, there is no reason to panic—we can take the recovery data and use a conditional overwrite:

```
$ recovery_table = spark.table("bronze.covid_nyt_by_date")
  partition_col = "date"
  partition_to_fix "2021-02-17"
  table_to_fix = "silver.covid_nyt_by_date"

(recovery_table
  .where(col(partition_col) == partition_to_fix)
  .write
  .format("delta")
  .mode("overwrite")
  .option("replaceWhere", f"{partition_col} == {partition_to_fix}")
  .saveAsTable("silver.covid_nyt_by_date")
)
```

This code showcases the replace overwrite pattern, as it can either replace missing data or overwrite the existing data conditionally in a table. This option allows you to fix tables that may have become corrupt or to resolve issues where data was missing and has become available. The `replaceWhere` with insert overwrite isn't bound only to partition columns and can be used to conditionally replace data in your tables.

It is important to ensure the `replaceWhere` condition matches the `WHERE` clause of the recovery table; otherwise, you may create a bigger problem and further corrupt the table you are fixing. Whenever possible, it is good to remove the chance of human error, so if you find yourself repairing (replacing or recovering) data in your tables often, it would be beneficial to create some guardrails to protect the integrity of your table. For example, say we write a simple command-line tool that takes a table and sets the conditions (`replaceWhere`, `overwrite`, or `restore`) and allows anyone to trigger a dry run—also known as a practice run—to see what would happen, to ensure the operation behaves correctly without causing additional problems. Rather than allowing teammates to run the command locally, and given that we are looking to remove human error, the command could be triggered using an API (with credentials) or via GitHub actions (after a PR and review to execute). In this way the operation intent can be recorded, and if things go wrong for any reason, the operation can be rolled back with limited impact and with no surprises.

Next, let's look at conditionally removing entire partitions.

Deleting Data and Removing Partitions

It is common to remove specific partitions from our Delta Lake tables to fulfill specific requests—for example, when deleting data older than a specific point in time, removing abnormal data, and generally cleaning up our tables.

Regardless of the case, if our intentions are simply to clear out a given partition, we can do so using a conditional delete on a partition column. The following statement conditionally deletes partitions (`date`) that are older than January 1, 2023:

```
(
    DeltaTable
     .forName(spark, 'default.covid_nyt_by_date')
     .delete(col("date") < "2023-01-01"))
```

Removing data, or dropping entire partitions, can be managed using conditional deletes. When you delete based on a partition column, this is an efficient way to delete data without the processing overhead of loading the physical table data into memory; instead, it uses the information contained in the table metadata to prune partitions based on the predicate. In the case of deleting based on nonpartitioned columns, the cost is higher, as a partial or full table scan can occur. However, there is an added bonus: whether you are removing entire partitions or conditionally removing a subset of each table, if for any reason you change your mind, you can "undo" the operation using time travel. We will learn how to restore our tables to an earlier point in time next.

Remember to never remove Delta Lake table data (files) outside the context of the Delta Lake operations, as doing so can corrupt your table and cause headaches. This also means that any process that is not Delta aware should follow the same rules. Take cloud storage life cycle policies, for example: if your files are being automatically deleted every N days, this can also corrupt your Delta Lake tables.

The Life Cycle of a Delta Lake Table

Over time, as each Delta Lake table is modified, older versions of the table remain on disk to support table restoration or the viewing of earlier points in table time (time travel), and to provide a clean experience for streaming jobs that may be reading from various points in the table (which relate to different points in time, or history across the table). This is why it is critical that you ensure you have a long enough lookback window for the `delta.logRetentionDuration`, so when you run vacuum on your table, you are not immediately flooded with pages or with unhappy customers because a stream of data just disappeared.

Restoring Your Table

In the case where a transaction has occurred—for example, an incorrect delete from your table (because life happens)—rather than reloading the data (in the case where we have a copy of the data), we can rewind and restore the table to an earlier version. This is an important capability, especially given that problems can arise when the only copy of your data was in fact the data that was just deleted. When there is nowhere left to go to recover the data, you can time travel back to an earlier version of your table.

What you'll need to restore your table is some additional information. We can get this from the table history:

```
$ dt = DeltaTable.forName(spark, "silver.covid_nyt_by_date")
  (dt.history(10)
    .select("version", "timestamp", "operation")
    .show())
```

The prior code will show the last 10 operations on the Delta Lake table. In the case where you want to rewind to a prior version, just look for the DELETE:

```
+-------+-------------------+-------------------+
|version|          timestamp|          operation|
+-------+-------------------+-------------------+
|      1|2023-06-09 19:11:...|             DELETE|
|      0|2023-06-09 19:04:...|CREATE TABLE AS S...|
+-------+-------------------+-------------------+
```

You'll see the DELETE transaction occurred at version 1, so let's restore the table back to version 0:

```
$ dt.restoreToVersion(0)
```

All it takes to restore your table is knowledge about the operation you want to remove. In our case, we removed the DELETE transaction. Because Delta Lake delete operations occur in the table metadata, unless you run a process called VACUUM (or REORG), you can safely return to the prior version of your table.

Cleaning Up

When we delete data from our Delta Lake tables, this action is not immediate. In fact, the operation itself simply removes the reference from the Delta Lake table snapshot, so it is as if the data is now invisible. This operation means that we have the ability to "undo" in cases where data is accidentally deleted. We can clean up the artifacts, the deleted files, and truly purge them from the Delta Lake table using a process called *vacuuming*.

Vacuum

The vacuum command will clean up deleted files or versions of the table that are no longer current, which can happen when you use the overwrite method on a table. If you overwrite the table, all you are really doing is creating new pointers to new files that are referenced by the table metadata. So if you overwrite a table often, the size of the table on disk will grow exponentially. With this in mind, it is best to utilize vacuum to enable short-lived time travel (up to 30 days is typical), and to employ a different strategy for storing strategic table backups. We'll look at the common scenario now.

Luckily, there are some table properties that help us control the behavior of the table as changes occur over time. These rules will govern the vacuuming process:

- delta.logRetentionDuration defaults to interval 30 days and keeps track of the history of the table. The more operations that occur, the more history that is retained. If you won't be using time travel operations, then you can try reducing the number of days of history down to a week.

- delta.deletedFileRetentionDuration defaults to interval 1 week and can be changed in cases where delete operations are not expected to be undone. For peace of mind, it is good to maintain at least one day for deleted files to be retained.

With the table properties set on our table, the vacuum command does most of the work for us. The following code example shows how to execute the vacuum operation:

```
$ (DeltaTable.forName(spark, "default.nonoptimal_covid_nyt")
    .vacuum()
```

Running vacuum on our table will result in the removal of all files that are no longer referenced by the table snapshot, including deleted files from prior versions of the table. While vacuuming is a necessary process to reduce the cost of maintaining older versions of a given table, there is a side effect, in that downstream data consumers can accidentally be left high and dry should they need to read an early version of your table.

If there is a need to store longer-retention table backups—for audit purposes, for disaster recovery, or for teams looking to read from earlier versions of the table—it is easiest to store the backup in another table. All we would need is the table version for the backup, and then a new Delta Lake table that can store the table permanently. Such backups could be postfixed with _version_x and can sit alongside the original table schema to reduce the number of places in which people need to look to find the earlier versions of the table.

Other issues that may arise will be covered in Chapter 7, where we tackle streaming data in and out of our Delta Lake tables.

The vacuum command will not run itself. When you are planning to bring your table into production and want to automate the process of keeping the table tidy, you can set up a cron job to call vacuum on a normal cadence (daily, weekly). It is also worth pointing out that vacuum relies on the timestamps of the files when they were written to disk, so if the entire table was imported, the vacuum command will not do anything until you hit your retention thresholds. This is due to the way that the filesystem marks file creation time versus the actual time the files were originally created.

Dropping tables

Dropping a table is an operation with no undo. If you execute delete from {table}, you are essentially truncating the table and can still utilize time travel to undo the operation. However, if you really want to remove all traces of a table, please read through the following warning box, and remember to plan ahead by creating a table copy (or clone (*https://oreil.ly/4jAKR*)) if you want a recovery strategy.

Dropping a table is an operation with no undo. If you truly want to remove all traces of a table, then read ahead.

Removing all traces of a Delta Lake Table

If you want to do a permanent delete and remove all traces of a managed Delta Lake table, and you understand the risks associated with what you are doing and really do intend to forgo any possibility of table recovery, then you can drop the table using the SQL DROP TABLE syntax:

```
$ spark.sql(f"drop silver.covid_nyt_by_date")
```

You can confirm the table is gone by attempting to list the files of the Delta Lake table:

```
$ docker exec \
  -it delta_quickstart bash \
  -c "ls -l /opt/spark/.../silver.db/covid_nyt_by_date/"
```

The preceding code will result in the following output, which shows that the table really no longer exists on disk:

```
ls: cannot access './spark-warehouse/silver.db/covid_nyt_by_date/': No such
file or directory
```

Conclusion

This chapter introduced you to the common utility functions provided within the Delta Lake project. We learned how to work with table properties, explored the table properties we'd most likely encounter, and learned how to optimize our tables to fix the small files problem. This led to our learning about partitioning and about restoring and replacing data within our tables. We explored using time travel to restore our tables, and we concluded the chapter with a dive into cleaning up after ourselves and, lastly, permanently deleting tables that are no longer necessary. While not every use case can fit cleanly into a book, we now have a great reference for common problems and their required solutions in maintaining your Delta Lake tables and keeping them running smoothly over time.

Building Native Applications with Delta Lake

By R. Tyler Croy

Delta Lake was created on the Java platform, but since the protocol became open source, it has been implemented with a number of different languages, allowing for new opportunities to use Delta Lake in native applications without requiring Apache Spark. The most mature implementation of the Delta Lake protocol after the original Spark-based library is delta-rs (*https://oreil.ly/ZtPkY*), which produces the deltalake library for both Python (*https://oreil.ly/jx3HV*) and Rust (*https://oreil.ly/dyRZm*) users.

In this chapter you will learn how to build a Python- or Rust-based application for loading, querying, and writing Delta Lake tables using these libraries. Along the way we will review some of the tools in the larger Python and Rust ecosystems that support Delta Lake, giving users substantial flexibility and performance when building data applications. Unlike its Spark-based counterpart, the deltalake library has no specific infrastructure requirements and can easily run in your command line, a Jupyter Notebook, an AWS Lambda, or anywhere else Python or compiled Rust programs can be executed. This extreme portability comes with a trade-off: there is no "cluster," and therefore native Delta Lake applications generally cannot scale beyond the computational or memory resources of a single machine.[1]

To demonstrate the utility of this "low overhead" approach to utilizing Delta Lake, in this chapter you will create an AWS Lambda, which will receive new data via its trigger, query an existing Delta Lake table to enrich its data, and store the new results in

---

[1] Some really interesting efforts such as Ballista (*https://oreil.ly/OCsfq*) are underway that will enable users to build Python- or Rust-based programs that run on a cluster, but they are still early in their maturity.

a new silver Delta Lake table. The pricing model of AWS Lambda incentivizes short execution time and low memory utilization, which makes `deltalake` a powerful tool for building fast and cheap data applications. While the examples in this chapter run on AWS (*https://oreil.ly/XROdO*), the `deltalake` libraries for Python and Rust support a number of different storage backends from cloud providers such as Azure and Google Cloud Platform or on-premises tools like MinIO, HDFS, and more.

 The general requirements for developing and deploying a Lambda function will be excluded from this chapter. To learn more, please consult with the AWS documentation for building a Python Lambda (*https://oreil.ly/rGuDN*) or a Rust Lambda (*https://oreil.ly/zdQLZ*).

Getting Started

To develop native Delta Lake applications, you will need to have Python 3 installed when building Python applications. Chances are your workstation either has Python 3 preinstalled or has it readily available as part of "developer tooling" packages. The Rust toolchain is necessary only when building Rust-based Delta Lake applications.[2] Rust, on the other hand, should be installed following the official documentation (*https://oreil.ly/l3Ndr*) for installing the compiler and associated tooling, such as `cargo`.

Python

This example will largely be developed in the terminal on your workstation using `virtualenv` to manage the project-specific dependencies of the Lambda function:

```
% cd ~/dldg       # Choose the directory of your choice
% virtualenv venv  # Configure a Python virtualenv for managing deps
                   # in the ./venv/ directory
% source ./venv/bin/activate  # Activate the virtualenv in this shell
```

Once the `virtualenv` has been activated, the `deltalake` package can be installed with `pip`. It is also helpful to install the `pandas` package to do some data querying. The following example demonstrates some basic `deltalake` and `pandas` invocations to load and display a test dataset that is partitioned between two separate columns (c1, c2) containing a series of numbers:

```
% pip install 'deltalake>=0.18.2' pandas

% python
>>> from deltalake import DeltaTable
```

---

2 The Rust compiler toolchain can easily be installed with the `rustup` installer (*https://oreil.ly/R9bkF*).

```
>>> dt = DeltaTable('./deltatbl-partitioned')
>>> dt.files()

['c2=foo0/part-00000-2bcc9ff6-0551-4401-bd22-d361a60627e3.c000.snappy.parquet',
 'c2=foo1/part-00000-786c7455-9587-454f-9a4c-de0b22b62bbd.c000.snappy.parquet',
 'c2=foo0/part-00001-ca647ee7-f1ad-4d70-bf02-5d1872324d6f.c000.snappy.parquet',
 'c2=foo1/part-00001-1c702e73-89b5-465a-9c6a-25f7559cd150.c000.snappy.parquet']

>>> df = dt.to_pandas()
>>> df

   c1    c2
0   0  foo0
1   2  foo0
2   4  foo0
3   1  foo1
4   3  foo1
5   6  foo0
6   8  foo0
7   5  foo1
8   7  foo1
9   9  foo1
```

Reading data from Delta Lake tables is very easy thanks to the `to_pandas()` function, which loads data from the `DeltaTable` and produces a `DataFrame` that can be used to further query or inspect the data stored in the Delta Lake table. With a Pandas `DataFrame`, a wide world of data analysis is available in your terminal or notebook; to learn more about Pandas specifically, check out *Python for Data Analysis* (O'Reilly).

Getting started with Pandas is simple, but when reading large datasets, `to_pandas()` has some limitations; those will be covered in the next section.

Reading large datasets

Using Pandas and Delta Lake is a great way to start exploring data from within the terminal on your workstation. Behind the scenes of the `to_pandas()` function call mentioned in the previous section, the Python process must do the following:

1. Collect references to the necessary data files—in essence, the *.parquet* files returned from `dt.files()`.

2. Retrieve those data files from storage (the local filesystem in this example).

3. Deserialize and load those data files into memory.

4. Construct the `pandas.DataFrame` object using the data loaded in memory.

Steps 2 and 3 pose scaling limitations as the size of the data in the Delta Lake table grows. Modern workstations have *lots* of memory, which often means that loading a few gigabytes of data into memory is not that much of a concern, but the *retrieval* of that data can be a problem. For example, if the Delta Lake table is stored in AWS

S3 but your Python terminal is running on your laptop, loading a few gigabytes over coffee shop WiFi is time consuming, and it's unnecessary if you do not intend to query the *entire* table.

The design of Delta Lake provides a few mechanisms for reducing the size of the data that must be loaded to help make queries fast and efficient:

Partitions

Structuring of data in storage to allow grouping of files by common prefixes, such as `mytable/year=2024/*.parquet`.

File statistics

Additional metadata included by the writer in the transaction log about the *.parquet* file, whether Apache Spark or a native Python/Rust, that indicates the minimum or maximum values of columns contained in that data column.

By reducing the number of files that need to be loaded to perform queries, partitions and file statistics help lower execution times to produce results *faster*, which reduces developer iteration time and makes data processing workloads cheaper to run. The following examples will use these features to reduce the number of files loaded from storage and also the amount of memory needed to work with the Delta Lake table in Pandas.

> The Delta protocol has a number of other design optimizations to allow for efficient operation, such as checkpoints, compaction, and Z-Ordering. These features are supported in the native Python and Rust libraries. They are discussed elsewhere in this book and will not be addressed explicitly in this chapter.

Partitions. Partitioning data into common prefixes is a pattern shared by several storage systems, including Delta Lake. Commonly referred to as *hive-style partitioning*, the `to_pandas()` function allows you to specify partitions with the optional parameter `partitions`. Consider the following example table layout:

```
deltatbl-partitioned
├── c2=foo0
│   ├── part-00000-2bcc9ff6-0551-4401-bd22-d361a60627e3.c000.snappy.parquet
│   └── part-00001-ca647ee7-f1ad-4d70-bf02-5d1872324d6f.c000.snappy.parquet
├── c2=foo1
│   ├── part-00000-786c7455-9587-454f-9a4c-de0b22b62bbd.c000.snappy.parquet
│   └── part-00001-1c702e73-89b5-465a-9c6a-25f7559cd150.c000.snappy.parquet
└── _delta_log
    └── 00000000000000000000.json
```

The table has a partition column of c2 with two partitions defined. To work only with data contained within the first partition (foo0), the to_pandas() invocation can be modified as follows to use a partition filter that restricts data loaded only to the specified partition(s):

```
>>> dt.to_pandas(partitions=[('c2', '=', 'foo0')])

   c1   c2
0   0  foo0
1   2  foo0
2   4  foo0
3   6  foo0
4   8  foo0
```

If the datasets are particularly large, the same partition filter can be passed to the files() function on the DeltaTable for a low-overhead preview of the files that the to_pandas call would load:

```
>>> dt.files([('c2', '=', 'foo0')])

['c2=foo0/part-00000-2bcc9ff6-0551-4401-bd22-d361a60627e3.c000.snappy.parquet',
 'c2=foo0/part-00001-ca647ee7-f1ad-4d70-bf02-5d1872324d6f.c000.snappy.parquet']
```

This partition filter shows that only two *.parquet* files must be loaded, rather than the four total in this table. That helps reduce the time spent retrieving data files from storage, but their contents must still be loaded into memory to build the pandas.DataFrame.

The to_pandas() function has two other optional parameters that are important to consider when trying to reduce the memory footprint while working with this dataset. The easiest one to use is columns, which simply restricts the columns that are projected from the *.parquet* file into the DataFrame. In this example, the c2 partition is helpful to reduce the amount of data loaded from the table, but it's not needed in the DataFrame and is excluded via the columns parameter:

```
>>> dt.to_pandas(partitions=[('c2', '=', 'foo0')], columns=['c1'])

   c1
0   0
1   2
2   4
3   6
4   8
```

For particularly wide tables, this can be a helpful trick to reduce both the amount of data loaded into memory *and* the amount of data displayed in the terminal, making the results easier to visually inspect.

The final optional parameter that can further reduce the memory footprint is filters, which accepts DNF-style filter predicates that support a number of operations such as <, >, <=, >=, =, and !=. The following snippet incorporates the optional parameters to to_pandas() that can be combined to produce a compact DataFrame containing only the desired data:

```
>>> dt.to_pandas(partitions=[('c2', '=', 'foo0')], columns=['c1'],
filters=[('c1', '<=', 4), ('c1', '>', 0)])

   c1
0  2
1  4
```

The semantics provided by the to_pandas() function are no substitute for the expressive power provided by the Pandas DataFrame API, but they offer a very useful mechanism for constraining the amount of data retrieved from a Delta Lake table and loaded into memory. Both are important to consider in the example discussed later in the "Building a Lambda" on page 131 section, in which the resource constraints of the AWS Lambda environment reward fast and lightweight runtimes.

File statistics. The Delta protocol allows for optional *file statistics* that can enable further optimization by query engines. When writing a *.parquet* file, most writers will put this additional metadata into the Delta transaction log, capturing each column's minimum and maximum values. The deltalake Python library can utilize this information to skip files that don't contain values in the specified column(s). This can be especially useful for append-only tables that have predictable and sequential data within a given partition.

Using an example dataset[3] that is partitioned by year but contains multiple Parquet files within each partition, the transaction log includes the following entry:

```
{
  "add": {
    "path": "year=2022/0-ec9935aa-a154-4ba4-ab7e-92a53369c433-2.parquet",
    "partitionValues": {
      "year": "2022"
    },
    "size": 3025,
    "modificationTime": 1705178628881,
    "dataChange": true,
    "stats": "{\"numRecords\": 4, \"minValues\": {\"month\": 9,
    \"decimal date\": 2022.7083, \"average\": 415.74,
    \"deseasonalized\": 419.02, \"ndays\": 24, \"sdev\": 0.27,
    \"unc\": 0.1}, \"maxValues\": {\"month\": 12, \"decimal date\": 2022.9583,
    \"average\": 418.99, \"deseasonalized\": 419.72, \"ndays\": 30,
    \"sdev\": 0.57, \"unc\": 0.22}, \"nullCount\": {\"month\": 0,
    \"decimal date\": 0, \"average\": 0, \"deseasonalized\": 0, \"ndays\": 0,
```

---

3 Scripts to download this sample data can be found in this book's GitHub repository (*https://oreil.ly/2m8Kv*). This particular example uses data from NOAA (*https://oreil.ly/G61ce*) that tracks global CO_2 concentrations.

```
    \"sdev\": 0, \"unc\": 0}}",
    "tags": null,
    "deletionVector": null,
    "baseRowId": null,
    "defaultRowCommitVersion": null,
    "clusteringProvider": null
  }
}
```

The `stats` portion contains the relevant information for the file statistics–based optimization. Inspecting `minValues` and `maxValues` shows that *0-ec9935aa-a154-4ba4-*
ab7e-92a53369c433-2.parquet contains data only for the months September to
December in the year 2022. The following Pandas invocation will create a `DataFrame`
that has loaded data *only* from this specific file utilizing the partition column and the
month column. The file statistics help the underlying engine avoid loading *every* file
in the `year=2022/` partition; instead, it selects only the one containing values where
the month is greater than or equal to 9, leading to a much faster and more efficient
execution of data retrieval:

```
>>> from deltalake import DeltaTable
>>> dt = DeltaTable('./data/gen/filestats')
>>> len(dt.files())

198

>>> df = dt.to_pandas(filters=[('year', '=', 2022), ('month', '>=', 9)])
>>> df

    year  month  decimal date  average  deseasonalized  ndays  sdev  unc
0   2022      9     2022.7083   415.91          419.36     28  0.41  0.15
1   2022     10     2022.7917   415.74          419.02     30  0.27  0.10
2   2022     11     2022.8750   417.47          419.44     25  0.52  0.20
3   2022     12     2022.9583   418.99          419.72     24  0.57  0.22
```

Rather than loading every one of the files in the Delta Lake table to produce a
`DataFrame` for experimentation, `filters` utilizes Delta's partitioning and file statistics
to load a *single file* from storage for this example.

The Delta Lake transaction log provides a wealth of information that the `deltalake`
native Python library utilizes to provide fast and efficient reads of tables; more
examples can be found in the online documentation (*https://oreil.ly/7bVLN*). Reading
existing Delta Lake tables is exciting, but for many Python users, the *writing* of
Delta Lake tables helps unlock new superpowers in the Python-based data analysis or
machine learning environment.

Writing data

Numerous examples for performing data analysis or machine learning in Python
start with loading data into a DataFrame of some form (typically Pandas) from
a CSV- or TSV-formatted dataset. Comma-separated values (CSV) files are fairly

easy to produce and reason about and can be streamed into and out of different applications. The major downside for CSV datasets is that, to perform data analysis, they *typically* must fully be loaded into memory whenever they are needed; this can become problematic when they are quite large or slow to load.

This section will utilize the same small (tens of kilobytes) publicly available CSV dataset used earlier to demonstrate file statistics. The dataset contains annual atmospheric CO_2 concentrations provided by NOAA and demonstrates the ease with which Delta Lake tables can be created in Python using the `deltalake` package.

There are a couple of different options for writing Delta Lake tables, but this initial example will focus on the simple case of writing an unpartitioned Delta Lake table from a `pandas.DataFrame`:

```
>>> import pandas as pd
>>> from deltalake import write_deltalake, DeltaTable
>>> df = pd.read_csv('./data/co2_mm_mlo.csv', comment='#')
>>> len(df)

790

>>> write_deltalake('./data/co2_monthly', df)
>>> dt = DeltaTable('./data/co2_monthly')
>>> dt.files()

['0-6db689af-10fe-4350-82e8-bef6d962330a-0.parquet']

>>> df = dt.to_pandas()
>>> df
```

	year	month	decimal date	average	deseasonalized	ndays	sdev	unc
0	1958	3	1958.2027	315.70	314.43	-1	-9.99	-0.99
1	1958	4	1958.2877	317.45	315.16	-1	-9.99	-0.99
2	1958	5	1958.3699	317.51	314.71	-1	-9.99	-0.99
3	1958	6	1958.4548	317.24	315.14	-1	-9.99	-0.99
4	1958	7	1958.5370	315.86	315.18	-1	-9.99	-0.99
..	...	...	...	...	...	...	...	...
785	2023	8	2023.6250	419.68	421.57	21	0.45	0.19
786	2023	9	2023.7083	418.51	421.96	18	0.30	0.14
787	2023	10	2023.7917	418.82	422.11	27	0.47	0.17
788	2023	11	2023.8750	420.46	422.43	21	0.91	0.38
789	2023	12	2023.9583	421.86	422.58	20	0.69	0.29

```
[790 rows x 8 columns]
```

The resulting Delta Lake table is simple and includes only a single *.parquet* data file due to the compact size of the source dataset; for datasets in the tens of megabytes or larger, the `deltalake` writer may produce multiple data files when creating new transactions on the table. The `write_deltalake()` function has a number of optional parameters that allow for more advanced behaviors, such as partitioning:

```
>>> df = pd.read_csv('./data/co2_mm_mlo.csv', comment='#')
>>> write_deltalake('./data/gen/co2_monthly_partitioned', data=df,
partition_by=['year'])
```

This snippet will write the new Delta Lake table with hive-style partitions based on the year column of the provided DataFrame. The resulting table in storage is cleanly partitioned as follows:

```
co2_monthly_partitioned
├── _delta_log
│   └── 00000000000000000000.json
├── year=1958
│   └── 0-50ffe4cc-864d-4753-8f47-b0b55618a31a-0.parquet
├── year=1959
│   └── 0-50ffe4cc-864d-4753-8f47-b0b55618a31a-0.parquet
├── year=1960
│   └── 0-50ffe4cc-864d-4753-8f47-b0b55618a31a-0.parquet
```

In this example, the uncompressed dataset is small and easily fits entirely in memory, but for larger datasets, write_deltalake() can accept larger and more lazily loaded datasets and iterators, which allows for writing data incrementally.

 To append or overwrite data, use the mode optional parameter, which currently supports the following modes:

- error (default): return an error if the table already exists
- append: add the provided data to the table
- overwrite: replace the table contents with the provided data
- ignore: do not write the table, or return an error if it already exists

The ability to write a Delta Lake table easily can accelerate local development or model training; in addition, it can enable building simple and fast ingestion applications in environments such as AWS Lambda, which will be covered later in the chapter.

Merging/updating

The DeltaTable object contains a number of simple functions for common merge or update tasks on the Delta Lake table, such as delete, merge, and update. These functions can be used in much the same way as delete, merge, and update operations in a relational database, but underneath the covers the Delta transaction log is doing a lot of important work to keep track of the data being modified.

For example, consider a Delta Lake table with 100 rows stored in a single *first.parquet* file, added via a single add transaction. A subsequent `delete` operation that deletes every other row will produce a new *second.parquet* file containing 50 records. Committing the deletion will create a new transaction on the table containing two actions —one removing the *first.parquet*, and a second action adding *second.parquet*:

```
>>> import pyarrow as pa
>>> from deltalake import DeltaTable, write_deltalake
>>> data = pa.table({'id' : list(range(100))}) # Create a sample dataset
>>> write_deltalake('delete-test', data)
>>> dt = DeltaTable('delete-test')
>>> dt.version()

0

>>> dt.to_pandas().count()

Id      100
dtype: int64

>>> dt.delete('id % 2 == 0')

{'num_added_files': 1, 'num_removed_files': 1, 'num_deleted_rows': 50,
 'num_copied_rows': 50, 'execution_time_ms': 35187, 'scan_time_ms': 33442,
 'rewrite_time_ms': 1}

>>> dt.version()  # There is a new version

1
```

Inspecting the *./delete-test/_delta_log/* directory after the `delete()` operation reveals two transaction entries; *00000000000000000001.json* contains the actions representing the `delete()` operation, revealing exactly how table modifications typically work:

```
{
  "add": {
    "path": "part-00001-4bc82516-2371-4004-9ff8...c000.snappy.parquet",
    "partitionValues": {},
    "size": 799,
    "modificationTime": 1708794006394,
    "dataChange": true,
    "stats": "{\"numRecords\":50,\"minValues\":{\"id\":1},\"maxValues\":
{\"id\":99},\"nullCount\":{\"id\":0}}",
    "tags": null,
    "deletionVector": null,
    "baseRowId": null,
    "defaultRowCommitVersion": null,
    "clusteringProvider": null
  }
}
{
  "remove": {
    "path": "0-2684b307-3947-49ce-bc07-02688b10a204-0.parquet",
    "dataChange": true,
```

```
      "deletionTimestamp": 1708794006394,
      "extendedFileMetadata": true,
      "partitionValues": {},
      "size": 1074
    }
  }
}
{
  "commitInfo": {
    "timestamp": 1708794006394,
    "operation": "DELETE",
    "operationParameters": {
      "predicate": "id % 2 = 0"
    },
    "clientVersion": "delta-rs.0.17.0"
  }
}
```

The preceding snippet contains the two key actions: remove and add, with their respective files. There is an additional action called commitInfo that is optional in the Delta Lake table protocol but may contain additional information about what triggered this particular transaction. In this case, it describes the DELETE operation with its predicate, giving us insight into *why* the remove and add were necessary.

Whether the operation is a delete, update, or merge, when data is changed in the Delta Lake table, there is typically a removal of outdated Parquet files and a creation of *new* Parquet files with the modified data. This is the case except when using the newer *deletion vectors* feature, which the Python or Rust libraries do not support at the time of this writing.[4]

Going beyond Pandas

The deltalake Python package provides support for the Delta Lake table format to a number of different query engines and implementations. While this chapter utilizes the Pandas library as an example for reading, writing, and so on, integrations exist for using the deltalake package from DataFrame libraries such as Polars or Datafusion. Each of those libraries provides a compelling feature set for Python data applications.

The foundational library pyarrow binds all of these integrations together and implements shared abstractions such as RecordBatch, DataSet, and Table. In the documentation for deltalake, there are a number of functions that accept or return these objects. This chapter does not provide exhaustive documentation for each of these types, which are documented at a high level in the PyArrow project's online API documentation (*https://oreil.ly/zuzUd*).

---

4 Development of deletion vectors can be followed in the delta-rs issue tracker (*https://oreil.ly/9gA0_*).

RecordBatch. Most of the internal operations for reading and writing Delta Lake tables in Python will create or work with `RecordBatch` objects, which represent a collection of columns of equal length. Delta Lake data files are Apache Parquet formatted, which is a columnar data format, and `RecordBatch` is similarly columnar. Rather than expressing rows such as `[1, 'Will', True]`, `[2, 'Robert', True]`, `[3, 'Ion', True]`, and so on, the `RecordBatch` types are typically instantiated with *columns*, such as: `[1, 2, 3]`, `['Will', 'Robert', 'Ion']`, `[True, True, True]`.

Most applications can work with DataFrames built on top of the `RecordBatch` type, but there are a number of ways to squeeze higher performance or efficiency from a Python data application by understanding and working with `RecordBatch` objects directly.

Table. A `pyarrow.Table` is a collection of named, equal-length Arrow arrays and is effectively how "table" is commonly understood in most other data systems. As a container for schema plus data, the `DeltaTable` object can expose a PyArrow `Table` directly with the `to_pyarrow_table()` function that accepts filtering options similar to `to_pandas()`, such as `partitions` or `filters` keyword parameters. Calling `to_pyarrow_table()` will *also* load all the available data into memory.

When possible, it is more efficient to rely on `DataSet` rather than `Table`, as described below.

DataSet. A `pyarrow.DataSet` is similar to `Table` in that it has an associated schema of the full dataset, but unlike `Table`, it is lazily loaded and provides substantial flexibility for working with larger datasets. A `DataSet` object is very low overhead to create, since it usually results in very little data being read from storage and can be created from a `DeltaTable` object with `to_pyarrow_dataset()`.

Once a `DataSet` has been created, it is possible to lazily load data using functions such as `filter`, which provides a *new* filtered `DataSet` from which you can invoke `to_batches()` to provide a lazy iterator of `RecordBatch` data or invoke `to_table()` to produce a `pyarrow.Table` with all the data from the filtered dataset.

In many cases, `deltalake` uses `DataSet` internally to produce or consume data; it is a very flexible, efficient, and well-documented data type (*https://oreil.ly/HafAW*).

From simple data ingestion to transformation or complex query and machine learning tasks, the ability to interact with Delta Lake tables from practically any Python environment opens up innumerable possibilities and applications for data stored in Delta Lake.

Rust

Underneath the Python library described in the beginning of this chapter is a full implementation of the Delta Lake protocol in Rust, commonly referred to as delta-rs (*https://oreil.ly/ZtPkY*), which can also be used directly to build high-performance data applications. Adding the `deltalake` package to *Cargo.toml* in a Rust project is typically all that is needed to get started. The `deltalake` crate includes feature flags and dependencies that can optionally add dependencies to enable support for AWS, Azure, or Google Cloud. The `datafusion` feature flag can also be used to add integration with the Apache Arrow DataFusion project for doing sophisticated query, write, and merge operations within Rust.

There are many characteristics of Rust that make it increasingly sought after for handling data engineering tasks (*https://oreil.ly/5uzht*), such as its low memory overhead, ease of concurrency, and stability. In many cases, once a Delta Lake application is developed in Rust, it can and will run for years without issue.[5]

Examples in this section will assume the latest version of the `deltalake` package configured in a Rust project, with the `datafusion` feature enabled.

 Rust is a compiled language, and with a large project such as delta-rs and DataFusion, link times can suffer with the default Clang or GNU `ld`. The mold linker (*https://oreil.ly/Qiphy*) is worth installing and configuring to improve development cycle times.

Following the same patterns as the Python examples, start by opening a contrived Delta Lake table:

```
#[tokio::main]
async fn main() {
    println!(">> Loading `deltatbl-partitioned`");
    let table = deltalake::open_table("../data/deltatbl-partitioned").await
      .expect("Failed to open table");
    println!("..loaded version {}", table.version());
    for file in table.get_files_iter() {
      println!(" - {}", file.as_ref());
    }
}
```

---

5 One of the earliest open source applications developed with delta-rs, kafka-delta-ingest, has been running in production environments for years without incident or substantial change in system resource requirements.

The full source code is located in the GitHub repository associated with this book (*https://oreil.ly/2m8Kv*). This simple example creates a DeltaTable from the provided path and inspects the files associated with the latest version, outputting the following:

```
>> Loading `deltatbl-partitioned`
..loaded version 0
 - c2=foo0/part-00000-2bcc9ff6-0551-4401-bd22-d361a60627e3.c000.snappy.parquet
 - c2=foo1/part-00000-786c7455-9587-454f-9a4c-de0b22b62bbd.c000.snappy.parquet
 - c2=foo0/part-00001-ca647ee7-f1ad-4d70-bf02-5d1872324d6f.c000.snappy.parquet
 - c2=foo1/part-00001-1c702e73-89b5-465a-9c6a-25f7559cd150.c000.snappy.parquet
```

Inspecting the file listing of the table is not particularly interesting, so the following example utilizes some DataFusion tooling to provide a SQL query–like interface to the same Delta Lake table:

```
use std::sync::Arc;
use deltalake::datafusion::execution::context::SessionContext;
use deltalake::arrow::util::pretty::print_batches;

#[tokio::main]
async fn main() {
  let ctx = SessionContext::new();
  let table = deltalake::open_table("../data/deltatbl-partitioned")
      .await
      .unwrap();
  ctx.register_table("demo", Arc::new(table)).unwrap();

  let batches = ctx
      .sql("SELECT * FROM demo LIMIT 5").await.expect("Failed to execute SQL")
      .collect()
      .await.unwrap();
  print_batches(&batches).expect("Failed to print batches");
}
```

Running this example will print the first five records found in the Delta Lake table, providing a simple interface and a distinctly simple but *unrusty* API for querying data in the table:

```
+----+------+
| c1 | c2   |
+----+------+
| 0  | foo0 |
| 2  | foo0 |
| 4  | foo0 |
| 1  | foo1 |
| 3  | foo1 |
+----+------+
```

DataFusion (*https://oreil.ly/K6Rv0*) bundles its own SQL dialect but also provides a DataFrame API that should be familiar to users coming from Pandas or Apache Spark. In the book's GitHub repository (*https://oreil.ly/2m8Kv*), there are some additional examples that demonstrate the DataFrame equivalent of the DataFusion SQL examples. In fact, the `SessionContext::sql` function returns a `DataFrame` that allows the combining of simple SQL queries with more complex DataFrame chaining of logic for advanced use cases.

Reading large data

For Delta Lake tables that represent data larger than what could reasonably fit in memory on a single machine, the Rust `deltalake` library offers users partitioning and file statistics semantics that are similar to those of the Python library.

When reading large datasets in Python, partitions and filters must be specified *before* creating a Pandas DataFrame. With DataFusion, the filters can be specified inline with the creation of the DataFrame because of the tight integration that the `delta lake` Rust crate provides with the DataFusion APIs. The `deltatbl-partitioned` table has a partition on the `c2` column that can be included in the DataFusion SQL query to avoid reading *.parquet* files in the partitions that don't match the predicate—for example:

```
let df = ctx
        .sql("SELECT * FROM demo WHERE c2 = 'foo0'")
        .await
        .expect("Failed to create data frame");
```

The DataFusion SQL will also use file statistics in the Delta transaction log to generate the appropriate and optimal query plan when creating the `DataFrame`. Generally speaking, when using the DataFusion SQL or DataFrame APIs with Delta Lake, the default behavior is almost always the correct and optimal one.

Writing data

At a fundamental level, a Delta Lake table consists of data files, typically in the Apache Parquet format, and transaction log files in a JSON format. The `deltalake` Rust crate supports writing both data and transaction log files, or writing *only* transactions. For example, kafka-delta-ingest (*https://oreil.ly/ivqMr*) translates streams of JSON data into Apache Parquet before creating a transaction to add the data to the configured Delta Lake table. Other Rust applications may use Parquet data files created by an external system, such as oxbow (*https://oreil.ly/TT2ni*), which only needs to manage the Delta Lake table's transaction log.

Regardless of the specific application needs, the `deltalake` crate has several options. Covering each of the writer APIs in detail is out of the scope of this book,[6] but at present the crate supports:

- Transaction operations that allow direct interaction with the Delta log
- A DataFusion-based writer for inserting and/or merging records
- A simple high-level JSON writer that accepts `serde_json::Value` types
- A `RecordBatch` writer that allows developers to turn Arrow RecordBatches into Apache Parquet files written into Delta Lake tables

For most use cases, the decision about what *type* of writer is required will come down to whether the write should be an *append* or a *merge*.

For append-only writers, DataFusion is not necessary, and the `deltalake` package's `RecordBatchWriter` can be used to issue append-only writes to a `DeltaTable`.

 DataFusion is an incredibly powerful data processing engine built in Rust, but it also adds a nontrivial increase in binary size, link-time overhead, and API surface area. The `deltalake` crate contains several integrations with DataFusion for performing queries, merges, and more, but they must be enabled by specifying the `data fusion` feature, such as with `cargo add -features datafusion deltalake`. For example, when building an AWS Lambda using Delta Lake, the binary built without DataFusion produces a binary size of 4.8 MB. When enabling the `datafusion` feature flag in *Cargo.toml*, the resulting *bootstrap.zip* grows to 8.2 MB.

Frequently the most challenging part of using `RecordBatchWriter` is constructing the necessary Arrow `RecordBatch` objects, which contain a schema and are columnar by nature. There are some utilities in the `arrow` crate that help with constructing `Record Batch` objects, such as the JSON reader: `arrow::json::reader::ReaderBuilder`; but for the following example, an object will be manually created from in-memory data and assumes a Delta Lake table has already been created.

---

6 The writers are available as of the 0.19 release of the `deltalake` crate, but this may change as the project moves toward a 1.0 release.

Merging/updating

Modifying Delta Lake tables from Rust generally requires using the `datafusion` feature since the DataFusion engine provides the predicate handling required for deletes, merges, and updates of records. Unlike the Python library, which hangs these operations off the `DeltaTable` object, the Delta Lake table operations are available via the `DeltaOps` struct, which helps generate builders for various operations, such as the following `delete` example:

```
let table = deltalake::open_table("./test")?;
let (table, metrics) = DeltaOps::from(table).delete()
                        .with_predicate(col("id").rem(lit(2)).eq(lit(0)))
                        .await?
```

Similar to the Python example, this will produce a new transaction in the log with a remove and an add. The documentation for `DeltaOps` (*https://oreil.ly/anZD-*) contains more information on exactly how to use `delete`, `update`, or `merge`. DataFusion is at the core of these operations, so it is highly useful to consult with the DataFusion documentation to learn more about constructing predicates, dataframes (needed for merges), and expressions. DataFusion SQL can also be used instead of Rust dataframe semantics via the `deltalake` crate's table provider.

Building a Lambda

Serverless functions represent an ideal use case for building native applications for Delta Lake, such as with AWS Lambda. The billing model for Lambda encourages low memory usage and fast execution time, which makes it a great platform for compact and efficient data processing applications. This section will adapt some of this chapter's previous examples to run within AWS Lambda to handle data ingestion or processing using `deltalake`. Other cloud providers have similar serverless offerings, such as Azure Functions and Google Cloud Run. The concepts in this section can be ported into those environments, but some of the interfaces may change.

For most applications, AWS Lambda is triggered by an external event such as an inbound HTTP request, an SQS message, or a CloudWatch event. Lambda will then translate this external event into a JSON payload, which the Lambda function will receive and can act upon. Imagine, for example, an application that receives an HTTP POST with a JSON array containing thousands of records that should be written to S3, as sketched out via the request flow diagram in Figure 6-1. Upon invocation, the Lambda receives the JSON array, which it can then append to a preconfigured Delta Lake table. Lambdas should conceptually be simple and complete their task as quickly and efficiently as possible.

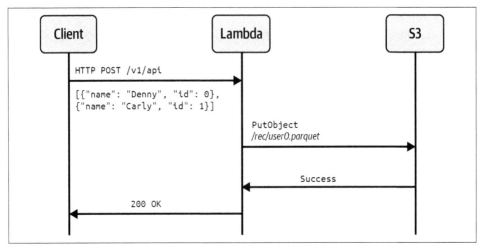

Figure 6-1. Request flow diagram of a hypothetical upload of user data for storage via AWS Lambda

Python

Lambdas can be written in Python directly within the AWS Lambda web UI. Unfortunately, the default Python runtime (*https://oreil.ly/9jahC*) has only minimal packages built in, and developers wishing to include `deltalake` will need to package their Lambdas either with layers (*https://oreil.ly/wH3hu*) or as containers. AWS provides an "AWS SDK with Pandas" layer that can be used to get started, but some care must be taken to include the `deltalake` dependency due to the 250 MB size limitation of Lambda layers. How the Lambda is packaged doesn't have a significant impact on its execution, so this section will not focus heavily on packaging and uploading the Lambda. Please refer to the book's GitHub repository (*https://oreil.ly/2m8Kv*), as it contains examples that use layers and container-based approaches, along with the infrastructure code necessary to deploy the examples.

The `hello-delta-rust` example demonstrates the simplest possible Delta Lake application in Lambda. This example looks only at the table's metadata, rather than querying any of the data.

The *lambda_function.py* simply opens the Delta Lake table and returns metadata to the HTTP client:

```python
import os
from deltalake import DeltaTable

def lambda_handler(event, context):
    url = os.environ['TABLE_URL']
    dt = DeltaTable(url)
    return { 'version' : dt.version(),
        'table' : url,
```

```
        'files' : dt.files(),
        'metadata' : {}}
```

This simple Python to create a `DeltaTable` object and then perform operations on the table (`dt`) demonstrates how easy interacting with Delta Lake from a Lambda can be. So long as the function returns a `list` or `dict` to the caller of `lambda_handler`, AWS Lambda will handle returning the information to the caller in JSON over HTTP.

The examples from the section "Reading large datasets" on page 117, which used Pandas or PyArrow for querying data in Python, can be reused inside the Lambda environment.

Similarly, the examples that cover *writing* data in Python can be reused in a Lambda. However, the Lambda execution environment is inherently *parallelized*, which presents concurrent write challenges when using AWS S3; these challenges and solutions are discussed later in this chapter. First we need the application, which will take the JSON array described above and append that to a Delta Lake table. Execution begins with the `lambda_handler` function, which is the entrypoint for AWS Lambda to execute your uploaded code:

```python
def lambda_handler(event, context):
    table_url = os.environ['TABLE_URL']
        try:
            input = pa.RecordBatch.from_pylist(json.loads(event['body']))
            dt = DeltaTable(table_url)
            write_deltalake(dt, data=input, schema=schema(), mode='append')
            status = 201
            body = json.dumps({'message' : 'Thanks for the data!'})
        except Exception as err:
            status = 400
            body = json.dumps({'message' : str(err),
               'type' : type(err).__name__})

    return {
            'statusCode' : status,
            'headers' : {'Content-Type' : 'application/json'},
            'isBase64Encoded' : False,
            'body' : body,
    }
```

The preceding is a shortened example of the `ingest-with-python` example from the GitHub repository (*https://oreil.ly/2m8Kv*) and could be taken and dropped into an arbitrary Python Lambda configuration. Upon uploading data, however, an error will be returned by default:

```
{"message": "Atomic rename requires a LockClient for S3 backends. Either con-
figure the LockClient, or set AWS_S3_ALLOW_UNSAFE_RENAME=true to opt out of
support for concurrent writers.",
"type": "DeltaProtocolError"}
```

By default, unsafe renames are *disabled* in the `deltalake` library. When you are faced with this error, it may be tempting to set `AWS_S3_ALLOW_UNSAFE_RENAME` to `true` in the configuration, but doing so can risk data loss or table corruption, because concurrent Delta writes cannot be done safely on AWS S3 without coordination. Skip ahead to the section "Concurrent writes on AWS S3" on page 135 to learn how to configure the Lambda to perform concurrent writes safely.

The append-only example can be further extended to load and merge data from other Delta Lake tables by creating more `DeltaTable` objects and then using the `pandas.DataFrame` functions for `merge`, `join`, or `concat`. Imagine a secondary table `s3://bucket/dietary_prefs` that needs to be joined with employee records being uploaded to the Lambda, which will produce the `s3://bucket/offsite_attendees` table:

```python
def lambda_handler(event, context):
    table_url = os.environ['TABLE_URL']
        try:
            input = pd.DataFrame(json.loads(event['body']))
        # Expecting both `input` and `prefs` to have an `id` column to
        # perform the inner join
        prefs = DeltaTable('s3://bucket/dietary_prefs').to_pandas()
            dt = DeltaTable(table_url)
            write_deltalake(dt,
              data=pd.merge(input, prefs),
              schema=schema(), mode='append')
            # …
```

When performing joins of datasets in Lambda, it is important to remember that the function operates in a memory- and CPU-constrained environment! Using predicates or adopting PyArrow directly rather than working with Pandas can allow for improved performance, should the simplistic approach become too memory- or CPU-intensive. If the working datasets cannot fit into memory within Lambda, then the workload should be considered for running in another environment, such as the standalone services ECS/EKS/EC2, or for porting to Spark to take advantage of multiple machines.

Rust

Building AWS Lambdas in Rust is similarly straightforward to building their Python counterparts. Unlike Python, however, Rust can be compiled to native code and does not require a "runtime" in AWS Lambda; instead, a custom-formatted *bootstrap.zip* file containing the compiled executable must be uploaded to AWS. Additional tools such as cargo-lambda (*https://oreil.ly/u0vi-*) should be installed on your workstation to provide generators and the build/cross-compiling functionality needed to build the *bootstrap.zip* files required by Lambda. The following examples and those in the book's GitHub repository (*https://oreil.ly/-X6Ob*) rely on cargo-lambda, and to begin writing a Rust Lambda, the necessary scaffolding should be created:

```
% cargo lambda new deltadog --event-type s3::S3Event
% cd deltadog
% cargo add –features s3 deltalake
% cargo lambda build –release –output-format zip
```

The last command above will produce ./target/lambda/deltadog/bootstrap.zip, which can be uploaded directly into AWS Lambda. Similar to the Python examples, there is a single entrypoint at which Rust code can be added. With the scaffolding above, any of the previous reading or writing Rust examples from this chapter can be copied and pasted into a Lambda function. Unlike their Python counterparts, the Rust Lambdas can typically process *much more* data because of the highly compact and efficient nature of Rust executables. Existing deltalake Rust code can be added into the function handler verbatim:

```
async fn function_handler(event: LambdaEvent<S3Event>) -> Result<(), Error> {
    // Extract some useful information from the request
    let _table = deltalake::open_table("s3://example/table").await?;
    Ok(())
}
```

The ingest-with-rust example in the GitHub repository (*https://oreil.ly/-X6Ob*) can be used as a starting point, similar to ingest-with-python.

Concurrent writes on AWS S3

Delta Lake has supported concurrent reads from multiple clusters since its inception, but safe concurrent writes require special care with AWS S3, since it lacks putIfAbsent consistency guarantees. Without separate coordination, there is no way to guarantee that writes originating from different writer processes—Python, Rust, or Spark—won't conflict with each other. Most Delta Lake applications built with AWS S3 use some variation of an AWS DynamoDB table to coordinate writers. Prior to the deltalake Python release 0.15 and the Rust release 0.17, those libraries used dynamodb_lock (*https://oreil.ly/vxwR-*), while more recent releases use the S3DynamoDB LogStore-compatible implementation, which allows Python and Rust applications to interoperate using the same protocol adopted by Delta Lake Spark writers (*https://oreil.ly/eqxtr*) requiring multicluster support (*https://oreil.ly/iiA8v*).

S3DynamoDBLogStore. The de facto standard for performing concurrent writes with AWS S3 relies on a DynamoDB table but utilizes it in a different fashion. Starting with the deltalake Rust crate version 0.17 and the deltalake Python version 0.15, native applications can interoperate seamlessly with Spark applications using the S3DynamoDBLogStore protocol. The protocol relies on the coordination of commits to the Delta log via a DynamoDB table, which provides both serialization of commits to the log *and* increased resiliency in case of unexpected crashes of writers (see Figure 6-2).

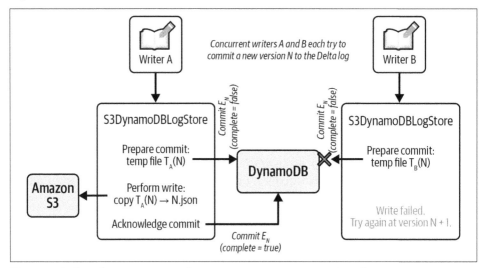

Figure 6-2. Coordination process for two concurrent writers using the S3DynamoDBLog Store *process*

The design considerations for S3DynamoDBLogStore are explained more in depth on the Delta Lake blog (*https://oreil.ly/eqxtr*). Consult the Delta Lake documentation (*https://oreil.ly/iiA8v*) for the most up-to-date details on configuring the required DynamoDB table, or start with some of the examples in this book's GitHub repository (*https://oreil.ly/-X6Ob*).

DynamoDB lock. Applications with older dependencies may still rely on dynamo db_lock, but since this approach is deprecated, this section will not dive too deeply into its function and design. At a high level, a DynamoDB table is configured as a simple key-value store alongside the Python or Rust application. Prior to executing a write operation, the deltalake library will check DynamoDB for the presence of a lock item—essentially a key representing the table it wishes to write against. If that key does not exist, the library will:

- Write a time-to-live (TTL) lock item with the table's identifier
- Commit its Delta transactions
- Delete the item from DynamoDB

If a key already exists, however, applications must enter a retry/backoff loop and wait until the lock item is cleared from the DynamoDB table. Aside from only supporting Python/Rust writers, this approach has been deprecated because it provides poor resiliency in cases of writer failures. If a writer crashes or exits with errors in the critical section after a lock item has been created, all other writers must wait until either the original writer is able to reclaim its lock *or* the TTL expires. There are few guarantees of recoverability with this approach, and "single giant table lock" leads to concurrency limitations, which can acutely affect Lambda invocations.[7]

Concurrency with S3-compatible stores

A number of other storage systems implement the AWS S3 APIs, such as the open source MinIO (*https://oreil.ly/Ilh87*) and Cloudflare R2 (*https://oreil.ly/ICkT8*). However, not every S3-like implementation suffers from the eventually consistent behaviors of AWS S3, which may mean there is no need for coordination among concurrent writers.

Consult the service's documentation to determine whether it can support an atomic "copy if not exists" operation (sometimes referred to as `putIfAbsent`). Cloudflare R2, for example, supports atomic behavior *only* when custom headers are supplied to its REST APIs, which can be toggled in the `deltalake` packages via the `AWS_COPY_IF_NOT_EXISTS` environment variable.

For other services, the environment variable `AWS_S3_ALLOW_UNSAFE_RENAME` can be set to true to disable the coordinator/locking requirements of the `deltalake` packages.

What's Next

The native data processing ecosystem is blossoming, with dozens of great tools in Python and Rust being developed and coming to maturity. Most of this innovation is being done by passionate and inspired developers in the larger open source ecosystem.

Delta Lake plays a pivotal role via the `deltalake` Python package or Rust crate, allowing data applications to benefit from the optimized storage and transactional nature of Delta. The list of integrations and great tools continues to grow; following is a list of interesting projects that are worth learning more about:

---

7 Check out the blog post "Concurrency Limitations for Delta Lake on AWS" (*https://oreil.ly/IrGnE*) for more details on the DynamoDB lock's limitations.

Python:
- Pandas (*https://oreil.ly/09Zu9*)
- Polars (*https://oreil.ly/fXqoz*)
- Dask (*https://oreil.ly/EqE8d*)
- Daft (*https://oreil.ly/rvXWj*)
- LakeFS (*https://oreil.ly/-mEdf*)
- PyArrow (*https://oreil.ly/zuzUd*)

Rust:
- ROAPI (*https://oreil.ly/qrCcK*)
- kafka-delta-ingest (*https://oreil.ly/ivqMr*)
- Ballista (*https://oreil.ly/AlRo5*)
- DataFusion (*https://oreil.ly/C7iWS*)
- arrow-rs (*https://oreil.ly/ywy7q*)
- Arroyo (*https://oreil.ly/U24fL*)
- ParadeDB (*https://oreil.ly/GyOGX*)

The delta-rs project and those listed here are only as productive as the people who show up, so you're invited to get involved! File bug reports, write user documentation, or create new open source projects that use Delta Lake to solve new problems!

Streaming In and Out of Your Delta Lake

Now more than ever, the world is infused with real-time data sources. From ecommerce, social network feeds, and airline flight data to network security and IoT devices, the volume of data sources is increasing alongside the speed with which you're able to access it. One problem with this is that, while some event-level operations make sense, much of the information we depend on lives in the aggregation of that information. So we are caught between the dueling priorities of (a) reducing the time to insights as much as possible and (b) capturing enough meaningful and actionable information from aggregates. For years we've seen processing technologies shifting in this direction, and it was this environment in which Delta Lake originated. What we got from Delta Lake was an open lakehouse format that supports seamless integrations of multiple batch and stream processes while delivering the necessary features like ACID transactions and scalable metadata processing that are commonly absent in most distributed data stores. With that in mind, in this chapter we dig into some of the details for stream processing with Delta Lake—namely, the functionality that is core to streaming processes, configuration options, specific usage methods, and the relationship of Delta Lake to Databricks Delta Live Tables.

Streaming and Delta Lake

As we go along, we want to cover some foundational concepts and then get into more of the nuts and bolts of actually using Delta Lake for stream processing. We'll start with an overview of concepts and some terminology, after which we will take a look at a few of the stream processing frameworks we can use with Delta Lake (for a more in-depth introduction to stream processing, see *Learning Spark* by Jules S. Damji, Brooke Wenig, Tathagata Das, and Denny Lee [O'Reilly]). Then we'll look at the core functionality, some of the options we have available, and some common more advanced cases with Apache Spark. And to finish out the chapter, we will cover a couple of related features used in Databricks, such as Delta Live Tables and how it relates to Delta Lake, and then review how to use the Change Data Feed functionality available in Delta Lake.

Streaming Versus Batch Processing

Data processing as a concept makes sense to us: during the data processing life cycle, we receive data, perform various operations on it, and then store it or ship it onward. So what primarily differentiates a batch data process from a streaming data process? Latency. There are different points at which to measure it, but *latency* is just the measure of time between records coming in and records going out. Above all other things, latency is the primary driver, because these processes tend not to differ in the business logic behind their design but instead focus on message/file sizes and processing speed. The choice of which method to use is generally driven by time requirements or service level/delivery agreements that should be part of requirements gathering at the start of a project. The requirements should also consider the latency in getting actionable insights from the raw data and will drive your decisions in processing methodology. One additional design choice we prefer is to use a framework that has a unified batch and streaming API because there are so few differences in the processing logic, which in turn provides us flexibility should requirements change over time. This is a simpler alternative to approaches like a lambda architecture running different systems for batch and stream processing.[1]

Each batch that we process has defined beginning and ending points—that is, there are boundaries placed in terms of time and format. For example, we might process data for each distinct calendar date as a batch. We may process "a file" or "a set of files" as a batch. In stream processing, we look at things a little differently and treat our data as unbounded and continuous instead. Even in the case of files arriving in storage, we can think of a stream of files (like log data) that continuously arrive. In the end, this unboundedness is really all that is needed to make a source a data stream. In Figure 7-1, the batch process equates to processing groups of six files for each scheduled run, where the stream process is always running and processes each file as it is available.

As we'll see shortly when we compare some of the frameworks with which we can use Delta Lake, stream processing engines such as Apache Flink or Apache Spark can work together with Delta Lake as either a starting point or an ending destination for data streams. These multiple roles mean Delta Lake can be used at multiple stages of different kinds of streaming workloads. Often we will see the storage layer as well

---

[1] For a review of the lambda architecture pattern, we suggest starting with the Wikipedia page (*https://oreil.ly/ YijEc*). It is essentially a parallel path architecture with a stream processing component and a batch processing component, both reading from the same source. The streaming process provides a faster view of the data, and the batch process ensures eventual accuracy.

as a processing engine present for multiple steps of more complicated data pipelines where we see both kinds of operation occurring. One common trait among most stream processing engines is that they are just processing engines. Once we have decoupled storage and compute, each must be considered and chosen, but neither can operate independently.

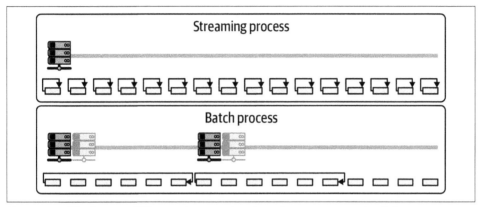

Figure 7-1. The biggest difference between batch and stream processing is latency; we can handle the files or messages individually as each becomes available or as a group

From a practical standpoint, the way we think about other related concepts such as processing time and table maintenance is affected by our choice between batch and streaming. If a batch process is scheduled to run at certain times, then we can easily measure the amount of time the process runs and how much data was processed and then chain it together with additional processes to handle table maintenance operations. We do need to think a little differently when it comes to measuring and maintaining stream processes, but many of the features we've already looked at—such as autocompaction and optimized writes, for example—can work in both realms. In Figure 7-2, we can see how, with modern systems, batch and streaming can converge, and we can focus instead on latency trade-offs once we depart from traditional frameworks. By choosing a framework that has a reasonably unified API minimizing the differences in programming for both batch and streaming use cases and then running it on top of a storage format like Delta Lake that simplifies the maintenance operations and provides for either method of processing, we wind up with a more robust yet flexible system that can handle all our data processing tasks, and we minimize the need to balance multiple tools and avoid other complications necessitated by running multiple systems. This makes Delta Lake the ideal storage solution for streaming workloads. Next, we'll consider some of the specific terminology for stream processing applications and follow up with a review of a few of the different framework integrations available for use with Delta Lake.

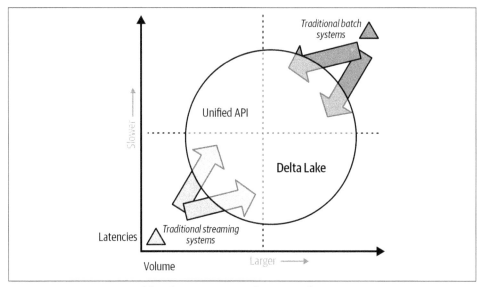

Figure 7-2. Streaming and batch processes overlap in modern systems

Streaming terminology

In many ways, streaming processes are quite the same as batch processes, with the difference being mostly one of latency and cadence. This does not mean, however, that streaming processes don't come with some of their own lingo. Some terms, such as *source* and *sink*, vary only a little from batch usage, while terms like *checkpoint* and *watermark* don't really apply to batch. It's useful to have some working familiarity with these terms, but you can dig into them at a greater depth in *Stream Processing with Apache Flink* by Fabian Hueske and Vasiliki Kalavri (O'Reilly) or *Learning Spark*.

Source.   A stream processing source is any of a variety of sources of data that can be treated as an unbounded dataset. Sources for data stream processing are varied and ultimately depend on the nature of the processing task in mind. There are a number of different message queue and pub/sub connectors used as data sources across the Spark and Flink ecosystems. These include many common favorites such as Apache Kafka, Amazon Kinesis, ActiveMQ, RabbitMQ, Azure Event Hubs, and Google's Pub/Sub. Both systems can also generate streams from files, for example, by monitoring cloud storage locations for new files. We will see shortly how Delta Lake fits in as a streaming data source.

Sink. Stream processing sinks similarly come in different shapes and forms. We often see many of the same message queues and pub/sub systems in play, but on the sink side in particular we quite often find some materialization layer such as a key-value store, RDBMS, or cloud storage like AWS S3 or Azure ADLS. Generally speaking, the final destination is usually one from the latter categories, and we'll see some type of mixture of methods in the middle, between origin and destination. Delta Lake functions extremely well as a sink, especially for managing large-volume, high-throughput streaming ingestion processes.

Checkpoint. It is usually important to make sure that you have implemented checkpointing in a streaming process. Checkpointing keeps track of the progress made in processing tasks and is what makes failure recovery possible without restarting processing from the beginning every time. This is accomplished by keeping some tracking record of the offsets for the stream, as well as any associated stateful information. In some processing engines, such as Flink and Spark, there are built-in mechanisms to make checkpointing operations simpler to use. We refer you to the respective documentation for usage details.

> All the examples and some other supporting code for this chapter can be found in the GitHub repository for the book (*https://oreil.ly/-X6Ob*).

Let's consider an example from Spark. When we start a stream writing process and define a suitable checkpoint location, it will in the background create a few directories at the target location. In the following example, we find a checkpoint written from a process we called "gold" (and named the directory similarly):

```
tree -L 1 /…/ckpt/gold/

/…/ckpt/gold/
├── __tmp_path_dir
├── commits
├── metadata
├── offsets
└── state
```

The metadata directory will contain some information about the streaming query, and the state directory will contain snapshots of the state information (if any) related to the query. The offsets and commits directories track at a microbatch level the progress of streaming from the source and writing to the sink, which for Delta Lake amounts to tracking the input or output files, respectively, as we'll see more of shortly.

Watermark.   Watermarking is a concept of time relative to the records being processed. The topic and usage are somewhat more complicated for our discussion, and
we would recommend reviewing the appropriate documentation. For our limited
purposes, we can just use a working definition: a *watermark* is basically a limit
on how late data can be accepted during processing. It is most especially used in
conjunction with windowed aggregation operations.[2]

Apache Flink

Apache Flink is one of the major distributed, in-memory processing engines that
supports both bounded and unbounded data manipulation. Flink supports many
predefined and built-in data stream sources and sink connectors.[3] On the data
source side, we see many message queues and pub/sub connectors supported, such as
RabbitMQ, Apache Pulsar, and Apache Kafka (see the Flink documentation (*https://
oreil.ly/_3MTd*) for more detailed streaming connector information). While some,
such as Kafka, are supported as an output destination, it's probably most common
to instead see something like writing to file storage or Elasticsearch or even a JDBC
connection to a database as the goal. You can find more information about Flink
connectors in their documentation.

With Delta Lake, we gain yet another source and destination for Flink, but one
that can be critical in multitool hybrid ecosystems or can simplify logical processing
transitions. For example, with Flink, we can focus on event stream processing and
then write directly to a Delta table in cloud storage, where we can access it for
subsequent processing in Spark. Alternatively, we could reverse this situation entirely
and feed a message queue from records in Delta Lake. A more in-depth review of the
connector, including both implementation and architectural details, is available as a
blog post on the delta.io website (*https://oreil.ly/b-Zld*).

Apache Spark

Apache Spark similarly supports many input sources and sinks.[4] Since Apache Spark
tends to hold more of a place on the large-scale ingestion and ETL side, we do
see a little bit of a skew in the direction of input sources available, in contrast
to the more event-processing-centered Flink system. In addition to file-based sources, there is a strong native integration with Kafka in Spark, as well as several

---

2 To explore watermarks in more detail, we suggest the "Event-Time and Stateful Processing" chapter of
  Spark: The Definitive Guide by Bill Chambers and Matei Zaharia (O'Reilly).

3 We understand many readers are more familiar with Apache Spark. For an introduction to concepts more
  specific to Apache Flink, we suggest the "Learn Flink" page of the Flink documentation (*https://oreil.ly/h8bJb*).

4 Apache Spark source and sink documentation can be found in the "Structured Streaming Programming
  Guide" (*https://oreil.ly/6166j*), which is generally seen as the go-to source for all things streaming with Spark.

---

separately maintained connector libraries, such as Azure Event Hubs (*https://oreil.ly/f_HF7*), Google Pub/Sub Lite (*https://oreil.ly/1NWJ_*), and Apache Pulsar (*https://oreil.ly/lzfeM*).

There are still several output sinks available too, but Delta Lake is easily among one of the largest-scale destinations for data with Spark. As we mentioned earlier, Delta Lake was essentially designed around solving the challenges of large-scale stream ingestion with the limitations of the Parquet file format. Due in large part to the origins of Delta Lake and the longer history with Apache Spark, much of what's covered here will be Spark-centric, but we should note that many of the concepts have corollaries with other frameworks as well.

Delta-rs

The Rust ecosystem also has additional processing engines and libraries of its own, and thanks to the implementation called delta-rs (*https://oreil.ly/ZtPkY*), we get further processing options that can run on Delta Lake. This area is one of the newer sides and has seen some intensive build-out in recent years. Polars (*https://oreil.ly/fXqoz*) and DataFusion (*https://oreil.ly/Tm-kG*) are just a couple of the other options for stream data processing, and both couple with delta-rs reasonably well. This is a rapidly developing area that we expect to see a lot more growth in going forward.

One other benefit of the delta-rs implementation is that there is a direct Python integration, which opens up additional possibilities for data stream processing tasks. This means that for smaller-scale jobs, it is possible to use a Python API (such as AWS Boto3, for example) for services that otherwise require larger-scale frameworks for interaction and thus cause unneeded overhead. While you may not be able to leverage some of the features from the frameworks that more naturally support streaming operations, you could benefit from a significant reduction in infrastructure requirements and still get lightning-fast performance.

The net result of the delta-rs implementation is that Delta Lake gives us a format through which we can simultaneously make use of multiple processing frameworks and engines without relying on an additional RDBMS and still operate outside of more Java-centered stacks. This means that, even when working in disparate systems, we can build data applications confidently without sacrificing the built-in benefits we gain through Delta Lake.

Delta as Source

Much of the original intent in Delta Lake's design was as a streaming sink that added the functionality and reliability that was previously found missing in practice. In particular, Delta Lake simplifies maintenance for processes that tend to have lots of smaller transactions and files and provides ACID transaction guarantees. Before we look at that side in more depth, though, let's think about Delta Lake as a streaming source. By way of the already incremental nature that we've seen in the transaction log, we have a straightforward source of JSON files with well-ordered ID values. This means that any engine can use the file ID values as offsets in streaming messages, with a complete transaction record of the files added during append operations, and see what new files exist. The inclusion of a flag in the transaction log, *dataChange*, helps separate out compaction or other table maintenance events that generate new files as well but do not need to be sent to downstream consumers. Since the IDs are monotonic, this also makes offset tracking simpler, so exactly-once semantics are still possible for downstream consumers.

The practical upside of all of this is that with Spark Structured Streaming, you can define the `readStream` format as `"delta"`, and it will begin by processing all previously available data from the targeted table or file and then add incremental updates as they are added. This allows for significant simplification of many processing architectures (such as the medallion architecture, which we have seen before and will discuss in more detail later), but for now, we should assume that creating additional data refinement layers becomes a natural operation with significantly reduced overhead costs.

With Spark, the `readStream` itself defines the operation mode, with `"delta"` denoting the format, and the operation proceeds as usual, with much of the action taking place behind the scenes. The approach is somewhat flipped with Flink, where you instead start by building off of the Delta source object in a `DataStream` class and then use the `forContinuousRowData` API to begin incremental processing:

```python
# Python
streamingDeltaDf = (
    spark
    .readStream
    .format("delta")
    .option("ignoreDeletes", "true")
    .load("/files/delta/user_events")
    )
```

Delta as Sink

Many of the features you would want for a streaming sink (such as asynchronous compaction operations) were not available or scalable in a way that could support modern, high-volume streaming ingestion. The availability and increased connectivity of user activity and devices, as well as the rapid growth in the Internet of Things (IoT), quickly accelerated the growth of large-scale streaming data sources. One of the most critical problems then comes in trying to answer the question *How can I efficiently and reliably capture all the data?*

Many of the features of Delta Lake are there specifically to remedy this problem. The way actions are committed to the transaction log, for example, fits naturally in the context of a stream processing engine, where you are tracking the progress of the stream against the source and ensuring that only completed transactions are committed to the log, while corrupted files are not; this allows you to make sure that you are actually capturing all the source data with some reliability guarantees. The metrics produced and emitted to the Delta log help you to analyze the consistency (or variability) of the streaming process, with counts of rows and files added during each transaction.

Most large-scale stream processing happens in *microbatches*, which in essence are smaller-scale transactions of similar larger batch processes. The result of this is that we may see many write operations coming from a stream processing engine as it captures the data in flight. When this processing is happening in an "always on" streaming process, it can become difficult to manage other aspects of the data ecosystem, such as running maintenance operations, backfilling, or modifying historical data. Table utility commands like `optimize` and the ability to interact with the Delta log from multiple processes in the environment mean that much of this was considered beforehand, and because of the incremental nature, we're able to interrupt these processes more easily in a predictable way. On the other hand, we might still have to think a little more often about what kinds of combinations of these operations might occasionally produce conflicts we wish to avoid.[5]

The medallion architecture with Delta Lake and Apache Spark in particular, which we will cover in depth in Chapter 9, becomes something of a middle ground in which we see Delta Lake as both a streaming sink and a streaming source working in tandem (see Figure 7-3). This actually eliminates the need for additional infrastructure in many cases and simplifies the overall architecture, while still providing mechanisms for low-latency, high-throughput stream processing and preserving clean data engineering practices.

---

5 You can find detailed descriptions, including error messages, in the "Concurrency Control" section of the Delta Lake documentation (*https://oreil.ly/Fko5I*).

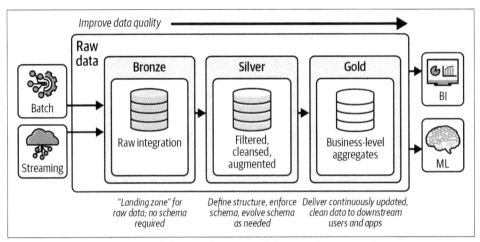

Figure 7-3. A visualization of the Databricks medallion architecture definition; you can see both a streaming source coming in with a Delta Lake table as a sink and then that table also becoming the source for the next process

Writing a streaming DataFrame object to Delta Lake is straightforward; it requires only the format specification and a directory location through the `writeStream` method:

```
# Python
(streamingDeltaDf
.writeStream
.format("delta")
.outputMode("append")
.start("/<delta_path>/")
)
```

Similarly, you can chain together a `readStream` definition (similarly formatted) and a `writeStream` definition to set up a whole input-transformation-output flow (transformation code omitted here for brevity):

```
# Python
(spark
.readStream
.format("delta")
.load("/files/delta/user_events")
...
# other transformation logic
...
.writeStream
.format("delta")
.outputMode("append")
.start("/<delta_path>/")
)
```

Delta Streaming Options

Now that we've discussed how streaming in and out of Delta Lake works conceptually, let's delve into the more technical side of the options we'll ultimately use in practice and go over a bit of background on instances in which you may wish to modify them. We'll start by looking at ways we might limit the input rate and, in particular, how we can leverage that in conjunction with some of the functionality we get in Apache Spark. After that, we'll delve into some cases where we might want to skip some transactions. Last, we'll follow up by considering a few aspects of the relationship between time and our processing job.

Limit the Input Rate

When we're talking about stream processing, we typically have to find a balance among three concerns: accuracy, latency, and cost. We generally don't want to forsake anything on the side of accuracy (except in cases where we might want to drop stale records or limit scope), and so this usually comes down to a trade-off between latency and cost—i.e., we can either accept higher costs and scale up our resources to process data as fast as possible, or we can limit the size and accept longer turnaround times on our data processing. Often this is largely under the control of the stream processing engine, but we have two additional options with Delta Lake that allow us more control over the size of microbatches:

maxFilesPerTrigger
> This sets the limit for how many new files will be considered in every microbatch. The default value is 1000.

maxBytesPerTrigger
> This sets an approximate limit for how much data gets processed in each microbatch. This option sets a *soft max*, meaning that a microbatch processes approximately this amount of data but can process more when the smallest input unit is larger than this limit. In other words, this size setting operates more like a threshold value that needs to be exceeded, whether with one file or with many files; however many files it takes to get past this threshold, it will use that many files—kind of like a dynamic setting for the number of files in each microbatch that uses an approximate size.

These two settings can be balanced with the use of triggers (*https://oreil.ly/Ik0hj*) in Structured Streaming to either increase or reduce the amount of data being processed in each microbatch. You can use these settings, for example, to lower the size of compute required for processing or to tailor the job for the expected file sizes you will be working with. If you use Trigger.Once for your streaming, these two options are ignored. This is not generally set by default. You can actually use both maxBytesPer

`Trigger` and `maxFilesPerTrigger` for the same streaming query, in which case the microbatch will just run until either limit is reached.

 We want to note here that it's possible to set a shorter `log RetentionDuration` with a longer trigger or job scheduling interval in such a way that older transactions can be skipped if cleanup occurs. Since it does not know what came before, processing will begin at the earliest available transaction in the log, which means data can be skipped in the processing. A simple example of where this could occur is when the `logRetentionDuration` is set to, say, a day or two, but a processing job intending to pick up the incremental changes is run only weekly. Since any vacuum operation in the intervening period would remove some of the older versions of the files, this will result in those changes not being propagated through the next run.

Ignore Updates or Deletes

So far in talking about streaming with Delta Lake, we've not really discussed something that we really ought to address. In earlier chapters we've seen how some features of Delta Lake improve the ease of performing CRUD operations, most notably those of updates and deletes. What we should call out here is that when we are streaming with Delta Lake, it assumes by default that we are streaming from an append-only type of source—that is, it assumes that the incremental changes that are happening are only the addition of new files. A question then arises: *What happens if I have update or delete operations in the stream source?*

To put it simply, the Spark `readStream` operation will fail, at least with the default settings. This is because as a stream source, we expect to receive only new files, and we must specify how to handle files that come from changes or deletions. This is usually fine for large-scale ingestion tables or for receiving change data capture (CDC) records, because those typically won't be subject to other types of operations. There are two ways you can deal with these situations. The harder way is to delete the output and checkpoint and restart the stream from the beginning. The easier way is to leverage the `ignoreDeletes` or `ignoreChanges` options, which have rather different behaviors from each other despite the similarity in their names. The biggest caveat is that when using either setting, you will have to manually track and make changes downstream, as we'll explain shortly.

The ignoreDeletes setting

The `ignoreDeletes` setting does exactly what it sounds like it does: it ignores delete operations as it comes across them *if a new file is not created*. The reason this matters is that if you delete an upstream file, those changes will not be propagated to downstream destinations, but we can use this setting to avoid failing the stream processing job and still support important delete operations, such as when we need to purge individual user data to comply with the GDPR's right to be forgotten (*https:// oreil.ly/IBEs2*). The catch is that the data would need to be partitioned by the same values we filter on for the delete operation so there are no remnants that would create a new file. This means that the same delete operations would need to be run across potentially several tables, but we can ignore these small delete operations in the stream process and continue as normal, leaving the downstream delete operations for a separate process.

The ignoreChanges setting

The `ignoreChanges` setting actually behaves a bit differently than `ignoreDeletes` does. Rather than skipping operations that are only removing files, `ignoreChanges` allows new files that result from changes to come through as though they are new files. This means that if we update some records within a particular file or delete a few records from a file so that a new version of the file is created, then the new version of the file is now interpreted as being a new file when propagated downstream. This helps to make sure we have the freshest version of our data available. However, it is important to understand the impact of this to avoid data duplication. What we then need in these cases is to ensure that we can handle duplicate records through `merge` logic or otherwise differentiate the data by inclusion of additional timekeeping information (i.e., add a `version_as_of` timestamp, or something similar). We've found that under many types of change operations, the majority of the records will be reprocessed without changes, so merging or deduplication is generally the preferred path.

Example

Let's consider an example. Suppose you have a Delta Lake table called `user_events` with `date`, `user_email`, and `action` columns, and it is partitioned by the `date` column. Let's also suppose that we are using the `user_events` table as a streaming source for a step in our larger pipeline process and that we need to delete data from it due to a GDPR-related request.

When you delete at a partition boundary (that is, the `WHERE` clause of the query filters data on a partition column), the files are already in directories based on those values, so the `delete` just drops any of those files from the table metadata.

So if you just want to delete data from some entire partitions aligning to specific dates, you can add the `ignoreDeletes` option to the `readStream`:

```python
# Python
streamingDeltaDf = (
    spark
```

```
    .readStream
    .format("delta")
    .option("ignoreDeletes", "true")
    .load("/files/delta/user_events")
    )
```

If you want to delete data based on a nonpartition column like user_email instead, then you will need to use the ignoreChanges option:

```
# Python
streamingDeltaDf = (
    spark
    .readStream
    .format("delta")
    .option("ignoreChanges", "true")
    .load("/files/delta/user_events")
    )
```

Similarly, if you update records against a nonpartition column like user_email, a new file is created that contains the changed records and any other records from the original file that were unchanged. With ignoreChanges set, this file will be seen by the readStream query, and so you will need to include additional logic against this stream to avoid duplicate data making its way into the output for this process.

Initial Processing Position

When you start a streaming process with a Delta Lake source, the default behavior will be to start with the earliest version of the table and then incrementally process through to the most recent version. There are going to be times, of course, when we don't actually want to start with the earliest version, such as when we need to delete a checkpoint for the streaming process and restart from some point in the middle, or even from the most recent point available. Thanks again to the transaction log, we can actually specify this starting point to keep from having to reprocess everything from the beginning of the log, similar to how checkpointing allows the stream to recover from a specific point.

What we can do here is to define an initial position to begin processing, and we can do that in one of two ways. The first is to specify the specific version from which we want to start processing, and the second is to specify the time from which we want to start processing. These options are available via startingVersion and startingTimestamp.

Specifying the startingVersion does pretty much what you might expect. Given a particular version from the transaction log, the files that were committed for that version will be the first data we begin processing, and the process will continue from there. In this way, all table changes starting from this version (inclusive) will be read by the streaming source. You can review the version parameter from the transaction logs to identify which specific version you might need, or you can alternatively specify "latest" to get only the latest changes.

 When using Apache Spark, this is most easily done by checking commit versions from the version column of the DESCRIBE HISTORY command output in the SQL context.

Similarly, we can specify a startingTimestamp option for a more temporal approach. With the timestamp option, we actually get a couple of slightly varying behaviors. If the given timestamp exactly matches a commit, it will include those files for processing; otherwise, the behavior is to process only files from versions occurring after that point in time. One particularly helpful feature here is that it does not strictly require a fully formatted timestamp string; we can also use a similar date string that can be interpreted for us. This means our startingTimestamp parameter should look like one of the following:

- A timestamp string, e.g., 2023-03-23T00:00:00.000Z
- A date string, e.g., 2023-03-23

Unlike with some of our other settings, we cannot use both options simultaneously here; we have to choose one or the other. If this setting is added to an existing streaming query with a checkpoint already defined, then they will both be ignored, as they apply only when starting a new query.

Another thing you will want to note is that even though you can start from any specified place in the source using these options, the schema will reflect the latest available version. This means that incorrect values or failures can occur if there is an incompatible schema change between the specified starting point and the current version.

Considering our user_events dataset again, suppose you want to read changes occurring since version 5. Then you would write something like the following:

```python
# Python
(spark
.readStream
.format("delta")
.option("startingVersion", "5")
.load("/files/delta/user_events")
)
```

Alternatively, if you wanted to read changes based on a date—say, any changes occurring since 2023-04-18—you would use something like this:

```python
# Python
(spark
.readStream
.format("delta")
.option("startingTimestamp", "2023-04-18")
.load("/files/delta/user_events")
)
```

Initial Snapshot with withEventTimeOrder

The default ordering when using Delta Lake as a streaming source is based on the modification date of the files. We have also seen that when we are initially running a query, it will naturally run until we are caught up to the current state of the table. We call this version of the table, the one covering the starting point through to the current state, the *initial snapshot* at the beginning of a streaming query. On Databricks, we get an additional option for interpreting time for this initial snapshot. We may want to consider whether, in the case of our dataset, this default ordering based on the modification time is correct, or if there is an event time field we can leverage in the dataset that might simplify the ordering of the data.

A timestamp associated with when a record was last modified (i.e., seen) doesn't necessarily align with the time an event happened. Think of IoT device data that gets delivered in bursts at varying intervals. This means that if you are relying on a `last_modified` timestamp column or something similar to that, records can get processed out of order, and this could lead to records being dropped as late events by the watermark. You can avoid this data drop issue by enabling the option `withEventTimeOrder`, which will prefer the event time over the modification time. Following is an example of setting the option on a `readStream` with an associated watermark option on the `event_time` column:

```python
# Python
(spark
.readStream
.format("delta")
.option("withEventTimeOrder", "true")
.load("/files/delta/user_events")
.withWatermark("event_time", "10 seconds")
)
```

When the option is enabled, the initial snapshot is analyzed to get a total time range and then divided into buckets, with each bucket getting processed in turn as a microbatch, which might result in some added shuffle operations. You can still use the `maxFilesPerTrigger` or `maxBytesPerTrigger` option to throttle the processing rate.

There are several callouts related to this situation that we want to make sure you're aware of:

- The data drop issue happens only when the initial Delta snapshot of a stateful streaming query is processed in the default order.

- `withEventTimeOrder` is another of those settings that takes effect only at the beginning of a streaming query, so it cannot be changed after the query is started and while the initial snapshot is still being processed. If you want to modify the `withEventTimeOrder` setting, you must delete the checkpoint and make use of the initial processing position options to proceed.

- If you are running a stream query with `withEventTimeOrder` enabled, you cannot downgrade it to a version that doesn't support this feature until the initial snapshot processing is completed. If you need to downgrade versions, you can either wait for the initial snapshot to finish or delete the checkpoint and restart the query.

- There are a few rarer scenarios in which you cannot use `withEventTimeOrder`:
  - If the event time column is a generated column and there are nonprojection transformations between the Delta source and the watermark
  - If there is a watermark with multiple Delta sources in the stream query

- Due to the potential for increased shuffle operations, the performance of the processing for the initial snapshot may be impacted.

Using the event time ordering triggers a scan of the initial snapshot to find the corresponding event time range for each microbatch. This suggests that for better performance we want to be sure that our event time column is among the columns we collect statistics for. This way our query can take advantage of data skipping, and we get faster filter action. You can increase the performance of the processing in cases where it makes sense to partition the data in relation to the event time column. Performance metrics should indicate how many files are being referenced in each microbatch.

The setting `spark.databricks.delta.withEventTimeOrder` `.enabled true` can be set as a cluster-level Spark configuration, but be aware that doing this will make it apply to all streaming queries that run on the cluster.

Advanced Usage with Apache Spark

Much of the functionality we've covered to this point can be applied from more than one of the frameworks listed earlier. Here we turn our attention to a couple of common cases we've encountered while using Apache Spark specifically. These are cases in which leveraging features of the framework can prevent us from using some of the built-in features in Delta Lake directly.

Idempotent Stream Writes

Much of the previous discussion is centered around the idea of running a processing task from a single source to a single destination. In the real world, however, we may not always have neat and simple pipelines like this; instead, we may find ourselves building out pipelines using multiple sources writing to multiple destinations, which may also wind up overlapping. With the transaction log and atomic commit behavior, we can support multiple writers to a single Delta Lake destination from a functional perspective, as we've already considered. How can we apply this in our stream processing pipelines, though?

In Apache Spark, we have the method `foreachBatch` available on a Structured Streaming DataFrame that allows us to define more customized logic for each stream microbatch. This is the method we would typically use to support writing a single stream source to multiple destinations. The problem we encounter is that if there are, say, two different destinations, and the transaction fails in writing to the second destination, then we have a scenario in which the processing state of each of the destinations is out of sync. More specifically, since the first write was completed and the second write failed, when the stream processing job is restarted it will consider the same offsets from the last run, since it did not complete successfully.

Consider this example in which we have a `sourceDf` DataFrame and we want to process it in batches to two different destinations. We define a function that takes an input DataFrame and just uses normal Spark operations to write out each microbatch. Then we can apply that function using the `foreachBatch` method available from the `writeStream` method:

```python
# Python
sourceDf = ... # Streaming source DataFrame

# Define a function writing to two destinations
def writeToDeltaLakeTables(batch_df):
    # location 1
    (batch_df
    .write
    .format("delta")
    .save("/<delta_path_1>/")
    )
```

```
# location 2
(batch_df
.write
.format("delta")
.save("/<delta_path_2>/")
)

# Apply the function against the microbatches using 'foreachBatch'
(sourceDf
.writeStream
.format("delta")
.queryName("Unclear status stream")
.foreachBatch(writeToDeltaLakeTables)
.start()
)
```

Now suppose an error occurs after writing to the first location but before the second write completes. Since the transaction failed, we know the second table won't have anything committed to the log, but in the first table the transaction was successful. When we restart the job, it will start at the same point and rerun the entire function for that microbatch, which can result in duplicated data being written to the first table. Thankfully, Delta Lake has something that can help us out by allowing us to specify more granular transaction tracking.

Idempotent writes

Let's suppose that we are leveraging foreachBatch from a streaming source and are writing to just two destinations. What we would like to do is take the structure of the foreachBatch transaction and combine it with some nifty Delta Lake functionality to make sure we commit the microbatch transaction across all the tables without winding up with duplicate transactions in some of the tables (i.e., we want idempotent writes to the tables). We have two options we can use to help get to this state:

txnAppId
    This should be a unique string identifier and acts as an application ID that you can pass for each DataFrame write operation. This identifies the source for each write. You can use a streaming query ID or some other meaningful name of your choice as txnAppId.

txnVersion
    This is a monotonically increasing number that acts as a transaction version and functionally becomes the offset identifier for a writeStream query.

The application ID (txnAppId) can be any user-generated unique string and does not have to be related to the stream ID, so you can use this to more functionally describe the application performing the operation or identifying the source of the data. The same DataFrameWriter options can actually be used to achieve similar idempotent writes in batch processing as well.

By including both of these options, we create a unique source and offset tracking at the write level, even inside a foreachBatch operation writing to multiple destinations. This allows, at a table level, for the detection of duplicate write attempts that can be ignored. This means that if a write is interrupted during the processing of just one of multiple table destinations, we can continue the processing without duplicating write operations to tables for which the transaction was already successful. When the stream restarts from the checkpoint, it will start again with the same microbatch, but then in the foreachBatch, with the write operations now being checked at a table level of granularity, we write only to the table or tables that were not able to complete successfully before, because we will have the same txnAppId and txnVersion identifiers.

In the case that you want to restart processing from a source and delete/recreate the streaming checkpoint, you must provide a new appId as well before restarting the query. If you don't, then all of the writes from the restarted query will be ignored because it will contain the same txnAppId, and the batch ID values will restart, so the destination table will see them as duplicate transactions.

If we wanted to update the function from our earlier example to write to multiple locations with idempotency using these options, we could specify the options for each destination like this:

```python
# Python
app_id = ... # A unique string used as an application ID.

def writeToDeltaLakeTableIdempotent(batch_df, batch_id):
    # location 1
    (batch_df
    .write
    .format("delta")
    .option("txnVersion", batch_id)
    .option("txnAppId", app_id)
    .save("/<delta_path>/")
    )
    # location 2
    (batch_df
    .write
    .format("delta")
```

```
.option("txnVersion", batch_id)
.option("txnAppId", app_id)
.save("/<delta_path>/")
)
```

Merge

There is another common case in which we tend to see `foreachBatch` used for stream processing. Think about some of the limitations we have seen where we might allow large amounts of unchanged records to be reprocessed through the pipeline, or where we might otherwise want more advanced matching and transformation logic, such as processing CDC records. To update values, we need to merge changes into an existing table rather than simply append the information. The bad news is that the default behavior in streaming kind of requires us to use append-type behaviors (unless we leverage `foreachBatch`, that is).

We looked at the merge operation in Chapter 3 and saw that it allows us to use matching criteria to update or delete existing records and append others that don't match the criteria—that is, we can perform upsert operations. Since `foreachBatch` lets us treat each microbatch like a regular DataFrame, then at the microbatch level we can actually perform these upsert operations with Delta Lake. You can upsert data from a source table, view, or DataFrame into a target Delta table by using the `MERGE` SQL operation or its corollary for the Scala, Java, and Python Delta Lake API (*https://oreil.ly/L--Ti*). It even supports extended syntax beyond the SQL standards to facilitate advanced use cases.

A merge operation on Delta Lake typically requires two passes over the source data. If you use nondeterministic functions such as `current_timestamp` or `random` in a source DataFrame, then multiple passes on the source data can produce different values in rows, causing incorrect results. You can avoid this by using more concrete functions or values for columns or by writing out results to an intermediate table. Caching the source data may help as well, because a cache invalidation can cause the source data to be partially or completely reprocessed, resulting in the same kind of value changes (for example, when a cluster loses some of its executors when scaling down). We've seen cases in which this can fail in surprising ways when trying to do something like using a salt column to restructure DataFrame partitioning based on random number generation (e.g., Spark cannot locate a shuffle partition on disk because the random prefix is different than expected on a retried run). The multiple passes for merge operations increase the possibility of this happening.

Let's consider an example of using merge operations in a stream using `foreachBatch` to update the most recent daily retail transaction summaries for a set of customers. In this case, we will match on a customer ID value and include the transaction date, number of items, and dollar amount. In practice what we do to use the `mergeBuilder` API here is to build a function to handle the logic for our streaming DataFrame.

Inside the function, we'll provide the customer ID as a matching criteria for the target table and our changes source, and then we'll allow for a delete mechanism and otherwise update existing customers or add new ones as they appear.[6] The flow of the operations in the function is to specify what to merge, with arguments for the matching conditions, and which actions we want to take when a record is matched or not (for which we can add some additional conditions):

```python
# Python
from delta.tables import *

def upsertToDelta(microBatchDf, batchId):
    Target_table = "retail_db.transactions_silver"
    deltaTable = DeltaTable.forName(spark, target_table)
    (deltaTable.alias("dt")
    .merge(source=microBatchDf.alias("sdf"),
        condition="sdf.t_id = dt.t_id")
    .whenMatchedDelete(condition="sdf.operation='DELETE'")
    .whenMatchedUpdate(set={
        "t_id": "sdf.t_id",
        "transaction_date": "sdf.transaction_date",
        "item_count": "sdf.item_count",
        "amount": "sdf.amount"
        })
    .whenNotMatchedInsert(values={
        "t_id": "sdf.t_id",
        "transaction_date": "sdf.transaction_date",
        "item_count": "sdf.item_count",
        "amount": "sdf.amount"
        })
    .execute())
```

The function body itself is similar to how we specify merge logic with regular batch processes already. The only real difference in this case is that we will run the merge operation for every received batch rather than for an entire source all at once. Now with our function already defined, we can read in a stream of changes and apply our customized merge logic with the `foreachBatch` in Spark and write it back out to another table:

```python
# Python
changesStream = ... # Streaming DataFrame with CDC records

# Write the output of a streaming aggregation query into Delta table
(changesStream
.writeStream
.format("delta")
.queryName("Summaries Silver Pipeline")
```

---

6 For additional details and examples on using merge in `foreachBatch`, e.g., for SCD Type II merges, see the Delta Lake documentation (*https://oreil.ly/z5Iy8*).

```
    .foreachBatch(upsertToDelta)
    .outputMode("update")
    .start()
    )
```

So each microbatch of the changes stream will have the merge logic applied to it and will be written to the destination table or even to multiple tables, as we did in the example for idempotent writes.

Delta Lake Performance Metrics

An often overlooked but very helpful thing to have for any data processing pipeline is insight into the operations that are taking place. Having metrics that help us to understand the speed and scale at which processing is taking place can be valuable information for cost estimating, capacity planning, or troubleshooting when issues arise. We've already seen a couple of cases in which we are receiving metrics information when streaming with Delta Lake, but here we'll look more carefully at what we are actually receiving.

Metrics

As we've seen, there are cases in which we want to manually set starting and ending boundary points for processing with Delta Lake, and these are generally aligned to versions or timestamps. Within those boundaries, we can have differing numbers of files and so forth, and one of the concepts we've seen is important to streaming processes in particular is tracking the offsets, or the progress, through those files. In the metrics reported out for Spark Structured Streaming, we see several details tracking these offsets.

When running the process on Databricks as well, there are some additional metrics that help to track backpressure—that is, how much outstanding work there is to be done at the current point in time. The performance metrics we see get output are numInputRows, inputRowsPerSecond, and processedRowsPerSecond. The backpressure metrics are numBytesOutstanding and numFilesOutstanding. These metrics are fairly self-explanatory by design, so we won't explore them individually.

 Comparing the inputRowsPerSecond metric with the processed RowsPerSecond metric provides a ratio that can be used to measure relative performance and that might indicate whether a job should have more resources allocated to it or whether triggers should be throttled down a bit.

Custom metrics

For both Apache Flink and Apache Spark, there are also custom metrics options you can use to extend the metrics information tracked in your application. One method we've seen using this concept is to send additional custom metrics information from inside a `foreachBatch` operation in Spark. See the documentation for each processing framework as needed to pursue this option. This provides the highest degree of customization but also requires the most manual effort.

Auto Loader and Delta Live Tables

The majority of our focus is on everything freely available in the Delta Lake open source project. However, there are a couple of major topics available only in Databricks that rely on or frequently work in conjunction with Delta Lake and that deserve mention.

Auto Loader

Databricks has a somewhat unique Spark Structured Streaming source known as Auto Loader (*https://oreil.ly/tOgPU*), though it is really better thought of as the `cloud Files` source. On the whole, the `cloudFiles` source is more of a streaming source definition in Structured Streaming on Databricks, but it has rapidly become an easier entrypoint for streaming for many organizations in which Delta Lake is commonly the destination sink. This is partly because it provides a natural way to incrementalize batch processes so as to integrate some of the benefits of stream processing, such as offset tracking.

The `cloudFiles` source actually has two different methods of operation: one is to directly run file-listing operations on a storage location, and the other is to listen on a notifications queue tied to a storage location. Whichever method is used, it will quickly become apparent that this is a scalable and efficient mechanism for regular ingestion of files from cloud storage, as the offsets it uses for tracking progress are the actual filenames in the specified source directories. Refer to the section "Delta Live Tables" on page 163 for an example of the most common usage.

One fairly standard application of Auto Loader is to use it as a part of the medallion architecture design, with a process ingesting files and feeding the data into Delta Lake tables with additional levels of transformation, enrichment, and aggregation up to gold layer aggregate data tables. This is quite commonly done with additional data layer processing taking place, with Delta Lake as both the source and the sink of streaming processes, which provides low-latency, high-throughput, end-to-end data transformation pipelines. This process has become somewhat of a standard for file-based ingestion and has eliminated some of the need for more complicated processes based on lambda architecture—so much so that Databricks also built a framework largely centered around this approach.

Delta Live Tables

Databricks offers a data engineering pipeline framework running on top of Delta Lake called Delta Live Tables (DLT) (*https://oreil.ly/cXZln*) that combines incremental ingestion, streamlined ETL, and automated data quality processes like *expectations*. DLT serves to simplify building pipelines like those we just described in investigating the cloudFiles source, which actually explains the main reason for including it here in our discussion about streaming with Delta Lake: it is a product built around Delta Lake that captures some of the key principles noted throughout this guide in an easy-to-manage framework.

Rather than building out a processing pipeline piece by piece, the declarative framework allows you to simply define some tables and views with less syntax than a lot of the features we discussed by automating many of the best practices commonly used across the field. The things that it can manage on your behalf include compute resources, data quality monitoring, processing pipeline health, and optimized task orchestration.

DLT offers static tables, streaming tables, views, and materialized views to chain together many otherwise more complicated tasks. On the streaming side, we see Auto Loader as a prominent and common initial source feeding downstream incremental processes across Delta Lake–backed tables. Here is some example pipeline code based on examples in the Delta Live Tables documentation (*https://oreil.ly/1Y3PY*):

```python
# Python
import dlt

@dlt.table
def autoloader_dlt_bronze():
    return (
        spark
        .readStream
        .format("cloudFiles")
        .option("cloudFiles.format", "json")
        .load("<data path>")
    )

@dlt.table
def delta_dlt_silver():
    return (
        dlt
        .read_stream("autoloader_dlt_bronze")
        ...
        <transformation logic>
        ...
```

```
    )

@dlt.table
def live_delta_gold():
    return (
        dlt
        .read("delta_dlt_silver")
        ...
        <aggregation logic>
        ...
    )
```

Since the initial source is a streaming process, the silver and gold tables there are also incrementally processed. One of the advantages we gain for streaming sources specifically is simplification. By not having to define checkpoint locations or programmatically create table entries in a metastore, we can build out pipelines with a reduced level of effort. In short, DLT gives us many of the same benefits of building data pipelines on top of Delta Lake but abstracts away many of the details, making it simpler and easier to use.

Change Data Feed

Earlier we looked at the integration of change data capture (CDC) data into a streaming Delta Lake pipeline. Does Delta Lake have any options for supporting this type of feed? The short answer is *yes*. To get around to the longer answer, let's first make sure we're on level terms of understanding.

By this point, we have worked through quite a few examples of using Delta Lake, and we've seen that we basically have just three major operations for any particular row of data: inserting a record, updating a record, or deleting a record. This is similar to pretty much any other data system. So then where exactly does CDC come into play?

As defined by Joe Reis and Matt Housley in *Fundamentals of Data Engineering*, "Change data capture (CDC) is a method for extracting each change event (insert, update, delete) that occurs in a database. CDC is frequently leveraged to replicate between databases in near real time or create an event stream for downstream processing." Or as they put it more succinctly, CDC "is the process of ingesting changes from a source database system."[7]

Bringing this back around to our initial inquiry, tracking changes is supported in Delta Lake via a feature called Change Data Feed (CDF) (*https://oreil.ly/dJeON*). What CDF does is to let you track the changes to a Delta Lake table. Once it is enabled, you get all the changes to the table as they occur. Updates, merges, and deletes will

---

7 Joe Reis and Matt Housley, *Fundamentals of Data Engineering: Plan and Build Robust Data Systems* (O'Reilly), 163, 256.

be put into a new _change_data_ folder, while append operations already have their own entries in the table history, so they don't require additional files. Through this tracking, we can read the combined operations as a feed of changes from the table to use downstream. The changes will have the required row data with some additional metadata showing the change type.

 CDF is available in Delta Lake 2.0.0 and above. Levels of support for using CDF on tables with column mapping vary by the version you are using:

- Versions ≤ 2.0 do not support streaming or batch reads for CDF on tables that have column mapping enabled.

- For version 2.1, only batch reads are supported for tables with column mapping enabled. It also requires that there are no nonadditive schema changes (no renaming or reordering).

- For version 2.2, both batch and streaming reads are supported for CDF from tables with column mapping enabled as long as there still are no nonadditive schema changes.

- For versions ≥ 2.3, batch reads for CDF for tables with column mapping enabled can now support nonadditive schema changes. CDF uses the schema of the ending version used in the query rather than the latest version of the table available. You can still encounter failures in cases in which the version range specified spans a nonadditive schema change.

Using Change Data Feed

While ultimately it is up to you whether or not to leverage the CDF feature in building out a data pipeline, there are some common use cases in which you can make good use of it to simplify or rethink the way you are handling some processing tasks. Here are a few examples of the way you might think about leveraging CDF:

Curating downstream tables
> You can improve the performance of downstream Delta Lake tables by processing only row-level changes following initial operations to the source table to simplify ETL (extract, transform, load) and ELT (extract, load, transform) operations, because CDF provides a reduction in logical complexity. This happens because you will already know how a record is being changed before checking against its current state.

Propagating changes

You can send a change data feed to downstream systems such as another streaming sink like Kafka or to some other RDBMS that can use it to incrementally process in later stages of data pipelines.

Creating an audit trail

You could also capture the change data feed as a Delta table. This could provide perpetual storage and efficient query capability to see all changes over time, including when deletes occur and what updates were made. This could be useful for tracking changes across reference tables over time or for security auditing of sensitive data.

We should also note that using CDF may not necessarily add any additional storage. Once it is enabled, what we actually find is that there is no significant impact on processing overhead. The size of change records is pretty small; in most cases their size is much less than that of actual data files written during change operations This means there's very little performance implication for enabling the feature.

Change data for operations is located in the *_change_data* folder under the Delta table directory, similar to the transaction log. Operations like appending files or deleting whole partitions are much simpler than other types of changes. When the changes are of this simpler type, Delta Lake detects that it can efficiently compute the change data feed directly from the transaction log, and thus these records can be skipped altogether in the folder. Since these are often among the most common operations, this capacity strongly aids in reducing overhead.

> Since the *_change_data* folder is not part of the current version of table data, the files in the folder follow the retention policy of the table. This means it is subject to removal during vacuum operations, just like other transaction log files that fall outside the retention policy.

Enabling the change data feed

On the whole, there's not much you need to do as far as configuring CDF for Delta Lake. The gist of it really is to just turn it on, but how you do this will differ slightly depending on whether you are creating a new table or you are implementing the feature for an existing one.

For a new table, simply set the table property `delta.enableChangeDataFeed` to `true` within the `CREATE TABLE` command:

```sql
-- SQL
CREATE TABLE student (id INT, name STRING, age INT)
TBLPROPERTIES (delta.enableChangeDataFeed = true)
```

For an existing table, you can instead alter the table properties with the `ALTER TABLE` command to set `delta.enableChangeDataFeed` to `true`:

```sql
-- SQL
ALTER TABLE myDeltaTable SET TBLPROPERTIES (delta.enableChangeDataFeed = true)
```

If you are using Apache Spark, you can set this as the default behavior for the SparkSession object by setting `spark.databricks.delta.properties.defaults.enableChangeDataFeed` to `true`.

Reading the changes feed

Reading the change feed is similar to most read operations with Delta Lake. The key difference is that we need to specify in the read that we want to change the feed itself rather than just the data as it is by setting `readChangeFeed` to `true`. Otherwise, the syntax looks pretty similar to setting options for time travel or typical streaming reads. The behavior between reading the change feed as a batch operation and reading it as a stream processing operation differs, so we'll consider each in turn. We won't actually use it in our examples, but rate limiting with `maxFilesPerTrigger` or `maxBytesPerTrigger` can be applied to versions other than the initial snapshot version. When that is used, either the entire commit version being read will be rate-limited as expected or the entire commit will be returned when below the threshold.

Specifying boundaries for batch processes. Since batch operations are a bounded process, we need to tell Delta Lake what bounds we want to use to read the change feed. You can provide either version numbers or timestamp strings to set both the starting and ending boundaries. The boundaries you set will be inclusive in the queries—that is, if the final timestamp or version number exactly matches a commit, then the changes from that commit will be included in the change feed. If you want to read the changes from any particular point all the way up to the latest available changes, then only specify the starting version or timestamp.

When setting boundary points, you need to use either an integer to specify a version or a string in the format `yyyy-MM-dd[ HH:mm:ss[.SSS]]` for timestamps in a similar way to how we set time travel options. An error will be thrown letting you know that the change data feed was not enabled if a timestamp or version you give is lower or older than any that precedes when the change data feed was enabled:

```python
# Python
# version as ints or longs
(spark.read.format("delta")
  .option("readChangeFeed", "true")
  .option("startingVersion", 0)
  .option("endingVersion", 10)
  .table("myDeltaTable")
)
```

```
# timestamps as formatted timestamp
(spark.read.format("delta")
  .option("readChangeFeed", "true")
  .option("startingTimestamp", '2023-04-01 05:45:46')
  .option("endingTimestamp", '2023-04-21 12:00:00')
  .table("myDeltaTable")
)

# providing only the startingVersion/timestamp
(spark.read.format("delta")
  .option("readChangeFeed", "true")
  .option("startingTimestamp", '2023-04-21 12:00:00.001')
  .table("myDeltaTable")
)

# similar for a file location
(spark.read.format("delta")
  .option("readChangeFeed", "true")
  .option("startingTimestamp", '2021-04-21 05:45:46')
  .load("/pathToMyDeltaTable")
)
```

Specifying boundaries for streaming processes.   If we want to use a readStream on the change feed for a table, we can still set a startingVersion or startingTimestamp, but they are more optional than they are in the batch case—if the options are not provided, the stream returns the latest snapshot of the table at the time of streaming as an INSERT and then all future changes as change data.

Another difference for streaming is that we won't configure an ending position, since a stream is unbounded and so does not have an ending boundary. Options like rate limits (maxFilesPerTrigger, maxBytesPerTrigger) and excludeRegex are also supported when reading change data, so we otherwise proceed as we would normally:

```
# Python
# providing a starting version
(spark.readStream.format("delta")
  .option("readChangeFeed", "true")
  .option("startingVersion", 0)
  .load("/pathToMyDeltaTable")
)

# providing a starting timestamp
(spark.readStream.format("delta")
  .option("readChangeFeed", "true")
  .option("startingTimestamp", "2021-04-21 05:35:43")
  .load("/pathToMyDeltaTable")
)

# not providing either
(spark.readStream.format("delta")
  .option("readChangeFeed", "true")
```

```
    .load("/pathToMyDeltaTable")
)
```

 If the specified starting version or timestamp is beyond the latest found in the table, then you will get an error: `timestampGreater ThanLatestCommit`. You can avoid this error, which would mean choosing to receive an empty result set instead, by setting this option:

```
-- SQL
set
delta.changeDataFeed.timestampOutOfRange.enabled
=true;
```

If the starting version or timestamp value is in range of what is found in the table but an ending version or timestamp is out of bounds, you will see, with this feature enabled, that all available versions falling within the specified range will be returned.

Schema

At this point, you might wonder exactly how the data we are receiving in a change feed looks as it comes across. We get all the same columns in your data as before. This makes sense, because otherwise it wouldn't match up with the schema of the table. We do, however, get some additional columns so we can understand things like the change type taking place. We get these three new columns in the data when we read it as a change feed:

Change type
> The `_change_type` column is a string type column that, for each row, will identify whether the change taking place is an `insert`, an `update_preimage`, an `update_postimage`, or a `delete` operation. In this case, the preimage is the matched value before the update, and the postimage is the matched value after the update.

Commit version
> The `_commit_version` column is a long integer type column noting the Delta Lake file/table version from the transaction log that the change belongs to. When reading the change feed as a batch process, it will be at or in between the boundaries defined for the query. When read as a stream, it will be at or greater than the starting version and will continue to increase over time.

Commit timestamp
> The `_commit_timestamp` column is a timestamp type column (formatted as `yyyy-MM-dd[ HH:mm:ss[.SSS]]`) noting the time at which the version in `_commit_version` was created and committed to the log.

As an example, suppose there was a (fictional) discrepancy in the People 10 M dataset (*https://oreil.ly/XPFuO*) because the details actually belonged to a relative. We can update the errant record, and when we view the change feed, we will see the original record values denoted as the preimage and the updated values denoted as the postimage. We'll update the set on the mistakenly input name and correct the name and gender of the individual. Afterward, we'll view a subset of the table highlighting the before and after change feed records to see what it looks like. We can also note that it captures both the version and the timestamp from the commit at the same time:

```sql
-- SQL
UPDATE
people10m
SET
gender = 'F',
firstName='Leah'
WHERE
firstName='Leo'
and lastName='Conkay';
```

```python
# Python
(
  spark
  .read.format("delta")
  .option("readChangeFeed", "true")
  .option("startingVersion", 5)
  .option("endingVersion", 5)
  .table("tristen.people10m")
  .select(
    col("firstName"),
    col("lastName"),
    col("gender"),
    col("_change_type"),
    col("_commit_version"))
  ).show()
```

```
+---------+--------+------+----------------+---------------+-------------------+
|firstName|lastName|gender|    _change_type|_commit_version|   _commit_timestamp|
+---------+--------+------+----------------+---------------+-------------------+
|      Leo|  Conkay|     M|  update_preimage|              5|2023-04-05 13:14:40|
|     Leah|  Conkay|     F| update_postimage|              5|2023-04-05 13:14:40|
+---------+--------+------+----------------+---------------+-------------------+
```

Conclusion

In this chapter we have built upon many of the concepts covered in previous chapters and seen how they can be applied across several different kinds of uses. We explored several fundamental concepts used in stream data processing and how they come into play with Delta Lake. We indirectly saw how the core streaming functionality (particularly in Spark) is simplified with the use of a unified API due to the similarity in how it is used. Then we explored some different options for providing more direct control over the behavior of streaming reads and writes with Delta Lake. We followed this by looking a bit at some areas that are closely related to stream processing with Apache Spark or Databricks but are built on top of Delta Lake. We finished by reviewing the Change Data Feed functionality available in Delta Lake and how we can use it in streaming or nonstreaming applications. We hope this helps to answer many of the questions or curiosities you might have had about this area of using Delta Lake. Next, we're going to explore some of the other more advanced features available in Delta Lake.

Advanced Features

In this chapter the focus is a bit less on how to interact with and use Delta Lake tables than you may have found in other chapters. Instead, the main focus here is a handful of advanced features that you'll find useful. At heart, these Delta Lake features have more to do with metadata than anything else. The first thing we'll look at is how you can use generated columns as part of table definitions to reduce the amount of insertion or transformation work required for data loading operations. After that, we'll look at how Delta Lake metadata helps drive higher data quality standards and provides richer information to users through constraints and comments. Last, we'll share some insight into how deletion vectors can speed up many operations against applicable tables. Each of these features shows how the power of Delta Lake is enhanced through well-thought-out uses of table metadata and the transaction log.

Generated Columns, Keys, and IDs

One of Delta Lake's lesser-utilized features is the ability to use generated columns in Spark to create column values dynamically. Put simply, generated columns allow you to add simple statements to a table definition that will create the values of a column when applied, rather than relying on the insertion of values for those columns as new data is inserted into the table. The use of these can vary, from identity columns to new columns that perform simple conversions of input columns.

 All the examples and some other supporting code for this chapter can be found in the GitHub repository for the book (*https://oreil.ly/ 2m8Kv*).

You can include two types of generation expressions in a table definition that allow you to control whether values will always be generated or are generated by default. Columns that are always generated cannot be overwritten, whereas you can specify values during insertion operations for columns that are generated by default. Usually, the choice is to always generate columns because that option is simpler, but you may have cases in which you wish to explicitly be able to override a generated value with a specific value. For example, suppose you want to set a transaction at the beginning of each month to increment the beginning values of keys to the next thousand or million; you would then use generate by default so you could manually set that initial monthly transaction. Regardless, if you want to generate columns, you need to add the generation expression in your original table definition. In the following example, you can apply a Spark SQL function to an incoming date column to extract the year as a column. This can also be done to typecast columns or even to create more complex data structures such as structs out of incoming columns:

```sql
-- SQL
CREATE TABLE if not exists summary_cases(
    state STRING,
    fips INT,
    cases INT,
    deaths INT,
    county STRING,
    year INT GENERATED ALWAYS AS (YEAR(date))
    )
USING DELTA
```

One of the most common applications of generated columns is to create identity or surrogate key columns.[1] In the past you've been able to do this with other methods, such as leveraging external libraries to create UUIDs or using hashing methods to create unique keys. Delta Lake offers some advantages over these methods. By baking the ability to generate columns into the foundation of the format, you can avoid running into issues that stem from the nondeterminism of many of these previous methods and get simpler ID columns that are more human-readable than the results of the hashing methods.

Defining identity columns is just a slight extension of the generation expressions, except that there is no required SQL statement to perform some transformation. Instead, using the IDENTITY keyword triggers some actions behind the scenes that make this work. What you get is, in essence, a bit of automated tracking that maintains the incremental nature of the identity column(s):

---

1 If you'd like to further explore the use of various kinds of key-based relationships, we recommend *Learning SQL*, 3rd ed., by Alan Beaulieu (O'Reilly), *Deciphering Data Architectures* by James Serra (O'Reilly), and *Data Management at Scale*, 2nd ed., by Piethein Strengholt (O'Reilly).

```
-- SQL
id BIGINT GENERATED BY DEFAULT AS IDENTITY
```

```
-- SQL
id BIGINT GENERATED ALWAYS AS IDENTITY
```

These identity columns serve as surrogate keys that can be leveraged throughout your downstream applications to create primary and foreign key relationships, or potentially even for slowly changing dimension (SCD) types of tables. It's relevant to note that Databricks has a feature to make these primary and foreign key relationships enforceable via Unity Catalog.[2]

At an implementation level, there are a few secrets to the recipe to be learned from the Delta Lake protocol definitions for identity columns (*https://oreil.ly/ejOWG*). The main takeaway is that whenever overwriting values is disallowed, a simple monotonic function generates the values for the column. This means you can also feel assured that the generation of values is an efficient operation, as it primarily relies on table metadata and simple integer mathematics.[3]

There are a couple of things under the covers that you will want to be aware of. First, when columns are generated using ALWAYS, there is a constraint applied to the table (you will find more information on constraints later in this chapter). This means that attempting to provide values for generated columns during insertion operations will yield an error for your transaction. Second, using generated columns poses some limitations on usage; for example, you cannot partition a table by a generated identity column, and concurrent transactions are disallowed. Last, for identity columns specifically, you must use the BIGINT type, whereas with other generated columns the type definition is more flexible, depending on your actual application.

Comments and Constraints

Delta Lake metadata helps to describe and/or provide you with more granular information about the table than would otherwise be available. Here the focus is on two specific components of the table metadata, *comments* and *constraints*, with each used distinctly. The creators and maintainers of tables commonly use the first kind, namely table comments. You can use these to provide richer context to column or table data. Savvy users, consumers of the data, may be able to gain a lot of additional information or save a lot of time by not having to reverse-engineer features. The second kind of metadata is more operational. Constraints are overall less common

---

2 See the Databricks documentation (*https://oreil.ly/GiV3i*) for usage examples and additional details.

3 For an extended discussion of the benefits and use of surrogate keys, see the blog post "Identity Columns to Generate Surrogate Keys Are Now Available in a Lakehouse Near You!" (*https://oreil.ly/AyiOG*) by Franco Patano.

in many applications, but they can play a huge role in improving the quality of data tables and detecting aberrations earlier than other methods.

 Tags are map objects that contain additional metadata about transactional operations. They are an optional field in add or remove files, deletion vector files, and CDC files. When using the checkpoint V2 space, both the checkpoint and the associated sidecar files can also have tags. Note that remove actions in the checkpoint are tombstones used only by VACUUM and do not contain the stats field or the tags field. These are mostly intended for use at the implementation level to support or add new features to a particular Delta Lake implementation. A common use of tags is to annotate table properties in different processing engines. These are not explored in depth here, as most users will not use them, but we want to mention them, as they are distinctly different from the tags used in catalogs.

Comments

Comments should be used often and well. There are many kinds of comments you might wish to include for different kinds of informational purposes. They can convey important information about ownership or column design information. Possibilities for types of constructive comments might include:

Instructive
> Sometimes when creating different datasets, we make decisions about the layout that may not be transparent to end users. If a table does not have a unique key column but requires a combination of multiple columns to have a unique key, we might wish to capture in the comments for those columns which columns they can be combined with to have a unique key.

Explanatory
> In some cases, it might be useful to annotate the origin of data residing in a column, its security classification level, its intended users, or information about the derivation of calculated fields. Denoting the data origin is even more valuable when Delta Lake is used outside of environments that automatically capture lineage information. All of these provide enriched information to consumers on demand and can increase the delivered value of data products. This can be particularly useful in cases in which a table includes nonstandard key performance indicators (KPIs) with a reference to design documentation.

What you include in the comments is ultimately up to you and your organization. We recommend that you come up with a standard definition for usage and stick with it, as the many benefits that may potentially be gained from the additional information can greatly improve the experience.

We highly recommend the use of a catalog, such as Unity Catalog (*https://oreil.ly/21G-5*), that also supports table-level comments (and ideally tags) as well as additional features like lineage. Downstream consumers of a table, especially when accessing the table from multiple systems, might benefit from information about its maintainers or a point of contact, in case any issues arise with a means of contacting them (such as an email address). In many cases, information captured in table comments may also be beneficial if replicated to this table level for convenience.

Here is a quick example showing how you can easily add columns to a table at the time of creation. This allows you to provide clarifying or explanatory quick notes for all columns in the table at the same time; all you need to do is include the comments as part of the table schema definition:

```
-- SQL
CREATE TABLE example_table (
  id INT COMMENT 'uid column',
  content STRING COMMENT 'payload column for text'
)
USING delta
```

Sometimes your initial comments may not be as clear to table consumers as intended. In those cases, you can update individual column comments to refine them. This also gives you the flexibility you might need to include additional information not available at the time of table creation:

```
-- SQL
ALTER TABLE example_table
ALTER COLUMN id
COMMENT 'unique id column'
```

One last area that can be rather useful in many cases is adding transactional comments to table changes. You can set this option during individual operations as part of the table options when using the Python API, set it for a session in SQL and reuse it until you are done with those updates, or change it as many times as needed throughout the session.

When using the Python API as a table option, you just want to set the `userMetadata` option with your custom metadata:

```
# Python
(spark
 .read
 .table(<source>)
 .write
 .format("delta")
 .option("path", <destination>)
 .option("userMetadata", "custom commit metadata for the creation operation")
```

```
    .save()
    )
```

In SQL the same option is set, but as mentioned, it will happen at a session level. This means you will need to remember to update it if you do not want the message to continue:

```
-- SQL
SET spark.databricks.delta.commitInfo.userMetadata='comment here'
```

You might find this useful, for example, when you are running multiple deletes and updates or other operations and want to denote that they all belong to the same set of actions. You can reset the userMetadata to NULL if you want to return to the default behavior.

Delta Table Constraints

Delta Lake table metadata can be used for more than just providing additional information about the table. In some cases, metadata can also create additional actions that help to provide safeguards and guarantees for your data assets in Delta Lake. You've already seen this with table versions stored in the metadata (Chapter 3) and how they allow for time travel views of the table to see prior versions without necessarily trying to roll back operations. Another kind of action-inducing metadata is when you include constraints on a table.[4]

> Tables using writer version 7 and above need to have the feature name checkConstraints in the writerFeatures. Versions 3–6, however, always support CHECK constraints.

CHECK constraints are stored in your table metadata just like userMetadata and column comments. They are stored as key-value pair objects. You can see the value of any constraint for a particular table by name under the attribute delta .constraints.<name>. The value is stored as a SQL expression that will return a Boolean value. Because of this expression's nature, the columns specified in the expression must exist in the table. All rows in the table must satisfy the constraint expression by returning true when expressions are evaluated.

When you add a constraint to a table, it will check the existing table data to make sure it is compliant. In cases where it is not, the ALTER TABLE execution will fail. Similarly, when writing data to the table after a constraint has been added, every row

---

4 For an extended overview, we suggest Matt Powers's blog post on constraints for Delta Lake (*https://oreil.ly/ ZUm78*).

must satisfy the constraint expression or the write operation will fail. This can help you avoid writing malformed or noncompliant data to your table.

One of the most common uses of this feature is just adding a NOT NULL argument to guarantee that certain columns always get populated.[5]

To do this during table creation, you can include it as part of the column arguments, similar to and alongside column comments:

```
-- SQL
CREATE TABLE IF NOT EXISTS example_table (
  id INT COMMENT 'uid column' NOT NULL,
  content STRING COMMENT 'payload column for text'
)
USING delta
```

It's important to note here that only CHECK constraints added via ALTER TABLE commands will be represented in the table metadata, but you can feel assured that the null constraints set at creation will also be effective. Setting constraints via ALTER TABLE is also relatively straightforward. Consider the following example you could use to ensure you have nonnegative ID column values:

```
-- SQL
ALTER TABLE example_table
ADD CONSTRAINT id CHECK (id > 0)
```

Whichever way you choose to set various constraints, they are an effective way to increase data quality and enhance confidence in your data platform.

Deletion Vectors

Sometimes we can look at a problem and think of different ways to solve it. A feature in Delta Lake called *deletion vectors* is a great example of this idea. Chapter 10 provides a look at several ways you can optimize for either the table readers or the table writers for performance and the trade-offs you might need to make in that process. While deletion vectors certainly have a place in that discussion, they also deserve treatment and investigation as one of the advanced features in Delta Lake, so they are referenced here instead. The reason for this is that the way they work introduces a new concept that deserves a bit of explanation. Another reason is that the term *deletion vector* defines more the form and function of what the process does rather than how it helps you as a feature. One of the key benefits is that it gives you the ability to do a Merge-on-Read (MoR) operation. It dramatically reduces the

---

5 For an explanation of the relationship between constraints and nullability in Spark, as well as additional examples, see Matt Powers's blog post (*https://oreil.ly/ZUm78*).

performance impact of doing simple delete operations and instead postpones those operations to run as a batch at a more convenient time in the future.

Merge-on-Read

What does *Merge-on-Read* mean? It means that, rather than going through the operation of rewriting a file at the time of deleting a record or set of records from a particular file, you instead make some kind of a note that the record or records are deleted. Thus you get to postpone the performance impact of actually performing the delete operation until a later time. Usually you will do this when you can run an `OPTIMIZE` operation or a more complicated `UPDATE` statement. With columnar files (Parquet, Delta, Iceberg, etc.), row-level deletions invoke relatively expensive rewrite operations of entire files containing those rows. Of course, if someone were to read the table after a Merge-on-Read operation has been initiated, then it will merge during that read operation. That's kind of the point, because it allows us to minimize the performance impact of performing a simple delete operation and to just perform it at a later time, when you are already filtering on the same set of files while reading them. For other cases, you can then avoid the deletions in situations where you don't need them to happen straight away. This further allows you to push multiple (or many) deletes into a single large batch later.

Deletion vectors are a way to get this kind of Merge-on-Read behavior.[6] Put simply, deletion vectors are just a file (or multiple files) adjacent to a data file that allows you to know which records are to be deleted out of the data file and to save the delete (rewrite) operation for a later point in time that is more efficient and convenient. *Adjacent* in this case is relative: deletion vector files are part of the larger set of files that make up a Delta Lake table, but in partitioned tables you will notice that the deletion vector files sit at the top directory level rather than within the partition directories. You can observe this in the coming examples.

 We might call a deletion vector file a *sidecar* file since it is a file that sits alongside the other files in a table. In Delta Lake, however, we would want to distinguish this from sidecar files (*https://oreil.ly/0Ylh5*) that are a formal component of the V2 checkpoint specification and that specify add or remove file operations.

For most cases in which performance is being optimized for the Delta Lake writer operations, deletion vectors present a unique opportunity to reduce latency in the write operations, as their use avoids cases of rewriting files where otherwise there is no data change. This does come at a small cost of an additional filtering operation

---

6 There's an excellent blog post by Nick Karpov (*https://oreil.ly/Tzf2M*) exploring deletion vectors in great detail.

during subsequent read operations, but overall the performance impact is not very large.

To read a table with deletion vectors, you must use a client with at least reader version 3. This presents an area for potential conflicts. If you have an environment using older clients with lower reader versions, this could make tables inaccessible from those environments. Writing merely requires writer version 7. For example, in Databricks you need to use a Databricks Runtime (DBR) version of 14 or higher to write deletion vectors, but you only need to be on DBR version 12.1 or higher to be able to read them. Deletion vectors will work only when they are enabled via the enableDeletionVectors table property.

Setting the property is a simple ALTER TABLE command:

```
-- SQL
ALTER TABLE tblName
SET TBLPROPERTIES ('delta.enableDeletionVectors' = true);
```

Stepping Through Deletion Vectors

In this section we present an extended example to highlight the file-level changes that occur while using deletion vectors. You will see the familiar covid_nyt dataset used throughout the book, but with the size reduced and partitioned in such a way as to highlight deletion vector behavior specifically. As a bit of a roadmap to guide you, we'll show you these steps:

1. Create a table and identify some specific values to delete.

2. Enable deletion vectors.

3. Apply deletion operations against the table and inspect the file structure after each operation.

This example should help you to understand the nature of how the deletion vectors are operating. It's worth mentioning here that the original table creation does not need to occur in an environment that supports deletion vectors, but once the feature is enabled, read and write operations will be subject to the aforementioned version constraints.

First, create the reduced-size table; this makes it easier to view all the files simultaneously:

```
# Python
from pyspark.sql.functions import col
(
spark
 .read
 .load("rs/data/COVID-19_NYT/")
 .filter(col("state")=="Florida")
```

```
  .filter(
col("county").isin(
['Hillsborough', 'Pasco', 'Pinellas', 'Sarasota']
))
  .repartition("county")
  .write
  .format("delta")
  .partitionBy("county")
  .option("path", "nyt_covid_19/")
  .save()
  )

(
spark
.read
.load("nyt_covid_19/")
.write
.mode("overwrite")
.format("delta")
.saveAsTable("nyt")
)
```

Next, identify a single record from the table as a deletion target (for partition-level delete operations, you will be able to use any partition value):

```
# Python
spark.sql("""
select
  date,
  county,
  state,
  count(1) as rec_count
from
  nyt
where
  county="Pinellas"
and
  date="2020-03-11"
group by
  date,
  county,
  state
order by
  date
""").show()

date          county     state       rec_count
2020-03-11    Pinellas   Florida     1
```

Now enable deletion vectors on the table:

```python
# Python
spark.sql("
ALTER TABLE nyt SET TBLPROPERTIES ('delta.enableDeletionVectors' = true);
")
```

Using `tree` or a file browser, verify the table structure before making any further changes. Since the table data was partitioned by county, you will see four resulting partition directories. Also, when the deletion vector operation was enabled, it incremented the table version and added a transaction to the *_delta_log* subdirectory. This allows for traceability across table transactions, which is useful if something downstream is not working right later:

```bash
# BASH
!tree spark-warehouse/nyt/
spark-warehouse/nyt/
├── county=Hillsborough
│   └── part-00000-6cf1fac7-1237-48b5-a7ca-ce824054a997.c000.snappy.parquet
├── county=Pasco
│   └── part-00003-dc22f540-c7f7-449c-8dc1-816f0f357075.c000.snappy.parquet
├── county=Pinellas
│   └── part-00001-42060e31-83e8-48d2-9174-02325ca5e686.c000.snappy.parquet
├── county=Sarasota
│   └── part-00002-dfb35d92-25bc-4caf-8aa0-1228143444a7.c000.snappy.parquet
└── _delta_log
    ├── 00000000000000000000.json
    └── 00000000000000000001.json
```

Apply a single deletion against the previously identified record:[7]

```python
# Python
spark.sql("""
delete from
  nyt
where
  county='Pinellas'
and
  date='2020-03-11'
""").show()
```

---

7 Adding the `show` command at the end of the delete operations yields the number of affected rows in your output; otherwise you don't see this until checking the transaction log.

Check the results, and notice that all the original files still exist in the table. The only addition is a new file outside of the partition directories at the top level of the table. This is the deletion vector file from the delete operation:

```
# BASH
!tree spark-warehouse/nyt/
spark-warehouse/nyt/
├── county=Hillsborough
│   └── part-00000-6cf1fac7-1237-48b5-a7ca-ce824054a997.c000.snappy.parquet
├── county=Pasco
│   └── part-00003-dc22f540-c7f7-449c-8dc1-816f0f357075.c000.snappy.parquet
├── county=Pinellas
│   └── part-00001-42060e31-83e8-48d2-9174-02325ca5e686.c000.snappy.parquet
├── county=Sarasota
│   └── part-00002-dfb35d92-25bc-4caf-8aa0-1228143444a7.c000.snappy.parquet
├── deletion_vector_7de8988e-d96d-447c-9f99-1428e354907a.bin
└── _delta_log
    ├── 00000000000000000000.json
    ├── 00000000000000000001.json
    └── 00000000000000000002.json
```

Now apply two more deletion operations—one that aligns to a partition, and another that traverses multiple partitions:

```python
# Python
spark.sql("""
delete
from
  nyt
where
  county='Pasco' # This is an entire partition
""").show()

spark.sql("""
delete
from
  nyt
where
  date='2020-03-13'# This has records in multiple partitions
""").show()
```

Inspect the files again. Notice that only one new deletion vector appears in this case:

```
# BASH
!tree spark-warehouse/nyt/
spark-warehouse/nyt/
├── county=Hillsborough
│   └── part-00000-6cf1fac7-1237-48b5-a7ca-ce824054a997.c000.snappy.parquet
├── county=Pasco
│   └── part-00003-dc22f540-c7f7-449c-8dc1-816f0f357075.c000.snappy.parquet
├── county=Pinellas
│   └── part-00001-42060e31-83e8-48d2-9174-02325ca5e686.c000.snappy.parquet
├── county=Sarasota
```

```
|   └── part-00002-dfb35d92-25bc-4caf-8aa0-1228143444a7.c000.snappy.parquet
├── deletion_vector_7de8988e-d96d-447c-9f99-1428e354907a.bin
├── deletion_vector_eda97b62-a3df-4b8f-885d-68295f324c2d.bin
└── _delta_log
    ├── 00000000000000000000.json
    ├── 00000000000000000001.json
    ├── 00000000000000000002.json
    ├── 00000000000000000003.json
    └── 00000000000000000004.json
```

So what happened? The answer is rather straightforward and is partially revealed if you check the `operationMetrics` from the transaction log. It shows that in the first delete operation, you get `numDeletionVectorsAdded: "1"`, which corresponds to the number of records we deleted (`numDeletedRows: "1"`) because it lies within a single partition file. The third deletion operation instead shows `numDeletionVectorsAdded: "3"`, which also directly corresponds to `numDeletedRows: "3"` as before. However, two additional entries appear that you should note: `numDeletionVectorsRemoved: "1"` and `numDeletionVectorsUpdated: "1"`. Delta Lake is compacting the deletion vectors into a single file when they apply to the same partition. You might then ask: *Why didn't I get another file for the second delete operation?* Since the operation aligned with the boundaries of the entire partition, Delta Lake simply removed the file that appears in the transaction log as `numRemovedFiles: "1"`. The original deletion vector is now a stale file, and the byte-level information in the new deletion vector also contains the old information. The extra data file and the original deletion vector file still behave by normal retention rules, so until you run a vacuum operation, they remain alongside the active table files.

The schema of these deletion vectors themselves is relatively straightforward. A deletion vector will specify the application storage type, a path or inline specification, an offset when applicable (depending on the specified storage type), the size in bytes when applicable (also depending on the storage type), and the cardinality of the deletion operation. These specifications will also be present in the transaction log as part of later affected operations, like an `add` action taking place in the presence of a deletion vector. Since these operations are typically implemented at the engine level, there's no need to explore them further, but if you are curious and want additional details on the exact schema definition, check out the "Deletion Vector Descriptor Schema" section of the protocol document (*https://oreil.ly/dG9SJ*).

Conclusion

Delta Lake's advanced features such as generated columns, constraints, comments, and deletion vectors, while minimal to implement, can yield enormous impacts. These features enhance data quality, provide richer metadata, and optimize performance for deletion-related operations.

Generated columns allow for the dynamic creation of column values based on expressions, reducing data loading work. Constraints such as CHECK constraints enforce data quality rules and detect issues earlier. Comments enable the annotation of tables and columns with valuable context for users. Deletion vectors enable a Merge-on-Read approach, postponing the performance impact of deletes until a more convenient time, such as during reads or optimizations. Overall, these advanced Delta Lake metadata capabilities show how the power of Delta Lake is augmented through strategic uses of table metadata and the transaction log, delivering higher data quality standards and richer information to provide an enhanced experience for data consumers.

Architecting Your Lakehouse

Successful engineering initiatives begin with a clear vision and sense of purpose (what we are doing and why) as well as with a solid design and architecture (how we plan to achieve the vision). Combining a thoughtful plan with the right building blocks (tools, resources, and engineering capabilities) ensures that the final result reflects the mission and performs well at scale. Delta Lake provides key building blocks that enable us to design, construct, test, deploy, and maintain enterprise-grade data lakehouses.

Our goal for this chapter is not just to offer a collection of ideas, patterns, and best practices but to offer you a field guide. We've provided the right information, reasoning, and mental models so that the lessons learned here can coalesce into clear blueprints for architecting your own data lakehouse. Whether you are new to the concept of the lakehouse, unfamiliar with the medallion architecture for incremental data quality, or attempting your first foray into working with streaming data, we'll take this journey together.

What we'll learn:

- What the lakehouse architecture is
- Using Delta Lake as the foundation for implementing the lakehouse architecture
- The medallion architecture
- Streaming medallion architecture

The Lakehouse Architecture

If successful engineering initiatives begin with a clear vision and purpose, and our goal is ultimately to lay the foundation for our own data lakehouses, then we'll need to first define what a lakehouse is.

What Is a Lakehouse?

> *The lakehouse is an open data management architecture that combines the flexibility, cost efficiency, and scale of the data lake with the data management, schema enforcement, and ACID transactions of the traditional data warehouse.*
>
> —Databricks

There is a lot to unpack from this definition—namely, assumptions are being made that require some hands-on experience, or shared mental models, from both an engineering and a data management perspective. Specifically, the definition assumes a familiarity with data warehouses and data lakes, as well as with the trade-offs people must make when selecting one technology over another. The following section will cover the pros and cons of each choice and describe how the lakehouse came to be.

The history and myriad use cases shared across the data warehouse and data lake should be second nature for anyone who has previously worked in roles spanning the delivery and consumption spaces. For those of you who are just setting out on your data journey, are transitioning from data warehousing, or have only worked with data in a data lake, this section is also for you.

To understand where the lakehouse architecture evolved from, we'll need to be able to answer the following:

- If the lakehouse is a hybrid architecture combining the best of the data lake and the data warehouse, then mustn't it be better than the sum of its parts?
- Why does the flexibility, cost efficiency, and unbounded data scaling inspired by traditional data lakes matter for all of us today?
- Why do the benefits of the data lake only truly matter when coupled with the benefits of schema enforcement and evolution, ACID transactions, and proper data management, as inspired by traditional data warehouses?

Learning from Data Warehouses

The data warehouse emerged to fix the issue of data silos within large enterprises and to simplify business intelligence (BI) and analytical decision making. While the data warehouse exists as a centralized solution to solve structured data problems within a given data domain, physical limitations within the data warehouse architecture meant costs would increase proportionally to the size and scale of the data within the warehouse. These physical limitations were attributable to data being stored locally (nondistributed) in what is known as a vertically scaling architecture.

While cost is a limiting factor of large-scale data warehouses (due to vertical scaling), the benefits of running the data warehouse can outweigh the higher bills when compared to operating many independent data silos. Architected with safe data management, access policies, and the enforcement of rules and standards in mind, data warehouses are built for consistency first. This means a lot when considering the correctness of data, which now falls under its own umbrella of *data quality*. With the support of type-safe structured data and schema enforcement, the data warehouse is commonly utilized for foundational business intelligence and operational data systems that must provide consistent tables and clear data definitions.

On the data management front, support for access control through user- and role-based permissions (called *grants*) enable a secure and rule-based system to gate which users can execute reads (select), writes (insert), updates, and deletes of the data within the warehouse's subsequent tables and views.

Outside of cost, issues preventing the data warehouse architecture from scaling to meet the demands of today reside in a lack of flexibility supporting various kinds of workloads, including data science and machine learning.

Today, support for common machine learning and data science workflows—which require custom data types and formats supporting unstructured (images), semistructured (CSV, JSON), and fully structured data (Parquet/ORC), as well as the ability to easily read entire tables into memory using efficient file skipping, column pruning, and other data reduction techniques—is missing from traditional data warehouses. Rather than relying on the raw data required to train and test models, teams must actively query the warehouse to produce the correct input datasets, which can be tricky, especially when utilizing iterative algorithms due to multiple roundtrips if explicit cache points are skipped.

Learning from Data Lakes

The data lake emerged to store raw (unprocessed) data in a wide variety of formats (CSV, JSON, ORC, text, binary) within a distributed filesystem, the popular choice at the time being the Hadoop Distributed File System (HDFS). Utilizing commodity hardware, the data lake could be utilized to run distributed processing jobs (Map-Reduce) or be leveraged to act as a staging area for data to be loaded into the data warehouse. Today, many workloads still follow similar patterns, utilizing cloud-based object stores or other managed elastic storage and elastic compute to power data lakes. So how does this fit into the lakehouse story?

The data lake provides a solution for storing raw feeds of data (as files) that can be processed directly for data science and machine learning use cases, supporting data formats that are unavailable within the data warehouse. These feeds of data found another use through being transformed to *keep the data warehouse in sync* using the dual-tier data architecture, which is covered in the next section.

The benefits of the data lake are associated with its cost, which is comparatively low when weighed against data warehouse, as well as with its general support for file format flexibility.

The file format flexibility acts as a double-edged sword. What exists in one format today can just as easily shift tomorrow, as the data lake remains schema-less, allowing anything to be stored inside its filesystem.

On the upside, the separation of storage and compute means that costs remain low, requiring minimal overhead, until the point at which data will be called into action. Sadly, due to the schema-less nature of the data lake, things don't always go well when older datasets are pulled out of storage. Corrupt data is one of the big reasons why the data lake has also been given the name "data swamp."

Further distancing itself from the data warehouse, the data lake doesn't support transactions or operation-level isolation, and as a consequence it lacks support for multiple data producers or consumers sharing the same set of resources simultaneously. With respect to consistency, it is nearly impossible to achieve a consistent state between active readers and writers, or to support multiple access modes, something that is more common today with batch and streaming jobs operating on the same physical table.

Out of our understanding that a data lake *without rules* eventually leads to data instability, unusable data, and, in the worst examples, completely "polluted" or "toxic" data lakes, there emerged this radical idea: what if you could achieve the best of both worlds?

The Dual-Tier Data Architecture

The dual-tier architecture is the natural evolution in the relationship between the data lake and the data warehouse. Set into your mind an orchestration platform like Airflow: Airflow's popularity rests on the fact that it is difficult to manage consistency between the data lake and the data warehouse. What if we had a way to manage both?

Rather than having a single hop from the operational data system (siloed data) into the data warehouse (shared) or into the data lake, the dual-tier architecture relies on extract, transform, load (ETL) jobs to manage consistency, utilizing data from the data lake to populate the data warehouse. This is what is shown in Figure 9-1.

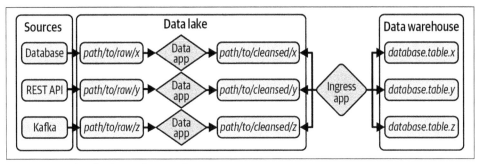

Figure 9-1. The dual-tier data architecture

The diagram shows the following flow:

1. Extract operational data from *siloed sources* for writing into landing zones (*/raw/**).

2. Read, clean, and transform the data from */raw* and write the changes to */cleansed*.

3. Read from */cleansed* (could do additional joining and normalizing with other data) before writing out to the data warehouse.

As long as the workflow completes, the data in the data lake will always be in sync with the warehouse. This pattern also enables support for unloading or reloading tables to save cost in the data warehouse. This makes sense in hindsight.

In order to support direct read access on the data, the data lake is required for supporting machine learning use cases, while the data warehouse is required to support the business and analytical processing. However, the added complexity inadvertently puts a greater burden on data engineers to manage multiple sources of truth as well as the cost of maintaining multiple copies of all the same data (one or more times in the data lake, and once in the data warehouse) and the headache of figuring out what data is stale, and where and why.

If you have ever played the game Two Truths and a Lie, this is the architectural equivalent, but rather than it being a fun game, the stakes are much higher; this is, after all, our precious operational data. Having two sources of truth by definition means that the systems can (and probably will) be out of sync, each telling its own version of the truth. This also means each source of truth is also lying. They just aren't aware.

So the question is still up in the air: what if you could achieve the best of both worlds and efficiently combine the data lake and the data warehouse? Well, that is where the data lakehouse was born.

Lakehouse Architecture

The lakehouse is a hybrid data architecture that combines the best of the data warehouse with the best of the data lake. Figure 9-2 provides a simple flow of concepts through the lens of what use cases can be attributed to each of the three data architectures: the data warehouse, the data lake, and the data lakehouse.

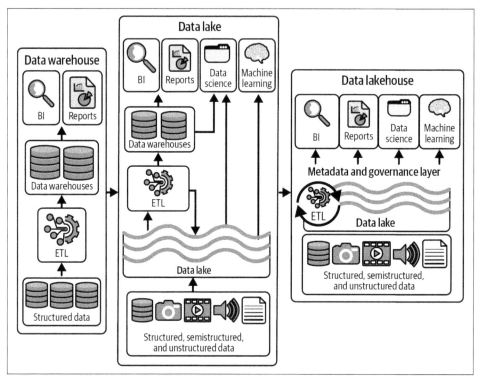

Figure 9-2. The data lakehouse provides a common interface for BI and reporting while ensuring that data science and machine learning workflows are supported in a single, unified way

This new architecture is enabled by marrying open standards in an opinionated overarching systems design—implementing data structures and data management features similar to those in a data warehouse directly on the kind of low-cost storage used for data lakes.

In fact, the lakehouse architecture intelligently provides the following:

- Transaction support
- Schema enforcement and governance/audit log and data integrity

- BI support through SQL and open interfaces such as JDBC
- Separation between storage and compute
- Open standards, open APIs, and open data formats
- End-to-end streaming
- Support for diverse workloads, from traditional SQL to deep learning

By merging the best of both worlds, we gain a single system that data teams can utilize to move faster, as they can utilize data for its explicit purpose without needing to access multiple systems (which always increases complexity). The dissolution of boundaries between the data warehouse and the data lake also makes it easier to utilize a single source of table truth. When compared against the dual-tier architecture, this is a huge win. This also prevents the problem of figuring out which side (warehouse or lake) has the correct data, who isn't in sync, and all the costly work involved to come up with a straight answer. The benefits also ensure teams have the most complete and up-to-date data available for data science, machine learning, and business analytics projects.

Foundations with Delta Lake

We just learned about the successful marriage of ideas resulting in the lakehouse, whose design isn't limited in the way of the data warehouse and which benefits from the high availability, near-boundless scalability, and cost-effective separation of storage and compute of the data lake.

This section will cover what we gain out of the box with Delta Lake and why it's the right tool to power the lakehouse.

Open Source on Open Standards in an Open Ecosystem

Architecting your lakehouse with Delta Lake comes with open standards and a commitment to an open ecosystem focused on open protocols, common sense, and standard conventions.

Open file format

Apache Parquet is the physical file format for the data stored in our Delta tables. Parquet, being widely supported within the big data community, has already proved its value with respect to speed and scalability, but it becomes difficult to maintain, as data naturally evolves over time. Parquet on its own doesn't provide schema validations or evolution, nor does it support column remapping.

The big difference that Delta brings to the table is consistency and column-level guarantees, enabling the underlying Parquet to survive schema transformations and subtle changes over time that would leave standard Parquet corrupted when processed as a contiguous collection of data over time.

Parquet is the standard file format for column-oriented analytical data. So rather than our having to implement an internal, proprietary table format and access protocol, the Delta protocol is freely available to be used by the community to build new tooling and connectors (which we looked at in Chapter 4) and can be used natively within many offerings provided by key cloud service vendors such as Amazon and Microsoft, as well as Starburst and Databricks.

Self-describing table metadata

The metadata for each Delta table is stored alongside the physical table data. This design eliminates the need to maintain a separate metastore, like the Hive Metastore, simply to describe a given table. The design decision enables static tables to be more efficiently copied and moved using standard filesystem tools, while also enabling the existence of metadata-only copies of tables, which can be explored using the SHALLOW CLONE command (*https://oreil.ly/yTc-g*).

Open table specification

Last, there is no fear of vendor lock-in; the entire Delta Lake project itself is provided freely to the entire open source community through the Linux Foundation and has a good community around it.

Delta Universal Format (UniForm)

UniForm is a Delta feature introduced in Delta Lake 3.0. It enables reading Delta tables in the format needed by an application even if that application requires Iceberg or Hudi formats. By committing to interoperability, we can continue to utilize our Delta tables in an ever-expanding data ecosystem with ease of mind.

UniForm automatically generates the metadata needed for Apache Iceberg or Apache Hudi, so we don't need to decide on a given lakehouse format up-front or do manual conversions between formats, which can be error-prone. With UniForm, Delta is the universal format that works across ecosystems, providing interoperability for the lakehouse.

Enabling Delta UniForm Iceberg requires the Delta table feature `IcebergCompatV2`, a write protocol feature. Only clients that support this table feature can write to enabled tables. You must use Delta Lake 3.1 or above to write to Delta tables with this feature enabled.

Enabling Delta UniForm Iceberg requires `delta-iceberg` to be provided to Spark shell:

```
-packages io.delta:io.delta:delta-iceberg_2.12:<version>
```

Enabling Delta UniForm Hudi requires `delta-hudi` to be provided to Spark shell:

```
-packages io.delta:io.delta:delta-hudi_2.12:<version>
```

You can enable Iceberg or Hudi support using the Delta table properties:

```
% 'delta.universalFormat.enabledFormats' = 'iceberg, hudi'
```

You can create a table with support for Iceberg and Hudi as follows:

```
% CREATE TABLE T(c1 INT) USING DELTA TBLPROPERTIES(
    'delta.universalFormat.enabledFormats' = 'iceberg, hudi');
```

Or to add support for Iceberg after table creation:

```
ALTER TABLE T SET TBLPROPERTIES(
    'delta.columnMapping.mode' = 'name',
    'delta.enableIcebergCompatV2' = 'true',
    'delta.universalFormat.enabledFormats' = 'iceberg');
```

UniForm works by asynchronously generating the metadata for our Iceberg or Hudi tables after each successful Delta transaction.

Transaction Support

Support for *transactions* is critical whenever data accuracy and sequential insertion order are important. Arguably this is required for nearly all production cases. *We should concern ourselves with achieving a minimally high bar at all times.* While transactions mean there are additional checks and balances, if, for example, there are multiple writers making changes to a table, there will always be the possibility of collisions. Understanding the behavior of the distributed Delta transaction protocol means we know exactly which write should win and how, and we can guarantee the insertion order of data to be exact for reads.

Serializable writes

Delta provides ACID guarantees for transactions while enabling multiple concurrent writers using a technique called *write serialization*. When new rows are simply being appended to the table, as with INSERT operations, the table metadata doesn't need to be read before a commit can occur. However, if the table is being modified in a more complex way—for example, if rows are being deleted or updated—then the table metadata will be read before the write operation can be committed. This process ensures that before any changes are committed, the changes don't collide, as that could potentially corrupt the true sequential insert and operation order on a Delta table. Rather than risking corruption, collisions result in a specific set of exceptions raised by the type of concurrent modification.

Snapshot isolation for reads

Processes reading a given Delta table are insulated from the complexities of multiple simultaneous writers and are guaranteed to read a consistent snapshot of the Delta table in exact serial order.

Support for incremental processing

Each table contains a single serial history of the atomic versions of the table, and for each version of the table the state is contained in a snapshot. This means that processes (jobs) reading from the Delta table at specific versions (points in time) can intuitively read only the specific changes between their local table snapshot and the current (latest) version of the table.

Incremental processing reduces the operational burden of maintaining a cursor (last offsets, IDs) or more complex state. Consider Example 9-1. We've probably seen a job like this in our careers, or can surmise that it is taking a starting timestamp and a set number of records to read, write, or maybe delete, and is also taking the last record identified of the last successful batch. The state management of traditional batch jobs can be tricky depending on the complexity of the job, due to the fact that we must maintain a manual checkpoint. Example 9-1 shows three variables that must be tracked: `startTime`, `recordsPerBatch`, and `lastRecordId`. The `startTime` variable in this example is intended to help create a time-based cursor in conjunction with the `lastRecordId`.

Example 9-1. Providing state to a stateless batch job

```
% ./run-some-batch-job.py \
    --startTime x \
    --recordsPerBatch 10000 \
    --lastRecordId z
```

With Delta Lake, we can ignore the `startTime` and `lastRecordId` and simply use the `startingVersion` of the transaction log. This provides a specific point for us to read from. Example 9-2 shows the modified job.

Example 9-2. Providing the Delta `startingVersion` to a stateless batch job

```
% ./run-some-batch-job.py --startingVersion 10 --recordsPerBatch 10000
```

While there may not be a clear "Aha!" moment with this example, the power of incremental processing with Delta is that there is a transaction log that informs us of all the changes that happened on a table since our last run.

Support for time travel

The biggest gain from transactions, aside from the ability to rewind and reset tables based on incorrect inserts, is the ability to harness this power (time travel) to do new things such as viewing the state of a given table at specific points in time in order to compare changes. This is a vantage point that few data engineers know they need, and a capability that can drastically reduce mean time to resolution (MTTR), thus minimizing data downtime, since each table has a history, and that history is very similar to Git history or Git blames for those familiar.

Schema Enforcement and Governance

Governance in the following context applies to the rules governing the structure of a given table definition (data definition language, or DDL); these rules manage the columns, column types, and descriptive metadata that make up a table. Schema enforcement pertains to the consequences of attempting to write invalid content into a table.

Delta Lake uses schema-on-write to achieve the high level of consistency required by the classic databases and supports the governance that people have come to rely on within database management systems (DBMS). For clarity, we'll cover the differences between schema-on-write and schema-on-read next.

Schema-on-write

Because Delta Lake supports schema-on-write and declarative schema evolution, the onus of being correct falls to the producers of the data for a given Delta Lake table. However, this doesn't mean that anything goes just because you wear the producer-of-the-data hat. Remember that data lakes only become data swamps due to a lack of governance. With Delta Lake, the initial successful transaction committed automatically sets the stage for identifying the table columns and types. With a governance hat on, we now must abide by the rules written into the transaction log. This may sound a little scary, but rest assured, it is for the betterment of the data ecosystem. With clear rules around schema enforcement and proper procedures in place to handle schema evolution, the rules governing how the structure of a table is modified ultimately protect the consumers of a given table from problematic surprises.

Consistent Data and Quality Expectations

In the real world, having invariants in place reduces the conversation about who broke what, when, and where. With Delta Lake, this means using the `mergeSchema` option infrequently and being very concerned if people want to use `overwriteSchema`. When you are using Delta Lake with some established ways of working, the Delta log will be your source of truth for arbitration, effectively removing useless meetings, since you can more or less automatically pinpoint root cause just by looking at the table history in the event that things do end up going off the rails—for example, we can take a look at the last 10 transactions using the `history` function from an instance of the `DeltaTable` class, like so: `DeltaTable.for Name(spark, …).history(10)`. The result provides us with the exact sequence of changes made to the table and is an invaluable resource for root cause analysis.

Schema-on-read

Data lakes use the schema-on-read approach because there is no consistent form of governance or metadata native to the data lake, which is essentially a glorified distributed filesystem. While *schema-on-read* is flexible, its flexibility is also why data lakes are categorized as being like the Wild West—ungoverned, chaotic, and, more often than not, problematic.

What this means is that when there is data in some location (directory root) with some filetype (JSON, CSV, binary, Parquet, text, or other), with the ability of files being written to a specific location to grow unbounded, there is a high potential for problems to grow as the dataset ages.

As a consumer of the data in the data lake at a specific location, you may be able to extract and parse the data, if you're lucky—it may even have some kind of documentation, if you're really lucky—and with enough lead time and compute, you can probably accomplish your job. Without proper governance and type safety, however, the data lake can quickly grow to multiple terabytes (or petabytes, if you love burning money), or essentially data garbage with a low cost of storage overhead. While this is an extreme statement, it is also a reality in many data organizations.

Separation between storage and compute

Delta Lake provides a clear separation between storage and compute. One of the biggest benefits of the data lake architecture is the flexibility of unbounded storage and filesystem scalability. The lakehouse architecture adopts the benefits of the data lake, since producing and consuming tons of data comes with the territory of modern data analytics and machine learning.

In theory, as long as you have strict governance in place around schema enforcement, conformance, and evolution—that comes with the invariants of schema-on-write—coupled with opinionated support for the underlying file format (Parquet), you gain near limitless scalability (within reason) for the data living in your data lakehouse, using a file format that is interoperable and extremely portable. The portability aspect can be broken down even further. You can take your Delta Lake tables (i.e., pack the whole lakehouse up and go) from one cloud to another cloud, while retaining the integrity of all your tables—including the transaction logs.

Separation Between Logical Action and Physical Reaction

It is worth pointing out that there is even more separation between logical action within Delta Lake and the resulting physical action on the underlying physical storage layer. Take the example of cleaning up our tables from Chapter 5; there is a separation between calling DELETE FROM on a given table and when the physical files are affected (actually deleted). This is due to the time travel capabilities (rewind/undo) that enable us to remove accidental deletes —deletes that can otherwise harm the data integrity with no chance of restoration. The accidental deletion of data has happened to everyone at one point or another in their career; it's just that not everyone admits to it! This is why the VACUUM and REORG operations are so valuable. To really delete files, an action with a physical reaction must occur.

Support for transactional streaming

We introduced Delta's streaming capabilities in Chapter 7. The ability to switch easily between batch and streaming, across transactional tables, regardless of the specific operation (inbound reads or outbound writes) with Delta, may initially sound magical. Many the streaming pipeline has met its unexpected end due to distributed files suddenly disappearing on source tables due to changes made to tables by outside forces (such as overwrite jobs to replace missing data), but with Delta there is complete support for multiversion concurrency control, which means a streaming application reading from a table won't be interrupted due to a concurrent writer's operation.[1]

Delta Lake supports full end-to-end streaming without sacrificing quality for speed. Everything has trade-offs, and it is easy to go fast and operate blindly. In the real world, it is better to weigh the cost of delay against the need for speed and come to a general agreement on what trade-offs the business or data team is willing to make to

---

1 This is true for common append-style writes to the table. Other operations such as overwriting a table or deleting the table can affect streaming applications.

achieve the correct balance. While we can't guarantee that everything will always go smoothly, the safeguards provided to us when using Delta Lake can help calm even the choppiest of waters.

Unified access for analytical and ML workloads

Rounding things out, Delta provides a balanced approach to a wide range of data-related solutions. Data analysts and BI engineers can easily query using simple SQL, while there is also simultaneous support for efficient and direct physical file access for the data encompassing the Delta Lake tables; the latter provides the correct operating model for data science and ML workloads, where direct access to all columnar data, including the ability to run iterative algorithms (in place) within the scope of a job, is required.

The Delta Sharing Protocol

Sharing data safely and reliably between internal and external stakeholders is one of the hardest problems after data modeling. It is common practice to see ETL jobs that export data out of the data lake—for example, from one S3 bucket to another. The reason for essentially using file transfer protocol (FTP) to send and receive data rests on missing standards for identity and access management (IAM) and interoperable data formats. The Delta Sharing Protocol solves this problem.

Figure 9-3 shows the Delta Sharing Protocol (*https://oreil.ly/mgFVx*). The physical Delta table exists as a single source of truth, and the introduction of the Delta Sharing server adds the missing access controls and governance required to provide a safe and reliable exchange of data.

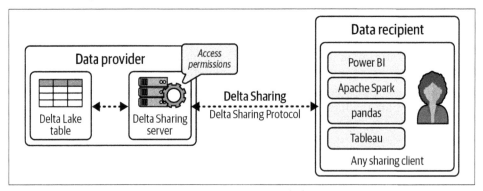

Figure 9-3. The Delta Sharing Protocol is the industry's first open protocol for secure data sharing, making it simple to share data with other organizations, regardless of which computing platforms they use

Using the Delta Sharing Protocol gives internal or external stakeholders secure direct access to Delta tables. This removes the operational costs incurred when exporting data, while saving time, money, and engineering sanity and providing a shared source of truth that is platform agnostic. We conclude this book with a deep dive into the Delta Sharing Protocol in Chapter 14.

The general capabilities provided by the Delta protocol support the foundational capabilities required by the data lakehouse. Now it is time for us to shift gears and look more specifically at architecting for data quality within the lakehouse using a purpose-driven, layered data architecture called the medallion architecture.

The Medallion Architecture

Data in flight is messy, as it arrives in all shapes and sizes and with varying degrees of accuracy and completeness. Accepting that data will not always adhere to the myriad end-user expectations, existing data contracts, and established data quality checks, or even arrive on time—or ever—is key to addressing these data quality problems. Such challenges place a high degree of pressure on data engineering teams to continuously deliver across a dynamic landscape of subjective and objective requirements, and born from this collective toil is the *medallion architecture*.

The medallion architecture is a data design pattern used to logically organize data in the lakehouse. This is accomplished using a series of isolated data layers to provide a framework for progressively refining datasets. Figure 9-4 shows a high-level view of the architecture, with data flowing from *batch* or *streaming* sources across a variable lineage—from the point of initial ingestion (bronze) across multiple processing and enhancement phases, or stages.

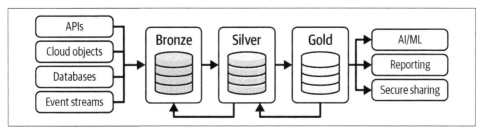

Figure 9-4. The medallion architecture is a procedural framework providing quality gates and tiers from the point of ingestion onward to the purpose-built curated data product

The medallion architecture provides a flexible framework for dealing with progressive enhancement of data in a structured way. It is worth pointing out that, while it is common to see three tiers (bronze, silver, gold), there is no rule stating that all use cases *require* three tiers. It may be that more mature data practitioners will have a two-tier system in which golden tables are joined with other golden tables to create even more golden tables. So the separation between silver and gold or between bronze and silver may be fuzzy at times. The key reason for having a three-tiered framework is that it enables you to have a place to recover, or fall back on, when things go wrong or when requirements change.

Exploring the Bronze Layer

The bronze layer represents the initial point for our data lineage within the lakehouse. A common practice here is to apply minimal transformations (if any) on the data. These are the transformations that can't be ignored, like converting the source format into a compatible type for writing to Delta Lake. Going with the minimal transformations approach means we leave open the option to reprocess this raw data to support additional use cases, or modified requirements in the future.[2]

The Bronze Layer Is for Minimal Augmentation

The bronze layer is commonly used to transform source data for writing into Delta Lake. When you take a minimal augmentation approach, it is also worth exploring ways to simplify and even automate this initial ingestion step. Using open data protocols that are interoperable with the DataFrame APIs—for example, by using a type-safe, binary, serializable exchange format such as Apache Avro or Google Protocol Buffers—means you can spend more time solving better problems than ingestion. For a small number of tables, it is arguable that you can ignore automation, but as the surface area increases, ignoring automation is simply bad for engineering mental health.

Minimal transformations and augmentation

Because we are ingesting data that is as close to "raw" as possible, we need to remember to maintain a limited schema and do as little to transform the data as possible. Let's use a concrete example: say we are reading data from a streaming source such as Kafka, and we want to capture the topic name, binary key, and value as well as the timestamp for each record and write them into a Delta Lake table. These properties all exist in the Kafka DataFrame structure (if we are using the KafkaSource APIs (*https://oreil.ly/14ftH*) with Spark) and can be extracted with the *kafka-delta-ingest* library (*https://oreil.ly/ivqMr*) (first explored in Chapter 4) as well.

Example 9-3 (*ch09/notebooks/medallion_bronze.ipynb*) is a concise example of minimal transformation and augmentation.

---

2 Remember that anything containing user data must be captured and processed according to the end-user agreed-upon consent and according to data governance bylaws and standards.

Example 9-3. This shows a simple bronze-style pipeline reading from Kafka, applying minimal transformations, and writing the data out to Delta

```
% reader_opts: Dict[str, str] = …
  writer_opts: Dict[str, str] = …
  bronze_layer_stream = (
    spark.readStream
    .options(**reader_opts)
    .format("kafka").load()
    .select(col("key"),col("value"),col("topic"),col("timestamp"))
    .withColumn("event_date", to_date(col("timestamp")))
    .writeStream
    .format('delta')
    .options(**writer_opts)
    .partitionBy("event_date")
)
streaming_query = bronze_layer.toTable(...)
```

The extreme minimal approach applied in Example 9-3 takes only the information needed to preserve the data as close to its raw form as possible. This technique puts the onus on the silver layer to extract and transform the data from the value column.

While we are creating a minor amount of additional work, this bare-bones approach enables the future ability to reprocess (reread) the raw data as it landed from Kafka without worrying about the data expiring (which can lead to data loss). Most data retention periods for delete in Kafka are between 24 hours and 7 days.

In cases in which we are reading from an external database, such as Postgres, the minimum schema is simply the table DDL. We already have explicit guarantees and row-wide expected behavior given the schema-on-write nature of the database, and thus we can simplify the work required in the silver layer when compared to the example shown in Example 9-3.

As a rule of thumb, if the data source has a *type-safe* schema (Avro, Protobuf), or the data source implements *schema-on-write*, then we will typically see a significant reduction in the work required in the bronze layer. This doesn't mean we can blindly write directly to silver either, since the bronze layer is the first guardian blocking unexpected or corrupt rows of data from its progression toward gold. In the case where we are importing non-type-safe data—as seen with CSV or JSON data—the bronze tier is incredibly important to weeding out corrupt and otherwise problematic data.

Guarding the Bronze Layer with Permissive Mode in Spark

Example 9-4 shows a technique called *permissive passthrough* with Spark. This option allows us to add a gating mechanism using a predefined (consistent) schema to block corrupt data, while preserving the nonconformant rows for debugging.

Example 9-4. Preventing bad data with permissive passthrough

```
% from pyspark.sql.types import StructType, StructField, StringType
known_schema: StructType = (
  StructType.fromJson(...) ❶
  .add(StructField('_corrupt', StringType(), True, { ❷
    'comment': 'invalid rows go into _corrupt rather than simply being dropped'
}))
happy_df = (
  spark.read.options(**{ ❸
    "inferSchema": "false",
    "columnNameOfCorruptRecord": "_corrupt",
    "mode": "PERMISSIVE",
})
.schema(known_schema)
.json(...)
```

❶ We begin by loading a known schema using the `StructType.fromJson` method. We could just as easily have manually built the schema using the `Struct Type().add(...)` pattern.

❷ We then append the `_corrupt` field to our schema. This will provide a container for our bad data to sit in. Think of this as either the `_corrupt` column is null or it contains a value. The data can then be read using a filter `where(col("_corrupt").isNotNull())` or the inverse to separate the good from the bad.

❸ We then apply the reader options: `"inferSchema": "false"`, `"mode": "PERMISSIVE"`, `"columnNameOfCorruptRecord": "_corrupt"`. By turning off schema inference, we can opt into schema changes only by explicitly providing an updated schema. This means no runtime surprises. Schema inference is a powerful technique that scans (samples) a large number of rows of semistructured data (like CSV or JSON) to generate what it believes to be a stable `Struct Type` (schema). The problem with schema inference is that it doesn't understand the historical structure of the data and is limited to generating assumptions based on what it is provided in an initial batch.

The technique from Example 9-4 can be applied to streaming transforms just as easily using the `from_json` native function, which is located in the `sql.functions` package (`pyspark.sql.functions.*`, `spark.sql.functions.*`). This means we can test things in batch and then turn on the streaming fire hose, understanding the exact behavior of our ingestion pipelines even in the inconsistent world of semistructured data.

While the bronze layer may feel limited in scope and responsibility, it plays an incredibly important role in debugging and recovery, and as a source for new ideas in the future. Due to the raw nature of the bronze layer tables, it is also unadvisable to broadcast the availability of these tables widely. There is nothing worse than getting paged or called into an incident for issues arising from the misuse of raw tables.

Exploring the Silver Layer

While the bronze layer represents the initial point of lineage in the medallion architecture, the silver layer represents the point at which raw data is filtered, cleaned, and dressed up, and even augmented by joining across one or many other tables. If the bronze layer is data in its infancy, the silver layer is data in its teenage years, and as was true for all of us in our teens, our data coming-of-age story has its ups and downs.

Used for cleaning and filtering data

Depending on the source of the data that first landed in the bronze layer, we may be in for a wild ride. Just as no two people are exactly alike, the general consistency and baseline quality of data sources can vary wildly. This is where initial cleaning and filtering come into play.

We clean up our data to normalize and present a consistent source of reliable data for downstream consumption. Our downstream consumers may be ourselves, teams within our organization, or even external stakeholders. At one extreme, we may be extracting and decoding binary data that originated from streaming sources—such as Kafka—to convert from Avro or Protobuf and then applying additional transformations on the resulting data. The output of our pipeline may result in nested or flattened rows.

It is also normal to be filtering or even dropping some columns at this point. In Example 9-4, we saw the inclusion of the _corrupt column pattern. This information isn't valid for consumption in the silver or golden layer of the medallion architecture and is provided only to support data preservation techniques in the bronze layer and as a way of communicating problems to engineers.

It isn't uncommon for engineers to provide _* columns like _corrupt or _debug that contain simple information or more specific structs or maps. This technique can also be used to carry observability metadata or additional context for reporting purposes.

Example 9-5 provides a continuation of Example 9-4, showing how we would pick up reading from the bronze Delta table and then filter, drop, and transform rows for receipt into the cleansed silver tables.

Example 9-5. Filtering, dropping, and transformations—all the things needed for writing to silver

```
% medallion_stream = (
  delta_source.readStream.format("delta")
  .options(**reader_options)
  .load()
  .transform(transform_from_json)
  .transform(transform_for_silver)
  .writeStream.format("delta")
  .options(**writer_options))
  .option('mergeSchema': 'false'))
  streaming_query = (
    medallion_stream
    .toTable(f"{managed_silver_table}"))
```

The pipeline shown in Example 9-5 reads from the bronze Delta table (from Example 9-3) and decodes the binary data received (from the `value` column), while also enabling permissive mode, which we explored in Example 9-4:

```
def transform_from_json(input_df: DataFrame) -> DataFrame:
    return input_df.withColumn("ecomm",
        from_json(
            col("value").cast(StringType()),
            known_schema,
            options={
                'mode': 'PERMISSIVE',
                'columnNameOfCorruptRecord': '_corrupt'
            }
        ))
```

Then a second transformation is required as we make preparations for writing into the silver layer. This is a minor secondary transformation removing any corrupt rows and applying aliasing to declare the ingestion data and timestamp, which could be different from the event timestamp and date:

```
def transform_for_silver(input_df: DataFrame) -> DataFrame:
    return (
        input_df.select(
            col("event_date").alias("ingest_date"),
            col("timestamp").alias("ingest_timestamp"),
            col("ecomm.*")
        )
        .where(col("_corrupt").isNull())
        .drop("_corrupt"))
```

After the transformations are taken care of, we write the data out to our silver Delta table. We also explicitly set the `mergeSchema:false`. While this is the default behavior, it is an important callout, since it flags for other engineers what the expected behavior is and ensures accidental columns don't mistakenly make their way to silver from bronze. We covered alternatives to automatic schema evolution using `ALTER TABLE` in Chapter 5.

Regardless of why we clean and filter the bronze data, the results of our efforts provide our stakeholders with more consistent and reliable data to power their myriad use cases. We can consider the silver layer to be the first stable layer in the medallion architecture.

Establishes a layer for augmenting data

There is no rule stating that a silver table must read from a bronze table. In fact, it is common for the silver layer to be used to join from one or many silver and even golden tables. For example, if the results of cleaning and filtering one of our bronze tables can be used to power multiple additional use cases, then we can save ourselves both time and additional complexity by reusing the fruits of our internal teams' and external partners' labor. Conceptually, Figure 9-5 shows the table lineage from left to right, starting with two bronze tables (on the left), followed by a series of joins and transformations (the silver layer), before yielding golden tables (on the right).

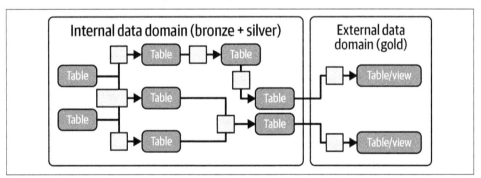

Figure 9-5. Each layer of the medallion architecture can be simple or complex; it can be easier to visualize the transformation of data across a lineage in terms of what is internal (left-hand side of the figure) and what is external (right-hand side)

Being able to view the lineage between bronze, silver, and gold can help provide additional context as the number of tables and views increases, and as the total data products and their owners naturally grow over time. We cover lineage in more detail in Chapter 13.

Enable data quality checks and balances

Delta provides capabilities for column-based constraints to enhance the functionality that can't be provided with simple schema enforcement alone. (Recall that schema enforcement and evolution was covered in Chapter 5.)

With column-level constraints, we can enforce more complex rules directly at the table level by applying predicates in the form of CHECKs:

```
ALTER TABLE <tablename>
ADD CONSTRAINT <name>
CHECK <sql-predicate>
```

The upside here is that we can guarantee that the data in our table will never fail to meet the constraint criteria. The downside is that if any row doesn't meet the constraint's check, a DeltaInvariantViolationException will be thrown, short-circuiting the job.

Data quality frameworks can help simplify table constraints by separating the rules from the underlying physical table definition. Some popular open source frameworks are Great Expectations (*https://oreil.ly/-rK9y*), Spark Expectations (*https://oreil.ly/TBpsY*), and Delta Live Tables (DLT) expectations (*https://oreil.ly/h5ohR*) (the last of which is a paid offering from Databricks). Data quality is an important part of DataOps; it can help to block bad data before it leaves a specific layer within the medallion architecture.

Remember: as data engineers, we need to act like owners and provide excellent customer service to our data stakeholders. The earlier in the refinement process we can establish good quality gates, the happier our downstream data consumers will be.

Exploring the Gold Layer

The gold layer is the most mature data layer in the medallion architecture. Data in the gold layer has undergone multiple transformations and has been specifically curated, and it has a specific place in the data world. This is because data in the gold layer is purpose-built to solve explicit intended goals. If the bronze layer represents data as an infant, and silver is a teenager, then golden tables represent data in its late thirties or early forties — or at a point where it has established a concrete identity.

Establishes high trust and high consistency

While the analogy of data as people at different points in their lives might not be accurate, as a mental model it works. Data in the golden layer is much less likely to change drastically from day to day, in the same way that our personalities, wants, and wishes change at a slower pace as we age. Example 9-6 explores generating topN reports from the transformations out of our silver layer (Example 9-5).

Example 9-6. Creating intentional tables for business-level consumption

```
% pyspark
silver_table = spark.read.format("delta")...
top5 = (
  silver_table
  .groupBy("ingest_date", "category_id")
  .agg(
    count(col("product_id")).alias("impressions"),
    min(col("price")).alias("min_price"),
    avg(col("price")).alias("avg_price"),
    max(col("price")).alias("max_price")
  )
  .orderBy(desc("impressions"))
  .limit(5))
(top5
  .write.format("delta")
  .mode("overwrite")
  .options(**view_options)
  .saveAsTable(f"gold.{topN_products_daily}"))
```

Example 9-6 shows how to do daily aggregations. It is typical for reporting data to be stored in the gold layer. This is the data we (and the business) care most about. It is our job to ensure that we provide purpose-built tables (or views) to ensure that business-critical data is available, reliable, and accurate.

For foundational tables—and really with any business-critical data—surprise changes are upsetting and may lead to broken reporting as well as to inaccurate runtime inference for machine learning models. This can cost the company more than just money; it can be the difference in whether or not the company retains its customers and reputation in a highly competitive industry.

The gold layer can be implemented using physical tables or virtual tables (views). This provides us with ways of optimizing our curated tables that result in either a full physical table when not using a view, or simple metadata providing any filters, column aliases, or join criteria required when interacting with the virtual table. The performance requirements will ultimately dictate the usage of tables versus views, but a view is good enough to support the needs of many gold layer use cases.

Now that we've explored the medallion architecture, the last stop on our journey will be to dive into patterns for decreasing the effort level and time requirements from the point of data ingestion to the time when the data becomes available for consumption by downstream stakeholders at the gold edge.

Streaming Medallion Architecture

Earlier we learned that the medallion architecture is a data design pattern enabling us to solve common data problems encountered with any data in flight—such problems being:

- Lack of replay or recovery (which is solved with the bronze layer)
- Broken column-level expectations (which can be solved with the Delta protocol and by turning off `mergeSchema` and ignoring `overwriteSchema` unless needed as a last resort)
- Issues with column-specific data quality and correctness (which can be solved with constraints or by using utility libraries such as spark-expectations (*https:// oreil.ly/TBpsY*) or Delta Live Tables (*https://oreil.ly/XOz85*) with `@dlt.expect`)

While we've already looked at patterns to refine data using the medallion architecture to remove imperfections, adhere to explicitly defined schemas, and provide data checks and balances, what we didn't cover was how to provide a seamless flow for transformations from bronze to silver and silver to gold.

Time tends to get in the way more often than not—with too little time, there is not enough information to make informed decisions, and with too much time, there is a tendency to become complacent and sometimes even a little bit lazy. Thus time is something of a Goldilocks problem (*https://oreil.ly/v8ZIc*), especially when we concern ourselves with reducing the end-to-end latency for data traversing our lakehouse. In the next section, we will look at common patterns for reducing the latency of each tier within the medallion architecture, focusing on end-to-end streaming.

As we've seen across the book, the Delta protocol supports both batch or streaming access to tables. We can deploy our pipelines to take specific steps ensuring that the datasets that are output meet our quality standards and result in the ability to trust the upstream sources of data, enabling us to drastically reduce the end-to-end latency, from data ingestion (bronze) on through (silver) and ultimately to the business or data product owners in the gold layer.

By crafting our pipelines to block and correct data quality problems before they become more widespread, we can use the lessons learned across Examples 9-3 through 9-6 to stitch together end-to-end streaming workflows.

Figure 9-6 provides an example of the streaming workflow. Data arrives from our Kafka topic, as we saw in Example 9-3. The dataset is then appended to our bronze Delta table (`ecomm_raw`), which enables us to pick up the incremental changes in our silver application. The example providing the transformations was shown in Example 9-5. Last, either we create and replace temporary views (or materialized views in Databricks), or we create another golden application with the responsibility of periodically ingesting data from `ecomm_silver` to produce purpose-built tables or views. Extending the pattern seen in Example 9-6, we can stitch together an end-to-end pipeline that incrementally ingests from its direct upstream, allowing us to trace the lineage of transformations all the way back to the initial point of inception (Kafka).

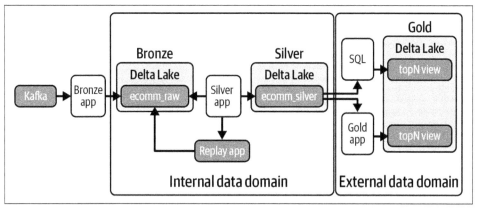

Figure 9-6. Streaming medallion architecture as viewed from the workflow level

There are many ways to orchestrate end-to-end workflows using scheduled jobs or full-fledged frameworks like Apache Airflow, Databricks Workflows, or Delta Live Tables. The end result provides us with reduced latency from the edge all the way to our most important and business-critical golden tables.

For Delta Lake and Spark Structured Streaming

If you are migrating from a batch-first to a streaming-first architecture, it can be easiest to lean on triggers while you are ramping up—for example, `df.writeStream…trigger(available Now=True).toTable(...`—so that you can continue to operate as if you are in batch while enabling your data applications to be easily converted into always-on streaming applications. A benefit of using structured streaming here is that all complex state management is handled via your application checkpoint; another added benefit is that `availableNow` triggering honors any rate-limiting options on the `DataStreamReader`, such as `maxFilesPerTrigger`.

Conclusion

This chapter introduced the architectural tenets of the modern lakehouse architecture and showed how Delta Lake can be used for foundational support for this mission.

The lakehouse architecture is built on open standards, with open protocols and formats, supporting ACID transactions, table-level time travel, and simplified interoperability with UniForm, as well as out-of-the-box data sharing protocols to simplify the exchange of data both for internal and external stakeholders. We skimmed the surface of the Delta protocol and learned more about the invariants that provide us with rules of engagement, as well as table-level guarantees, by looking at how schema-on-write and schema enforcement protect our downstream data consumers from accidental leakage of corrupt or low-quality data.

We then looked at how the medallion architecture can be used to provide a standard framework for data quality, and how each layer is utilized across the common bronze-silver-gold model.

The quality gating pattern enables us to build a consistent data strategy and provide guarantees and expectations based on a model of incremental quality from bronze (raw) to silver (cleansed and normalized) and on up to gold (curated and purpose driven). How data flows within the lakehouse and between these gates enables a higher level of trust within the lakehouse and even allows us to reduce the end-to-end latency by enabling end-to-end streaming in the lakehouse.

Performance Tuning: Optimizing Your Data Pipelines with Delta Lake

Up to this point, you've explored various ways of working with Delta Lake. You've seen many of the features that make Delta Lake a better and more reliable choice as a storage format for your data. Tuning your Delta Lake tables for performance, however, requires a solid understanding of the basic mechanics of table maintenance, which was covered in Chapter 5, as well as a bit of knowledge about and practice at manipulating or implementing some of the internal and advanced features introduced in Chapter 8. This performance side becomes the focus now, as we'll look at the impact of pulling the levers of some of those features in a bit more detail. We encourage you to review the topics laid out in Chapter 5 if you have not recently used or reviewed them.

In general, you will often want to maximize reliability and the efficiency with which you can accomplish data creation, consumption, and maintenance tasks without adding unnecessary costs to your data processing pipelines. By taking the time to optimize your workloads properly, you can balance the overhead costs of these tasks with various performance considerations to align with your objectives. What you should be able to gain here is an understanding of how tuning some of the features you've already seen can help to achieve your objectives.

First, there's some background work to provide a bit of clarity about the nature of your objectives. After that, there is an exploration into several of Delta Lake's features and how they impact these objectives. While Delta Lake can generally be used suitably with limited changes, when you think about the requirements put on modern data stacks, you should realize that you could always do better. In the end, taking on performance tuning involves striking balances and considering trade-offs to gain advantages where you need them. Because of this, it is best to make sure you think about what other settings are affected when you consider modifying some parameters.

Performance Objectives

One of the biggest factors you need to consider is whether you want to try and optimize best for data producers or consumers. As discussed in Chapter 9, the medallion architecture is an example of a data architecture that allows you to optimize for both reading and writing where needed through data curation layers. This separation of processes helps you to streamline the process at the point of data creation and at the point of consumption by focusing on the goals of each at different points in the pipeline. Let's first consider some of the different objectives toward which you might want to orient your tuning efforts.

Maximizing Read Performance

Optimizing your processes for data consumers can be more simply thought of as improving the read performance on your datasets. You might have data scientists who rely on repeated reads on subsets of a dataset to build accurate machine learning models, or business analysts looking to derive specific information to convey to business stakeholders. The data consumer's needs should be considered in the design and layout of your processes. While this section won't contain a deep dive into requirements gathering or entity-relationship (ER) diagrams, proper data modeling is a high-value prerequisite to building a successful data platform, whether curation and governance happen centrally or are more distributed, such as with a data mesh architecture.[1] The data consumer needs you are primarily concerned with here are how those data consumers will access data the majority of the time. Broadly speaking, queries will fall into one of three types of patterns: narrow point queries, broader range queries, or aggregations.

Point queries

A *point query* is a query submitted by a data consumer, or user, with the intention of returning a single record from a dataset. For example, a user may access a database to look up individual records on a case-by-case basis. Such users are less likely to use advanced query patterns involving SQL-based join logic or advanced filtering conditions. Another example is a robust web-server process retrieving results programmatically and dynamically on a case-by-case basis. These queries are more likely to be evaluated with higher levels of scrutiny concerning perceived performance metrics

---

[1] If you wish to read more about data modeling and ER diagrams, check out Appendix A in *Learning SQL*, 3rd ed., by Alan Beaulieu (O'Reilly), or see the Wikipedia pages for data modeling (*https://oreil.ly/kO3bN*) and the entity–relationship model (*https://oreil.ly/eUTLO*).

(*https://oreil.ly/qq6y7*). In both scenarios there is a human at the other end who is impacted by the query's performance, so you want to avoid any delays in record lookup without incurring high costs. This could mean that in some scenarios—such as the latter one, potentially—a high-performance, dedicated transactional system is required to meet latency requirements; this is often not the case, however, and through the tuning methods seen here you may be able to meet targets adequately without the need for secondary systems.

One of the things you'll consider is how things like file sizes, keys or indexing, and partitioning strategies can impact point query performance. As a rule of thumb, you should tend to steer toward smaller file sizes and try to use features such as indexes that reduce latency when searching for a needle in a haystack, even if the haystack is an entire field. You'll also see how statistics and file distribution impact lookup performance.

Range queries

A *range query* retrieves a set of records instead of retrieving a single record result like in a point query (which you can think of as just a special case with narrow boundaries). Rather than having an exact filter-matching condition, you'll find that range queries look for data within boundaries. Some common phrases that suggest such situations might be:

- Between
- At least
- Prior to
- Such that

Lots of other phrases are possible, but the general idea is that many records could satisfy such a condition (though it's still possible to wind up with just a single record). You will still encounter range queries when you use exact matching criteria describing broad categories, such as selecting *cats* as the type of animal from a list of pet species and breeds—you would have only one species but many different breeds. In other words, the result you look to obtain with a range query will generally be greater than one. Usually, you wouldn't know the specific number of records without adding some ordering element and further restricting the range.

Aggregations

On the surface, an *aggregation query* is similar to a range query, except that, instead of selecting down to a particular set of records, you'll use additional logical operations to perform some operation on each group of records. Borrowing from the pets example, you might want to get a count of the number of breeds per species or some other summary type of information. In such cases, you'll often see some type of partitioning of the data by category or by breaking fine-grained timestamps down to larger periods (e.g., by year). Since aggregation queries will perform many of the same scanning and filtering operations as range queries, they will similarly benefit from the same kinds of optimizations.

One of the things you'll find here is that your preferences for how you create files in terms of size and organization depend on how you generally select the boundaries or define the groups for this type of usage. Similarly, indexing and partitioning should generally be aligned with the query patterns to produce more performant reads.

The similarities between point queries, range queries, and aggregation queries can be summarized as follows: *to deliver the best performance, you need to align the overall data strategy with the way the data is consumed.* This means you'll want to consider the data layout strategy in addition to the consumption patterns as you optimize tables. To do so, you will also have to consider how you maintain the data, and you'll have to consider how running maintenance processes such as OPTIMIZE or collecting statistics with ANALYZE TABLE impacts performance and then schedule any downtime as needed.

Maximizing Write Performance

Optimizing the performance for data producers is more than just reducing *latency*, the time lapse between receipt (ingestion) of a record and writing (committing) it to storage, where it is then available for consumption. While you usually will want to minimize this time as much as possible, striking a balance between SLAs, performance objectives, and cost, there is more you must consider. You've already seen a few of the ways you'll want to think about how the strategy you use for your data architecture should be driven by the data consumers, principally by aligning optimization goals to the kinds of query patterns that are used. What you must also remember is that you usually are not fortunate enough to have so much control as to be able to specify exactly how you'd like to receive data, and so you also have constraints driven by the upstream data producers—that is, the systems generating the data.

You might have to join numerous different data sources together to deliver the data asset your business requires. These sources can range from infrequently uploaded files in shared cloud storage locations and legacy RDBMS instances to memory stores and high-volume message bus pipelines. The types of systems that are involved will drive much of your decision making, because the volume of the data and the frequency with which you receive it will influence how your data application needs to perform. You'll also likely find that these sources will further impact the overall data strategy you choose to adopt.

Trade-offs

As has been noted, many of the constraints on your write processes will be determined by the producer systems. If you are thinking of large file-based ingestion or event- or microbatch-level stream processing, then the size and number of transactions will vary considerably. Similarly, if you are working with a single-node Python application or using larger distributed frameworks, you will have such variance. You will also need to consider the amount of time required for processing, as well as the cadence. Many of these things must be balanced, and so again, the medallion architecture lends a hand, because you can separate some of these concerns by optimizing for your core data-producing process at the bronze level and for your data consumers at the gold level, with the silver level forming a kind of bridge between them. Refer back to Chapter 9 if you want to review the medallion architecture.

Conflict avoidance

How frequently you perform write operations can limit when you can run table maintenance operations—for example, when you are using Z-Ordering. If you are using Structured Streaming with Apache Spark to write microbatch-level transactions to a Delta Lake table partitioned by the hour, then you have to consider the impacts of running other processes against that partition while it is still active.[2] How you choose options like autocompaction and optimized writes also impacts when or whether you need to run additional maintenance operations. Building indexes takes time to compute and could conflict with other processes too. It's up to you to make sure you avoid conflicts when needed, though it is much easier to do so than it was with things like read/write locks involved in every file access.

Performance Considerations

So far you've seen some of the criteria on which you'll want to base much of your decision making as far as how you interact with Delta Lake. You have many different tools built in, and how you use them usually will depend on how a particular table is interacted with. Our goal now is to look at the different levers you can pull and think about how the way you set different parameters can be better for any of the above cases. Some of this will review concepts discussed in Chapter 6 in the context of data producer/consumer trade-offs.

---

2 You can find detailed descriptions, including error messages, in the "Concurrency Control" section of the Delta Lake documentation (*https://oreil.ly/Fko5I*).

Partitioning

One of the great things about Delta Lake is that data can still be partitioned like Parquet files using Hive-style partitioning.[3] However, being able to partition tables in this way is also one of the drawbacks (be sure not to miss the section on liquid clustering, "Cluster By" on page 236). You can partition a Delta table by a column or even by multiple columns. The most commonly used partition column is date, but in high-volume processes it's not uncommon to find tables with multiple levels of partitioning using even hour and minute columns. This is a bit excessive for most processes, but technically you're not limited in how fine-grained you can make your partitioning structure. However, you may do so at your own peril, as overpartitioned tables can yield many headaches in terms of poor performance.

Structure

The easiest way to think about what partitioning does is that it breaks a set of files into sorted directories tied to your partitioning column(s). Suppose you have a customer membership category column in which every customer record will fall into either a "paid" membership or a "free" membership, as in the following example. If you partition by this `membership_type` column, then all the files with "paid" member records will be in one subdirectory, while all the files with "free" member records will be in a second directory:

```python
# Python
from deltalake.writer import write_deltalake
import pandas as pd

df = pd.DataFrame(data=[
    (1, "Customer 1", "free"),
    (2, "Customer 2", "paid"),
    (3, "Customer 3", "free"),
    (4, "Customer 4", "paid")],
    columns=["id", "name", "membership_type"])

write_deltalake(
    "/tmp/delta/partitioning.example.delta",
    data=df,
    mode="overwrite",
    partition_by=["membership_type"])
```

---

3 For a more in-depth look at the Hive side of data layouts, see *Programming Hive* by Edward Capriolo, Dean Wampler, and Jason Rutherglen (O'Reilly).

All the examples and some other supporting code for this chapter can be found in the GitHub repository for the book (*https://oreil.ly/2m8Kv*).

By forcing the partitioning down and simultaneously partitioning by the member ship_type column, you should see when you check the write path directory that you get a subdirectory for each of the distinct values in the membership_type column:

```
# Bash
tree /tmp/delta/partitioning.example.delta

/tmp/delta/partitioning.example.delta
├── _delta_log
│   └── 00000000000000000000.json
├── membership_type=free
│   └── 0-9bfd1aed-43ce-4201-9ef0-1d6b1a42db8a-0.parquet
└── membership_type=paid
    └── 0-9bfd1aed-43ce-4201-9ef0-1d6b1a42db8a-0.parquet
```

The following section can help you figure out when (or when not to) partition tables and the impact such decisions bear on other performance features, but understanding the larger partitioning concept is important, as even if you don't choose to partition tables yourself, you could inherit ownership of partitioned tables from someone who did.

Pitfalls

There are some cautions laid out for you here with regard to the partitioning structure in Delta Lake (remember the table partitioning rules from Chapter 5!). Your decision about the actual file sizes to use will be impacted by what kind of data consumers will use the table, but the way you partition your files has downstream consequences too. Generally, you will want to make sure that the total amount of data in a given partition is at least 1 GB, and you don't want partitioning at all for total table sizes under 1 TB. Anything less, and you can incur large amounts of unnecessary overhead with file and directory listing operations, especially if you are using Delta Lake in the cloud.[4] This means that if you have a high cardinality column, you should not use it as a partitioning column in most cases unless the sizing is still appropriate. In cases in which you need to revise the partitioning structure, you should use methods such as those outlined in Chapter 5 to replace the table with a more optimized layout. Overpartitioning tables is a problem that has been seen as

---

4 See more on this in the whitepaper "Delta Lake: High-Performance ACID Table Storage over Cloud Object Stores" (*https://oreil.ly/boPCR*).

causing performance problems for numerous people over time. It's far better to take the time to fix the problem than to pass poorer performance downstream.

File sizes

One direct implication of overpartitioning is that file sizes often turn out to be too small. File sizes of about 1 GB are recommended to handle large-scale data processes with relative ease. There are many cases, however, in which leveraging smaller file sizes, typically in the 32 MB to 128 MB range, can have performance benefits for read operations. A decision about the optimal file size comes down to the nature of the data consumer. High-volume append-only tables in the bronze layer generally function better with larger file sizes, as the larger sizes maximize throughput per operation with little regard to anything else. The smaller sizes will help a lot more with finer-grained read operations such as point queries, or in cases in which you have lots of merge operations, because of the higher number of file rewrites generated.

In the end, file size will often wind up being determined by the way you apply maintenance operations. When you run OPTIMIZE, and in particular when you run it with the included Z-Ordering option, you'll see that it affects your resulting file sizes. You do, however, have a couple of base options for trying to control the file sizes.

Table Utilities

You're probably pretty familiar with some version of the small files problem. While it was originally a condition largely affecting *elephantine* MapReduce processing, the underlying nature of the problem extends to more recent large-scale distributed processing systems as well.[5] In Chapter 5, you saw the need to maintain your Delta Lake tables and some of the tools available to do that. One of the scenarios covered was that for streaming use cases, where the transactions tend to be smaller, you need to make sure you rewrite those files into bigger ones to avoid a similar small files problem. Here you'll see how leveraging these tools can affect read and write performance while interacting with Delta Lake.

OPTIMIZE

The OPTIMIZE operation on its own is intended to reduce the number of files contained in a Delta Lake table (recall the exploration in Chapter 5). This is true in particular of streaming workloads, where you may have microbatches creating files and commits measured in just a couple of MB or less, and thus you can wind up with many comparatively small files. *Compaction* is a term used to describe the process of

---

[5] If you're not familiar with this problem, the blog post "The Small Files Problem" (*https://oreil.ly/yapTU*) is probably worth a read.

packing smaller files together, and it's one that is often used when talking about this operation. One of the most common performance implications of compaction is the failure to do it. While there could be some minute benefits to such small files (like rather fine-grained column statistics), these are generally heavily outweighed by the costs of listing and opening many files.

How it works is that when you run OPTIMIZE, you kick off a listing operation that lists all the files that are active in the table and their sizes. Then any files that can be combined will be combined into files around the target size of 1 GB. This helps to reduce issues that might occur from, for example, several concurrent processes committing smaller transactions to the same Delta Lake destination. In other words, OPTIMIZE is a mechanism to help avoid the small files problem.

Remember, there is some overhead to the operation; it has to read multiple files and combine them into the files that eventually get written, so it is a heavy I/O operation. Removing the file overhead is part of what helps to improve the read time for downstream data consumers. If you are using an optimized table downstream as a streaming source, as you explored in Chapter 9, the resulting files are not data change files and are ignored.

It's important to recall that there are some file size settings with OPTIMIZE that you can tweak to tune performance more to your preference. These settings and their behavior are covered in depth in Chapter 5. Next, we take a deeper look at Z-Ordering, which is instructive even if you're planning on using liquid clustering, as the underlying concepts are strongly related.

Z-Ordering

Sometimes the way you insert files or model the data you're working with will provide a kind of natural clustering of records. Say you insert one file to a table from something like customer transaction records, or you aggregate playback events from a video device every 10 minutes. Then say you want to go back an hour later to compute some KPIs from the data. How many files will you have to read? You already know it's six because of the natural time element you're working with (assuming you used event or transaction times). You might describe the data as having a natural, linear clustering behavior. You can apply the same description to any cases in which a natural sort order is inherent to the data. You could also artificially create a sorting or partitioning of the data by alphabetizing, using unique universal identifiers (UUIDs), or using a file insertion time and then reordering as needed.

At other times, however, your data may not have a native clustering that also lends itself to how it will be consumed. Sorting by an additional second range might improve things, but filtering for the first sorting range will almost always yield the strongest results. This trend continues to diminish in value as additional columns are added because it's still too linear.

There's a method used in multiple applications, one that extends well beyond just data applications, and it relies on remapping the data using a space-filling curve.[6] Without getting into too much of the rigorous detail (yet), this is a construction that lets us map multidimensional information, such as the values of multiple columns, into something more linear, such as a *cluster ID* in a sorted range. To be a bit more specific, what you need are locality-preserving, space-filling curves such as a Z-Order curve or a Hilbert curve, which are among the most commonly used options.[7] These allow us to create clusters of data in a far less linear style, which can provide great gains in performance for data consumers, especially for fine-grained point queries or more complex range queries.

In other words, this multidimensional approach means you can more easily filter on disjoint conditions. Consider a case in which you have a customer or device ID number column and an additional location information column. These columns wouldn't have any particular correlation, so there's no natural, linear clustering order. Space-filling curves would allow you to impose a clustering order on them anyway. You'll see more detail about how it works, but from a practical perspective, this means you can filter down to the combined clusters rather than get stuck having to read a full dataset.

For data producers, this represents an additional step in data production, which slows down processes, so the need for it downstream should be determined in advance. If no one benefits, then it wouldn't be worth the cost of applying it. That being said, the process is largely incremental and can be run on individual partitions when specified.

Compaction with OPTIMIZE using ZORDER BY is not idempotent (this is one of those cases in which the data change flag will be False) but is designed to be incremental when it runs. That is to say, when no new data is added to a partition (or to the table in the case of unpartitioned tables), then it will not try to cluster that partition or table again. This behavior expects that you are using the same column specifications for Z-Ordering, which makes sense, because a new column specification would require reclustering over the whole partition (or table).

---

6 For more information, see the Wikipedia article on space-filling curves (*https://oreil.ly/dFPcw*).

7 See the original Databricks Engineering blog post (*https://oreil.ly/h1D4F*) on the initial implementation in Delta Lake. See Wikipedia for more information on Z-Order curves (*https://oreil.ly/hbj9g*) and Hilbert curves (*https://oreil.ly/ySQcI*).

Z-Ordering attempts to create clusters of similar size in memory, which typically will be directly correlated with the size on disk, but there are situations in which this can become untrue. In those cases, task skewing can occur during the compaction process.

For example, if you have a string column containing JSON values, and this column has significantly increased in size over time, then when Z-Ordering by date, both the task durations and the resulting file sizes can become skewed during later processing.

Except for the most extreme cases, this should generally not significantly affect downstream consumers or processes.

One thing you might notice if you experiment with and without Z-Ordering of files in your table is that it changes the distribution of the sizes of the files. While OPTIMIZE, when left to its defaults, will generally create files that are fairly uniform in size, the clustering behavior you put in place means that file sizes can become smaller (or larger) than the built-in file size limiter (or one specified when available). This preference for the clustering behavior over strict file sizing is intended to provide the best performance by making sure the data gets colocated as desired.[8]

Optimization automation in Spark

Two settings available in Databricks—*autocompaction* and *optimized writes*—help make some of these table utilities easier to use and less interruptive (e.g., stream processing workloads). In the past, their combined usage was often called *auto-optimize*. Now they can be treated individually, because not only can they be used together, but they also can be flexibly used independently as needed in different situations, to great advantage.

Autocompaction. The first setting, delta.autoCompact, has been available in the Databricks Runtimes for a few years but is expected to become available across Delta Lake. The idea of autoCompact is that it can run OPTIMIZE on your table while a process is already running without additional commands. One of the biggest advantages is that you don't need to have a secondary process running that might conflict with a stream processing application, for example. The downside is that there could be a relatively minor effect on the processing latency. This is because after a file is committed, Spark will perform an OPTIMIZE operation as part of the same process. It analyzes the files available in the table and applies the compaction as necessary. This can be especially helpful with a streaming write based on a message bus, as the transactions tend to be smaller than you would find in many other workload

---

8 There is a more detailed example of Z-Ordering later in this chapter, but if you're in a hurry, the blog post "Optimize by Clustering not Partitioning Data with Delta Lake" (*https://oreil.ly/XIiP0*) by Denny Lee is a good and fast end-to-end walkthrough.

types, but it does come as a trade-off since it will insert additional tasks to do the compaction, which can hold up processing time. This means that for cases with tight SLA margins, you may wish to avoid using it.

Enabling the feature is just a Spark configuration setting:

```
delta.autoCompact.enabled true
```

There are a few additional settings that provide added flexibility and allow you to align the behavior of the compaction operations to your choosing.

 While this feature can improve the way you use OPTIMIZE with Delta Lake, it will not allow the option of including a ZORDER on the files. You may still need additional processes, even when auto Compact is used to provide the best performance for downstream data consumers.

You can control the target output size of autoCompact with spark.databricks .delta.autoCompact.maxFileSize. While the default of 128 MB is often sufficient in practice, you might wish to tune this to a higher or lower number to balance between the impacts of rewriting multiple files during processing, whether or not you plan to run periodic table maintenance operations, and your desired target end state for file sizes.

The number of files required before compaction will be initiated is set through spark.databricks.delta.autoCompact.minNumFiles. The default number is 50. This just makes sure you have a lower threshold to avoid any negative impact of additional operations on small tables with small numbers of files. Tables that are small but have many append and delete operations might benefit from setting this number lower, as this would create fewer files but would have less performance impacts due to the smaller size. A higher setting might be beneficial for rather large-scale processes where the number of writes to Delta Lake in a single transaction is generally higher. This would avoid running an OPTIMIZE step for every write stage, which could become burdensome in terms of added operational costs for each transaction.

Optimized writes.   This setting is also a Databricks-specific implementation on Delta Lake that may become available in other versions.[9] In the past, you might often have ended up in scenarios in which the number of DataFrame partitions you were using grew much larger than the number of files you might want to write into, because the size of each file would be too small and create additional unneeded overhead. To

---

9 You can find additional configuration options in the Databricks documentation for this feature (*https:// oreil.ly/zcdeZ*).

solve this, you'd generally do something like coalesce(*n*) or repartition(*n*) before the actual write operation to get your results compacted down to just *n* files being written. *Optimized writes* are a way to avoid needing to do this.

If you set delta.optimizeWrites to true on your table—or similarly, if you set spark.databricks.delta.optimizeWrites.enabled to true in your Databricks SparkSession—you get this different behavior. The latter setting will apply the former option setting to all newly created tables from the SparkSession. You might be wondering how this magical automation gets applied behind the scenes. How it works is that before the write part of the operation happens, you will get additional shuffle operations (as needed) to combine memory partitions so that fewer files can be added during the commit. This is beneficial on partitioned tables because the partitioning tends to make files even more granular. The added shuffle step can add some latency into write operations, so for data producer–optimized scenarios you might want to skip it, but it provides some additional compaction automatically, similar to autoCompact above, except that it occurs prior to the write operation rather than happening afterward. Figure 10-1 illustrates a case in which the distribution of the data across multiple executors would result in multiple files written to each partition (at left) and how the added shuffle improves the arrangement (at right).

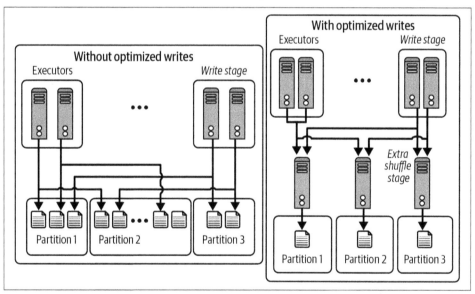

Figure 10-1. A comparison of how optimized writes add a shuffle before writing files

Vacuum

Because things like failed writes are not committed to the transaction log, you need to make sure you vacuum even append-only tables that don't have OPTIMIZE run on them. Write failures do occur from time to time, whether due to some cloud provider failure or perhaps because of something else, and the resulting stubs still live inside your Delta Lake directory and could do with a little cleaning up. Not doing it early is another issue that can cause some pain. We've seen some fairly large Delta tables in production where cleaning up got overlooked during planning, and it wound up becoming a larger and costlier chore to handle later on, because by that point, millions of files needed removal (it took around three full days to fix in one case). In addition to the unnecessary associated storage costs, any external transactions hitting partitions containing extra files have many more files to sift through. It's much better to have a daily or weekly cleanup task or even to include maintenance operations in your processing pipeline. The details around the operation of vacuuming were shared in Chapter 5, but the implications of not doing it are worth mentioning here.[10]

Databricks autotuning

Databricks includes a couple of scenarios in which the respective options, when enabled, automatically adjust the `delta.targetFileSize` setting. One case is based on workload types, and the second is on the table size.

In Databricks Runtime (DBR) 8.2 and later, when `delta.tuneFileSizesForRewrites` is set to `true`, the runtime will check whether nine out of the last ten operations against the table were `merge` operations. In cases where that is the case, the target file size will be reduced to improve write efficiencies (at least some of the reasoning has to do with statistics and file skipping, which will be covered in the next section).

From DBR 8.4 onward, the table size is accounted for in determining this setting. For tables less than about 2.5 TB, the `delta.targetFileSize` setting will be put at a lower value of 256 MB. If the table is larger than 10 TB, the target will be set at a larger size of 1 GB. For sizes that fall in the intermediate range between 2.5 TB and 10 TB, there is a linearly increasing scale for the target, from 256 MB up to the 1 GB value. Please refer to the documentation for additional details, including a reference table for this scale.

Table Statistics

Up to this point, most of the focus has been centered around the layout and distribution of the files in your tables. The reason for this has a great deal to do with the underlying arrangement of the data within those files. The primary way to see what that data looks like is based on the file statistics in the metadata. Now you will see how you get statistics information and why it matters to you. You'll see what the process looks like, what the stats look like, and how they influence performance.

---

10 Matthew Powers and Nick Karpov's blog post on the `vacuum` command (*https://oreil.ly/-aR3R*) provides a more in-depth exploration of vacuuming, with examples and exploration of some of the nuances.

How statistics help

Statistics about our data can be pretty useful. You'll see more about what this means and what it looks like in a moment, but first, let's think about some reasons why you might want statistics on the files in your Delta Lake. Suppose that you have a table with a "color" field that takes 1 of 100 possible values, and each color value occurs in exactly 100 rows. This gives you 10,000 total rows. If these color values are randomly distributed throughout the rows, then finding all the "green" records would require scanning the whole set. Suppose you now add some more structure to the set by breaking it into ten files. In this case, you might guess that there are green records in each of the ten files. How could you know whether that is true without scanning all ten files? This is part of the motivation for having statistics on your files—namely, that if you do some counting operations at the time of writing the files or as part of your maintenance operations, then you can know from your table metadata whether or not specific values occur within files. If your records are sorted, this impact gets even bigger, because then you can drastically reduce the number of files that need to be read to find all your green records, or to find the row numbers between 50 and 150, as you can see in Figure 10-2. While this example is just conceptual, it should help to convince you why table statistics are important—but before you turn to a more detailed practical example, see first how statistics operate in Delta Lake.

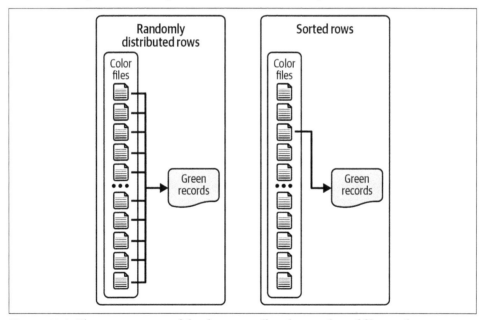

Figure 10-2. The arrangement of the data can affect the number of files read

File statistics

If you go back to the customer data table you created earlier, you can get a simple view of how statistics are generated during file creation by digging into the Delta Log. It's recommended to check the values or the relevant section of the Delta Lake protocol (*https://oreil.ly/sWGA3*) to see additional statistics that are added over time. Here you can use the path definition of your table and then add to that the initial JSON record from the table's creation in the *_delta_log* directory:

```python
# Python
import json

basepath = "/tmp/delta/partitioning.example.delta/"
fname = basepath + "_delta_log/00000000000000000000.json"
with open(fname) as f:
    for i in f.readlines():
        parsed = json.loads(i)
        if 'add' in parsed.keys():
            stats = json.loads(parsed['add']['stats'])
            print(json.dumps(stats))
```

When you run this, you will get a collection of the statistics generated for each of the created files added to the Delta Lake table:

```
{
  "numRecords": 2,
  "minValues": {"id": 2, "name": "Customer 2"},
  "maxValues": {"id": 4, "name": "Customer 4"},
  "nullCount": {"id": 0, "name": 0}
}
{
  "numRecords": 2,
  "minValues": {"id": 1, "name": "Customer 1"},
  "maxValues": {"id": 3, "name": "Customer 3"},
  "nullCount": {"id": 0, "name": 0}
}
```

In this case, you see all the data values since the table has only four records, and there were no null values inserted, so those metrics are returned as zeros.

 Notice in the example statistics pulled from the partitioning demonstration table that there is a count of records for each file. Apache Spark leverages this count to avoid reading any actual data files when running simple count operations that span partitions or entire tables by summing the statistics rather than scanning any data files, providing a significant performance advantage in many applications. Similarly, Spark can leverage these stats to performantly answer similar queries—for example:

```sql
-- SQL
SELECT max(id) FROM example_table
```

In Databricks (DBR 8.3 and above), you can additionally run an ANALYZE TABLE command to collect additional statistics, such as the number of distinct values, average length, and maximum length. These added statistics values can yield further performance improvements, so be sure to leverage them if you're using a compatible compute engine.

If you'll recall from Chapter 5, one of the settings you have available to you is delta.dataSkippingNumIndexedCols, which, with a default value of 32, determines how many columns statistics will be collected on. If you have a situation in which you are unlikely to run SELECT queries against the table, as in a bronze to silver layer stream process, for example, you can reduce this value to avoid additional overhead from the write operations. You could also increase the number of columns indexed in cases where query behavior against wider tables varies considerably more than would make sense to ZORDER BY (anything more than a few columns is usually not very beneficial). One other item to note here is that you can alter the table order to directly place larger valued columns after the number of indexed columns using ALTER TABLE CHANGE *COLUMN* (FIRST | AFTER).[11]

If you want to make sure statistics are collected on columns you add after the initial table is created, you would use the FIRST parameter. You can reduce the number of columns and move a long text column, for example, after something like a timestamp column to avoid trying to collect statistics on the large text column and ensure that you still include your timestamp information to take advantage of filtering better. Setting each is fairly straightforward, but note that the after argument requires a *named* column:

```
-- SQL
ALTER TABLE
    delta.`example`
    set tblproperties("delta.dataSkippingNumIndexedCols"=5);
ALTER TABLE
    delta.`example`
    CHANGE articleDate first;
ALTER TABLE
    delta.`example` CHANGE textCol after revisionTimestamp;
```

Partition pruning and data skipping

So what's the actual goal of optimizing partitioning and collecting file-level statistics? The idea is to reduce the amount of data that needs to be read. Logically, the more you can skip reading, the faster you'll be able to retrieve the results of a query. At a surface level, you've already seen how statistics collection can be used to look for the maximum value of a column or to count the number of records without needing to

---

11 There is an example in the section covering the CLUSTER BY command that demonstrates this practice.

read the actual files. This is because the read part of that operation was done when the files were created, and by storing that result in the metadata, you get something like you'd expect from cached results because you don't have all the overhead required to reread all the data to compute the results. So that's great, but what about when you're doing something that isn't as trivial as getting a count of the records?

The next best thing would be to skip reading as many files as possible to retrieve results. Since these statistics are collected per file, what you get is a set of boundaries you can use to check for membership. Let's look again at the statistics you had for our small example table:

```
{
    "numRecords": 2,
    "minValues": {"id": 2, "name": "Customer 2"},
    "maxValues": {"id": 4, "name": "Customer 4"},
    "nullCount": {"id": 0, "name": 0}
}
{
    "numRecords": 2,
    "minValues": {"id": 1, "name": "Customer 1"},
    "maxValues": {"id": 3, "name": "Customer 3"},
    "nullCount": {"id": 0, "name": 0}
}
```

If you wanted to pull all the records contained for Customer 1, then you can easily see that you need to read only one of the two available files. That reduced the workload by half just in this simple case. This begins to highlight the impact of some of the points you've already seen, such as decisions you can make about file sizes or partitioning, and really kind of brings together the larger point.

Knowing that this behavior exists, you should try to target a partition layout and column organization that can leverage these statistics to maximize the performance according to your goals. If you are optimizing for write performance but frequently have to backfill values with a merge function to some previous point in time, then you will likely want to organize your data so that you can skip reading as many other days' data as possible to eliminate wasted processing time.

Similarly, if you want to maximize read performance, and you understand how your end users are accessing the data at the point of consumption, then you can seek a targeted layout that provides the most opportunity for skipping files at read time. There are some other cautions about overpartitioning tables because of the additional processing overhead, so next you'll see how you can use ZORDER to impact the downstream performance in conjunction with this knowledge of the statistics contained in each file.

Z-Ordering revisited

File skipping creates great performance improvements by reducing the number of files that need to be read for many kinds of queries. You might ask, though: how does adding the clustering behavior from ZORDER BY affect this process? This is fairly straightforward. Remember, Z-Ordering creates clusters of records using a space-filling curve. The implication of doing this is that the files in your tables are arranged according to the clustering of the data. This means that when statistics are collected on the files, you get boundary information that aligns with how your record clusters are segregated in the process. So now when seeking records that align with your Z-Ordered clusters, you can further reduce the number of files that need to be read.

You might further wonder how the clusters in the data get created in the first place. Consider the goal of optimizing the read task for a more straightforward case. Suppose you have a dataset with a timestamp column. If you wanted to create some same-sized files with definite boundaries, then a straightforward answer appears. You can sort the data linearly by the timestamp column and then just divide it into chunks that are the same size. What if you want to use more than one column, though, and create real clusters according to the keys, instead of just some linear sort you could have done on your own?

The more advanced task of using space-filling curves on multiple columns is not that hard to understand once you see the idea, but it's not as simple as the linearly sorted case either. At least not yet it isn't. That's actually part of the idea. You need to perform some additional work to construct a way to be able to similarly range partition data across multiple columns. To do this, you need a mapping function that can translate multiple dimensions onto a single dimension so that you can do the dividing step, just like in the linear ordering case. The actual implementation used in Delta Lake might be a little tricky to digest out of context, but consider this snippet from the Delta Lake repository (*https://oreil.ly/FoV_4*):

```scala
// Scala
object ZOrderClustering extends SpaceFillingCurveClustering {
  override protected[skipping] def getClusteringExpression(
    cols: Seq[Column], numRanges: Int): Column = {
    assert(cols.size >= 1, "Cannot do Z-Order clustering by zero columns!")
    val rangeIdCols = cols.map(range_partition_id(_, numRanges))
    interleave_bits(rangeIdCols: _*).cast(StringType)
  }
}
```

This takes the multiple columns passed to the Z-Order modifier and then alternates the column bits to create a new temporary column that provides a linear dimension you can now sort on and then partition as a range. Now that you know how it works, consider a more discrete example that demonstrates this approach.

Lead by example

This example will show you how the differences in the layout can affect the number of files that need to be read with Z-Order clustering involved. In Figure 10-3, you have a two-dimensional array within which you want to match data files. Both the x range and the y range are numbered 1 to 9. The points are partitioned by the x values, and you want to find all the points at which both x and y are either 5 or 6.

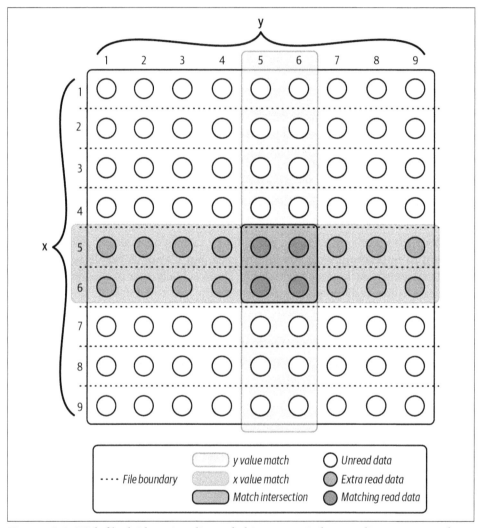

Figure 10-3. With files laid out in a linear fashion, you wind up reading extra records

First, find the rows that match the conditions $x = 5$ or $x = 6$. Then find the columns matching the conditions $y = 5$ or $y = 6$. The points where they intersect are the target values you want, but if the condition matches for a file, you have to read the whole file. So for the files you read (the ones that contain matching conditions), you can sort the data into two categories: data that matches your conditions specifically, and extra data in the files that you still have to read anyway.

As you can see, you have to read the entirety of the files (rows) where $x = 5$ or $x = 6$ to capture the values of y that match as well, which means nearly 80% of our read operation was unnecessary.

Now update your set to be arranged with a space-filling Z-Order curve instead. In both cases, you have a total of nine data files, but now the layout of the data (as shown in Figure 10-4) is such that by *analyzing the metadata* (checking the min/max values per file), you can skip additional files and avoid a large chunk of unnecessary records being read.

After applying the clustering technique to the example, you only have to read a single file. This is partly why Z-Ordering goes alongside an OPTIMIZE action. The data needs to be sorted and arranged according to the clusters. You might wonder if you still need to partition the data in these cases since the data is organized efficiently. The short answer is *yes*, as you may still want to partition the data, for example, in cases where you are not using liquid clustering and might run into concurrency issues. When the data is partitioned, OPTIMIZE and ZORDER will only cluster and compact data already colocated within the same partition. In other words, clusters will be created only within the scope of data inside a single partition, so the benefits of ZORDER still directly rely on a good choice of partitioning scheme.

The method for determining the closeness, or cluster membership, relies on inter-leaving the column bits and then range partitioning the dataset.[12]

---

12 There is a version of this written in Python to encourage additional exploration in the Chapter 10 section of the book's repository (*https://oreil.ly/Hms_d*).

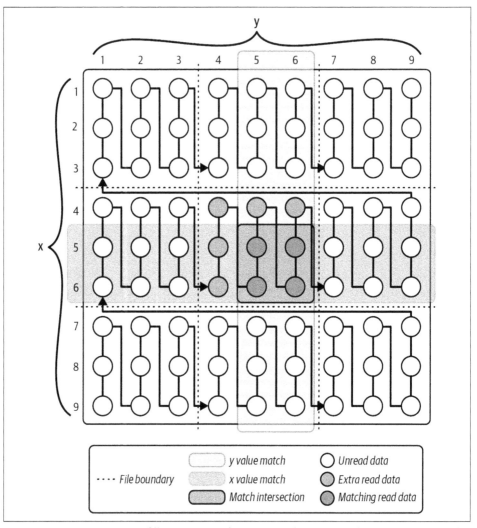

Figure 10-4. Using a space-filling curve such as a Z-Order curve reduces the number of files and unneeded data reads required for operations

You can use these steps to accomplish this:

1. Create columns containing the coordinate positions as integers.
2. Map them to binary values.
3. Bitwise interleave the binary values.
4. Map the resulting binary values back to integers.

5. Range partition the new one-dimensional column.

6. Plot the points by coordinates and bin identifier.

The results are shown in Figure 10-5. They don't show quite the same behavior as Figure 10-4, which is very neat and orderly, but they do clearly show that even with a self-generated and directly calculated approach, you could create your own Z-Ordering on a dataset.

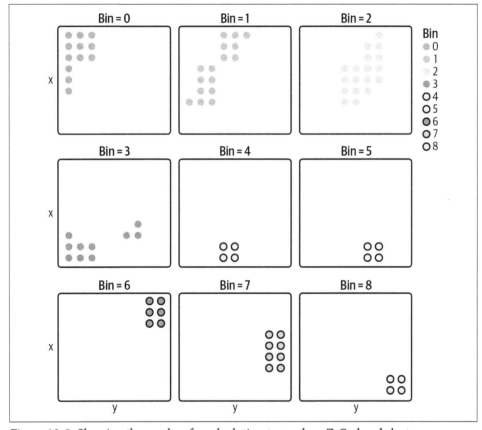

Figure 10-5. Showing the results of a calculation to produce Z-Ordered clusters

From a mathematical perspective, there are more details and even some enhancements that could be considered, but this algorithm is already built into Delta Lake, so for the sake of our sanity, this is the current limit of our rigor.[13]

---

13 For more technical details, refer to Mohamed F. Mokbel, Walid G. Aref, and Ibrahim Kamel, "Performance of Multi-dimensional Space-Filling Curves" (*https://oreil.ly/yLR53*), in *Proceedings of the 10th ACM International Symposium on Advances in Geographic Information Systems (GIS '02)* (New York: Association for Computing Machinery, 2002), 149–54.

More recently, there have been questions about whether any table ought to be partitioned so that there are fewer constraints on the further development of ideas like Z-Ordering. This is partly because it can be very difficult to settle on the right partitioning columns from the outset, outside of highly static processes. Needs can also change over time, leading to added maintenance work in updating the table structure (see the example in Chapter 6 if you need to do this). One development in this area may reduce these maintenance burdens and decisions for good.

Cluster By

The end of partitioning? That's the idea. The newest and best-performing method for taking advantage of data skipping came in Delta Lake 3.0. Liquid clustering takes the place of traditional Hive-style partitioning with the introduction of the `CLUSTER BY` parameter during table creation. Like `ZORDER`, `CLUSTER BY` uses a space-filling curve to determine the best data layout but changes to other curve types that yield more efficiency. Figure 10-6 shows how different *partitions* may either get coalesced together or be broken down in different combinations within the same table structure.

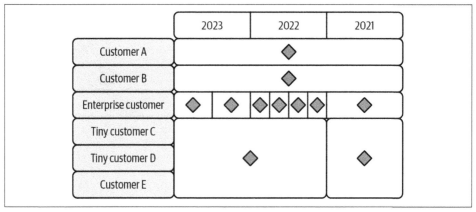

Figure 10-6. An example file layout resulting from applying liquid clustering on a dataset[14]

Where it starts to get different is in how you use it. Liquid clustering *must* be declared during table creation to enable it, and it is incompatible with partitioning, so you can't define both. When set, it creates a table property, `clusteringColumns`, which can be used to validate that liquid clustering is in effect for the table. Functionally, it

---

14 This example comes from a fuller walk-through highlighting how liquid clustering works both to split apart larger partitions as well as to coalesce smaller ones. For the full example, check out Denny Lee's blog post "How Delta Lake Liquid Clustering Conceptually Works" (*https://oreil.ly/raq79*).

operates similarly to ZORDER BY in that it still helps to know which columns might yield the greatest filtering behaviors on queries, so you should still make sure to keep our optimization goals in sight.

You also will not be able to ZORDER the table independently, as the action takes place primarily during compaction operations. A small side benefit worth mentioning is that liquid clustering reduces the specific information needed to run OPTIMIZE against a set of tables because there are no extra parameters to set, allowing you to even loop through a list of tables to run OPTIMIZE without worrying about matching up the correct clustering keys for each table. You also get row-level concurrency—a must-have feature for a partitionless table—which means that most of the time you can stop trying to schedule processes around one another and reduce downtime, since even OPTIMIZE can be run during write operations. The only conflicts that happen are when two operations try to modify the same row at the same time.

File clustering, like that shown in Figure 10-6, gets applied to compaction in two different ways. For normal OPTIMIZE operations, it will check for changes to the layout distribution and adjust as needed. This newer clustering enables a best-effort application of clustering the data during write processes, which makes it far more reliably incremental to apply. This means less work is required to rewrite files during compaction, which also makes that process more efficient as well. This feature is called *eager clustering*. This means that for data under the threshold (512 GB by default), new data appended to the table will be partially clustered at the time of the write (the best-effort part). In some cases, the size of these files will vary from the larger table until a larger amount of data accumulates and OPTIMIZE is run again. This is because the file sizes are still driven by the OPTIMIZE command.

 To use the CLUSTER BY argument, you need at least a writer version of 7 (*https://oreil.ly/EuuJm*) in a Delta Lake release with the liquid clustering table feature present and enabled. To only consume the tables, you need a reader version of 3 (*https://oreil.ly/eVeJW*). This means that if you have other/older consumers in the environment, you are at risk of breaking workflows while migrating to newer versions and protocols.

Explanation

CLUSTER BY uses a different space-filling curve than ZORDER, but without the presence of partitions, it creates clusters across the whole table. Using it is fairly straightforward, as you simply include a CLUSTER BY argument as part of your table creation statement. You must do so at creation or else the table will not be compatible as a liquid partitioning table—it cannot be added afterward. You can, however, later update the columns chosen for the operation or even remove all columns from the clustering by using an ALTER TABLE statement and CLUSTER BY (use NONE instead of providing a column name or names for the latter case—there's an example of this soon). This means you gain great flexibility with clustering keys, because they can be changed as needs arise or as consumption patterns evolve.

As you're creating tables that are optimized for either the downstream consumers or your write process, this presents an area in which you can make just such a decision between the two. Similar to other cases, if the goal is to get the speediest write performance, then you can elect not to include any clustering at all or to include as little as you wish. For the downstream consumers, though, you gain a considerable advantage. You saw in Chapter 5 that although it's possible to repartition a given table, it's not the most straightforward operation. Now you can adapt to downstream consumer needs more optimally by redefining the clustering columns, and this will be picked up during the next compaction process to apply the layout to the underlying files. This means that as usage patterns change, or even if you made questionable assumptions or errors in your original layout, they are more easily rectifiable. The following example shows how you can leverage liquid clustering in the Databricks environment.

 If the initial write to a table is larger than 10 TB—for example, if you use a CTAS (CREATE TABLE AS SELECT) statement to do a one-time conversion—the first compaction operation can suffer from performance issues and take some time to complete. The clustering quality may also be affected somewhat. It is recommended to run the process in batches for large tables as a result, but otherwise even tables of 100 TB can have liquid clustering applied to them.

Hopefully, it has become apparent that liquid clustering offers several advantages over Hive-style partitioning and Z-Ordering tables whenever it's a good fit. You get faster write operations with similar read performance to other well-tuned tables. You can avoid problems with partitioning. You get more consistent file sizes, which makes downstream processes more resistant to task skewing. Any column can be a clustering column, and you gain much more flexibility to shift these keys as required. Last, thanks to row-level concurrency, conflicts with processes are minimized, allowing workflows to be more dynamic and adaptable.

Example

In this example, you'll see the Wikipedia articles dataset found in the */databricks-datasets/* directory available in any Databricks workspace. This Parquet directory has roughly 11 GB of data (disk size) across almost 1,100 gzipped files.

Start by creating a DataFrame to work with, add a regular date column to the set, and then create a temporary view to work with in SQL afterward:

```
# Python
articles _path = (
"/databricks-datasets/wikipedia-datasets/" +
"data-001/en_wikipedia/articles-only-parquet")

parquetDf = (
    spark
    .read
    .parquet(articles_path)
)
parquetDf.createOrReplaceTempView("source_view")
```

With a temporary view in place to read from, you can create a table simply by adding the CLUSTER BY argument to a regular CTAS statement to define the table:

```
-- SQL
CREATE TABLE
    example.wikipages
CLUSTER BY
    (id)
AS (SELECT *,
    date(revisionTimestamp) AS articleDate
    FROM source_view
    )
```

You still have a normal statistics collection action to think about, so you probably want to exclude the actual article text from that process, but you also created the articleDate column, which you probably want to use for clustering. To do this, you can add the following steps: reduce the number of columns you collect statistics on to only the first five, move both the articleDate and text columns, and then define the new CLUSTER BY column. You can do all of these using ALTER TABLE statements:

```
-- SQL
ALTER TABLE example.wikipages
   SET tblproperties ("delta.dataSkippingNumIndexedCols"=5);
ALTER TABLE example.wikipages CHANGE articleDate first;
ALTER TABLE example.wikipages CHANGE `text` after revisionTimestamp;
ALTER TABLE example.wikipages CLUSTER BY (articleDate);
```

After this step, you can run your OPTIMIZE command, and everything else will be handled for you. Then you can use a simple query like the following for testing:

```
-- SQL
SELECT
  year(articleDate) AS PublishingYear,
  count(distinct title) AS Articles
FROM
  example.wikipages
WHERE
  month(articleDate)=3
AND
  day(articleDate)=4
```

```
GROUP BY
  year(articleDate)
ORDER BY
  publishingYear
```

Overall, the process was easy, and the performance was comparable—only slightly faster than the Z-Ordered Delta Lake table. The initial write for liquid partitioning also took about the same amount of time. These results should be expected, because the arrangement is still basically linear. One of the biggest gains in value here, however, is the added flexibility. If at some point you decide to revert to clustering by the id column as in the original definition, you just need to run another ALTER TABLE statement and then plan for a bigger-than-usual OPTIMIZE process later on. Whether you end up using liquid clustering or rely on the familiar Z-Ordering, there's still an additional indexing tool you can put in place that further improves the query performance of chosen tables.

Bloom Filter Index

A *Bloom filter index* is a hashmap index that identifies whether a value *probably* exists in a file or *definitely* does not.[15] Hashmap indexes are considered space-efficient because an index file containing the hashed value (in a single row) is stored alongside the associated data file, and you can specify which columns you wish to be indexed. The catch is that you want to have a reasonable idea of the number of distinct values that need to be indexed, because this will determine the length of hashes needed to avoid collisions if that number is set too small or to avoid wasting space if it is set too large.

Bloom filter indexes can be used by either Parquet or Delta Lake tables in Apache Spark, even if they use liquid clustering. At runtime, Spark checks for the existence of the directory and uses the index if it exists. It does not need to be specified during query time.

A deeper look

A Bloom filter index is created at the time of writing files, so this has some implications to consider if you want to use the option. In particular, if you want all the data indexed, then you should define the index immediately after defining a table but before you write any data into it. The trick to this part is that defining the index correctly requires you to know the number of distinct values of any columns you want to index ahead of time. This may require some additional processing overhead, but for the example, you can add a COUNT DISTINCT statement and get the value

---

15 If you wish to dive more deeply into the mechanisms and calculations used to create Bloom filter indexes, consider starting with the "Bloom filter" Wikipedia article (*https://oreil.ly/qlQqc*).

as part of the process to accomplish this using only metadata (another Delta Lake benefit). Use the same table from the CLUSTER BY example, but now insert a Bloom filter creation process right after the table definition statement (before you run the OPTIMIZE process):

```python
# Python
from pyspark.sql.functions import countDistinct

cdf = spark.table("example.wikipages")
raw_items = cdf.agg(countDistinct(cdf.id)).collect()[0][0]
num_items = int(raw_items * 1.25)

spark.sql(f"""
    create bloomfilter index
    on table
        example.wikipages
    for columns
        (id options (fpp=0.05, numItems={num_items}))
""")
```

Here the previously created table is loaded, and you can bring in the Spark SQL function countDistinct to get the number of items for the column you want to add an index for. Since this number determines the overall hash length, it's probably a good idea to pad it—for example, where raw_items is multiplied by 1.25, there was an additional 25% added to get num_items to allow for some growth to the table (adjust according to your projected needs). Then define the Bloom filter index itself using SQL. Note that the syntax of the creation statement details exactly what you wish to do for the table and is pretty straightforward. Then specify the column(s) to index and set a value for fpp (more details are in the following section on configuration) and the number of distinct items you want to be able to index (as already calculated).

Configuration

The fpp value in the parameters is short for *false positive probability*. This number sets a limit on what rate of false positives is acceptable during reads. A lower value increases the accuracy of the index but takes a little bit of a performance hit. This is because the fpp value determines how many bits are required for each element to be stored, so increasing the accuracy increases the size of the index itself.

The less commonly used configuration option, maxExpectedFpp, is a threshold value set to 1.0 by default, which disables it. Setting any other value in the interval [0, 1) sets the maximum expected false positive probability. If the calculated fpp value exceeds the threshold, the filter is deemed to be more costly to use than it is beneficial, and so it is not written to disk. Reads on the associated data file would then fall back to normal Spark operation, since no index remains for it.

You can define a Bloom filter index on numeric types, datetime types, strings, and bytes, but you cannot use Bloom filter indexes on nested columns. The filtering actions that work with these columns are and, or, in, equals, and equalsnullsafe. One additional limitation is that null values are not indexed in the process, so filtering actions related to null values will still require a metadata or file scan.

Conclusion

When you set out to refine the way you engineer data tables and pipelines with Delta Lake, you may have a clear optimization target, or you might have conflicting objectives. In this chapter, you saw how partitioning and file sizes influence the statistics generated for Delta Lake tables. Further, you saw how compaction and space-filling curves can influence those statistics. In any case, you should be well equipped with knowledge about the different kinds of optimization tools you have available to you in working with Delta Lake. Most specifically, note that file statistics and data skipping are probably the most valuable tools for improving downstream query performance, and you have many levers you can use to impact those statistics and optimize for any situation. Whatever your goal is, this should prove to be a valuable reference as you evaluate and design data processes with Delta Lake.

Successful Design Patterns

Considering Delta Lake's flexibility and applicability to data applications, trying to capture all the cases for which you can use Delta Lake is like trying to describe all the potential uses of paper. The variety feels limitless, and its value is legion. That said, we will do our best in this chapter to capture exemplary cases of using Delta Lake and to highlight the value in doing so.

We will start by showing how the performance optimizations and simplified maintenance operations in Delta Lake helped Comcast slash the amount of resources needed to run its smart remote process by a factor of 10. We will then describe how Scribd helped evolve the Delta Lake landscape and created the Delta Rust implementation, which is one hundred times cheaper than the equivalent structured streaming applications. Finally, we'll see how Delta Lake feeds high-volume operational CDC ingestion and supports real-time workloads from Flink at DoorDash, creating a single-source-of-truth lakehouse from many different operational systems. Each section is accompanied by several resources you may wish to review to explore the stories found here in greater detail.

Slashing Compute Costs

The focus of this section reaches many audiences—literally! It's no secret that there has been somewhat of an eruption in the number of streaming entertainment services over the last several years. Organizations supporting these kinds of services tend to have large volumes of high-throughput streaming data that they need to manage to help support the service.

High-Speed Solutions

Streaming media services usually capture data from individual end-user devices, which include several different components. To run such services successfully, you may require varying kinds of information about device health, application status, playback event information, and interaction information. This usually translates to a need for building high-throughput stream processing applications and solutions.

One of the most critical components of these streaming applications is ensuring the capture of the data with reliability and efficiency. In Chapter 7, several implementation methods and their benefits demonstrate how Delta Lake can play a critical role in doing exactly these kinds of data capture tasks. Delta Lake is often the destination for many of these ingestion processes because it has ACID transaction guarantees and additional features like optimized writes that make high-volume stream processing better and easier.

Let's say you want to monitor the Quality of Service (QoS) across all your users in near real time. To accomplish this task, you usually need not just playback event information but also the relevant context from each user's session, a sequence of interactions bound together over some time span. Sessionization is often an important cornerstone of many downstream operations beyond ingestion and typically falls into the data engineering stages of a larger data process, as shown in Figure 11-1. With session information and other system information in Delta Lake, you can power downstream analytics use cases such as Quality of Service measurement or trending item recommendations while maintaining a low turnaround time in processing.

Building out these pipelines is often fairly complex and will involve the interaction of multiple pipelines and processes. At the core, you will find that each component boils down to the idea of needing to build a robust data processing pipeline to serve multiple business needs.

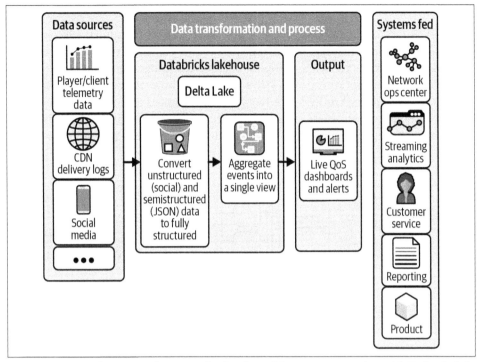

Figure 11-1. A reference architecture for Quality of Service monitoring with Delta Lake[1]

Smart Device Integration

Comcast developed a successful smart remote control device to change the way people watch television. The crux of the company's data problem was that this kind of system requires large amounts of data processing and poses several technical and organizational challenges. Through the use of Delta Lake as a data format, many of these challenges were overcome, and Comcast was able to slash the cloud infrastructure requirements for one of its most critical workloads by 90%. It was also able to solve many quality-of-life issues around these data processes. Here you can see how Comcast solved many of those challenges.

---

[1] For an extended exploration of a QoS solution end-to-end, we recommend the blog post "How to Build a Quality of Service (QoS) Analytics Solution for Streaming Video Services" (*https://oreil.ly/2s3oO*) and its accompanying notebooks from Databricks.

Comcast's smart remote

Comcast (*https://oreil.ly/uYhkA*) is the largest American multinational telecommunications and media conglomerate, and in this section you will see how the company was able to drastically reduce the amount of cloud resources required to run its most important workloads. Comcast has strived to change how people interact with their televisions through its Xfinity Voice Remote, which acts as a central point of access. So, as you might expect, there are a lot of critical data workloads that center around the device at the edge. Figure 11-2 shows a high-level example of the interaction flow.

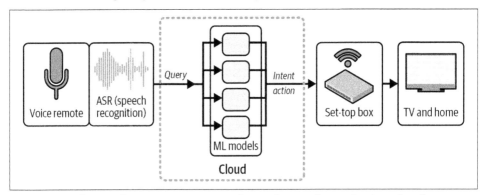

Figure 11-2. Comcast's smart remote control provides an alternative interface for entertainment

Before we explore how Comcast is building its solutions on Delta Lake, it might be useful to review more specific information about the scale of its operations. Comcast drives interactions through its voice remote, and its customers used this remote 14 billion times in 2018–2019 (Figure 11-3 illustrates the relative scale to data processing).[2] Users expect many things in their experience with the applications, such as getting accurate searches and feeling enabled to find the right content for consumption. Each user's individual experience should also have elements of personalization that make the experience their own. With the voice remote, users can interact with the whole system; anything they want is just a quick phrase away. On top of this, Comcast uses user data to create personalized experiences.

---

2 For additional detail, see the Databricks videos "Comcast Makes Home Entertainment Accessible to Everyone with Voice, Data and AI" (*https://oreil.ly/mr9eJ*) and "Winning the Audience with AI: How Comcast Built an Agile Data and AI Platform at Scale" (*https://oreil.ly/LR50z*).

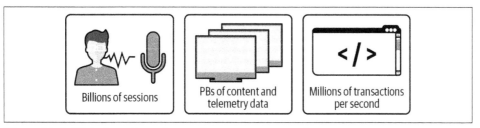

Figure 11-3. High data throughput volumes occur across large consumer groups

Consider the technical components essential to running such services behind the scenes. First, receiving voice commands as input (something that's exploded in popularity more recently) is a technically challenging problem. There's the transformation of voice to a digital signal, which then has to be mapped to each needed command. There's often an additional component to this mapping of correcting for intent. Is it more likely for someone to be searching for a show called *How It's Made* or to be asking about other shows that explain how some particular thing is made? If it is a search command, there is still a need to find similar content through a matching algorithm. All of this gets wrapped together into a single interface point in a setting in which the user experience needs to be measured against accuracy, so getting bits of data about these processes and enabling analytics to assess immediate problems or long-term trends is also critical.

So now we have voice inputs that have to be converted to embedding vectors (vectors of numeric data capturing semantic meaning as "tokens"), as well as contextual data (this could be what type of page the user is on, other recent searches, date-time parameters, etc.) for each interaction with the remote.[3] The goal is to collect all this and provide inference back through the user interface (UI) in nearly real time. From a functional standpoint, there's also a large amount of telemetry information that needs to be collected to maintain insights into things such as device health, connectivity status, viewing session data, and other similar concerns.

Once the problem of getting this data from individual devices to a centralized processing platform is solved, there are still additional challenges in deciding how to standardize the data sources, as multiple versions of devices may have differing available information, or usage regions may have differing collection laws that mean fuller or lesser contents of captured events. Downstream from standardization, there is still a need to organize the data and create actionable steps in a fit-for-function format.

---

3 For a more robust treatment of embeddings, see Marcos Garcia, "Embeddings in Natural Language Processing: Theory and Advances in Vector Representations of Meaning" (*https://oreil.ly/UEtL_*), *Computational Linguistics* 47, no. 3 (2021): 699–701.

For all of this to happen from a single team would require a huge amount of effort and a lengthy amount of time, so enabling multiple teams to collaborate to tackle the complexity would be beneficial, if not an absolute necessity.

Earlier attempts

To support the voice remote, Comcast needed to be able to analyze queries and look at user journeys to do things like measure the intention of a query. At a rate of up to 15 million transactions per second, Comcast needed to enable sessionization across billions of sessions on multiple petabytes of data. Running on native AWS services, it would overrun limits and increase the concurrency it was using until it was eventually running 32 concurrent job runs across 640 virtual machines to be able to get to the scale it needed for sessionization. The processing flow is shown in Figure 11-4. This led Comcast to seek a scalable, reliable, and performant solution.

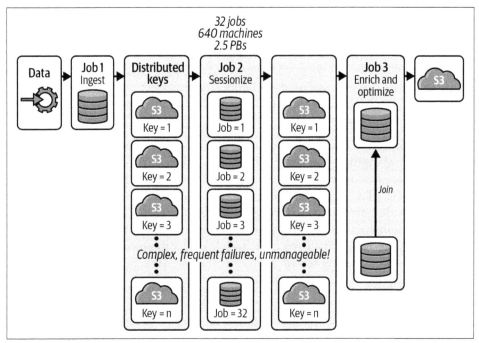

Figure 11-4. To scale the earlier data ingestion pipeline, Comcast had to crank up the concurrency

Delta Lake reduces the complexity

Delta Lake was built to help solve exactly these kinds of problems. ACID transactions and support for multiple writers with features like optimized writes and autocompaction each play a role in simplifying and overcoming the challenges involved with large-scale stream processing tasks. The problem here originates in the nature of the data and the partitioning by key values. Many natural keys (e.g., user ID values) will result in skewing of the data. This means that high-volume key lookups become increasingly burdensome as data volumes increase, and the highest-frequency keys can become a bottleneck in your application.[4] Enabling additional features such as `delta.randomFilePrefixes` for high transaction rates with cloud providers allows you as an engineer to achieve massive scale with improved efficiency, as doing so removes potential barriers caused by prefix limitations.[5] By allowing a distributed framework to handle the key partitioning rather than forcing a manual parallelization of the tasks, you can gain significant performance improvements. By making this change, Comcast was able to run the same ingestion process with a single Spark job on just 64 virtual machines. The resulting process flow is shown in Figure 11-5.[6]

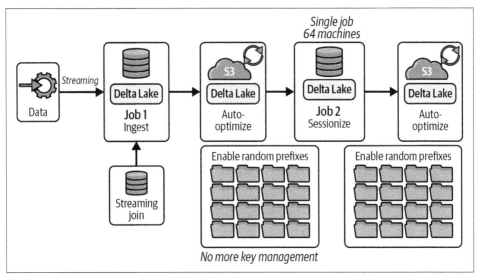

Figure 11-5. Delta Lake provides the foundation for optimized ingestion and sessionization

If this was the whole story, you would probably already be convinced of the value Delta Lake can bring to ease processing burdens. What's great is that it's *not* the whole story. In its Databricks environment, Comcast was able to readily access this sessionized data for multiple downstream purposes.

---

4 There is some good discussion of hot-spot keys in key-value stores in the section "Partitioning of Key-Value Data" in Martin Kleppmann's *Designing Data-Intensive Applications* (O'Reilly).

5 AWS states in its performance guidance for S3 (*https://oreil.ly/N2kZt*) that sequential prefixes can also be effective.

6 Databricks, "Customer Story: Comcast" (*https://oreil.ly/iDgXL*).

It was mentioned already that building a process like this may involve different kinds of machine learning tasks, such as the creation of embedding vectors or model inference. In particular, there would be a need to transform that voice input into meaningful action. By capturing the sessionized data and storing it efficiently, data scientists can build modeling pipelines quickly and easily.

 MLflow (*https://oreil.ly/iHwzE*), another open source product, offers many features for improving the end-to-end MLOps process. MLflow's key features include tracking and comparing multiple model versions in experiments, a registry for management, and mechanisms enabling the easier deployment of model objects. MLflow also includes support for large language models (LLMs), other generative models, and AI agents in addition to traditional machine learning models.

Since Comcast is using MLflow, it gets additional side benefits from Delta Lake in its machine learning processes. With the data source tracking available in the experiment for a project, MLflow can track information about the Delta Lake table being used for the experiment without having to make a copy of the data, in the same way as you would with a CSV file or other data sources.[7] Figure 11-6 shows where MLflow sits in the data life cycle. Since Delta Lake also has time travel capabilities, machine learning experiments can have enhanced reproducibility, which would benefit anyone maintaining data science products in production.

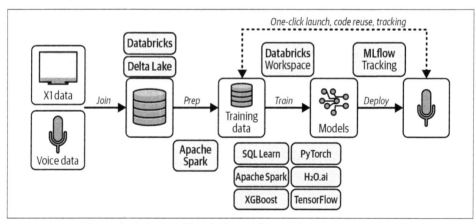

Figure 11-6. Delta Lake helps enable reliable end-to-end MLOps processes

---

7 To compare the entire capabilities for tracking different kinds of files in MLflow experiments, we suggest you look at the "mlflow.data" section of their documentation (*https://oreil.ly/Sp7Sz*).

Another important target is to be able to monitor the telemetry data involved for QoS or similar types of analytical applications. In Comcast's case, it used Databricks SQL to run analytical workloads directly on its Delta Lake tables instead of in Redshift, as it had previously.[8] The company reported for a pilot of this approach that it chose its 10 worst-performing queries to evaluate the performance. It observed a reduction of more than 70% in the time spent running queries (see Figure 11-7).

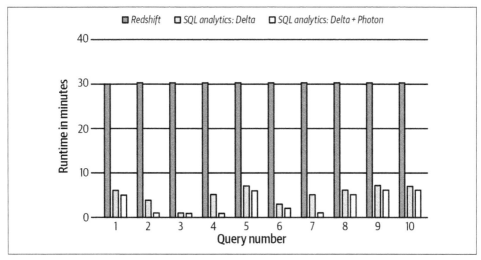

Figure 11-7. Performance comparison results for query running times in Databricks SQL on Delta Lake versus Redshift

In the end, it's looking to be highly advantageous for Comcast to continue innovating with Delta Lake. It has so far experienced huge savings gains in its data ingestion processes and has a promising outlook on improving reporting. This should allow Comcast to further improve end-user experiences for its smart remotes and increase overall satisfaction rates.

---

8 Molly Nagamuthu and Suraj Nesamani, "SQL Analytics Powering Telemetry Analysis at Comcast" (*https://oreil.ly/OcgQf*), posted September 16, 2021, by Databricks, YouTube.

Efficient Streaming Ingestion

Suppose you have some large ingestion pipelines running on Kafka and Databricks to feed your Delta Lake environment. Now suppose you have a crack engineering team that decides to invest significant effort into reducing costs by crafting a solution for small streams that doesn't require the heavy-lifting capabilities of Spark. You also want to bring all that data together downstream from those ingestion processes. What you might be looking for then is something like what the team at Scribd (*https:// oreil.ly/nCrpV*) has done.

Streaming Ingestion

Stream processing applications for ingestion tasks are relatively common. We have a large array of streaming frameworks out there to choose from. Among the most common ones are the open source Apache Kafka, Kinesis from AWS, Event Hubs in Azure, and Google's Pub/Sub.

While there is certainly a wide variety of applicability covering interesting subjects like real-time telemetry monitoring of IoT devices and fraudulent transaction monitoring or alerting, one of the most common cases for stream processing is large-scale and dynamic data ingestion.[9] For many organizations, collecting data about activities by end users on mobile applications or point-of-sale (POS) data from retailers directly translates to success in supporting mission-critical business analytics applications. Acquiring large amounts of data from widely dispersed sources quickly and correctly allows businesses to become more rapidly adaptable to changing conditions as well (Figure 11-8 shows a unified architecture across many streaming sources).

Great flexibility, as achieved through the enablement of real-time processes and the use of artificial intelligence applications, is fueled by dynamic and resilient data pipelines often falling into this category.[10] In all of these, there's usually an element of capturing inbound data for later analytical or evaluation purposes, so while there might be additional components in some processing pipelines, at the end of the day this process applies to most stream processing applications.[11]

---

9 Many teams document their own journey of landing streaming data sources in Delta Lake; for example, the Michelin team captured a step-by-step implementation guide (*https://oreil.ly/XCGXN*) to building a Kafka + Avro + Spark + Delta Lake IoT data ingestion pipeline in a Microsoft Azure environment.

10 The term *artificial intelligence* is used here in the classical software development sense of "narrow AI," meaning the application of machine learning algorithms to make automated business decisions without human interaction—see the definitions of artificial intelligence posted by the Stanford Institute of Human-Centered Artificial Intelligence (*https://oreil.ly/rjFV9*).

11 Refer to the discussion of the medallion architecture in Chapter 7 or 9 for more details on implementing stream processing applications and Delta Lake.

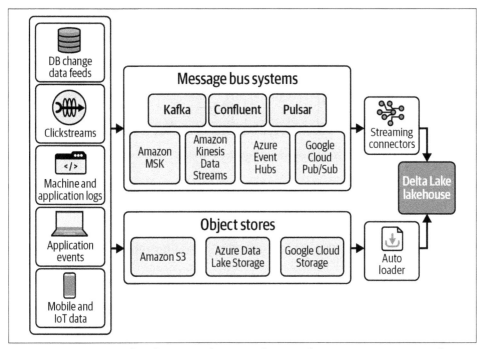

Figure 11-8. An example reference architecture diagram for stream processing applications with a Delta Lake sink from Databricks[12]

Consider the case of IoT data coming in from devices. If you send all the data into Kafka, you can build a Spark application to consume that stream and capture all the original data as it is received, following the model of the medallion architecture. Then you can create business-level reporting and send those results out to be consumed in a downstream application. Naturally, there are many variations on this approach, but the general pipeline model is similar, as shown in Figure 11-9. At Scribd, this application was so common that they built a new framework around implementing this process.

---

12 This architecture diagram comes from the Databricks blog post "Simplifying Streaming Data Ingestion into Delta Lake" (*https://oreil.ly/A6Rag*) (accessed December 7, 2023).

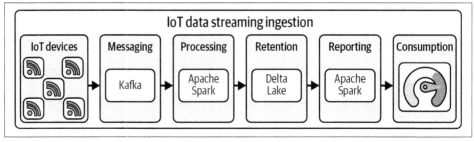

Figure 11-9. A simplified streaming data ingestion architecture for IoT devices specific to Kafka

The Inception of Delta Rust

While it started as an open publishing platform, Scribd (*https://oreil.ly/nCrpV*) is now a digital document library, with over 170 million documents in more than 150 categories and counting. Part of Scribd's mission is to change the way the world reads. Scribd aims to do so by providing a wide range of reading material at a fair price for both creators and consumers, providing intellectual property protection for creators, and keeping costs low, preferring to build its brand on community rather than on advertising.

Inherent to its existence as a digital library, Scribd runs its website as well as mobile applications.[13] Users can utilize Scribd's website and mobile applications to browse through a digital library with millions of presentations, research papers, templates, and other kinds of documents. All the documents in the library are uploaded by creators, writers, and editors using multiple common document formats like *.pdf*, *.txt*, *.doc*, *.ppt*, *.xls*, and *.docx*. There is also a subscription system. All these different system components translate to events that must be collected and handled accordingly. Scribd accomplishes this by using a fairly large number of event streams through Kafka.

Building a streaming ingestion pipeline typically requires multiple components. Putting this into the immediate context, a straightforward design approach would be to build a stream processing application for each topic stream coming from Kafka. In the case of Scribd, we can easily build a list of some of the probable event topic streams: creator uploads, reading events, system login or authentication events, subscription events, web traffic events, searches, item bookmarking or saving events, and item sharing events. This means many different stream processing applications will be involved, which usually leads to the development of some kind of framework to reduce development and maintenance overhead across all the applications.

---

13 Christian Williams, "Streaming Data into Delta Lake with Rust and Kafka" (*https://oreil.ly/dwPgy*), posted July 19, 2022, by Databricks, YouTube.

Maintaining a stream processing framework for many event streams can be quite a complex task, and without careful planning it can be quite expensive as well. Here is the story of the evolution of Scribd's stream processing framework, leading up to its creation of the *kafka-delta-ingest* library (*https://oreil.ly/ivqMr*), and of how it cut ingestion costs by 95%.

The Evolution of Ingestion

The stream processing platform at Scribd has been revamped a couple of different times. Early on, all the processing was done in Kafka and Hadoop, which used to be a fairly standard stream processing approach. This version of the platform was later subsumed by a move to Kafka and Databricks using Spark Structured Streaming and Delta Lake. This was a favorable move for Scribd, in part because of Delta Lake's features, such as the `optimize` and `vacuum` utilities and the addition of ACID transactions.

However, in Scribd's case, there were many topic streams, and many of them were on the small side. This led to some attempts to reduce spiraling ingestion costs. At Scribd, larger dedicated clusters were still used "when it didn't seem wasteful" to do so—that is, when there were large tasks that efficiently utilized the cluster resources. Many small streams were instead *stacked* (run simultaneously on the same cluster), which produces a similar level of efficient resource utilization and thus reduces overall processing costs. There are still some challenges in doing this, however. Making decisions about how to logically group topics can be frustrating. There's always the possibility that one of the processing tasks could fail, causing all the stacked streams on that cluster to subsequently fail. This is in addition to the already slightly challenging task of trying to accommodate maintenance tasks in your ingestion processes.

The Scribd team had a few desires for improving the situation:

- Further reducing the costs, if possible
- Different observability of the ingestion processes
- Better handling of job failures
- More flexible adjustment to changes in the throughput size of event streams

This also led to thoughtful reflection on how the team might approach the problem. Would it be possible to do this without Spark or to find some more minimal overhead method? How would the team still maintain its standardization on Delta Lake, since that made stewardship so much easier?

To the Scribd team at the time, it seemed like with some invested effort, there might be another way to approach the problem. The team has relatively simple ingestion processes that are append-only operations with no filters, joins, or aggregations and uses only a subset of Delta Lake's features, which proved to simplify the development of an alternative.

The scenario at Scribd led to its investment in developing two projects that are now well-supported and accepted parts of the larger Delta Lake ecosystem. The first project is delta-rs (*https://oreil.ly/ZtPkY*), the Rust-based implementation of the Delta Lake protocol (*https://oreil.ly/CPxmm*) explored in depth in Chapter 6. The second project is *kafka-delta-ingest* (a short guide to using *kafka-delta-ingest* can be found in Chapter 4), a lightweight companion framework designed to quickly and easily ingest data from a Kafka topic stream into a Delta Lake table.[14] Together the projects form an efficient operating pair (Figure 11-10 shows the simplified data flow).

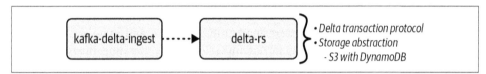

Figure 11-10. Scribd's kafka-delta-ingest in tandem with delta-rs for efficient ingestion

Undertaking such an endeavor was not without risks or potential blocking issues. The risk of corrupting the Delta log posed one challenge, as did the need to manually control offset tracking in Kafka to avoid duplicate or dropped records. Scribd also needs to support multiple writers to tables, and furthermore, some limitations in AWS S3 require specific handling (e.g., S3 lock coordination).[15]

Scribd runs anywhere from 70 to 90 of these *kafka-delta-ingest* and delta-rs pipelines in production. It runs serverless computation of these pipelines through AWS Fargate (*https://oreil.ly/uMffX*) and monitors everything in Datadog (*https://oreil.ly/FyOGF*). Some of the things it monitors include message deserialization logs and several metrics: the number of transformations and failures, the number of Arrow batches in memory, the sizes of Parquet data files written, and the current time lag in Kafka streams.

---

14 Christian Williams, "Kafka to Delta Lake, as Fast as Possible" (*https://oreil.ly/2LRy2*), *Scribd Technology* (blog), Scribd, May 19, 2021.

15 Some of these S3 issues are discussed in the D3L2 web series episode "The Inception of Delta Rust" (*https://oreil.ly/C70Fe*) on YouTube.

All of this led to rather significant cost savings in ingestion processing, as with the tools the Scribd team built, the cost for running some of the stream processing applications is reduced to as much as 100 times lower (shown in Figure 11-11). Another feature that rounds out this fantastic achievement is that this is accomplished in such a way (by remaining standardized on Delta Lake) that the ingested data is immediately available for analytics and machine learning processes or for further integration with other batch processes in Scribd's Databricks environment, and it maintains queryability.

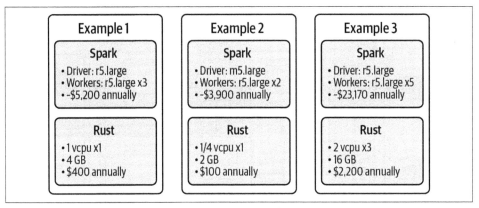

Figure 11-11. Some of the cost-saving examples Scribd shared during Data+AI Summit 2022 that show the cost of running a process originally in Spark and then using delta-rs[16]

Coordinating Complex Systems

From smart devices and entertainment to security and digital payment systems, there is no shortage of high-volume data sources. With Scribd, much of the focus was on simple event capture, with less stress on the operational systems where *kafka-delta-ingest* is a viable solution. Now let's consider cases in which the edge of interaction with the outside world is less straightforward and requires more services. It's more messy and more human. Complex applications that continuously evolve tend to have many more integrated operational components that need to stay in harmony over time, or else you might find yourself spending too much time curating existing data, rather than thinking about new requirements, sources, or processes as you would probably prefer.

The inclusion of multiple real-time operational databases and the demand for generating business value often mean that the information from those databases needs to

---

16 Note that the Rust resources show individual vCPU and memory allocation, whereas the Spark resources show clusters composed of multiple EC2 instances; r5.large EC2 instances each have two vCPUs and 16 GB of RAM. Amazon EC2 R5 instance metrics can be found on the AWS website (*https://oreil.ly/uhaoO*).

be collected into a unified location for the development of analytics and machine learning applications. Other systems may not have operational databases but rely on event-driven systems. Oftentimes this data will be needed in conjunction with data from other systems, creating a relatively complex data ecosystem, such as customer transaction data with anonymized trend data available on the open market, for example. Figure 11-12 shows how to combine data sources such as these to support multiple downstream applications. Relying on a lakehouse format such as Delta Lake with its broad array of connectors for different systems reduces this complexity and enables analytical and artificial intelligence–based applications.

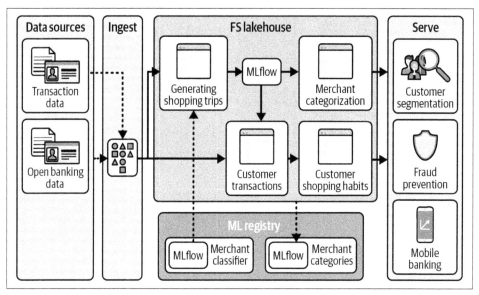

Figure 11-12. Retail merchant credit transactions present just one area in which we might see complex system interactions

Combining Operational Data Stores at DoorDash

Many people have found themselves in situations in which it would be convenient if someone could pick up meals, groceries, electronics, or pretty much anything else for them and maybe save them a trip out. DoorDash helps to fill all kinds of needs by providing flexibility and convenience through its delivery services. While most are familiar with DoorDash's gig-based operating methodology, it may be helpful to consider a particular couple of points.

Multiple parties are involved in the purchase process through DoorDash. Typically there are the requesters, the people who make deliveries, and restaurants or merchants who will prepare orders or make products available. Without even stepping into the larger IT ecosystem of the DoorDash organization, there is already an apparent need for large-scale low-latency data pipelines, i.e., streaming data applications, because each "event" itself is a collation of many events as it steps through the process.

DoorDash is leveraging Delta Lake as part of its data ecosystem in two ways. The first is to simplify the management of large-scale change data capture and downstream exposure of data for analytics. The second is in support of real-time workloads in Flink. Both capture some of the benefits of utilizing Delta Lake in your architectural designs.

Change Data Capture

Change data capture, or CDC, is a common application pattern that often needs to be supported for a variety of reasons (see Chapter 7 for some additional discussion of CDC).[17] DoorDash uses CDC for replication of operational databases supporting multiple services into the analytical environment.[18] This is driven by a historical need to answer the question "How many orders did DoorDash do yesterday?" Earlier on this was an easier task, as the question could be answered by creating a copy of the database and using queries against the copy to answer analytical questions or perform data science tasks.

As DoorDash grew, its service architecture evolved, leading to an environment with multiple operational databases that also come in multiple flavors, such as Cock-roachDB (*https://oreil.ly/vOvNj*), PostgreSQL (*https://oreil.ly/wfVXl*), and Apache Cassandra (*https://oreil.ly/vT5AX*). Seeking to get data from these databases in the simplest way, the DoorDash team initially got snapshots from the databases and pulled them in daily. While this approach worked, it did pose problems—specifically, the challenge of tracking data versioning, and a need to filter the snapshots to incrementalize the data process efficiently. After trying various changes in the environment, the team eventually set out to develop a more robust system.

For our purpose, the key system requirements were:

- Maintain less than a day of data latency
- Use a lakehouse design pattern
- Support schema evolution
- Allow for data backfilling
- Enable analytical workloads

---

17 If you want to spend more time exploring CDC, also known as logical log replication, we recommend *Designing Data-Intensive Applications* by Martin Kleppmann (O'Reilly).

18 Ivan Peng and Phani Nalluri, "Unlocking Near Real Time Data Replication with CDC, Apache Spark Streaming, and Delta Lake" (*https://oreil.ly/GW2tc*), posted July 26, 2023, by Databricks, YouTube.

- Write once, read many times
- Avoid late-arriving data
- Build with open source software

The design that arose from these requirements (see Figure 11-13) is a streaming CDC framework built on Spark Structured Streaming that replicates change feeds into a unified source of truth built on Delta Lake that supports downstream integrations across a wide range of query interfaces. Features such as merge support and ACID transactions helped make Delta Lake a critical component of the design.

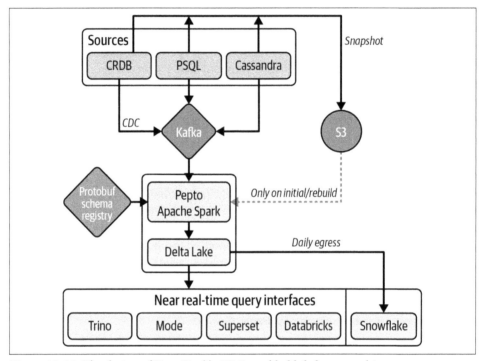

Figure 11-13. The design of DoorDash's CDC-enabled lakehouse architecture

The success of this design could be measured in many ways, but there are several aspects that the team highlights. The system supports 450 streams (one-to-one with tables) running 24/7 on more than one thousand EC2 nodes. This translates to about 800 GB ingested daily from Kafka, with a total daily processing volume of about 80 TB. The design far exceeded the initial requirements and attained a data freshness of less than 30 minutes. The team has enabled the self-service creation of tables for data users in the environment that become available in less than an hour.

Delta and Flink in Harmony

With real-time events being of central importance to DoorDash, its heavy use of Kafka is hardly surprising. Apache Spark is a natural choice for many stream processing applications; however, it's not the only choice. Some teams at DoorDash use Apache Flink for many real-time processes, and therefore it should also be easily supportable. In Chapter 4 you saw how the Flink/Delta Connector works operationally, but here it could be useful to see how this can be pulled into a larger data ecosystem to provide both flexibility and reliability.[19]

The real-time platform team at DoorDash is managing petabytes of vital customer events every day and needs to provide a platform to enable data users and applications to capture, create, or access this information (see Figure 11-14).[20] Adding the Flink/Delta Connector extends the number of ways that users and applications can interact with Delta Lake, which combines the fast operational nature of Flink with a storage format built to handle exactly those kinds of workloads and provides a common format usable across the whole data platform, even while different teams choose to leverage different application processing frameworks.

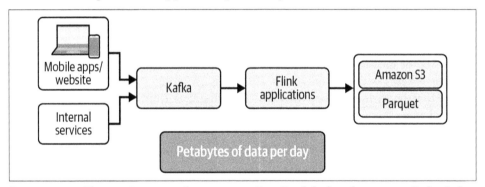

Figure 11-14. The starting state of processes at DoorDash before the move to Delta Lake

Figure 11-15 shows exactly what this change at DoorDash enabled: easy integration with its current tooling with the addition of ACID guarantees at a massive scale. Previously this process was taking place with regular Parquet files, adding additional complications in the form of write locks and other challenges. Additionally, the quality-of-life improvements gained through easy-to-use compaction operations and the ability to do these operations while stream processing applications are still

---

19 Fabian Paul, Pawel Kubit, Scott Sandre, Tathagata Das, and Denny Lee, "Writing to Delta Lake from Apache Flink" (*https://oreil.ly/_yzlC*), Delta Lake (blog), April 27, 2022.

20 Allen Wang, "Building Scalable Real Time Event Processing with Kafka and Flink" (*https://oreil.ly/N78Ch*), *DoorDash Engineering* (blog), DoorDash, August 2, 2022; Allison Cheng, "Flink + Delta: Driving Real-Time Pipelines at DoorDash" (*https://oreil.ly/uzkwT*), posted July 26, 2023, by Databricks, YouTube.

running are highly valuable, as is the efficiently queryable state achieved through the inclusion of Z-Ordering clusters on the data.

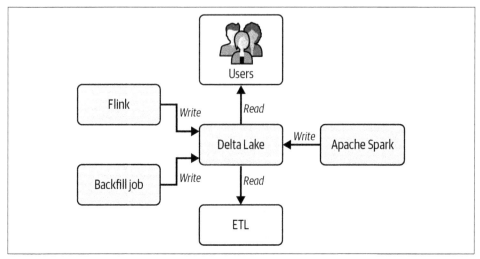

Figure 11-15. The resulting state of the data ecosystem at DoorDash after the move to Delta Lake

The moral of the story of the DoorDash decision to adopt Delta Lake is this: even for data systems with multiple types of tooling operating at massive scale and with a need to support things like efficiently capturing data from real-time event streams or the changes coming through operational databases, Delta Lake provides reliability and usability, making it a winning choice.

Conclusion

Data applications come in many different forms and formats. Authoring those data applications can be complex and painful. In this chapter you've seen a few ways to alleviate this pain through the many benefits of Delta Lake. In particular, the features of Delta Lake help create a robust data environment that supports broad tooling choices, reduces costs, and improves your quality of life as a developer.

Foundations of Lakehouse Governance and Security

We do many things every day without consciously thinking about them. These rote actions, or automatic behaviors, are based on our daily routines and on information we've grown to trust over time. Our routines can be simple or complex, with actions grouped and categorized into different logical buckets. Consider, for example, the routine of locking up before leaving for the day; this is a common behavior for mitigating risk, because we simply can't trust everyone to have our best interests in mind. Think about this risk mitigation as a simple story: *to prevent unauthorized access to a physical location (entity: home, car, office), access controls (locking mechanism) have been introduced to secure a physical space (resource) and provide authorized admittance only when trust can be confirmed (key, credentials).*

In the simplest sense, the only thing preventing intrusion is *the key.* While a key grants access to a given physical space via a lock, the bearer of a given key must also know the physical location of a protected resource; otherwise, the key has no use. This is an example of site security, and as a mental model, it is useful when constructing a plan for the layered governance and security model for resources contained within our lakehouse. After all, the lakehouse is a safe space that protects what we hold near and dear *only* if we collectively govern the resources contained within.

But what exactly is the governance of a data resource, and how do we get started when there are many components of the governance landscape?

This chapter provides a foundation for architecting a scalable data governance strategy for the data assets (resources) contained within the lakehouse. While we aim to cover as much surface area here as possible, consider this a referential chapter just scratching the surface of the myriad components of lakehouse data governance. For example, we won't cover governance with respect to compliance and enforcement of region-specific rules and regulations (GDPR, CCPA, right-to-be-forgotten policies, and so on), nor will we cover general governance from a nonengineering or nontechnical perspective.

Lakehouse Governance

Before we dive deeper into lakehouse governance, it is important to introduce the many components of governance today. The reason for this is that *governance* is an overloaded term that means many different things, depending on who you ask. Therefore, in order to go beyond basic access controls and traditional database-level governance, we need to introduce the systems and services that can come together to provide a comprehensive governance solution for our lakehouse.

There are many components to lakehouse governance, as seen in Figure 12-1, but at a high level, we can simply break them down between *identity and access management* or IAM (1) and *catalog services* (2–8). This allows us to build a working model that is easier to adopt.

For example, unless we understand who (or what) is requesting access to our data (identity services), we cannot manage the permissions enabling access—seen as the union between identity services and policies. Furthermore, without integrating the policies and rules contained within our IAM services (1) with the physical filesystem (3), we will not be capable of governing the databases (schemas), tables, views, and other assets stored in our catalog metastores (2). Given the modern separation between metadata management (2) and physical filesystem resources (3), the foundation for any lakehouse governance begins with the basic delegation of access to resources in a unified and controlled way.

Modern lakehouse governance includes (4) robust auditing across data management operations on a per-action basis, commonly captured through event logs for state changes made via IAM (1) for the resources registered within the catalog or metastore (3).

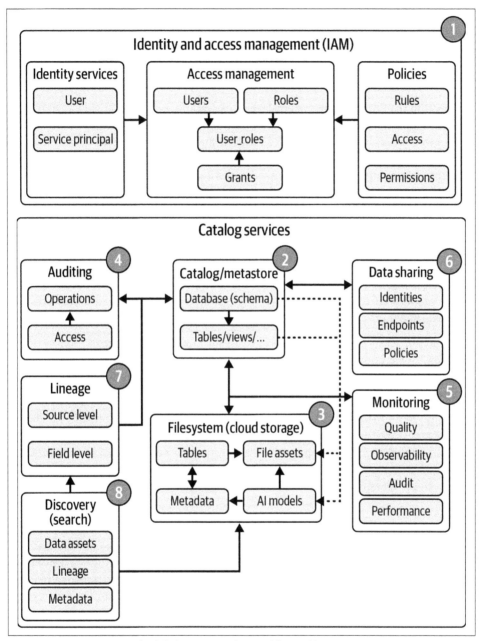

Figure 12-1. Governing the lakehouse goes beyond basic filesystem access controls

Building off the audit event logs, integrated monitoring (5) allows the governance platform to notify when things don't seem right, or when resources are out of compliance (via tracing and active monitoring). Using techniques similar to the audit logging, performance and runtime metrics and other statistics can be captured during job runs to enable data quality and system-level observability.

Connecting the dots for true system-level observability requires (7) data asset lineage (at least from the catalog -> schema -> table), including the tracking of ownership (who owns what) and of where (the location and point in the end-to-end lineage) and how the data is accessed, transformed, and otherwise "used." Understanding the objective data quality for mission-critical tables and the general performance of active data pipelines provides a bird's-eye view over the complete behavior of the lakehouse. It is also worth mentioning that the same metrics used for auditing, performance, and observability can be reused to track total cost-of-ownership insights, which are especially useful when looking to reduce spend or deprecate tables.

We dedicate Chapter 14 to data sharing (via Delta Sharing), but without the integrated services discussed here (1, 2, 3, 4, 5), including data lineage (7), it becomes much more complicated to effectively share single-source-of-truth data in a cost-effective and governed way.

Last but not least, the icing on the cake of all our hard work is the ability to tie together "all we know about our data" to provide powerful data discovery (8), which is arguably one of the most widespread issues given the sprawl of data across a vast number of silos, platforms, and systems and services.

The core components of lakehouse governance include access controls, lakehouse data catalogs and metastores, elastic data management, audit logging, monitoring, data sharing, data lineage, and data discovery. It is common to see all of these components neatly bundled under a single catalog solution. For now we will discuss what each component is and then dive deeper into each facet:

Access controls (1)
   Access controls provide capabilities to secure and govern the data assets within a lakehouse through leakproof abstractions—in the case of Delta Lake table access, this means there is zero direct access to the underlying storage. Without the ability to identify a user or service, there would be no way to approve or deny access or to authorize permissions to create, read (view), write (insert), update (or upsert), or delete. It would be the Wild West.

Lakehouse data catalogs and metastores (2)
   This component enables capabilities to find and view data assets, including catalogs, databases (schemas), tables, views, volumes, and files, and to govern

permissions for access to and control of these resources. The catalog[1] provides critical metadata about each resource—defining where it resides (the location in cloud storage, for example), as well as the associated owner and specific data relating to the type of resource, such as the columns, constraints, and table properties for each table (like we explored in Chapter 5), and metadata specific to the database (`dbproperties`) containing a set of managed or external tables.

So access controls and data catalogs go hand in hand, as we can't have one without the other.

Elastic data management (3)

The last core component of the lakehouse architecture is the data lake. We know by now that the Delta protocol aids in providing schema enforcement and evolution capabilities (as seen in Chapter 5), and that by having invariants on the table level, thanks to the Delta protocol, we reduce the complexity of managing data. The data lake provides elastic scalability to the databases and tables contained within our metastore and made available broadly via our data catalog. And as we will learn soon, identity and access management plays a key role in governing data assets securely.

Together, a strong foundational model can be constructed to power the lakehouse, paving the way for additional critical capabilities, including audit services and comprehensive monitoring of access and the generation of insights on data operations and actions:

Audit logging (4)

Audit logging can be as simple as capturing changes in the behavior of the lakehouse—for example, a change to a role or policy affecting which identities can execute critical operations such as create or delete on highly controlled resources like catalogs, databases, and tables. Another common use case is logging when critical changes take place, such as an ALTER TABLE operation on a table (recording the table version of the operation), or when a table is *deleted*, *truncated*, or even *dropped*. Last, it is also wise to capture when a job fails due to *failed permissions*. The reason for capturing access failure is that it helps to surface which workflows (jobs, pipelines) are attempting to access data that may contain highly sensitive data (and therefore access is blocked for the right reasons); the same process can capture when permissions are missing (could have been revoked for other reasons), and this information can help get a broken job back on track more quickly.

---

1 The term *data catalog* can mean a metastore like Hive, or it can also encapsulate a full "enterprise" data catalog. This chapter caters to the engineering side of the house, and so we won't be discussing the integration of "data catalogs" for use by nonengineering personas in a typical enterprise.

Audit logs can be stored directly in Delta Lake tables to simplify their integration into more robust security-based workflows and to provide the data source to power active monitoring.

Monitoring (5)

Capturing the behavior of the lakehouse through the lens of audit logs (for security purposes) and at the catalog, database, and table levels (for engineers, analysts, and scientists) simply provides a recording (timeseries) of metrics or events. Assuming that the audit logs are stored in Delta Lake, and that data asset changelogs are also stored in Delta Lake, these data sources can be used to create active monitoring solutions.

Monitoring requires you to aggregate the metrics and transform them to generate key performance indicators (KPIs), and to convert events (audit events) into metrics (KPIs) to generate insights. Each KPI provides a measurement that can be used to understand trends within the lakehouse or on a specific data asset and is critical for sounding the alarm (via alerting or paging) or to providing a central communication channel for teams. A good place to begin when monitoring audit level events is with the access frequency to specific data assets. The same access data can also be used to surface when a data asset is popular, infrequently accessed, or never accessed for read or write.

Unified data quality metrics, access and permissions history, and system-wide event tracking come together to act like a flight recorder observing changes with respect to a data asset—stitching important historical moments in time together with the state of the many systems and services in the governance stack. Without proper monitoring and audit logging, advanced capabilities like read-only data sharing or zero-copy shares and data lineage recording simply wouldn't be as powerful:

Data sharing and zero-copy sharing (6)

We were first introduced to the concept of data sharing in Chapter 9 and will spend the entirety of Chapter 14 looking at data sharing with the Delta Sharing Protocol. Data sharing is a complicated component of lakehouse governance, as it requires operational maturity to first establish a high-trust data ecosystem. When we share data with users and services outside of our control, it costs less and reduces the data management overhead *only if* the data can be read (in place) without requiring any export out of our lakehouse. The Delta Sharing protocol therefore requires the foundation (1, 2, 3, 4, and 5, and really 7 as well) to be in place, since the addition of managing shares and recipients is just an extension of the internal access management paradigm.

Data lineage (7)

Data lineage can be active or passive. *Active lineage* is automatically generated during the runtime of a data application. This can be done by utilizing a framework that allows you to record the upstream sources through the use of additional job-level metadata; that will automatically create and maintain the downstream resource metadata simply by successfully running the job. Unlike active lineage, *passive lineage* tells the story of what was and what could be. This means that the lineage is registered and recorded offline and isn't directly modified or synchronized when a job is run.

Each data application (pipeline, workflow, streaming, or batch) takes data from one or more sources (via reads), transforms the data, and sends it (via writes) to other locations (tables) inside or outside the lakehouse, or on to stream processors such as Apache Kafka or Pulsar. Using what we know about each data application, we can construct the directional lineage graph (DLAG) from each active application and use the lineage data to run downstream impact analysis when outages or data quality issues are identified in a source. We will cover data lineage more broadly in Chapter 13.

We capture data about the observable state changes, operations, and actions for our important data assets in order to create a history of what has occurred. This information is useful for managing compliance audits (GDPR, CCPA, and others), identifying risk, tracking data quality over time, and taking action if expectations diverge, and even for automating alerting to pinpoint data outages.

Last but not least is the addition of data discovery:

Data discovery (8)
> Data discovery is used differently depending on the personas within the enterprise and is commonly split into *engineering-specific* data discovery and *business-based* data discovery.

> The first set of capabilities is more of a schema repository for data assets (databases, tables, *queries, *dashboards, *monitors, and *alerts) inside the lakehouse that is targeted toward engineers, scientists, and analysts. The second is more of an organizational search engine for data that reaches across many data sources and suborganizations. The common persona for this second data discovery engine is targeted more toward business users who are looking for data that is not yet residing within the lakehouse.

> Data discovery becomes an essential component to ensure that different personas can quickly identify the best starting point for their work—without the need to create a long series of meetings or complicated coordinated efforts. By reusing insights for access frequency (from auditing [4]) on specific tables, as well as a crowd-sourced usability score (1–5), a popularity score (or data NPS score) can also be defined to help surface data assets by usage and general usability.

As any data engineer can tell you, all sorts of issues can and will occur at runtime—for example, access to data assets can be revoked (for the right or wrong reasons), causing data pipelines to fail or become degraded. Tables can be deprecated, go into read-only mode where they are no longer being updated, or even accidentally be deleted (without the proper governance checks and balances). Without a clear history of changes to permissions, table state, or established patterns for communicating state changes or degradations to data stakeholders, trust degrades.

Trust is easily broken without clear lines of communication. Data governance is one way to maintain a high-trust environment, with reliable tools and services that go beyond security and compliance to help connect disparate data teams working to solve complex problems.

 This chapter skips over regional data governance and compliance regulations, as well as design patterns for managing cross-region data access. These topics are outside the scope of the book but remain a critical central tenet of any complete governance solution. However, the topics discussed here will support your work to achieve compliance. For those looking to dive deeper into the topic of data governance, please take a look at *The Enterprise Data Catalog* by Ole Olesen-Bagneux (O'Reilly).

The Emergence of Data Governance

Data governance is defined as an umbrella that brings together various principles and practices, as well as tools and workflows, to govern an organization's data assets throughout their complete life cycle. The life cycle of data encapsulates the full end-to-end journey from creation to deletion, including all transformations and any access and utilization of the data at any point in time along the way (within the data's existence).

Consider the life cycle of our data through the lens of a Delta table:

- The conduit for our data is the *table* itself.
- Each table provides a container that stores a bounded or unbounded set of data over time alongside a transaction log of the *who*, *what*, *where*, and *how* of each change made to the table.
- Tables don't just blink into and out of existence. Each table must first be created, rows must be inserted, read, modified, or deleted, and the table must also be deleted (dropped) to complete the full journey.

To expand the scope of table-level data life cycle management, the simple diagram in Figure 12-2 provides a lens into common steps, from data creation to archiving and ultimately to destruction.

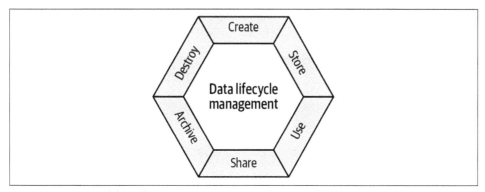

Figure 12-2. Data life cycle management

Similar to other common cycles, such as the software development cycle, the common data life cycle starts with (1) creation and continues to (2) storage, (3) usage, (4) sharing, (5) archiving, and ultimately (6) destruction. This life cycle encapsulates a complete history of actions and operations (a timeline) occurring at the resource level.

These observable moments in time are critical for the purposes of data governance, as well as for the maintenance and usability of the table from an engineering perspective. Each table is a *governable resource* referred to as a data asset.

> It is important to consider the use of the term *asset* here. A data asset (*table*) is directly owned, managed, and governed by a person (or team) representing an organization. The organization in turn provides the funding to manage the data asset and to pay the responsible parties across engineering, product, security, privacy, and governance.
>
> As a rule of thumb, data assets should be maintained only for as long as they are still providing value. *Data life cycle management* begins to make more sense when we think of data as existing only until it is no longer useful.

We learned about the medallion architecture for data quality in Chapter 9. This novel design pattern introduced the three-tiered approach for data refinement, from bronze to silver and into gold. This architecture plays a practical role when we're thinking about managing the life cycle of our data assets over time and when we're considering how long to retain data at a specific tier.

Aided by Figure 12-3, we can visualize the value of data assets as they are refined over time and across the logical data quality boundaries represented by bronze, silver, and gold.

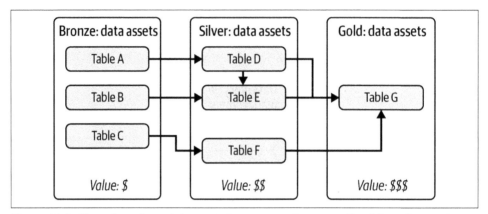

Bronze: data assets | Silver: data assets | Gold: data assets

Table A | Table D | Table G
Table B | Table E
Table C | Table F

Value: $ | Value: $$ | Value: $$$

Figure 12-3. The value of our data assets increases as they are refined from bronze to silver and from silver to gold. The medallion architecture is a helpful framework when considering how long to retain data and, more specifically, which tables to retain at which point in the lineage (from bronze to gold).

Figure 12-3 shows the source tables and lineage of transformations for a curated *data product* named *(table G)*. Working backward from the gold data assets, we see that there is a decrease in the value of the tables as we retrace the lineage back through the silver tier (D–F), concluding with our bronze data assets (A–C). *Why is the single table worth more conceptually than the collection of the prior six tables?*

Simply put, the complexity to build, manage, monitor, and maintain the collection of data asset dependencies for table G represents a higher cost than that of the individual parts. Consider that the raw data represented by the bronze data assets (A–C) *is expected to survive only as long as necessary* in order to be accessed and further refined, joined with, or generally utilized by the direct downstream data consumers (D–F), and that the same expectations are in turn made of our silver-tier data assets by the gold tier—they must exist only as long as they are needed,[2] and they must provide a simplification and general increase in data quality the further down the lineage chain they go.

A helpful way of thinking about the end-to-end lineage is through the lens of data products.

---

2 Drawing a line between data value and data hoarding is difficult. If there is value yet to be discovered, then I would suggest keeping that data in bronze, or archiving it for a later point in time.

For data that isn't being refined through the traditional medallion architecture, for example, you may have Salesforce data being ingested into the lakehouse. This data is already fit for purpose and is of high quality, so it is justifiable to say that that data is ingested directly into your curated layer (gold). In most cases, as your data becomes more refined, it adds more value to the enterprise.

Data Products and Their Relationship to Data Assets

The term *data product* represents the *code*, *data*, and *metadata*, as well as the *logical infrastructure* required to build, produce, and manage a given curated data product. Figure 12-4 shows in detail the intersection between code, data, and the data about said data (metadata), as well as the infrastructure to run and serve up a data product (*https://oreil.ly/Z2SrL*).

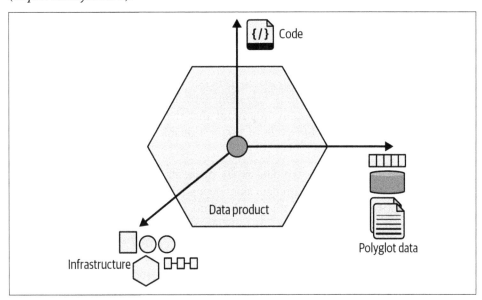

Figure 12-4. Data products are the sum of all their parts (adapted from Zhamak Dehghani)

Zhamak Dehghani introduced the novel idea of data products as part of her architectural paradigm the *data mesh*, where she proposed a rule that any curated data product must be purpose-built and capable of being used *as is* without requiring additional joins to other tables.[3] Essentially, the expense and effort of producing the data product should be paid in full on behalf of the consumers of the data product itself. This rule also helps tie together the simple idea that a data product is tied to a

---

3 Zhamak Dehghani, *Data Mesh: Delivering Data-Driven Value at Scale* (O'Reilly).

service, and that service is the production of useful, fit-for-purpose data. You can still join together the data from individual data products to create new data products, but the fact remains that additional joins *won't* need to be made by consumers of your data product for it to be usable for their given purpose.

Logically, it is also safe to assume that a data product can't exist without one or more data assets. Therefore, when we talk about data assets and data products, we are ultimately talking about data that is valuable enough to an organization that work went into designing, building, testing, releasing, monitoring, and maintaining the required applications and workflows to generate the set of valuable data assets encapsulating a specific data product. If this level of rigor and commitment to operations is ringing the traditional software project bell, that is correct.

Creating high-quality data requires engineers to follow the standard software development life cycle (SDLC). Essentially, this means designing for "no surprises" at runtime for the data product life cycle.

Data Products in the Lakehouse

Given the tendency for organizations to generate what feels like ever-increasing volumes of data through large data ingestion networks with increasingly complex dependency graphs, it is incredibly important that the lakehouse provides general capabilities for tracking the life cycle of highly valuable data assets—streaming or static.

This means being able to track the data assets' metadata, including upstream dependencies, as well as any downstream data asset dependencies. This is especially critical for downstream consumers, who must understand and react to changes in the volume of data and to modifications to the schema and structure of a given source or table, as well as other considerations and expectations in terms of the cadence of data being produced.

Maintaining High Trust

To maintain implicit trust in our data products, we must ensure that explicit and intentional additional metadata—including the union of data lineage, data quality, and end-to-end data observability—is available for our data products. For example, by being able to show that all processes involved in the production of a given mission-critical table utilize the same discipline, we can ensure our data consumers have the right information to feel confident, and this practice establishes a high-trust environment. You can also say that high trust is a consequence of following strict disciplines that come together to create a high-fidelity data product. More recently, data stewards and data product owners have come together to ensure that trust is part of the contractual agreement between the data producers and the data consumers of a given data product, thus providing a human touch in addition to metrics and monitoring.

If we take a step back to consider what tools, workflows (lakehouse orchestration), metadata, processes, architectural principles, and engineering best practices are required to manage the data contained by a Delta table representing a point in the lineage of a data journey from ingestion to deletion, across systems and services, users and their personas, data classification and access policies, and the curated *data products* representing data management at its finest, we quickly begin to realize the size and scale that is the umbrella of modern data governance.

Data Assets and Access

In the early days of traditional database management, there weren't large teams dedicated to governing how an organization managed the efficient collection, ingestion, transformation, cataloging, tagging, accessibility, and deprecation of data as seen with data governance organizations today; rather, the responsibility of managing access to a database was in the hands of the database administrator. This administrator was "in charge" of granting privileges to users, running expensive queries, and ensuring the database continued to operate.

The governance of which operations a user or group can execute is managed with privileges using the following SQL syntax groups: data control language, data definition language, and data manipulation language. We'll look at the data asset model next.

The Data Asset Model

The governance of a resource with respect to the lakehouse commonly describes the relationship between a policy and a governable object known as a *data asset*. In the simplest traditional sense, a data asset is a TABLE or VIEW, and a policy is a GRANT permission. The database, or schema, containing the table resource is also a data asset, as a policy grants access for a user, known as a *principal*, to execute an operation (show or select) on the data asset (database, table, or view). Before any principal can execute an action on resources, a data asset must first be created.

This data asset model is presented in Figure 12-5 and can pertain to any securable object that requires access and use controls through common SQL permissions.

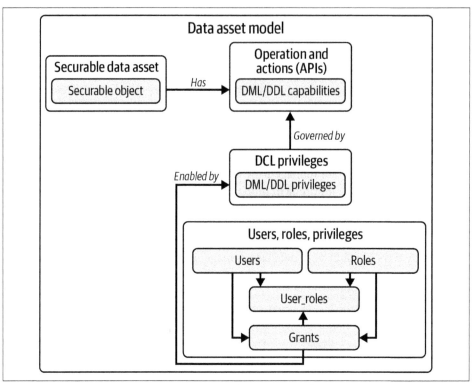

Figure 12-5. Data assets can generally be defined as securable objects that require a set of one or more permissions authorizing their access and general usage

The set of operations and actions that a principal can execute on a data asset is contained under the umbrella of *data definition language* (DDL), which contains CREATE, ALTER, DROP operations, and via *data manipulation language* (DML), which enables the INSERT and UPDATE actions, while the ability to execute one or more actions and operations is managed using *data control language* (DCL) by way of GRANT and REVOKE statements.

Nowadays, data assets have evolved to also encapsulate other resources that require access and use control (authorization) policies governing how they can be interacted with—for example, dashboards, queries (which in turn power dashboards), notebooks, machine learning models, and more.

Governing Data Access with SQL Grants

The governance of operations within SQL-like systems is handled through the grammar of DCL, DDL, and DML. Here is a quick refresher on these capabilities.

Data Control Language (DCL)

This special syntax is used for access management within SQL-like systems. Through the use of GRANT and REVOKE operations, a set of authorized actions (privileges) are associated with a set of USERs or GROUPs, enabling them to execute operations defined by DDL and DML, or removing one or more privileges that had previously been granted.

The syntax for GRANT permissions will vary depending on the flavor of the database, but they generally support ANSI-SQL standard syntax:

```
% GRANT priv_type [(column list)]
    ON [object_type]
    TO user_or_role, [user_or_role]
```

Controlling what actions a user or group can take isn't simply additive. In many cases, permissions are granted only for a finite amount of time before they are removed again. To fulfill the requirements of granting temporary permissions, the ability to remove permissions is enabled via the REVOKE syntax:

```
% REVOKE priv_type [(column list)]
    ON [object_type]
    TO user_or_role, [user_or_role]
```

Data Definition Language (DDL)

This syntax provides the following standard actions: CREATE, ALTER, DROP, COMMENT, and RENAME. We've used DDL in action directly as well as indirectly through the use of the Delta Scala, Python, and Rust companion libraries. In Chapter 5, we learned to create and alter tables, modify comments on columns, and even drop tables when we were through with them.

The CREATE syntax is used to define governable data assets. An example of the syntax for a standard SQL CREATE is shown next:

```
% CREATE [OR REPLACE] TABLE [IF NOT EXISTS] table_name (
    [column_name, type, ...]
  ) USING DELTA
  TBLPROPERTIES ('key'='value')
  CLUSTER BY (...)
```

The ALTER syntax is used to modify a governable data asset. The following examples show how to modify the properties of a table and how to add columns to a known table:

```
% ALTER TABLE table_name
  SET TBLPROPERTIES ('key'='value')

% ALTER TABLE table_name
  ADD COLUMNS (
    [column_name, type, ...],
  )
```

Data Manipulation Language (DML)

This syntax provides privileges to govern the operations a user or group can execute on a resource using the standard actions SELECT, INSERT, UPDATE, and DELETE:

```
% select [column,] from [table or inner select]
  [where,] [group by,] [having,] [order by], [limit]
```

Together DCL enables privileges to be assigned to users or groups that allow them to execute some or all of the actions governed by the resources created using DDL and the operations enabled by DML.

While the size and scale of data operations continues to grow across the globe, the paradigm of using simple GRANT and REVOKE privileges to control both access and authorization of data assets is still the simplest path toward adopting a unified governance strategy. Challenges arise almost immediately as we begin to consider interoperability with systems and services that simply don't speak SQL.

Unifying Governance Between Data Warehouses and Lakes

In the preceding section, we discovered that traditional data governance capabilities began with the addition of DCL syntax for SQL databases, which enabled the ability to allow or deny access to specific resources using GRANT and REVOKE statements.

Together the use of grants authorizes specific permissions associated with a user or role, enabling the execution of a set of actions on a secured resource (data asset). Governance for access using DCL works for traditional siloed databases (RDBMS) such as MySQL and Postgres as well as for most modern data warehouses via vendors like Databricks, AWS, and Snowflake.

There is a challenge, however, in using traditional SQL grants for governance of our lakehouse: *not all systems and services understand SQL.* To make matters worse, we don't have the ability to simply use one governance model to secure all data assets.

Consider the simple fact that the lakehouse still houses a traditional data lake just beneath the surface. This means we need to address the permissions and access model for the underlying data in order to provide a SQL-like interface to unify governance for the lakehouse.

Permissions Management

Just below the surface of the lakehouse lies the data lake. As we all know by now, the data lake is a data management paradigm that assists in the organization of raw data using primitives from the traditional filesystem. In most cases, cloud object stores are used, and at the root of these elastic systems are *buckets containing objects in a flat structure.*

Buckets encapsulate a resource root "/" representing a logical structure similar to the standard filesystem, but within a cloud object store. Figure 12-6 shows the breakdown of the bucket into its constituent parts. For example, just off the root we have top-level directories (paths and partitions) and their underlying files.

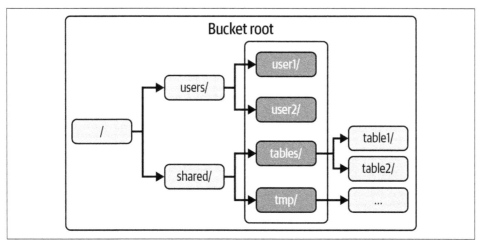

Figure 12-6. Data lakes are commonly built using cloud object stores. The primitives for these collections begin with the bucket, or root of the filesystem, and descend in an orderly fashion across directories and their subcollections of files or additional directories.

Each directory contains a collection of unstructured (raw) data—as commonly seen with log files, images, videos, or shareable assets such as configuration files (properties, YAML, JSON, etc.) and libraries (JARs, wheels, eggs)—as well as our structured but unprocessed data.

For structured data, it is advisable to use a well-known row-based format such as Apache Avro (*https://oreil.ly/tdP9j*) or Google's Protobuf (*https://oreil.ly/zAxPu*), or a column-based format like Apache Parquet (*https://oreil.ly/X2AcJ*), which is simple to convert into Delta's table format using the Delta utilities,[4] as shown here:

```
% from delta.tables import *
    deltaTable = DeltaTable.convertToDelta(
                    spark,
                    "parquet.`<path-to-table>`")
```

In addition to all other types of unstructured and structured data, the data lake stores our managed (or unmanaged) Delta tables. So we have many possible kinds of files stored behind the scenes.

Understanding how to secure the underlying filesystem from unauthorized access is critical for lakehouse governance, and luckily, SQL-like permissions share a similar data management paradigm to that of the classic operating system (OS) filesystem permissions—access to files and directories is controlled using users, groups (akin to roles), and permissions granting *read*, *write*, and *execute* actions.

Filesystem Permissions

The OS running on our laptops and the OS running remotely on servers we've provisioned share similar access and delegation patterns. For example, it is the responsibility of the OS to oversee the distribution of finite resources (compute, RAM, storage) among many short- and long-lived processes (operations). Each process is itself the result of executing a command (action), and the execution is associated with a *user*, *group*, and *set of permissions*. Using this model, the OS is able to construct simple rules of governance.

Let's look at the `ls` command as a practical example:

```
% ls -lah /lakehouse/bronze/
```

The output of the command is a listing of filesystem resources (files, directories) as well as their metadata. The *metadata* includes the resource type (file or directory), the access mode (permissions), references (resources relying on this resource), ownership (user), and group association, as well as the file size, the last modified date, and the filename or directory name:

File type
This is represented by a single character. Files are represented by a –, while directories are represented with *d*.

---

4 See "Convert a Parquet Table to a Delta Table" (*https://oreil.ly/hamBh*) in the Delta Lake documentation.

Permissions

These include read (*r*), write (*w*), and execute (*x*). Permissions are managed separately for the resource owner, a specific access group, and lastly anyone else (known as *others*).

References

This tracks how many other resources link to a resource.

Owner

Each resource has an owner. The owner is a known user in the OS. The owner of a resource has full control over how other users and processes interact through the assignment of group-level permissions.

Group

Users are associated with one or more groups. Groups enable multiple users and processes to work together while restricting certain privileges. Groups within the context of the operating system are similar to roles within the context of the data warehouse. For each resource, a specific group can be granted permissions (outside of the owner of the resource), and for unknown group membership, default permissions can be applied as well.

When everything comes together, we can start to see the connection between filesystem permissions and how they can apply to the governance of our lakehouse as well. Consider what the output of the following example tells us about the *ecomm_aggs_table*:

```
% ls -lh /lakehouse/bronze/ecomm_aggs_table/
drwxr-x---@ 338 dataeng eng_analysts   11K Oct 23 12:53 _delta_log
drwxr-x---@ 130 dataeng eng_analysts  4.1K Oct 23 12:34 date=2019-10-01
drwxr-x---@ 130 dataeng eng_analysts  4.1K Oct 23 12:34 date=2019-10-02
```

First off, the *_delta_log* directory informs us we are looking at a Delta table. It is owned by a user named *dataeng* who has full read-write-execute permissions (*rwx*). Additionally, the table is accessible for reading and execution by the *eng_analysts* group, but members of that group cannot modify the table since they are authorized for read-only access. For any other user in the OS, they would get an exception (not authorized) while attempting to interact with the files at this path.

A similar permissions model can be applied to our cloud object stores as well. The main difference is the way we identify users and manage groups.

Cloud Object Store Access Controls

The separation between storage and computation of the data lake ensures a physical boundary between the location of our data assets and the servers running our compute processes. If we dig further into the separation of concerns, we'll also discover that we are additionally cut off from the traditional OS-level user permissions model, since the user (identity) bound to a local compute process is not directly known to the object store without the addition of a key (or token) signaling to the remote process that we are in fact allowed to execute a given action. This key helps to identify the request and authorize a simple rule set that will allow or deny the requested action in the form of a remote execution (read or write or delete).

In the absence of a shared operating system, we establish trust relationships between where we process data (compute) and where we store our data, utilizing identities. Identities help us to answer the following:

- What is the identity (user) of a given runtime process, and how does that apply to the traditional user permissions model?
- How can we *enable access* to one or more cloud-based resources?
- Once identified, in what ways can we *authorize* specific actions and operations to occur for a given user?

The paradigm shifts away from classic filesystem permissions (user, group, permission) and into a more flexible system called identity and access management, or IAM for short.

Identity and Access Management

If you heard a knock at the door, would you answer it? Would you let a stranger in? The whole reason why IAM exists is to ensure there is a *mutual trust-based relationship* between an unknown entity (who could be who they say they are) and your internal systems. So how do we identify a user, system, or service in a dynamic cloud-based world?

Identity

Each identity represents a user (human) or a service (API, pipeline job, task, etc.). Identities encapsulate both individual users as well as service principals, who are jokingly referred to as *headless users*, since they are not human but still represent a system doing things on behalf of a user. An identity acts like a passport, certifying the legitimacy of the user. In addition, the identity is used to connect the user to a set of permissions through the use of policies.

It is common to see access tokens issued for individual users, and for both long-lived tokens and certificates (certs) to be issued for service principals.

Authentication

While an identity might be legitimate, the whole point of authentication is to test to be absolutely certain. Most systems issue (generate) keys or tokens for only a specific period of time; this forces the identity to reauthenticate from time to time, proving they are still legitimate. In the case of bad actors (hackers, spoofers) attempting to reuse a token they lifted for illegitimate purposes, a low time to live (TTL) on the token limits the potential impact of stolen identities. As a rule of thumb, the more secure the system, the lower the TTL for tokens.

Authorization

The identity and authentication mechanics come together to provide a guarantee that a user isn't simply an imposter. These two concepts are tightly coupled to the authorization process. Authorization is akin to GRANT permissions. We can assume that we know the identity of a user (since they have passed the test and proved that they are who they say they are), as they were able to gain entrance to the physical location of our resource (using a key, cert, or token to access data assets in the lakehouse). The authorization process is the bridge between the user and a set of policy files that describe what a user is allowed to do within a given system.

Access management

In a nutshell, access management is all about providing methods to control access to data and enforce security checks and balances, and it is the cornerstone of governance. Access controls provide a means of identifying what kinds of operations and actions can be executed on a given resource (data asset, file, directory, ML model) and provide capabilities to approve or deny based on policies.

The entire process of creating a user (identity), issuing credentials (tokens), and authenticating and authorizing access to resources is really no different than the GRANT mechanisms—the reverse being REVOKE, which would invalidate active credentials. No process is complete without the ability to also remove an identity, which completes the full-access life cycle.

IAM provides the missing capabilities enabling the implementation of GRANT-like permissions management for our lakehouse through the use of identities and access policies.

In the next section, we'll look at access policies and see how role-based access controls help simplify data access management through the use of personas (or actors), and we'll learn about creating and using policies as code.

Data Security

There are many pieces to the governance story, and in order to effectively scale a solution, there are important rules and ways of working that must be established up front—or carefully integrated into an existing solution.

For example, you might be familiar with the duck test: *if it looks like a duck, swims like a duck, and quacks like a duck, then it probably is a duck.* This refers to our ability to reason about something unfamiliar and to group it into a category of things "that are known to us." With respect to the various personas, or actors, operating within our lakehouse, we can use a modified duck test to create a limited number of roles that identify who has what level of access to which data assets as a first step on the path to more complex policy generation for authentication.

Role-based access controls

Role-based access controls (RBAC) are used to approve or deny system access and to authorize a subset of permissions on resources required to carry out the duties of specific personas using a role or roles within an organization.

For the lakehouse, consider the roles we play at our daily jobs (engineer, scientist, analyst, business functions), the team(s) and organization(s) we are part of, the logical dividing lines of our business (which can help establish data domains), the runtime environment for our systems, services, and data products (dev, stage, prod), and last, the classification of the data we are managing and accessing (all-access, restricted, sensitive, highly sensitive). The lines of what a role personifies can be a bit blurry at times, and for that reason, the R in RBAC can also denote *resource*.

Let's approach RBAC through a story. For the sake of the story, we all are employed at a global grocery chain called Complete Foods that sells local organic produce. Complete Foods sells products in physical stores, as well as online for delivery purposes. Each store operates in a specific geography, and the shopping trends will differ locally and regionally, as well as seasonally. This means that while all stores operate under the same corporate umbrella and share a majority of the same common products, regional inventory, vendor relationships, sales, and customers will differ based on where in the world the store is located.

However, the roles and responsibilities for employees requiring access to the lakehouse data will remain primarily the same, with level of access being based on need and reason (use case), as well as on required training on data privacy, governance, and sovereignty when it comes to accessing highly confidential data or when accessing customer data that is required for marketing and advertising campaigns.

Roles are not people. Each role can be assumed by a person or service. It is important to start simply and categorize the *who*, *what*, *where*, and *how*.

Establishing roles around personas

Understanding the who, what, where, how, and why is simplified when we abstract the roles associated with common personas within an organization. Let's explore some common dividing lines for personas within a typical organization:

Engineering role

This can be applied to any developer role across hardware, software, security, platform, data, and machine learning, including headless users. The responsibilities include maintaining the systems for point of sale (in store and online), writing and maintaining mobile applications, defining event data, establishing data capture and ingestion networks, and handling personal data such as credit card numbers and users' home addresses, as well as learning from customer shopping habits to ensure that the right products are available in the right regions at the right time of year.

Access patterns: All (read, read-write, admin)

Role name: `role/developerRole`

Analyst role

This includes business analysts or specialists. This role is responsible for working with business and engineering teams to ensure the right data is available to accurately capture critical business operations, and to assist in the decision-making process through the generation of insights, such as when to get pumpkin spice products back on the shelves, and what kinds of nondairy milk to continue to offer in what regions.

Access patterns: Primarily read-only for data, with the ability to create and share queries, build dashboards, and analyze historical data or emerging trends

Role name: `role/analystRole`

Scientist role

This includes data and behavioral scientists. Responsibilities include working with the engineers and analysts to ensure the right data flows into the right places at the right time to power recommendations and other inference models.

Access patterns: Primarily read-only, with the ability to create tables to power the training of models and to capture results for tests and experimentation

Role name: `role/scientistRole`

Business role

This includes manager, director, human resources, and even leadership. This role is responsible and accountable for building and maintaining the Complete Foods brand. There are local and global responsibilities, as well as regional store managers or buyers, and everyone will require access to sales numbers, forecasts, and subsets of data relating to employees or to concerns outside their line of business. Additionally, engineering leadership will require different access and capabilities than engineering managers and directors.

Access patterns: Mostly read-only; HR may need to create, modify, and delete employees

Role name: `role/businessRole`

The process for authorizing access to a given data asset (resource) in our lakehouse can be determined via a union of the following:

- The user's *role and responsibility* (*who* and *what*)
- The *resource location* (bucket and prefix) (*where*)
- The *environment where* they operate (dev, stage, prod)
- The *data classifications* (generally available, restricted, sensitive, etc.), which denote *what*
- The *operation* (*action*): read (view), modify (read, write), or admin (read, write, create, or delete) as the *how*

So remember: we always need to keep in mind the *who, what, where,* and *how,* as well as the *if.*

Think about it this way: *If we grant access to a given identity (who), then (what) operations are necessary to accomplish a given set of tasks (how), and in what environment (where) do they need user-level access versus headless user access? And last, what potential risks are involved in granting read-level versus read-write-level access?*

Additionally, aside from the considerations around whether access should be granted, the other question that must always be back of mind is whether the identity is allowed to view (read) all the data residing in the table. It is common to have data that is divided into groups based on the security and privacy considerations for the data access.

We will look at data classification patterns next.

Data classification

The following classifiers are a useful way to identify what kind of data is stored within a resource at a specific location in the data lake.

As a simple abstraction, let's think about data classification in terms of the stop-light pattern. A stop light signals to a driver to continue (green), slow down (yellow), or stop (red). As an analogy, when thinking about governing access to our data assets, the stop-light pattern provides a simple mental model to tag or label (identify) data that can be green, yellow, or red.

When in Doubt About Classifications

Every organization deals with different kinds of data. When in doubt, think about the damage to the company if a specific dataset (a table, raw data, etc.) was to leak to the public. Given the strict laws governing personal user data, some things will automatically come with a yellow or red classification. The guidelines and standards provided by GDPR, CCPA, and SOC2, for example, provide a compass to help you along your way. Each company is required to follow standards, and standards defined through policies make it easier to do the right thing. The more you work with different datasets, the easier it will be to intuit what is appropriate.

For example, access to data classified as "green" could be automated, assuming there are appropriate checks in place to ensure the resources are not leaking sensitive data. A practical example for "green" would be the earthquake and hazard data made generally available by the United States Geological Survey.

Access to data classified as "yellow" or "red" would require the grantee to consider who would have access, why they would need access and for how long, and how the access could benefit or harm the organization. When in doubt, always consider the *if*. *If we grant access to this data, do we trust the grantee(s) to do the right thing?*

Establishing rules and common ways of working can help to ensure that data is classified in a common way, reducing decision making to a scientific process:

General access
This classification assumes the data is available to a general audience. For example, let's say Complete Foods believes it can sell more groceries by enabling services like Instacart, Uber Eats, and DoorDash to access our inventory data. By enabling open access—sign up, get a token, and hit the Delta sharing endpoint—we can ensure that any external organization can access specific tables associated with the general access role limited to read-only.

Stop-light pattern: Green-level access

Restricted access
This classification assumes data is read-only, with approval on a need-to-know (use) basis. Continuing the Complete Foods example from before, while external access to the inventory data (via the general-access classification) enables a mutually beneficial relationship to extend the reach of our grocery business and brand, there is data that represents our competitive advantage that must remain internal only, or restricted to external domains.

For example, let's say we have a price per product offered that is public (in store and via our partner services), but we also have an internal price representing the actual true cost to acquire a given product. In most cases, the margin (the delta between the cost to acquire a good and the price at the time of sale) isn't something we would like to advertise, as it represents our competitive advantage, as well as pricing negotiations that cost us very real money.

Stop-light pattern: Green-, yellow-, or red-level access

Sensitive access
This classification applies to any sensitive data. Sensitive data would be damaging to the organization if leaked, but it doesn't contain critical information such as credit card numbers, Social Security numbers, payroll information, or medical or health information (which would cause compliance problems with HIPAA data). Sensitive data may contain personally identifiable information (PII) like users' first and last names, addresses, email addresses, birthdays, information about vendors (like the farms we purchase produce from), and other data relating to the operation of a business. Sensitive data may also contain information such as consumer behavior data, though without exposing a user's name or address or other PII. In the case in which daily aggregate data would be damaging if leaked, for example, if the data shows that the company's quarterly numbers are on a downward trend, even if the trend is represented as percentages versus actuals, this can still hurt the reputation of the company and would be a reason to tag the data as *highly sensitive access.*

Stop-light pattern: Yellow- or red-level access

Highly sensitive access
This classification applies to the most critically sensitive data available to an organization and to the user. This includes employee payroll information, company financial records, user credit card data as well as health-care data and home addresses, and more. Access to these data assets typically requires the completion of internal training, as well as a full audit trail related to access. Much of this data is traditionally reserved for human resources (HR) as well as payroll, and for specific actors within the business.

Stop-light pattern: Red-level access

Now that we've identified the basic personas and roles related to data access (`developerRole`, `analystRole`, `scientistRole`, `businessRole`), as well as common classifiers for our data (general-access, restricted-access, sensitive-access, highly-sensitive-access), we can finish connecting the dots between IAM and data access policies and then finish up with a brief introduction to policy-as-code.

Using Prefix Patterns for Organizational Success

When it comes to S3 buckets and policies, one of the most useful things we can do is to take time up front to organize our data lake in order to simplify how we manage our Delta tables—which commonly involves setting up an S3 bucket, adding a warehouse directory, and hoping that teams do the right thing. Rather, the prework should include the setup of key patterns required for seamless runtime execution across environments, top-level catalogs, various databases (schemas), and their underlying tables, as well as dedicated space for data applications and their metadata, libraries, and configurations.

Let's look at the lakehouse structure in Example 12-1.

Example 12-1. Exploring the lakehouse namespace pattern

```
├─ s3://com.common_foods.[dev|prod]
│   └─ common_foods
│       ├─ consumer
│       │   ├─ _apps
│       │   │   └─ clickstream
│       │   │       ├─ app.yaml
│       │   │       └─ v1.0.0
│       │   │           ├─ _checkpoints
│       │   │           │   ├─ commits
│       │   │           │   ├─ metadata
│       │   │           │   ├─ offsets
│       │   │           │   └─ state
│       │   │           ├─ config
│       │   │           │   └─ app.properties
│       │   │           └─ sources
│       │   │               └─ clickstream_app_v1.0.0.whl
│       │   └─ clickstream
│       │       ├─ _delta_log
│       │       ├─ event_date=2024-02-17
│       │       └─ event_date=2024-02-18
│       ├─ {table}
```

The lakehouse namespace pattern allows us to colocate our data applications alongside the physical Delta tables they produce. This reduces the number of policies required to manage the basics such as team-based access, line-of-business-level data management, and other concerns, like which environment to provide access to. When everything is done correctly, the development environment can act as a proving ground for new ideas, primed with mock data and built using anonymized production data (there is higher risk here, so remember the who, what, where, how, why, and if rules), and having two environments separated by a physical bucket makes it easier to follow the stop-light pattern, since dev and staging are traditionally all-access, while our production environment is almost always justifiably yellow- or red-level access, at least when it comes to personal data.

If you think back to the filesystem ownership pattern from earlier in the chapter, we have top-level ownership that defaults to admin over a given resource (file, application, directory), and then group-level access for approved identities becomes "read-only," while access for everyone else is simply blocked.

This pattern of default group-membership for engineers responsible for a data domain and the set of data applications powering the mission-critical data for a given domain should be part of the onboarding process for new team members once they have been trained and brought up to speed on the organization's ways of working.

From the lakehouse layout provided in Example 12-1, we see the data application and table resources for a clickstream data application underneath the consumer umbrella in the *common_foods* catalog. The directories contain the following:

Metadata (app.yaml)
> This can include resource configurations and other important application metadata, including the owning team, PagerDuty, or Slack channel information. Additionally, the *app.yaml* can include any runtime requirements in the form of CPU cores, RAM, min and max number of executors, access policies—you name it.

Source libraries (.whl, *.jar, *.py, etc.)*
> These libraries can be published directly to S3—or as an alternative, if you are working with containerized data applications, everything required for your application can be written to the container filesystem layer.

Configuration (app.properties, spark.conf)
> The application configuration can be supplied to your application using Config-Maps for Kubernetes, as spark.conf or spark.properties for traditional Spark applications, or as any type of configuration that you support within your data applications. The important thing is that for each version (v1.0.0 in the example), all resources are self-contained. This pattern allows you to easily roll back to the "last" version if mistakes are made (we all make mistakes) without corrupting your checkpoints (from what was working).

Streaming checkpoints (_checkpoints)
> This collection contains the metadata for the stateful application (Structured Streaming or other). For example, if our upstream is another Delta table, the *_checkpoints* contain the last read version from Delta (reservoir version) that was processed, and the sink information, including the last "observed" commit version.

Table metadata and physical files
> The Delta table is included within the umbrella of the data product to minimize the number of policies, files, and roles needed to enable a team to operate within the lakehouse.

All application resources are located using a simple namespace pattern on the S3 prefix—*{catalog}/{database_or_schema}/_apps/{app_name}/**—with all versioned resources and assets contained within the semantic versioned (*https://oreil.ly/DYS8N*) release (v1.0.0). When we connect continuous integration and continuous delivery (CI/CD) with the GitHub repositories containing our data applications, it becomes simple to tie the version of the application alongside the Git tag of a Git release (*https://oreil.ly/EcAVN*). This also enables automatic rollbacks in the case of failure by looking at the current release – 1.

Now let's move on to the actual Delta tables. The output tables of our data applications exist underneath the same relative path as the data application itself. The common ancestor of both the data application and the table is the database (or schema) contained within a specific catalog. This pattern might not always be possible, especially in the case where a data application is reading from multiple bronze tables to produce a silver-based output table.

For our application configuration, using Spark as an example, we can set the config property `spark.sql.warehouse.dir=s3://com.common_foods.prod/common_foods` to enable our application to read or write to tables contained under the *common_foods* catalog.

Data assets and policy-as-code

We can simplify the security and governance of our lakehouse using common access patterns. Take, for example, the introduction of Amazon S3 Access Grants: this abstraction simplifies the management of roles and the delegation of SQL-style `GRANT` permissions across traditional S3 buckets.

 The following section explores using Amazon S3 Access Grants (*https://oreil.ly/Gj9hO*) at a high level. This section assumes prior experience with Amazon S3 as well as with how policy management works.

Create an S3 bucket. The S3 bucket will act as a container encapsulating our production lakehouse. Using the Amazon CLI (shown in Example 12-2), we set up the bucket and call it *production.v1*.

Example 12-2. Setting up a bucket for our lakehouse

```
aws s3api create-bucket \
    --bucket com.dldgv2.production.v1 \
    --region us-west-1 \
    --create-bucket-configuration LocationConstraint=us-west-1
```

Once we have succeeded in setting up our bucket, the bucket location is returned. This means we have a unique ARN (Amazon Resource Name)—for example, *arn:aws:s3:::com.dldgv2.production.v1*.

Create an S3 Access Grants instance.   An S3 Access Grants instance is a container for logically grouping one or more registered S3 locations and the grants that define who has what level of access to what for our S3 data for each location. There is one instance per AWS region within a single AWS account—the process to create the grant instance is shown in Example 12-3. This means that regional data access controls are honored even when global access is possible for S3 buckets.

Example 12-3. Creating an S3 Access Grants instance

```
% ACCOUNT_ID="123456789012" && \
    aws s3control create-access-grants-instance \
    --account-id $ACCOUNT_ID
```

Here are the results of creating the new grant instance:

```
{
    "CreatedAt": "2024-01-15T22:54:18.587000+00:00",
    "AccessGrantsInstanceId": "default",
    "AccessGrantsInstanceArn": "arn:aws:s3:us-west-1:123456789012:access-grants/
default"
}
```

Now that we have set up an S3 bucket and the Access Grants instance (both in us-west-1), we can create an IAM role and trust policy to use for our S3 Access Grants.

Create the trust policy.   A trust policy must be created to allow the AWS service (identified by the service access-grants.s3.amazon.com) permissions to generate temporary IAM credentials using the `GetDataAccess` action on an S3 resource. The trust policy is shown in Example 12-4.

Example 12-4. Create the trust-policy.json file

```
{
    "Version": "2012-10-17",
    "Statement": [
        {
            "Effect": "Allow",
            "Principal": {
                "Service": "access-grants.s3.amazonaws.com"
            },
            "Action": [
                "sts:AssumeRole",
                "sts:SetSourceIdentity",
```

```
            "sts:SetContext"
        ]
      }
    ]
}
```

Now execute the following:

```
% aws iam create-role --role-name s3ag-location-role \
--assume-role-policy-document file://trust-policy.json
```

The final step to finish setting up the access grants is to create a policy enabling read and read-write capabilities on an S3 bucket prefix.

Create the S3 data access policy.   The last step is simply to associate the generic read and write permissions on our S3 bucket:

```
% aws iam put-role-policy --role-name s3ag-location-role \
--policy-name s3ag-location-role --policy-document file://iam-policy.json
```

The *iam-policy.json* file is included in the book's GitHub materials for this chapter (*https://oreil.ly/ua0n0*).

Now that we have established the S3 Access Grants, we can move on to simplifying how we manage read and read-write permissions, or even admin-level permissions, for resources in our lakehouse.

Applying policies at the role level

Next we will apply the principles of RBAC to our policies. This enables us to provide general-purpose rules that enforce access control to a set of resources. In this case, the resources are Delta Lake tables located within our S3 buckets.

Read.   This will authorize read-only capabilities on a resource, or the ability to view metadata about a given data asset, including the table properties, ownership, lineage, and other related data. This capability is required to view the row-level data within a table, list the resources contained within a bucket prefix (filesystem path), or read table-level metadata. Example 12-5 shows how to use SQL Grants to enable READ for our analystRole.

Example 12-5. Applying an Amazon S3 Access Grants Read Policy

```
$ export ACCOUNT_ID="123456789012"

aws s3control create-access-grant \
--account-id $ACCOUNT_ID \
--access-grants-location-id default \
--access-grants-location-configuration S3SubPrefix="warehouse/gold/analysis/*" \
```

```
--permission READ \
--grantee GranteeType=IAM,GranteeIdentifier=arn:aws:iam::$ACCOUNT_ID:role/analystRole
```

This example shows a simplified method of granting permissions for Amazon S3 using access grants.

ReadWrite. In addition to the actions provided by *read*, the write capabilities add modify capabilities enabling the actor (identity) to insert (write) new data, update table metadata, and delete rows from a table. The simple policy is shown in Example 12-6.

Example 12-6. Applying an Amazon S3 Access Grants ReadWrite policy

```
$ export ACCOUNT_ID="123456789012"
export GRANT_ROLE="role/developerRole"

aws s3control create-access-grant \
  --account-id $ACCOUNT_ID \
  --access-grants-location-id default \
  --access-grants-location-configuration S3SubPrefix="warehouse/gold/analysis/*" \
  --permission READWRITE \
  --grantee GranteeType=IAM,GranteeIdentifier=arn:aws:iam::$ACCOUNT_ID:$GRANT_ROLE
```

Admin. In addition to the capabilities managed by *readwrite*, the admin role authorizes an actor to create—or delete—a data asset located at a specific location. For example, it is common to restrict destructive capabilities to only service principals; similarly, creating resources most often also means additional orchestration to manage and monitor a resource. Since headless users can act only on behalf of a user, this means they can only run workflows and commands and execute actions and operations that already exist. In other words, the service principal can trigger a specific action based on some external event, reducing the surface area of accidental "oops." It is best to use traditional IAM policies to control access to create and destroy lakehouse resource locations.

Limitations of RBAC. There are, of course, limitations when simply using roles alone to manage access; mainly what tends to happen is an explosion of roles. This can be considered "sprawl," and it is an unforeseen side effect of success. Let's be honest: if there are only four lines of business, and you have four supporting roles (developer, analyst, scientist, business), then you are looking at a max of $4 \times 4 \times n$ (with n being the number of tables within a line of business that require special rules to govern access) to handle the requirements of general governance across the company. What happens when you go from four lines of business to twenty? What about fifty? It is the what-ifs that define what to do next. If we are lucky and the company has taken off, and we've hired well and managed to maintain a robust set of engineering disciplines and practices, then we could technically begin to pivot into attribute-based access control (ABAC). This is also known as *tag-based policies* and can also live under the umbrella of *fine-grained access controls.*

Fine-Grained Access Controls for the Lakehouse

The solution to the problem of compounding complexity with coarse-grained access controls—or access based on allowing or denying read and write to data assets as a whole based on hierarchical roles—comes in the form of fine-grained access controls. There are many emerging techniques to provide fine-grained access controls using the notion of tags, or attributes.

For example, say we have a Delta Lake table that has twenty columns. This table could encapsulate orders for our customers. There is a high probability that the information about each order is important to many personas within the company, but access to the user information associated with the order could be out of compliance depending on the bylaws and rules governing access to customer data. Rather than the entire table being marked as "yellow" or "red" for its classification, the columns themselves can be tagged (using metadata) to denote whether the column can be read or whether it should be masked, or nullified, for general access.

The SQL in Example 12-7 shows how dynamic masking can be achieved within Databricks using Unity Catalog. To view the data stored in the user struct, the user or service principal querying the order data must be in the `consumer_privileged` account group, and in this case the user struct must also be tagged with the value of `pii`.

Example 12-7. Using dynamic views and tags for fine-grained access controls

```
-- SQL
CREATE VIEW consumer.prod.orders_redacted AS
SELECT
  order_id,
  region,
  items,
  amount,
  CASE
    WHEN has_tag_value('pii')
    AND is_account_group_member('consumer_privileged')
    THEN user
    ELSE named_struct(
      'user_id', sha1(user.user_id), 'email', null, 'age', null)
    AS user
  END
  FROM consumer.prod.orders
```

While the SQL shown in Example 12-7 provides us with a starting point to selectively redact data, the example utilizes the `has_tag_value` function alongside the `is_account_group_member` function, both of which are not available to the general public. Additionally, without the support of integrated generalized rule management, creating and maintaining dynamic views can become cumbersome over time. However, to end on a positive note, a simple solution to the problem can be to provide access to the physical table via views that explicitly redact any data marked as PII for the general public, while continuing to restrict direct access to the underlying physical table using the simpler coarse-grained access controls. This is a nice stopgap that can be achieved using open source alone.

Conclusion

The way we govern, secure, and store the precious assets inside our lakehouse can be complicated, complex, or simple; it all depends on size and scale (or the number of tables and other data assets) and at what point in time we realize the need for a more complete governance solution. No matter the point in the journey, start small—begin by creating separation between data catalogs at the bucket level to separate all-access data from highly sensitive data. Layer into your solution ways of synchronizing what people need from the data and what systems and services will need from that same data, and roll this into your strategy for who, what, and when.

In the next chapter, we will continue to look at metadata management, data flow, and lineage and round out what we started in this chapter.

Metadata Management, Data Flow, and Lineage

In the preceding chapter, you were introduced to the foundational components required to build a successful lakehouse governance solution. These components included identity and access management, data catalogs, and metastores, as well as the physical cloud-based storage powering the lakehouse. We showed you how roles and personas aid in the generation of secure building blocks for layered security and privacy, and we concluded with a look at utilizing SQL-like permissions management to simplify access controls for the lakehouse. This chapter continues where the last one left off, tying together the components of metadata management alongside the dynamic flow of data, as captured through the lens of data lineage and observable data applications.

Metadata Management

Have you ever been lost in the woods, or been driving in a new place without GPS or even an old-school map? Being lost is something we all have in common, and the same feeling can be expressed by data teams who are just trying to get to a set of tables they know *should* exist. But where are those tables? Metadata management systems provide the missing components between being lost and having directions. In our case, the location we are trying to get to is a set of known tables within one or more data products that we can trust to provide us with the correct information to solve our data problem. The metastore and services built on top of this metadata, like any data discovery services, act as a compass to help us reach our waypoint or final destination. The metadata, which is our data about our data, is required to solve our problem and can provide assistance when we are trying to arrive at the correct data destination.

What Is Metadata Management?

Just as in data management, the life cycle of our metadata provides a way to keep track of the data assets we hold near and dear, as well as notes, descriptions, comments, and tags. The centralized metadata layer—a foundational component of our lakehouse data catalogs—provides a representation of an organization's information architecture. This includes the hierarchy represented by our catalog(s) and databases (schemas) and the tables and views contained therein. This basic hierarchy was presented in Chapter 12, when introducing the prefix patterns for organizational success. The role of the metadata layer is to provide the necessary descriptive data to produce a macro view across the entire lakehouse regarding the current state of all data assets, and to provide a compass pointing to those data assets available for use.

 It is common to use the term *data catalog* or *metastore* when referring to the operational metadata layer. The terms *metastore* and *data catalog* are used interchangeably, as both terms describe a service that stores data about our data that can be accessed through APIs.

Data Catalogs

Depending on where you sit within your organization, you may find there are many interpretations of what a data catalog is. Essentially, in its most basic form, a data catalog is a tool that enables a user to locate the high-quality data they need to get their job done. At a minimum, the data catalog provides information about the components of a data product—the catalog, database (schema), tables, and views—along with a simple search component called the data discovery layer (or service).

> *The data catalog is used in the same way someone shopping at IKEA would use integrated search to locate something they want, be it a couch, table, or chair; this is very different from how someone would look through a paper catalog—there are expectations. For data, people have a general idea of what they need, and a good data catalog makes the journey simple.*
>
> —Andy Petrella

There are many different ways to solve the problem of looking things up, and what we are solving for and the definition of the problem should be actionable and based on real customer use cases.

For instance, we could create a manual list of all tables; the solution could be a simple shared spreadsheet—with the known limitation of the shared spreadsheet being the need to ensure that *someone* keeps the metadata up to date. This book is about solving problems, so the prior example is more an example of what *not* to do, but it might also be the simplest solution, depending on the size of your organization, and it ticks the boxes of enabling a user to search (filter) the spreadsheet (basic metastore) to narrow the set of tables and hopefully find (locate) what they need.

The problem with any process requiring manual human effort to maintain state is that without the right discipline, things will eventually and inevitably be out of sync just when you or someone else really needs them. This is the downside of offline or static data catalogs. They are, by definition, simply a promise of what *could be* rather than reflecting the true state of what *is*. Because manual synchronization doesn't scale, the trend in the industry has shifted toward automated cataloging and active data discovery.

Data Reliability, Stewards, and Permissions Management

The problem of maintaining the *who* (owners, producers, consumers), *what* (data product, data assets), *where* (location), *why* (can and should the consumers access and use this data?), *when* (is access limited to a specific start and end date? Is access required for batch or for streaming, or for both?), and *how* (is the data being used in part or completely? Is the data being copied or used only to materialize views?) is offloaded to the data stewards—or in some cases, to the data product owners.

The who, what, where, how, and why also have a role to play in regard to the reliability of the data product with respect to the data consumers. So you can say there is a reciprocal role to play in producing data as a product and ensuring that the consumers of a given data product abide by any associated rules and regulations for consumption of that data product.

The IAM capabilities provided by the lakehouse governance platform (as illustrated in Figure 12-1 in the previous chapter) should provide the data stewards with the ability to simplify access management for the data products that they oversee and are ultimately responsible for governing. This responsibility spreads a wide umbrella that covers the data producers, the life cycle of the data products themselves, and the contracts established for those data products.

In terms of contracts, it is typical to provide data product guarantees backed by a set of data-level objectives (DLOs)—no different than service-level objectives (SLOs) —that specify the minimum reliability that can be expected for a given data product. This helps standardize the way trust is defined across an organization. The DLOs are backed by a set of data-level indicators (DLIs)—likewise mirroring the traditional service-level indicators (SLIs)—which are the key performance metrics required to observe and confirm the reliability of a given data product.

For example, say we have a Delta Lake table that is generated by a streaming ingestion job. The DLO for the table specifies that all columns contained within the dataset will never be NULL. This guarantee can easily be enforced with the addition of simple constraints to our Delta Lake table, and due to the invariants of the Delta protocol, we can always meet the minimum requirements for the given DLO.

In practice, if the Delta Lake table is based on a streaming ingestion pipeline, then the DLO will typically also include the expected update or append frequency. We can produce statistics to articulate table freshness by measuring the delta between the streaming source timestamps and the available data within the table as our DLIs for each streaming microbatch. This measurement is commonly called the *table lag metric*, as it describes how far behind real time the ingestion pipeline is running, and therefore how stale or fresh our Delta Lake table is.

Outside of data-level guarantees, there are other obligations for the data producers, including table-level considerations like backward compatibility for table schemas, which provide a level of confidence and trust to the consumers of a given data product.

Ultimately, the data producers, stewards, and product owners hold the line to establish high trust for their data products. Providing data teams with high-trust data products can be achieved in part through the use of the metastore and catalog.

Why the Metastore Matters

It is nearly impossible to ignore the Hive Metastore when discussing the Lakehouse. This is because the Hive Metastore provides the capabilities for translating our file-based data lake tables into structures that can be queried like traditional SQL tables. Before Apache Spark SQL, the ability to query tables inside the data lake was achieved by using Hive SQL running MapReduce jobs inside Hadoop clusters. As Spark SQL became more widespread, the Hive Metastore continued to be maintained, but over time the industry no longer required a complete Hive distribution, and the Hive Metastore alone provided the missing pieces, enabling a Spark job to convert the Hive data into a Spark table object.

The Hive Metastore provides a set of basic features that can be utilized for data (database, table, and view) discovery, given the metastore itself resides in a traditional relational database (like Postgres or MySQL). This means that a user who has read access to the Hive Metastore can execute SHOW commands to list the databases, tables, views, and columns contained within, in order to discover what exists—or to query the resource metadata available through the tblproperties, dbproperties, or other system or discovery tables.

Because of the separations of concern between the physical metastore and our physical Delta Lake tables, IAM can provide filesystem management while SQL grants limit the surface area (which databases [schemas] and tables or columns a user can see within the metastore). Figure 13-1 shows the Hive access model as it relates to the metadata stored in the relational database (left) and the reference to the databases and tables located within our cloud object store or distributed filesystem (right).

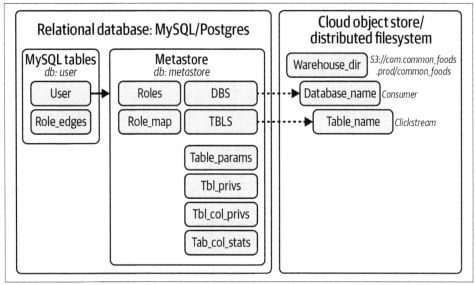

Figure 13-1. The Hive access model ensures a separation of concerns between access to database and table metadata and access to the physical files representing our Delta tables and located at a prefix within our storage layer

Figure 13-1 provides a high-level overview of the Hive Metastore. The metastore itself is a set of tables (>70) that enable the magic that provides us with a catalog of the where and what of our tables. However, the metastore is responsible only for storing the referential database and table data, including the *location* of these data assets with respect to their path on our cloud storage. The metadata also includes the table type, partitions, columns, and the schema.

While the basic information about the table is nice to have, we are missing a considerable amount of information that is really needed to operate our lakehouse at scale—not to mention, this is a book on Delta Lake and not on all table types or supported protocols. So we can safely ignore most of what the Hive Metastore provides, given that each Delta table contains a reference to its own metadata.

What the Hive Metastore provides to Delta for our lakehouse is the ability to identify the databases (schemas) and tables contained at a given cloud-storage prefix without requiring the object tree to be manually listed (which can be an expensive operation). Given that we have the Delta log (recording the table history), as well as the ability to fetch isolated snapshots of our tables (using time travel, or just for the current version of the table), we have limited use for the Hive Metastore outside of the general "listing" of catalogs, schemas, and the tables that reside within a known instance of the metastore.

In addition to the sparse capabilities mentioned above, there is one big limitation to address, especially if you are using the `delta-spark` library along with the Hive Metastore (or a variant such as AWS Glue, which is compatible with most of the Hive Metastore API). For any given data application, we can connect to only one catalog per session. This can be a bummer when we have requirements for joining tables contained across multiple catalogs. This limitation is due to setting the global `spark.sql.catalog.spark_catalog` as well as `spark.sql.warehouse.dir`. While this limiting factor can be worked around by creating copies of tables between different physical buckets (if we are using a bucket for each catalog), this reduces our ability to achieve a single source of data truth.

Unity Catalog

Unity Catalog is a universal catalog for data and AI. There are two versions of Unity Catalog at the time of writing—the internal proprietary version within Databricks and the open source software (OSS) version (*https://oreil.ly/21G-5*). The OSS version is interoperable with the Databricks version and provides the following key features: the metastore, a three-tiered namespace, governed assets, managed and unmanaged volumes, interoperability, and true system openness:

Metastore
Unity Catalog utilizes a centralized metadata layer called the *metastore*. This provides the ability to catalog and share data assets across the lakehouse, within regions, and even across clouds. Additionally, the metastore provides a three-tiered namespace in which data can be organized.

Three-tiered namespace
The namespace within Unity Catalog provides the following convention: `{catalog}.{database/schema}.{table}`. The namespace is a component of the metastore and enables us to organize our data and assets hierarchically.

The hierarchy is used for more than simple organization; it enables our data applications to read and join across boundaries that traditionally required copying data between Hive tables due to limitations of the two-tiered Hive namespace. Enabling a single job to read from multiple catalogs makes it simple for our data applications to join data between many tables residing across many catalogs.

As an added bonus, we can also utilize fully qualified table names (between cata-logs)—`spark.read.table('prod.consumer.clickstream')`, for example, which simplifies jobs that had previously relied on direct table paths to work around the limitations of the Hive Metastore.

Unified governance for data and AI
Assets within Unity Catalog include catalogs, databases (schemas), tables, note-books, workflows, queries, dashboards, filesystem volumes, ML models, and more. Using Unity Catalog's built-in governance and security—with strong authentication, secure credential vending, and asset-level access control—we can protect all our data and AI assets with a unified solution. This makes the solution to the complexities of providing filesystem-based access controls within a SQL-like system (covered in Chapter 12) much easier.

Managed and unmanaged UC volumes
One of the exciting features of OSS Unity Catalog—as included in the 0.1 release —is the availability of managed and unmanaged UC volumes with S3 credential vending. This feature allows us to centrally manage access to S3 bucket locations storing unstructured or nontabular data. This includes raw images and binary data for machine learning, application configuration, and artifacts (JARs, wheels, eggs) for running data applications, as well as a landing zone data layer to act as a primary ingestion source for our lakehouse, where applicable.

Interoperability
Unity Catalog supports Delta Lake, Apache Iceberg via UniForm, Parquet, CSV, JSON, and many other formats. It also implements the Iceberg REST Catalog APIs to interoperate with a broad ecosystem.

Openness
Unity Catalog is Apache 2.0–licensed, including an OpenAPI specification, server, and clients. Adoption of open standards maximizes flexibility and cus-tomer choice by ensuring extensive interoperability across various engines, tools, and platforms.

Getting Started with Unity Catalog OSS

If you are interested in using the open source version of Unity Catalog, the project has provided a really good quickstart (*https://oreil.ly/OSpjX*) that will have you up and running in under five minutes (depending on your internet speed!). Just clone the repo and start the server:

```
% git clone git@github.com:unitycatalog/unitycatalog.git &&
    cd unitycatalog &&
    bin/start-uc-server
```

If things go well, you will be greeted by the following:

```
#######################################################################
#    _     _      _  _      ____      _         _            #
#   | |   | |    (_) |     / ___|    | |       | |           #
#   | |   | |_ __ _| |_   _| |      __| | _ __ | |  ___    __ _  _    #
#   | |   | | '_ \| | __| | | |     / _` | '_/ _` | | |/ _ \ / _`  |  #
#   | |__| | | | | | | |_| || |__| (_| | || (_| | | (_) | (_| |  #
#   \___/|_| |_|_|\_|\__, |  \____\_,_|\_\_,_|_|\___/ \__, |  #
#                    _/ |                            _/ |  #
#                   |___/            v0.2.0-SNAPSHOT |___/  #
#######################################################################
```

There are a few example datasets to use in your exploration. Execute the following command to list out the available tables:

```
bin/uc table list --catalog unity --schema default
```

That is it for the quick introduction. Follow along with the quickstart docs online to learn to use the many features of Unity Catalog OSS available today.

Data Flow and Lineage

Data flows into our lakehouse in many different ways, and the way we capture the lineage of these data flows provides a view at the ingestion edge, or along the surface. On the surface, there is an understanding that tables must begin somewhere, and that the source of data powering a specific table today may and most likely *will* change at another point in time. The sources of data—outside the lakehouse—are impermanent. But the data product consumers shouldn't need to worry themselves with these internal data domain concerns.

For example, say we receive data from a third-party vendor every time an email or push notification is successfully sent. The data we ingest from each vendor is very specific to their APIs and internal data models and is also tied to whatever reliability contract we have established with that vendor at that point in time. The fact that we are using one vendor or another isn't the concern of data consumers, who are focused on insights into consumer behavior, or on increasing the open rate for emails, or on some conversion rate metric associated with the success of a marketing campaign.

It is the job of the data engineering team working under the consumer data domain (in the prior example) to transform the vendor-specific data into a common data format that eventually can be consumed by another team to produce insights within the external data domain (which is the gold layer of the medallion architecture). By providing common formats, we can transition from one vendor to another without interrupting the data flow into our mission-critical data assets (tables, reports, etc.).

So how does data lineage fit into this model?

Data Lineage

The purpose of data lineage is to record the movements, transformations, and refinements along a data journey, from the point of initial ingestion (data inception) within the lakehouse to the data's final destination—which can take the form of insights and other BI capabilities—or to provide a solid foundation for mission-critical ML models. Consider data lineage to be a sort of flight recorder, capturing important moments in time across our critical data applications—producing our data assets—with the purpose of being used to provide a measure of data quality, consistency, and overall compliance and to track the many data dependencies along that processing line.

Andy Petrella describes *lineage* as the intersection of "line" and "age," referring to the direct connection between data sources and how long they have shared a connection.[1]

The lineage of the many data sources and associated data applications comes together to provide an observable lens into the dependencies for our data products at runtime. In addition to helping with understanding the dependency graph, data lineage helps to ensure data teams understand the when, where, and why if any problems are experienced at runtime. Even with the best of intentions, things do inevitably go wrong, and flying blind is never a good look!

---

1 Andy Petrella, *Fundamentals of Data Observability: Implement Trustworthy End-to-End Data Solutions* (O'Reilly), 44.

Figure 13-2 supplies a visualization to aid in the discussion regarding data lineage. This diagram provides a simplistic view over the lineage, starting with data sources residing outside of the lakehouse (1) flowing into the internal data domain and utilizing a series of data applications (2) that produce a table or tables for each source (3). This data is then joined and further transformed by another data application before yielding the external data domain table (4).

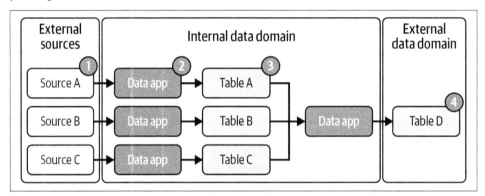

Figure 13-2. A starting point for data flow visualizations using data lineage

At the most rudimentary level, data lineage can be captured as a graph of sources to tables (or other data assets). However, this would ignore the fact that there are data applications (2) running to produce all tables other than the initial ingestion sources (1)—with respect to Figure 13-2. Therefore, we have both the concept of data lineage and that of data application lineage to consider.

Leaning on the data lineage to view the data flow allows us to quickly visualize "what changed" or to see "what is no longer behaving as expected," which can help to mitigate risk. To understand what changed, we need to go back to data application lineage (or workflow lineage).

Data application or workflow lineage

Data applications walk an interesting line with respect to complexity. At one extreme, a data application can be as simple as a SQL statement used to execute a transform, or as complex as a stateful aggregation application used to execute a complex operation like marketing funnel analysis. Regardless of the complexity, a good application exists in version control (like GitHub) and is associated with a release version (e.g., v1.0.0) and therefore has additional metadata that can be gathered to understand when things change. Furthermore, a data application requires resources to operate; this means there are compute resources associated with the runtime execution of each data application. Data applications add additional metadata to the data lineage graph, including the runtime version of each data application, the option of cluster configuration, and the Git SHA for the "current" version of the app. This additional metadata can be used for data application observability and can play a key role in providing a wider view on the operational data lineage.

There are many common uses for data lineage. It provides catalog, database, table/view, and columnar-schema-based linkage between data applications to help us understand how tabular data is accessed and used across the lakehouse. This includes additional data asset types (where supported), which can help us understand which sources of data are used to train machine learning models, or what specific tables or views are used to construct operational dashboards.

Data lineage can help us to identify important transitional points within the medallion architecture and to understand what data layer (internal or external) within a data domain provides the right level of refinement to solve a data problem. It can help in resolving upstream and downstream dependencies of a specific table or view or in building frequency graphs for access, and it can be used for audit awareness and to understand all active data customers of a data asset.

It can be used to derive insights for lakehouse-wide access and audit level insights to power monitoring and provide answers for centralized data governance teams with respect to audits (can and "should" a given principal [user or group] execute an action [read, write] on a given data asset [file, table, dashboard, etc.]).

There are many areas in which it makes sense to reuse our lineage data. These include access and compliance monitoring; impact analysis, to quickly triage when things go wrong; data change management, to understand the impact of critical schema changes; and to provide communication to the active data consumers—for example, when there is a need to migrate from a v1 to a v2 data asset or product.

Use case: Automating data lineage using OpenLineage

OpenLineage (*https://oreil.ly/ikdgv*) is an open source framework for the collection and analysis of data lineage. It is extensible and has a growing community surrounding it. The design of the framework provides an *open standard* for lineage metadata designed to record metadata for a Job within a specific execution.

The diagram in Figure 13-3 shows the generic operating model, consisting of a Dataset, a Job, and a Run entity. For each core entity (Dataset, Job, and Run), there is an extension object identified by the Facet keyword. These extension objects encapsulate user-defined metadata enabling enrichment of entities.

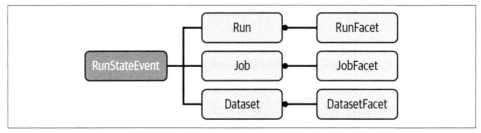

Figure 13-3. OpenLineage is built on top of simple entities encapsulating a Dataset, a Job, and a Run

Consider the fact that data doesn't simply exist in the lakehouse but requires a process (Job) to execute (Run) in order to ingest an initial table (Dataset) or to make modifications from one or more upstream tables (Datasets) in order to produce a new table or set of tables. This pattern and operating model essentially tracks the operational behavior of any data pipeline or simple data flow, as viewed through the lens of a data application (like we saw in Figure 13-2).

Getting started with OpenLineage

There are Java (*https://oreil.ly/lC3AO*) and Python (*https://oreil.ly/sm5AR*) client APIs available (at the time of writing). In the following examples, we'll be using the Python client APIs. If you would like to explore the full example, it is available in the book's GitHub content (*https://oreil.ly/Vto-D*).

Example 13-1 showcases how to create the OpenLineageClient instance and sets the metadata to assign the data producer, the upstream dataset, the named job, and the namespaced run instance, as well as simple functions to emit the start and complete events.

Example 13-1. Setting up the OpenLineage client to send start and complete events

```
client = OpenLineageClient.from_environment()
producer = 'common_foods.consumer.clickstream'
job_name = 'consumer.clickstream.orders'

datasets = {
  'clickstream': Dataset(namespace='consumer', name='consumer.clickstream')
}

cs_job: Job = Job(namespace='consumer', name=job_name)
```

```
# create the Run instance
run: Run = Run(f"{job_name}:{str(uuid4())}")

def emit_start(client, run, job, producer):
  run_event = RunEvent(
    RunState.START, datetime.now().isoformat(), run, job, producer)
    client.emit(run_event)

def emit_complete(
  client, run, job, producer, inputs: List[Dataset], outputs: List[Dataset]):
  run_event = (RunEvent(
    RunState.COMPLETE,
    datetime.now().isoformat(),
    run, job, producer,
    inputs, outputs,
  )
  client.emit(run_event)

# insert your data pipeline code
app = DataApplication(config)

# before you start the application
emit_start(client, run, job, producer)

# start your data application
app.run()

# before exiting the process
(if app.status() == 'complete':
  emit_complete(client, run, job, producer, app.inputs, app.outputs)
 else:
  emit_failed(client, run, job, producer, app.exception())
)
```

The code in Example 13-1 requires manual effort to construct string names and naming conventions in order to identify the data producer and the datasets, and to handle the construction of the Dataset, Job, Run, and RunEvent identifiers. Over time, it is much easier to use standard libraries and runtime environment variables, or common configurations, to streamline the generation of these lineage objects and remove the requirements of manual engineering effort—this helps to mitigate the risk that jobs end up reusing names and breaking the lineage. Just like with the "what not to do" covered in "Data Catalogs" on page 298, problems will arise when we ignore automation or convention-based engineering.

Simplified Lineage with Decorators and Abstractions

If you are familiar with Python decorators, then an avenue to simplifying how data and data application lineage is recorded could be provided as a function wrapping the run or execute method of your data application. When writing your integrations, ensure you provide a way to capture "failures," since we can also use data lineage to observe the current state of data in flight—even if that means there is no data in flight due to a breakdown in the runtime of a specific data application. If you are writing Scala or Java applications, then provide a simple trait or abstract base class that can be used to provide consistent hooks into the data lineage architecture.

The pseudo code in Example 13-2 provides a decorator over the run method of a PySpark application. The only expectation is that there is a `run` method that takes a `DataFrame` and returns a `StreamingQuery` object. This allows for the lineage recorder to parse the `StreamingQuery` object to gather more details about the sources and sinks, and to record the structure of the data flowing out of the application through the use of the schema method of the `DataFrame`.

Example 13-2. Decorating the run method for simplified data lineage

```
% python
 _app: Application = Application.fromEnv()
 @lineage.record(
   app: Application = _app,
   git: _app.git,
 )
 def run(df: DataFrame) -> StreamingQuery:
   …
```

While the code in Example 13-2 is just a snippet, it provides enough information to facilitate the generation of the Dataset, Job, Run, and RunEvent objects needed to track lineage via OpenLineage.

The way that data flows through the lakehouse and between our Delta Lake tables by way of our data applications ultimately provides the building blocks to create high-trust data products in a dynamic way—just like water moving between streams, rivers, and deltas and into reservoirs. Just like in nature, there will always be ebbs and flows, and ultimately certain areas that used to provide many downstreams will eventually dry up—but with the end of any data product, or the deprecation of an older source of data truth, there will always be new sources and new ways of connecting the data dots.

This is the beauty of capturing data lineage: when it is done correctly, the information provides a real-time or last "active" state of the what, when, and how, using a narrow or wide lens. This additional lineage-based metadata can then be combined with other Delta table metadata to provide invaluable information regarding the connectivity graphs as well as information to be used for monitoring, alerting, or data discovery. Together this information can answer questions like "When was the last update to a table?," "What data source can I use now that the old source is deprecated?," and more.

Data Sharing

What does it mean to share data or a data asset? In the simplest way, we provide the ability for a known identity (a stakeholder, customer, system, or service) to consume a collection of data by reading it directly from our single source of data truth. For our Delta tables, this means providing the capabilities to a known identity to read the Delta transaction log and generate a snapshot of the table so they can execute a table read.

Chapter 14 covers sharing with the Delta Sharing protocol; this is the simplest way to enable sharing within the lakehouse.

There are many reasons why we would want to make our data available to others—for example, we may be able to monetize our data to provide insights not available to other companies (as long as it abides by data use laws and isn't creepy), or we may need to provide data to our partners or suppliers, which is often the case in retail. And in the case of data that isn't exiting our company, sharing data between internal lines of business is critical to ensuring that everyone references the same sources of data truth.

Automating Data Life Cycles

Earlier in the chapter, we were introduced to the concept that data and data assets are expected to survive only as long as necessary. When it comes to the natural life cycle of data, sometimes we have a choice, and at other times we are bound by legal and regional requirements. Either way, data has an expiration date. Some data is more like milk—it needs to be used or it will spoil rather quickly—while at other times our data acts more like honey, crystalizing over time but easily returning to a perfectly healthy state with a minor amount of effort. *So how can we automate these data life cycles?*

Using table properties to manage data life cycles

We learned to apply properties to our Delta tables in Chapter 5. In the same way that the Delta protocol uses properties to control the utility-based functionality to ease the repetitive maintenance of our tables, we can utilize tables to unify the way we handle repetitive actions such as honoring data retention policies. The following techniques can be used to build a strategy for automatic data life cycle management or to run automatic compliance checks within your lakehouse.

Add the retention policy to the Delta table

The example shown in Example 13-3 introduces how to use the INTERVAL type to create a simple way of deleting data from our Delta tables. Three new table properties will be introduced; the naming conventions used in the book can be adjusted to fit the prefix patterns established in any lakehouse.

Using the properties prefix `catalog.table.gov.retention.*` will provide a name-space for our retention-specific use case.

Example 13-3. Add the table properties

```
% spark.sql(f"""
ALTER TABLE delta.`{table_path}`
SET TBLPROPERTIES (
  'catalog.table.gov.retention.enabled'='true',
  'catalog.table.gov.retention.date_col'='event_date',
  'catalog.table.gov.retention.policy'='interval 28 days'
)
""")
```

Whenever we add new governance behavior to our lakehouse, it is good to provide a way of opting into or out of a given feature. In this case, the `catalog.table.gov.retention.enabled` boolean can turn the feature on or off. Additionally, if the default state is false unless the property exists on the table, then it is much easier to opt in and ignore anything else.

Next, the code shown in Example 13-4 introduces a function to convert the interval value (28 days) into a `Column` object containing an `IntervalType`.

Example 13-4. Convert from a StringType to an IntervalType

```
% python
  def convert_to_interval(interval: str):
    target = str.lower(interval).lstrip()
    target = if target.startswith("interval"):
      target.replace("interval", "").lstrip()
    else:
      target
    number, interval_type = re.split("\s+", target)
    amount = int(number)

    dt_interval = [None, None, None, None]
    if interval_type == "days":
```

```python
        dt_interval[0] = lit(364 if amount > 365 else amount)
    elif interval_type == "hours":
        dt_interval[1] = lit(23 if amount > 24 else amount)
    elif interval_type == "mins":
        dt_interval[2] = lit(59 if amount > 60 else amount)
    elif interval_type == "secs":
        dt_interval[3] = lit(59 if amount > 60 else amount)
    else:
        raise RuntimeException(f"Unknown interval_type {interval_type}")

    return make_dt_interval(
        days=dt_interval[0],
        hours=dt_interval[1],
        mins=dt_interval[2],
        secs=dt_interval[3]
    )
```

The Python function from Example 13-4 can now be used to extract the
`catalog.table.gov.retention.policy` rule in the form of an Interval from a Delta
table. Next, we will use our new `convert_to_interval` function to take a Delta
table and return the earliest date that is acceptable to retain. This can be used to
automatically delete older data from the table, or even just to mark the table as out of
compliance. The final flow is shown in Example 13-5.

Example 13-5. Ensuring compliance through standards

```python
% python
table_path = "..."
dt = DeltaTable.forPath(spark, table_path)
props = dt.detail().first()['properties']
table_retention_enabled = bool(
  props.get('catalog.table.gov.retention.enabled', 'false'))
table_retention_policy = (props.get(
  'catalog.table.gov.retention.policy', 'interval 90 days'))

interval = convert_to_interval(table_retention_policy)

rules = (
  spark.sql("select current_timestamp() as now")
  .withColumn("retention_interval", interval)
  .withColumn("retain_after", to_date((col("now")-col("retention_interval"))))
)

rules.show(truncate=False)
```

We lean on the DeltaTable utility function to provide us with a simple means
of getting to our table properties. From the table properties, we extract out the
retention-related config. This includes the boolean (feature flag) that defaults to false,
as well as the retention policy, which defaults to 90 days. Using the *interval* variable,

which is the `IntervalType` column, we can then take the *current time* (when we run this expression), along with the results from `convert_to_interval`, and subtract the *interval* and then cast it to a `DateType` in the *retain_after* column. When we take a look at the rules `DataFrame`, we will see the following:

```
+------------------------+----------------------------------------+------------+
|now                     |retention_interval                      |retain_after|
+------------------------+----------------------------------------+------------+
|2024-03-24 20:11:27.759222|INTERVAL '28 00:00:00' DAY TO SECOND|2024-02-25  |
+------------------------+----------------------------------------+------------+
```

So, when we look back 28 days from March 24, we see that the date is February 25, due to the leap year.

The example starting in Example 13-3 and concluding in Example 13-5 shows a way to provide life cycle policy controls to our Delta tables. There are many places we can take this pattern, should we decide to extend outside of just data deletion, or we can choose simply to use this example to ensure we take control over how we delete older data. Remember the delete conditions presented in Chapter 6? You can use the column identity provided in the `catalog.table.gov.retention.date_col` to delete data older than the *retain_after* date.

Audit Logging

Audit is another critical component and important lens required for compliance within the lakehouse. Because each data asset has a specific set of rules (policies) and entitlements that must be enforced for compliance sake, we must therefore provide a simple way to query the access and permissions change log and general audit log of resources being created or removed from the lakehouse.

Thinking along the lines of what operations need to be recorded, we can use specific actions within the lakehouse like a flight recorder—similar to the recording of data as it flows to generate end-to-end lineage. Rather than tracking the journey in terms of the data life cycle and how the data flows through the data network making up the lakehouse, we are recording activity regarding the state changes for our data management.

In Chapter 12 we explained that audit logging can be as simple as capturing changes in the behavior of the lakehouse—for example, when there are changes to the roles or policies for critical operations on highly controlled resources like catalogs, databases, and tables.

Additionally, it is important to track operations for data in flight to provide a source of data (metrics) to help identify anomalies that can in turn help mitigate risks and identify threats or the potential for bad actors to take advantage of holes in security.

For example, say we want to understand what user or group has access (at any point in time) to any data asset (resource). Additionally, we would like to know which identity (user or group) performed a given operation (action), or the inverse, for any operation (action) performed to understand the resource, owners, and who "should" have been able to perform the given action.

To provide the security and governance personas with timely information and enable system-wide peace of mind, data must be collected and made available within the lakehouse to enable simplified audit event collection. Streamlining the audit trail is outside the scope of this book, however, considering that every data asset must have an accountable owner, and that each operation requires access controls that are handled via IAM permissions and role-based policies. We can start small by simply capturing the changes to IAM for resources owned by specific mission-critical data products.

This would provide a simple and humble beginning and enable streamlined audit capabilities to emerge using the collective metadata for tables and their lineage, and then building upon that with additional data about the frequency with which tables are accessed, refreshed, and deleted from, or even just to track what tables are out of compliance using the techniques introduced in Example 13-3 for automatic data life cycle management.

Monitoring and Alerting

It is essential for the success of our lakehouse to provide monitoring and alerting capabilities. These can be used solely for the purpose of data governance and security capabilities, or they can be extended to ensure each data product has proper operational observability, monitoring, and alerting capabilities as well.

General compliance monitoring

Returning to the use case for retention automation (Example 13-3), we discussed the fact that the retention duration could be used to check if a table was out of compliance. For example, say the governance organization required all table-based data assets to enable the `catalog.table.gov.retention.*` properties.

Aided by the data catalog, the governance engineers could easily set up a metadata read-only integration to check if the table owners have followed the rules and enabled retention policy configs to their tables. The scan could happen daily, recording which tables are out of general compliance, and could automatically use the `catalog .engineering.comms.[email|slack]` properties (introduced in Chapter 5) to send automated communications to the teams, or to escalate to the heads of the engineering organization. In this case, the alert isn't so much a PagerDuty alarm but could very well be integrated to page a team to be in compliance.

Data quality and pipeline degradations

We touched upon data quality when discussing the medallion architecture. For each table-based data asset (with a known data customer), if the pipeline fails, or if columns that once held important data go empty, this lets down the downstream consumers (the data customers). If there are table properties introduced to each Delta table to convey how often data is expected to land (the cadence of table refreshes, or freshness), then these can be used to automatically alert the data-producing team that things have gone wrong.

For a real scenario, the table properties introduced in Example 13-6 show four simple properties that provide a lot of powerful information.

Example 13-6. Declaring the intentions of each Delta table

```
% spark.sql(f"""
ALTER TABLE delta.`{table_path}`
SET TBLPROPERTIES (
  'catalog.table.deprecated'='false',
  'catalog.table.expectations.sla.refresh.frequency'='interval 1 hour',
  'catalog.table.expectations.checks.frequency'='interval 15 minutes',
  'catalog.table.expectations.checks.alert_after_num_failed'='3'
)
""")
```

Using the techniques introduced in Example 13-3 through Example 13-5, we can leverage a simple pattern to automatically run checks for a given table. The theory here is that unless a table is deprecated, there should be a known data service-level agreement (DSLA), or, at a minimum, specific DLOs and DLIs. With respect to our data assets (tables specifically), our downstream consumers tend to want to know the frequency with which data "becomes" available, or how often it is refreshed.

When making decisions based on when to use batch processing or microbatch processing, it usually comes down to the expectations of one or more upstream data sources. If nearly all sources usually refresh in under 15 minutes, but one source only updates daily, then if you need all data to provide specific data answers, you'll always be stuck in batch processing mode or be wasting money waiting on the laggard dataset. Making it easier to understand the average update frequency for a given table (without requiring meetings) can empower engineers and analysts to make decisions about whether streaming or batch processing makes the most sense to solve a problem.

Then when things go wrong, or when your pipelines stall due to "no new data" from your upstreams, you can check the DLOs for the laggard tables to understand what might have changed. Hopefully, if we've also incorporated data application lineage,

---

we can check to see how recently the data application that is powering the poorly behaving table was updated.

Leaning on the data lineage tables and some creative energy, a simple UI could also be built to provide up-to-date information about the data flow within your lakehouse and about what tables in the path are in compliance or are running slower than expected, or really any use case that can be automated to reduce meetings.

What Is Data Discovery?

Data discovery enables users to search (and explore) the data catalog to locate data assets (resources) within the lakehouse using a simple text-based interface. Behind the scenes, the discovery engine facilitates search by leaning on the metadata made available to it through the lakehouse data catalog and metastore. The same information required for metadata management, monitoring, and lineage comes together to enhance the search capabilities by providing a more robust search index.

Data discovery within the context of the lakehouse differs from that of traditional data catalog–based discovery, since the data that is present in the search index already resides within the lakehouse. It is common to see most sources of data within a large enterprise cataloged within a business data catalog; that capability is typically the starting point for business stakeholders to make informed decisions about what data to bring into the lakehouse.

For data discovery, a solution to the problem can be as simple as adding the table metadata (ownership and rules, as well as immediate upstream and downstream lineage) to an ElasticSearch index. If we wanted to layer in additional capabilities to the discovery engine—whether catalogs, databases/schemas, or other data asset types—we would only need to modify the types of metadata in our index and modify the search parameters to handle more complex discovery. Depending on the size and number of assets being maintained, the solution could be scaled accordingly, but for fewer than one million data assets, a simple ElasticSearch index would take us a very long way.

Considering what sorts of answers the customers of the lakehouse would be searching for can help inform what it means to be successful. In some cases, having validated "highly reliable" tables or "verified" owners is a useful step to reduce the number of tables matching the search criteria. As long as the process to get a specific tag or badge is a controlled process (meaning not just anyone can add their own tag), then the customers will trust that the process can't be gamed. If nothing else, think about how to balance complexity in terms of moving parts for the data discovery solution: How many sources of metadata need to be indexed, and how often? Is there a simple way to be notified when things change? Can we automate the process?

Having a good solution for data discovery can save countless hours and really raise the bar for a data organization. Just remember to balance speed and accuracy; a fast search result on bad data could waste company resources and lead to low trust in the lakehouse.

Conclusion

This chapter explored the value of metadata within the context of the lakehouse. Specifically, we looked at how metadata management acts as a critical component of the lakehouse platform and at how to utilize basic data asset information to capture more complex data flows through the use of data lineage. We spent time investigating how data lineage can be enhanced with data application lineage to enable context-aware insights, and we concluded with a brief overview of data discovery. In the next and final chapter, we will be looking at how data sharing with Delta Sharing completes the final component required for comprehensive lakehouse governance and security.

Data Sharing with the Delta Sharing Protocol

Sharing is a natural part of life. We share as an avenue to communicate pride with respect to accomplishments or to relay information related to our other emotions, be they joy, anger, frustration, bliss—really, the full gamut of human expression. As kids, we learn to share toys, whether we'd like to or not, as the simple act of sharing introduces others to an experience they may otherwise be excluded from. As we mature, we share meals with friends and family as a token of our gratitude, or simply to come together and reunite. So sharing is very much a natural part of our world.

With respect to our Delta tables, we share the fruits of our labor—whether internally to our organization, or externally—for myriad reasons to reduce the level of effort for other data teams who require access to the valuable data contained within the tables. However, the process of sharing data is itself not always so cut-and-dried.

For example, it is still common for data teams to set up periodic jobs with the sole purpose of extracting (copying) tabular data from one source of truth—say, their foundational Delta tables—before transforming each batch of rows into a common intermediate format, like JSON, and then writing the transformed data (again) into an alternative cloud storage location (either internally or externally). In other cases, data teams rely on SFTP (SSH File Transfer Protocol) and even good old email to send data back and forth. We might ask ourselves where the problem lies—isn't it safe to copy data from point A to point B? Isn't that essentially what data engineering is? We'd be correct in asking these questions.

The problem commonly encountered is actually a complexity problem based on divergent sources of data truth. Rather than having a single table representing a foundational dataset, we now must manage the complexity between all copies and deal with the expectations of all the teams represented by each downstream location to which we are actively exporting data.

Imagine that parts (partitions) of our table are exported to support 40 separate external locations, with each location representing a different cloud storage bucket, or prefix within a given bucket. Now, for each of our 40 separate locations, we include the added constraints of minimal permissions, and the sneaky problem of invalid (revoked) access permissions. What happens if we need to replace data in one or more partitions due to system failures or faults? Things tend to go wrong the more complex a system grows. Not to mention, there is a cost associated with reprocessing all the data again (for each downstream location), and this cost is included on both sides, represented by egress and ingress—when all along there has been an active single source of data truth represented by the original Delta table.

The problem described above is the issue with distributed synchronization—given that we can't assume that each export job will always succeed, we therefore must also *carry state* alongside each of our *simple* export jobs. So the simple act of periodic data export can easily become a complex and fragile process. Now for the good news: this chapter introduces the Delta Sharing Protocol, which is purpose-built to provide a secure and reliable way to share our Delta tables, regardless of where each table originates, and regardless of which cloud storage provider is used to store the table.

The Basics of Delta Sharing

The Delta Sharing Protocol provides an open solution to securely share live data from our lakehouse to any compute platform. Due to the open nature of the protocol, it is vendor and cloud agnostic, supporting the common cloud storage providers through the use of plug-ins without requiring one cloud over the other—or if we are running on prem, we can ditch the need for the cloud altogether.

In the chapter introduction, we were presented with the common problem of distributed synchronization, which introduces additional complexity, storage and compute costs, and complex state management to ensure that exported data is kept in sync with the originating Delta tables. A really impressive benefit when using Delta Sharing is that we remove the need to manage the complexity of managing exports altogether; rather, we need only concern ourselves with the creation of secure *shares*. Figure 14-1 shows this high-level concept. Each share provides the guardrails and access controls for our Delta tables and views, while removing the need to export data in the first place. Each share provides the *recipient* of the share with the ability to query any source-of-truth table or to view configuration by the share itself, with the bonus of being able to simply fetch table metadata (including the table properties and the table schema itself), and even to discover what tables are made available through the share itself.

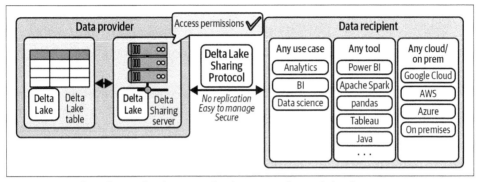

Figure 14-1. The relationship between the data provider and the data recipient

The relationship between the data provider and the data recipient can be thought of as being the same as the relationship between the data producer and the data consumer. On one side, the owner of the table or view is responsible for delegating a share. This share represents a presigned acknowledgment that the consumer of the data (the recipient) can access the Delta tables contained within the configuration of the respective share. Now let's look more closely at the notion of shares and recipients through the lens of data providers and recipients.

Data Providers

Data providers are responsible for managing access to their data products through the use of a share. A share represents a logical grouping of schemas, and of the tables or views accessible within each schema, to be shared with the recipients. Each recipient is an abstraction over an identity, known as a *principal*, which can act on behalf of a user, system, or service to provide read-only access to the tables or views allowed by a share (which we will go into in the next section).

Each share can be shared with one or more recipients, and each recipient can access all resources contained within a share. To put this information into perspective, an example share configuration is presented in Example 14-1. The share itself is configured in a similar way to an IAM-based policy file, providing the specific location of the tables or views that the recipient can access while reducing the complexity of managing cross-cloud (or on-prem) identity and access management (IAM). Lakehouse security and governance are covered in earlier chapters, if these concepts are new and a refresher is required.

Example 14-1. Configuring a share

```
version: 1
shares:
- name: "consumer_marketing_analysts_secure-read"
  schemas:
```

```
  - name: "consumer"
    tables:
    - name: "clickstream_hourly"
      location: "s3a://.../common_foods/consumer/clickstream_hourly"
      id: "eb6f82f5-a738-4bd8-943c-9cd8594b12ac"
```

Example 14-1 enables the recipient—in this case, the consumer marketing analysts—
to access hourly clickstream data. The configuration itself can contain many different
shares representing many different policies for many different recipients, and for each
uniquely identified share, a collection of one or more schemas can be configured,
with one or more tables or views per schema. This pattern enables us to simplify
access controls through the use of logical groups. We will be looking into how this
configuration is used later in the chapter when we explore the Delta Sharing server.

Data Recipients

The recipient of a share is a principal identified by a bearer token. While we go into
much more detail regarding identity and access management in earlier chapters, it
is worth pointing out that a principal represents a known identity, and the identity
can be at the user level, or represent a logical group like a team or even an entire
department or business unit, or be strictly headless—meaning it represents a system
or service that is not human acting on behalf of a human (hence the headlessness).

 With the Delta Sharing Protocol, there isn't a mechanism to support fine-grained access controls for individual users within a
group (team, business unit, etc.). If you want to provide variable
levels of access to individuals, you will need to provide each user
(identity) their own recipient profile.

All of the information required to authenticate against the Delta Sharing server is
packaged for the recipient in a simple profile file. Example 14-2 introduces us to the
format of the profile, which is represented by a JSON object.

Example 14-2. The recipient profile

```
{
  "shareCredentialsVersion": 1,
  "endpoint": "https://commonfoods.io/delta-sharing/",
  "bearerToken": "<token>",
  "expirationTime": "2023-08-11T00:00:00.0Z"
}
```

The profile contains all the information necessary to authenticate with the Delta
Sharing server from the delta-sharing client:

`shareCredentialsVersion`
> The file format version of the profile file. This version will be increased whenever non-forward-compatible changes are made to the profile format. When a client is running an unsupported profile file format version, it should show an error message instructing the user to upgrade to a newer version of their client.

`endpoint`
> The URL of the sharing server.

`bearerToken`
> The bearer token (*https://oreil.ly/6vwQe*) to access the server. This is just an opaque OAuth 2.0 token. The contents of the token can be as simple as a hash, or it can hold meaning, as with JWT tokens. It all depends on the authentication mechanism used and on whether we're using unstructured or structured tokens.

`expirationTime`
> The expiration time of the bearer token in ISO-8601 format (*https://oreil.ly/8dfZm*). This field is optional, and if it is not provided, the bearer token can be seen as never expiring.

> It is worth pointing out that while we can create long-lived or even perpetual tokens, it is a security antipattern and bad practice. Instead, always rotate your secrets (keep them secret, keep them safe!), and provide an API for external recipients to reauthenticate and retrieve their updated profile file and associated token. Being safe is much better than being sorry—especially when it comes to our Delta tables.

In the next section we will look at the Delta Sharing server. This service implements the Delta Sharing Protocol and offers a simple-to-use REST API powering the sharing service as well as the introspection API used by the Delta Sharing clients themselves.

Delta Sharing Server

The Delta Sharing Protocol provides a universal mechanism to create trust relationships between the data assets (schemas, tables, views, libraries, notebooks, AI models, dashboards, and more) owned by one identity and the one or many recipients of trust represented by a *share*. We can safely state that the promise of the sharing server is to act as both a bouncer—entrusted to accurately authenticate, authorize, and allow *recipients* access to a known share—and the authorized broker providing schema, table, and view metadata, as well as presigned access to the files making up a specific `Snapshot` of a given Delta table or view required to execute a table read.

We've briefly introduced the mechanics of the share (see Example 14-1) and the recipient (see Example 14-2), and we will now dive into the Delta Sharing REST APIs before discussing common strategies for managing the trust relationships encapsulated by the share and the recipients of a given share.

> The Delta Sharing OSS project provides a reference implementation of the Delta Sharing server that can be used as you get started in your open source journey. Head on over to the Delta Sharing GitHub repository (*https://oreil.ly/cgYwe*) to get started.

Using the REST APIs

The REST APIs provide capabilities for a recipient to explore their share, view what schemas and tables, or views, they have access to, and even query the tables and views directly. All API requests must be signed with a bearer token, which is conveniently made accessible to the Delta Sharing clients through the recipient profile file. We will look at the API routes and view examples to help build a working model of the capabilities provided by the Delta Sharing server, which we will call the *Delta Sharing service* from here on out.

> The REST APIs are intended to ensure that the Delta Sharing Protocol can be implemented easily by folks building Delta Sharing clients. If you are interested in using the Delta Sharing clients and want to skip the REST APIs section, then just move ahead to the section "Delta Sharing Clients" on page 332, as the rest of this section covers the REST API methods, all of which are encapsulated by most of the Delta Sharing clients.

Anatomy of the REST URI

The Delta Sharing service URI enables simplified scaling as well as routing using the concept of the sharing prefix:

```
% https://{endpoint}/{prefix}/{api-route}
```

It is common practice to enable load balancing and route redirection through the service URI. In this case, we can apply simple load-balancing requests using the `{prefix}` path. In addition to simple load balancing across the servers backing the deployment of our Delta Sharing service, we may also want to be intentional about how we route requests to different sharing instances based on their associated data domains.

For example, we could amend the prior example by adding more concrete use cases. Let's say we have established a set of four data domains—consumer, commercial, analytics, and insights. Now we can use name-based routing via the sharing prefix to direct each request to the appropriate sharing endpoint, enabling each data domain to fulfill a specific share-based request:

```
% https://{endpoint}/<consumer|commercial|analytics|insights>/{api-route}
```

Consider when we first introduced the recipient profile files. Whereas we previously had a common route prefix named delta-sharing under the endpoint property of the recipient profile file, we can now be more consistent with respect to where the share lives within the distributed ecosystem:

```
{
  "shareCredentialsVersion": 1,
  "endpoint": "https://sharing.commonfoods.io/consumer/",
  "bearerToken": "<token>",
  "expirationTime": "2023-08-11T00:00:00.0Z"
}
```

Now the recipient profile file is specifically pointing to the consumer prefix. In the case where we need to redirect or modify the prefix again in the future, we can use simple DNS, or force the recipient to reauthenticate and receive a new profile pointing to the new location endpoint.

When we use the sharing service to distribute requests across logical data domains, we end up embracing the decentralized nature of how data is distributed across natural organizational boundaries. This also makes it easier to scale based on specific workloads, rather than needing to arbitrarily scale up to meet "any" demands.

Next, we'll move onto the actual API methods and see how a recipient can explore the capabilities associated with their unique share.

List Shares

REST APIs commonly provide a list resource—the request parameters are shown in Table 14-1. In this case, the resource provides the means to view the variable number of shares that have been configured and assigned to the recipient identified by the provided bearer token on the request. Running the code in Example 14-3, we see how simple it is to explore what data assets we have access to, beginning with the most basic concept of the Delta Sharing Protocol—the humble share.

Table 14-1. List shares API request parameters

HTTP request	Value
Method	GET
Header	Authorization: Bearer {token}
URL	{prefix}/shares

HTTP request	Value
Query parameters	`maxResults` (type: Int32, optional): The maximum number of results per page that should be returned. If the number of available results is larger than `maxResults`, the response will provide a `nextPageToken` that can be used to get the next page of results in subsequent list requests. The server may return fewer than `maxResults` items even if there are more available. The client should check `nextPageToken` in the response to determine if there are more available. Must be nonnegative. 0 will return no results, but `nextPageToken` may be populated.
	`pageToken` (type: String, optional): Specifies a page token to use. Set `pageToken` to the `nextPageToken` returned by a previous list request to get the next page of results. `nextPageToken` will not be returned in a response if there are no more results available.

Example 14-3. Using the Delta Sharing Protocol to list configured shares

```
% export DELTA_SHARING_URL="https://sharing.delta.io"
  export DELTA_SHARING_PREFIX="delta-sharing"
  export DELTA_SHARING_ENDPOINT="$DELTA_SHARING_URL/$DELTA_SHARING_PREFIX"
  export BEARER_TOKEN="faaie590d541265bcab1f2de9813274bf233"
  export REQUEST_URI="shares"
  export REQUEST_URL="$DELTA_SHARING_ENDPOINT/$REQUEST_URI"
  export QUERY_PARAMS="maxResults=10"

  curl -XGET \
    --header 'Authorization: Bearer $BEARER_TOKEN' \
    --url "$REQUEST_URL?$QUERY_PARAMS"
```

The response from the sharing service will provide us with a list of the one or many shares that have been configured for us, the recipient. The response to our request is as follows:

```
{
  "items":[
    {"name":"delta_sharing"}
  ]
}
```

The object returned is a collection identified by items, with a single item representing a share with the `name` of `delta_sharing`. The protocol also allows the share record to contain an `id` field:

```
% {
    "name": "<unique_share_name>",
    "id": "<uuid_or_hash>"
  }
```

If the optional `id` field is present, the value of the `id` must be *immutable* for the lifetime of the share.

Using the shares as a starting point, we can introspect what is available in a given share using the share introspection endpoint—in this case, we are going to see what the *delta_sharing* share entails.

Get Share

Each share can contain one or more schemas, and within each schema, one or more tables or views (or other data assets) can be configured. To view a share, we must first use the list shares API to understand what shares are available for us to view. Next, we just need to send our request to the API endpoint. Example 14-4 shows the full request, while Table 14-2 shows the API request parameters required to complete the request.

Table 14-2. Get share API request parameters

HTTP request	Value
Method	GET
Header	Authorization: Bearer {token}
URL	{prefix}/shares/{share}
URL parameters	{share}: The share name to query. It's case insensitive.

Example 14-4. Sending a request to the share endpoint

```
% ...
  export REQUEST_URI="shares/delta_sharing"
  export REQUEST_URL="$DELTA_SHARING_ENDPOINT/$REQUEST_URI"
  curl -XGET \
    --header 'Authorization: Bearer $BEARER_TOKEN' \
    --url "$REQUEST_URL"
```

The result of issuing the request to the get share endpoint isn't much different from the list shares endpoint:

```
  % {
      "share":{
        "name":"delta_sharing"
      }
    }
```

The only change from the list shares endpoint is the result is now a single object rather than the array of items. The results of this request are unique to the shares configured for a recipient.

Next we will look at how to introspect the schemas associated with the share itself.

List Schemas in Share

To view the configured schemas we are authorized to access, we use the list schemas endpoint. Example 14-5 shows the full request, while Table 14-3 provides the API request parameters required to complete the request.

Table 14-3. List schemas API request parameters

HTTP request	Value
Method	GET
Header	Authorization: Bearer {token}
URL	{prefix}/shares/{share}/schemas
URL parameters	**{share}**: The share name to query. It's case insensitive.
Query parameters	maxResults (type: Int32, optional): The maximum number of results per page that should be returned. If the number of available results is larger than maxResults, the response will provide a nextPage Token that can be used to get the next page of results in subsequent list requests. The server may return fewer than maxResults items, even if there are more available. The client should check nextPageToken in the response to determine if there are more available. Must be nonnegative. 0 will return no results, but nextPageToken may be populated.
	pageToken (type: String, optional): Specifies a page token to use. Set pageToken to the nextPage Token returned by a previous list request to get the next page of results. nextPageToken will not be returned in a response if there are no more results available.

Example 14-5. Sending a request to the list schemas endpoint

```
% ...
  export REQUEST_URI="shares/delta_sharing/schemas"
  export REQUEST_URL="$DELTA_SHARING_ENDPOINT/$REQUEST_URI"
  export QUERY_PARAMS="maxResults=10"

  curl -XGET \
    --header 'Content-Type: application/json' \
    --header 'Authorization: Bearer $BEARER_TOKEN' \
    --url "$REQUEST_URL?$QUERY_PARAMS"
```

As we observed with the list shares endpoint, the list schemas endpoint provides capabilities to paginate over an arbitrary number of schemas. While pagination may not be required in all cases, the way pagination works is the same for all list resources:

```
% {
    "items":[
      {"name":"default","share":"delta_sharing"}
    ],
    "nextPageToken": "..."
  }
```

As we traverse the hierarchical tree from the share, now to the schemas, we are essentially unwrapping the exact same structure that represents our actual share itself. For context, look back at Example 14-1, where we learned to configure a share.

Next, we will learn to list the tables available underneath a specific schema, using the `default` schema returned from the request in Example 14-5.

List tables in schema

To view the configured tables of a given schema accessible by our recipient profile, we use the list tables endpoint. Example 14-6 shows the full request, while Table 14-4 provides the API request parameters required to complete the request.

Table 14-4. List tables API request parameters

HTTP request	Value
Method	GET
Header	Authorization: Bearer {token}
URL	{prefix}/shares/{share}/schemas/{schema}/tables
URL parameters	**{share}**: The share name to query. It's case insensitive.
	{schema}: The schema name to query, It's case insensitive.
Query parameters	maxResults (type: Int32, optional): The maximum number of results per page that should be returned. If the number of available results is larger than maxResults, the response will provide a nextPage Token that can be used to get the next page of results in subsequent list requests. The server may return fewer than maxResults items, even if there are more available. The client should check nextPage Token in the response to determine if there are more available. Must be nonnegative. 0 will return no results, but nextPageToken may be populated.
	pageToken (type: String, optional): Specifies a page token to use. Set pageToken to the nextPage Token returned by a previous list request to get the next page of results. nextPageToken will not be returned in a response if there are no more results available.

Example 14-6. Sending a request to the list tables endpoint

```
% ...
  export REQUEST_URI="shares/delta_sharing/schemas/default/tables"
  export REQUEST_URL="$DELTA_SHARING_ENDPOINT/$REQUEST_URI"
  export QUERY_PARAMS="maxResults=4"

  curl -XGET \
    --header 'Content-Type: application/json' \
    --header 'Authorization: Bearer $BEARER_TOKEN' \
    --url "$REQUEST_URL?$QUERY_PARAMS"
```

The response from the list tables request is shown next:

```
% {
    "items":[
    {"name":"COVID_19_NYT","schema":"default","share":"delta_sharing"},
    {"name":"boston-housing","schema":"default","share":"delta_sharing"},
    {"name":"flight-asa_2008","schema":"default","share":"delta_sharing"},
    {"name":"lending_club","schema":"default","share":"delta_sharing"}
    ],
    "nextPageToken":"CgE0Eg1kZWx0YV9zaGFyaW5GgdkZWZhdWx0"
}
```

We see that the service returned four tables in the result and is honoring the max Results query parameter. Because the nextPageToken is included in the response object, we can now return this to the service in order to fetch the next set of tables, as we see in Example 14-7. If there were no more results, then the absence of the nextPageToken declares that we are at the end of the list.

Example 14-7. Continuing the list tables query with pagination

```
% ...
export QUERY_PARAMS="maxResults=4&nextPageToken=CgE0Eg1kZWx0YV9zaGFyaW5GgdkZWZhdWx0"
curl \
  --request GET \
  --header 'Content-Type: application/json' \
  --header 'Authorization: Bearer $BEARER_TOKEN' \
  --url "$REQUEST_URL?$QUERY_PARAMS"
```

Given that the share is set up with a single schema (default), and underneath that schema there is a total of only seven tables—and because we are limiting the max Results per request to just four tables—it takes us two requests to get the full list of tables:

```
% {
    "items":[
    {"name":"nyctaxi_2019","schema":"default","share":"delta_sharing"},
    {"name":"nyctaxi_2019_part","schema":"default","share":"delta_sharing"},
    {"name":"owid-covid-data","schema":"default","share":"delta_sharing"}
    ]
}
```

Now there is a better way of quickly viewing all tables available to us, without requiring us to first descend the hierarchical tree from the shares to the schemas of an individual share, and then again descend into one or more schemas per share to view the configured tables. We can simply use the next API to query all tables available to us.

List All Tables in Share

To quickly view all configured tables for our share, we use the list all tables endpoint. Example 14-8 shows the full request, while Table 14-5 provides the API request parameters required to complete the request.

Table 14-5. List all tables API request parameters

HTTP request	Value
Method	GET
Header	Authorization: Bearer {token}
URL	{prefix}/shares/{share}/all-tables
URL parameters	**{share}**: The share name to query. It's case insensitive.
Query parameters	maxResults (type: Int32, optional): The maximum number of results per page that should be returned. If the number of available results is larger than maxResults, the response will provide a nextPageToken that can be used to get the next page of results in subsequent list requests. The server may return fewer than maxResults items, even if there are more available. The client should check nextPageToken in the response to determine if there are more available. Must be nonnegative. 0 will return no results, but nextPageToken may be populated.
	pageToken (type: String, optional): Specifies a page token to use. Set pageToken to the nextPageToken returned by a previous list request to get the next page of results. nextPageToken will not be returned in a response if there are no more results available.

Example 14-8. Sending a request to the list all tables endpoint

```
% ...
  export REQUEST_URI="shares/delta_sharing/all-tables"
  export REQUEST_URL="$DELTA_SHARING_ENDPOINT/$REQUEST_URI"
  export QUERY_PARAMS="maxResults=10"

  curl -XGET \
    --header 'Authorization: Bearer $BEARER_TOKEN' \
    --url "$REQUEST_URL?$QUERY_PARAMS"
```

The response from the endpoint is as follows:

```
% {
    "items":[
        {"name":"COVID_19_NYT","schema":"default","share":"delta_sharing"},
        {"name":"boston-housing","schema":"default","share":"delta_sharing"},
        {"name":"flight-asa_2008","schema":"default","share":"delta_sharing"},
        {"name":"lending_club","schema":"default","share":"delta_sharing"},
        {"name":"nyctaxi_2019","schema":"default","share":"delta_sharing"},
        {"name":"nyctaxi_2019_part","schema":"default","share":"delta_sharing"},
        {"name":"owid-covid-data","schema":"default","share":"delta_sharing"}
    ]
}
```

Now that we've learned the basics of the Delta Sharing service, it is time to start having a little more fun and embrace using the Delta Sharing clients. The next set of APIs we will learn about are more easily viewed through the lens of the Delta Sharing clients, as they are purpose-built to speak the same language.

Delta Sharing Clients

The next set of APIs are available using the Delta Sharing Clients. We will learn to query the table version and metadata and then finish by learning to query the physical tables themselves. We will start off basic and learn to simply read rows from the table, and then we'll learn about the more advanced change data feed capabilities—assuming a given table is configured to track changes, which we can introspect by using the table properties and looking for the presence of `delta.enable ChangeDataFeed=true`.

> The source code for the following examples is located in the book's GitHub repository under */ch14/delta-sharing/* (*https://oreil.ly/-X6Ob*).

Delta Sharing with Apache Spark

The Delta Sharing clients for the Apache Spark ecosystem are familiar and simple to get started with. Due to the nature of the Spark ecosystem, the core libraries are all written for the JVM, and wrapping libraries are provided to interact with the PySpark ecosystem and convert our Spark SQL queries into catalyst expressions. This section will look at using the PySpark client, then the Spark Scala client, and finally, the Spark SQL extension for Delta Sharing.

PySpark client

Getting started with the PySpark client requires the `delta-sharing` Python package, which can be installed locally using `pip install delta-sharing`. In addition to the Python wrappers, if you want to be able to run a local `pytest`, you will also need to bring the necessary JARs to your local `SparkSession`. We will walk through the end-to-end use case now, starting with Example 14-9, where we create an instance of the `SharingClient` and generate the share URL, which encapsulates the profile file as well as the share, schema, and table we will be reading.

Example 14-9. Generating the share URL to use the Delta Sharing client

```
%
profile_path = ...
sharing_client = SharingClient(f"{profile_path}/open-datasets.share")
shares = sharing_client.list_shares()
first_share: Share = shares[0]

schemas = sharing_client.list_schemas(first_share)
first_schema: Schema = schemas[0]

tables = sharing_client.list_tables(first_schema)

lending_club: Table = tables[3]
```

The code from Example 14-9 instantiates the `SharingClient` by passing a reference to the location on the filesystem where we've stored our recipient profile file. We then fetch the list of available shares and for simplicity's sake take the first entity—which is a `Share` object—from the results list to use to fetch our schemas. We repeat this same pattern, taking the first `Schema` from the results list to fetch what tables are available to us. Consider this series of operations to just be a hierarchical traversal from the share to the schema.

Last, we retrieve the list of tables and take the `Table` object representing the `lending_club` remote Delta table (since we will be querying the lending club Delta table). The `Table` object provides us with everything we need to generate the `table _url`, which is required by the sharing client to query the remote table.

The function in Example 14-10 is from the book's source code, and it provides a simple way to generate the full `table_url` required for reading the remote Delta table.

Example 14-10. Generate the Delta Sharing table URL

```
% def table_url(self, table: Table) -> str:
    table_uri = f"#{table.share}.{table.schema}.{table.name}"
    return f"{self._profile.as_posix()}{table_uri}"
```

This method allows us to pass a `Table` object to an instance of our Sharing helper class, and the end result is the Delta Sharing table URL required to query the table. The URL is the concatenation of the path to the share profile file along with the *<share>.<schema>.<table>*. For example, executing the function from Example 14-10—`self.table_url(lending_club)`—yields the following `table_url`:

.../delta-sharing/profiles/open-datasets.share#delta_sharing.default.lending_club

Now, in order to read the remote table using the Delta Sharing client, we'll need to generate a `SparkSession` that includes the `delta-sharing-spark` JAR:

```
spark: SparkSession = (
  SparkSession.builder
  .master("local[*]")
  .config("spark.jars.packages", "io.delta:delta-sharing-spark_2.12:3.1.0")
  .config("spark.sql.extensions", "io.delta.sql.DeltaSparkSessionExtension")
  .config(
    "spark.sql.catalog.spark_catalog",
    "org.apache.spark.sql.delta.catalog.DeltaCatalog"
  )
  .appName("delta_sharing_dldg")
  .getOrCreate()
)
```

Armed with our `SparkSession` and the `table_url` from Example 14-10, we can now read from the remote Delta table using the new `deltaSharing` format on our DataFrameReader. The code in Example 14-11 shows us how to do that.

Example 14-11. Reading a remote Delta table using `deltaSharing`

```
df = ((
  spark.read
  .format("deltaSharing")
  .option("responseFormat", "parquet")
  .option("startingVersion", 1)
  .load(table_url)
).select(
  col("loan_amnt"),
  col("funded_amnt"),
  col("term"),
  col("grade"),
  col("home_ownership"),
  col("annual_inc"),
  col("loan_status")
))
```

Behind the scenes, the `delta-sharing` Python library and the underlying `delta-sharing-spark` Scala library work together to negotiate the network calls to the Delta Sharing service, utilizing the table version API (`startingVersion = 1`), which if implemented on the sharing service allows our remote procedure call to time travel to a specific version of the remote Delta table. We also are using the `responseFormat` option on the reader. The available options at the time of writing are either Parquet (*https://oreil.ly/-g90j*) or Delta (*https://oreil.ly/Eaq0k*).

However, ignoring what is happening behind the scenes, the process is fairly transparent with respect to how we write our data applications. Given we can utilize the full set of DataFrame functions, there is no significant difference, except that we now can directly query a remote Delta table with the benefits of cloud-agnostic IAM and the complications presented in Chapter 12.

Spark Scala client

We just looked at the PySpark client in more detail. To use the Scala-based Delta Sharing client, we need a similar but simplified process. Rather than requiring the PySpark bindings, we can focus solely on using the `io.delta:delta-sharing-spark_2.12:3.1.0` package.

The code in Example 14-12 shows a simple example using the Spark Scala client.

Example 14-12. Reading a remote Delta table using the Scala Delta Sharing extensions

```
% import org.apache.spark.sql.functions.{col}

val dldg_path = "/path/to/book/github/chapter/"
val profile_file_location = f"$dldg_path/delta-sharing/profiles/open-datasets.share"

val table_url = f"$profile_file_location#delta_sharing.default.owid-covid-data"

val df = spark.read
        .format("deltaSharing")
        .load(table_url)
        .select("iso_code", "location", "date")
        .where(col("iso_code").equalTo("USA"))
        .limit(100)
```

The same DataFrameReader options are available for the PySpark and Spark Scala clients. The only difference between this and the code in Example 14-11 is the addition of the `where` and `limit` clauses.

Depending on how the Delta Sharing service has been implemented, the `where` clause can be handled as a direct predicate pushdown, or the client can handle the filtering. Given that the Delta Sharing server is based on an open standard, the service implementation (*https://oreil.ly/Ggh9i*) should be checked if we are experiencing less-than-ideal query times. The mechanism for handling modifications to the service response is through the use of hints. There are *jsonPredicateHints* as well as *limitHints*. These are all done using best effort and will evolve as the Delta Sharing Protocol does.

> The list of available DataFrameReader options for the `delta Sharing` reader is presented in Table 14-6.

Spark SQL client

The Delta Sharing SQL extension provided by the `delta-sharing-spark` JAR enables us to easily access remote tables in a secure and efficient way. Assuming we have a `SparkSession` generated, we can use the SQL method `spark.sql(...)` to query the remote table:

```
% sql
CREATE TABLE lending_club USING deltaSharing
LOCATION '<profile-file-path>#delta_sharing.default.lending_club';

SELECT * FROM lending_club;
```

This opens up myriad ways to securely access external data that can also be mixed with secure local or internal tables. For example, say we are tasked with building some business intelligence reports that require access to data that is provided by an external business partner or vendor. We can safely join our internal data with their external data and remove the problems that can pop up due to copying and divergent sources of data truth.

Stream Processing with Delta Shares

We were introduced to stream processing with Delta in Chapter 7 and are now familiar with the notion of incremental processing of unbounded tables. The same processing paradigms are available to us with Delta Sharing as well. Behind the scenes, the sharing client utilizes the remote table version API, along with the checkpoints of the structured streaming app; when combined, they enable us to read the remote transaction log and actively stay in sync with our remote sources of data truth:

```
% val tablePath = "<profile-file-path>#<share-name>.<schema-name>.<table-name>"
val df = spark.readStream.format("deltaSharing")
  .option("startingVersion", "1")
  .option("skipChangeCommits", "true")
  .load(tablePath)
```

Since the remote shared table acts just like any of our other tables (or data sources), we can simply treat it the same way when we write our streaming data applications. This makes life so much simpler, since the only real differences are (a) the way in which we identify the table and (b) the way in which we authenticate; the rest of the APIs remain the same.

Now that we've seen how to read streaming tables using the Delta Sharing client, we can close out this section with the available options for the Delta Sharing clients. Table 14-6 provides a handy overview of the different configuration options.

Table 14-6. Configuration options for the Delta Sharing reader

Delta Sharing option	Data type	Description
readChange Feed	Boolean	Enables the Delta Sharing client to read the change data feed.
maxVersions PerRpc	String	When incrementally processing table changes (readChangeFeed=true) using startingVersion and endingVersion, this option provides a mechanism to control the volume of data read per remote procedure call.
starting Version	Int	Supports *TimeTravel* on the remote shared table.
ending Version	Int	Supports reading of bounded sets. For example, if you want to read from table version 1 to 10, you can set startingVersion to 1, and endingVersion to 10; in this way, you can meter the volume of data being read for a given operation.
starting Timestamp	Timestamp	Read the shared table from the closest transaction available to the provided startingTimestamp. The timestamp must be parsable as a TimestampType—for example, 2024-05-26 04:30:00.
ending Timestamp	Timestamp	Set the bounds for the table read to the closest transaction available to the provided endingTimestamp. The timestamp must be parsable as a TimestampType—for example, 2024-05-26 05:30:00.
response Format	String	Changes the format of the read operation. The supported options are delta and parquet. To handle reading from tables with *deletionVectors* or *columnMapping* support, the responseFormat must be "delta." This list will continue growing to support additional UniForm types in the future.
maxFilesPer Trigger	Int	How many new files to be considered in every microbatch. The default is 1,000. (streaming only)
maxBytesPer Trigger	String	How much data gets processed in each microbatch. This option sets a "soft max," meaning that a batch processes approximately this amount of data and may process more than the limit in order to make the streaming query move forward in cases when the smallest input unit is larger than this limit. If you use Trigger.Once for your streaming, this option is ignored. This is not set by default. (streaming only)
ignore Changes	Boolean	Reprocess updates if files had to be rewritten in the source table due to a data changing operation such as UPDATE, MERGE INTO, DELETE (within partitions), or OVERWRITE. Unchanged rows may still be emitted; therefore your downstream consumers should be able to handle duplicates. Deletes are not propagated downstream. ignoreChanges subsumes ignoreDeletes. Thus if you use ignoreChanges, your stream will not be disrupted by either deletions or updates to the source table. (streaming only)
ignore Deletes	Boolean	Ignore transactions that delete data at partition boundaries. (streaming only)
skipChange Commits	Boolean	If set to true, transactions that delete or modify records on the source table are ignored. (streaming only)

Next, we will close this chapter with a listing of all the additional community-driven Delta Sharing connectors. These clients are lovingly built and shared to continue to extend the mission to bring Delta everywhere.

Delta Sharing Community Connectors

In addition to the common clients, there are even more connectors available from the community. Table 14-7 shows the connectors that are currently released (meaning they are ready for prime time).

Table 14-7. Additional Delta Sharing connectors[a]

Connector	Link	Status	Supported features
Power BI	Databricks owned (*https://oreil.ly/xlWW-*)	Released	QueryTableVersion QueryTableMetadata QueryTableLatestSnapshot
Node.js	goodwillpunning/nodejs-sharing-client (*https://oreil.ly/EWzHk*)	Released	QueryTableVersion QueryTableMetadata QueryTableLatestSnapshot
Java	databrickslabs/delta-sharing-java-connector (*https://oreil.ly/09UQd*)	Released	QueryTableVersion QueryTableMetadata QueryTableLatestSnapshot
Arcuate	databrickslabs/arcuate (*https://oreil.ly/wLdcs*)	Released	QueryTableVersion QueryTableMetadata QueryTableLatestSnapshot
Rust	r3stl355/delta-sharing-rust-client (*https://oreil.ly/nWgrL*)	Released	QueryTableVersion QueryTableMetadata QueryTableLatestSnapshot
Go	/magpierre/delta-sharing/tree/golangdev/golang/delta_sharing_go (*https://oreil.ly/LZiOr*)	Released	QueryTableVersion QueryTableMetadata QueryTableLatestSnapshot
C++	/magpierre/delta-sharing/tree/cppdev/cpp/DeltaSharingClient (*https://oreil.ly/1_XkF*)	Released	QueryTableVersion QueryTableLatestSnapshot

[a] All Delta Sharing connectors are located on GitHub, except for the Databricks-owned connector.

Conclusion

This chapter introduced us to Delta Sharing and showed us how we can move beyond traditional data export workflows to reduce complexity with secure, trust-based data sharing from a single source of data truth. When we reduce data sharing complexity, we in turn remove the common headaches related to distributed synchronization and the problem with many sources of fragmented truth. As long as we abide by the appropriate best practices with respect to table-level backward compatibility (see Chapter 5 for details on schema evolution), then we can rest easy at night knowing that the tables and views we've worked so hard to produce can bring joy and delight to the recipients of our shares.

Index

create, 40-45
delete, 49-52
read, 46-48
update, 49
CSV (comma-separated values) datasets, 121
CTAS (CREATE TABLE AS SELECT) statement, 44, 238
current_timestamp function, 159

D

Damji, Jules, 5
Das, Tathagata, 5
data asset model, 275-278
data assets
  governance of, 271
  life cycle of, 271
  relationship of data products to, 273
data catalogs, 266, 298
data classification patterns, 286-288
data control language (DCL), 276, 277
data definition language (DDL), 276, 277
data discovery, 269, 317
data engineering, 7
data files, 10, 11, 12
data governance, 263-296
  data assets
    data asset model, 275-278
    life cycle tracking, 274
    relationship of data products to, 273
  emergence of, 270-275
  maintaining high trust, 274
  overview of, 264-270
  unifying, between data warehouses and
    lakes, 278-296
    cloud object store access controls, 281
    data security, 283-295
    filesystem permissions, 280
    fine-grained access controls, 295
    identity and access management,
      282-283
    permissions management, 279
data lakehouses (see lakehouses)
data lakes
  corrupted data in, 190
  costs of, 190
  file format flexibility, 190
  lakehouses versus, 189
  modernizing, 7
  overview of, 2-4

shortcomings of, 4
data life cycle, 270
  automating, 311-314
    retention policies, 312
    using table properties, 311
data lineage, 268, 304-318
  audit logging, 314
  automating data life cycles, 311-314
    retention policies, 312-314
    table properties, 311
  automating using OpenLineage, 307-311
  data application or workflow lineage, 306
  data discovery, 317
  data sharing, 311
  monitoring and alerting, 315-317
    data quality and pipeline degradations,
      316
    general compliance monitoring, 315
  overview of, 305-311
  simplifying with decorators and abstractions, 310
data management operations, 39-56
  creation operations, 40-45
  delete, 49-52
  merge, 53
  Parquet conversions, 55
  read, 46-48
data manipulation language (DML), 9, 276, 278
data mesh, 273
data processing failure scenario, 14
data products, 273
data providers, 321
data quality and pipeline degradations, 316
data quality frameworks, 208
data science, 7
data service level agreement (DSLA), 316
data sharing, 268, 311, 319-338
  data providers, 321
  data recipients, 322-323
  Delta Sharing Clients, 332-338
    Apache Spark, 332-336
    community connectors, 338
    stream processing, 336-337
  Delta Sharing Protocol, 323-332
    get share, 327
    list shares, 325-327
    REST APIs, 324
    REST URI, 324
  overview of, 320-323

Docker image, 21-28
instructive comments, 176
INTEGER data type, 81
InternalTypeInfo, 67
IntervalType, 312
INTO parameter, 52
io.delta:delta-sharing-spark_2.12:3.1.0 package,
335
IoT (Internet of Things), streaming ingestion
for, 253
is_account_group_member function, 296

J
Java connector, 338
Java, setting up for Apache Spark, 30
JAVA_HOME environmental variable, 30
join function, 134
JSON files, 10, 12
jsonPredicateHints, 335
JupyterLab
attaching notebooks, 36
Delta Lake Docker image, 25
importing notebooks, 35

K
Kafka
DataFrame structure, 202
reading from and writing to Delta, 69-71
streaming ingestion for IoT devices specific
to, 253
kafka argument, 74
kafka-delta-ingest connector, 71-75
building, 73
building projects, 72
installing Rust, 72
running ingestion flow, 73-75
setting up environment, 72
kafka-delta-ingest library, 129, 202, 255, 256
KafkaSource, writing to DeltaSink, 69
KAFKA_BROKERS environment variable, 73
Kalavri, Vasiliki, 61
Kernel (see Delta Kernel)
key partitioning, 249
KPIs (key performance indicators), 268

L
lakehouse namespace pattern, 289
lakehouses (data lakehouses), 4

architecture, 187-212
dual-tier architecture, 190
medallion architecture, 201-211
open standards and open ecosystem,
193-195
overview of, 192
schema enforcement and governance,
197-201
transaction support, 195-197
data lakes versus, 189
data warehouses versus, 188
defined, 188
governance and security, 263-296
data asset model, 275-278
emergence of, 270-275
overview of, 264-270
unifying, between data warehouses and
lakes, 278-296
portability of data in, 199
reducing end-to-end latency within, 210
scalability of data in, 199
Lambdas, 131-137
concurrent writes on AWS S3, 135-137
writing in Python, 132-134
writing in Rust, 134
lambda_handler function, 133
lastRecordId variable, 196
Learning Spark (Damji, Wenig, Das, and Lee),
139
Lee, Denny, 5
libraries, native Delta Lake, 28-29
life cycle of data, 270
limit clause, 335
limitHints, 335
Linux Foundation, 9
liquid clustering, 236-240
localstack, 73
location property, CREATE TABLE, 82
logging, audit, 267
logRetentionDuration, 150
LONG data type, Delta, 81
ls command, 24, 280

M
machine learning, 7
MAP data type, 81
MapReduce operations, 29
masking, dynamic, 295
maxBytesPerTrigger option, 149, 167, 336

maxExpectedFpp option, 241
maxFilesPerTrigger option, 149, 167, 336
maxResults option, 325, 328-331
maxVersionsPerRpc option, 336
max_messages_per_batch argument, 74
mean time to resolution (MTTR), reducing, 197
medallion architecture, 147, 201-211
    bronze layer, 202-205
    gold layer, 208-209
    role in life cycle of data, 271
    silver layer, 205-208
        augmenting data, 207
        cleaning and filtering data, 205-207
        data quality checks and balances, 208
    streaming, 210-211
merge function, 134, 159, 230
Merge-on-Read (MoR), 180
mergeBuilder API, 159
mergeSchema option, 198
merging data, 53-55
metadata, 10, 11, 266, 297-303
    active lineage and, 269
    added to data lineage graph, 306
    centralized metadata layer, 298
    checking values of, 57
    comments, 175-178
    concurrent generation of lakehouse formats
        metadata with Delta format, 19
    constraints, 175
    coordinated and executed through Kernel
        library, 18
    data catalogs, 298
    data reliability, 299
    data stewards, 299
    decoupling logic around metadata from
        data, 18
    file skipping and, 233
    generated by UniForm, 194
    history of changes, 57
    Hive Metastore, 300-302
    metadata management defined, 298
    metadata–data interactions, 14-16
    migrating from nonpartitioned to parti-
        tioned tables, 107
    as output of ls command, 280
    permissions management, 299
    relationships between data and, 13

resolving all columns and their types using, 65
scalable, 8
self-describing, 194
table properties and, 98
Trino connector and, 85
trust and, 274
Unity Catalog, 302-303
viewing, 57
metastore (see data catalogs; Hive Metastore)
microbatch processing, 316
MinIO, 76
min_bytes_per_file argument, 74
MLflow, 250
mode parameter, 123
.mode(append) option, 43
mold linker, Rust, 127
monitoring, 268
    data quality and pipeline degradations, 316
    general compliance monitoring, 315
MoR (Merge-on-Read), 180
MTTR (mean time to resolution), reducing, 197
mutual trust-based relationship, 282
MVCC (multiversion concurrency control), 13
MySQL, 77

N

native Delta Lake libraries
    bindings, 29
    installing Python package, 29
native-application building, 115-138
    Lambdas, 131-137
    Python, 116-126, 137
    Rust, 127-131, 138
nextPageToken, 325, 328-331
Node.js connector, 338
nohup command, 27
notebooks (see JupyterLab)
numBytesOutstanding backpressure metric, 161
numFilesOutstanding backpressure metric, 161
numInputRows performance metric, 161

O

Olesen-Bagneux, Ole, 270
open source code, 9
OpenLineage, 307-311
operational metadata layer (see data catalogs)

UPDATE statement, 49, 180
updateCheckIntervalMillis (long) option, 65
upserting (see merging data)
use cases, 7
use delta.<schema> command, 82
userMetadata option, 177, 178
users, headless, 282
USING DELTA parameter, 41

V

vacuum operation, 14, 84, 111-112, 199, 225
VALUES argument, INSERT INTO operation, 43
VARBINARY data type, 81
VARCHAR data type, 81
VERSION AS OF, 48
virtualenv, 116
voice remote, 245-251

W

watermarking, 66, 144
whenMatchedUpdate, 54
whenNotMatchedInsert, 54
WHERE clause, 49, 50
where clause, 335

WITH clause, CREATE TABLE operation, 81
withColumn("date", to_date("date", "yyyy-MM-dd")), 93
withEventTimeOrder option, 154-155
withMergeSchema (boolean) option, 68
withPartitionColumns (string ...) option, 68
workloads, 6
write performance, maximizing, 216
write serialization, 195
writes, optimized, 224
writeStream method, 148, 156
write_deltalake() function, 122

X

Xfinity Voice Remote, 245-251

Y

Yavuz, Burak, 5

Ż

Z-ordering, 103, 221-223, 231-236
Zhu, Ryan, 5
ZORDER BY clause, 222, 229, 231
ZORDER clause, 224, 233

About the Authors

Denny Lee is a Unity Catalog, Apache Spark, and MLflow contributor, a Delta Lake maintainer, and a Principal Developer Advocate at Databricks. He is a hands-on distributed systems and data sciences engineer with extensive experience developing internet-scale data platforms and predictive analytics and AI systems. He has previously built enterprise DW/BI and big data systems at Microsoft, including Azure Cosmos DB, Project Isotope (HDInsight), and SQL Server. He was also the Senior Director of Data Sciences Engineering at SAP Concur. His current technical focuses include AI, distributed systems, Unity Catalog, Delta Lake, Apache Spark, deep learning, machine learning, and genomics.

Tristen Wentling is a Solutions Architect at Databricks, where he works with customers in the retail industry. Formerly a data scientist, he also has authored several blog posts covering topics such as best practices for production stream applications and building generative AI applications for ecommerce. Outside of technical work, Tristen spends a great deal of free time reading or heading to the beach. Tristen holds an MS in mathematics and a BS in applied mathematics.

Scott Haines is a Databricks Beacon and has been working with data, distributed systems, and real-time applications for over 15 years. His data journey began at Yahoo! and then took him to Twilio and more recently to Nike. He owns a consulting company named DataCircus and more recently wrote a book encapsulating his journey called *Modern Data Engineering with Apache Spark: A Hands-On Guide for Building Mission-Critical Streaming Applications* (Apress). He enjoys teaching people how to simplify data systems and data-intensive services and takes to the snow in the winter to pursue his love of snowboarding.

Prashanth Babu is a Databricks Certified Developer who helps guide design and implementation of customer use cases by building out reference architectures, best practices, frameworks, MVP, and prototypes, which enables customers to succeed in turning their data into value.

R. Tyler Croy helped create and still maintains the delta-rs project, which now helps thousands of organizations use Delta Lake from Rust, Python, and beyond. He also acts as a Databricks Beacon, helping teach others about Delta Lake and the Databricks platform. R. Tyler Croy contributed Chapter 6 of this book.

Colophon

The animal on the cover of *Delta Lake: The Definitive Guide* is an American pika (*Ochotona princeps*). Related to rabbits and hares, American pikas are small mammals that live in the mountains of western North America, from central British Columbia and Alberta in Canada to Oregon, Washington, Idaho, Montana, Wyoming, Colorado, Utah, Nevada, California, and New Mexico in the United States. They are typically found at or above the tree line.

American pikas often live in talus fields or among piles of broken rock or boulders, where they forage for the vegetation that makes up their diet. They rely on existing spaces in the talus for their homes and do not dig burrows.

The American pika has been classified by the IUCN as being of least concern from a conservation standpoint. However, the population is reportedly decreasing, especially at lower elevations in the southwestern United States. American pikas are highly sensitive to high temperatures, have limited dispersal ability and low fecundity, and are vulnerable to decreases in snowpack. Many of the animals on O'Reilly covers are endangered; all of them are important to the world.

The cover illustration is by Karen Montgomery, based on an antique line engraving from the Museum of Natural History. The series design is by Edie Freedman, Ellie Volckhausen, and Karen Montgomery. The cover fonts are Gilroy Semibold and Guardian Sans. The text font is Adobe Minion Pro; the heading font is Adobe Myriad Condensed; and the code font is Dalton Maag's Ubuntu Mono.